Madelen Robbins

HISTORY OF
MEDIEVAL AND MODERN EUROPE
IN EIGHT VOLUMES

Volume III
A HISTORY OF EUROPE
From 1198—1378

METHUEN'S
HISTORY OF MEDIEVAL & MODERN EUROPE

———

A History of Early Medieval Europe: 476–911
MARGARET DEANESLY

A History of Europe: 911–1198
Z. N. BROOKE

A History of Europe: 1198–1378
C. W. PREVITÉ-ORTON

A History of Europe: 1378–1494
W. T. WAUGH

A History of Europe: 1494–1610
A. J. GRANT

A History of Europe: 1610–1715
W. F. REDDAWAY

A History of Europe: 1715–1814
W. F. REDDAWAY

A History of Europe: 1815–1939
SIR J. A. R. MARRIOTT

A History of Europe

FROM 1198 TO 1378

—

C. W. PREVITÉ-ORTON

LONDON: METHUEN & CO. LTD.
NEW YORK: BARNES & NOBLE INC.

First published   .   .   *February 4th* 1937
Second Edition   .   .   1949
Third Edition, revised .   1951
Reprinted   .   .   .   1960
Reprinted   .   .   .   1964

*Reprinted by lithography in Great Britain
by Jarrold & Sons Ltd, Norwich and
bound by James Burn, Esher*

CATALOGUE NO. [METHUEN] 2/4352/10
3.3

PREFACE

ALTHOUGH this volume is restricted as a whole to the period 1198–1378, it has proved necessary to allow a little overlapping for a few years on occasion with the two volumes which precede and follow it. The reign of Charles V of France, for instance, could not well be cut short in the midst of closely connected events two years before its close, nor that of Philip Augustus begun without a brief account of its earlier years in which his consistent policy was first deployed.

The aim of the author has been to give a narrative of events and institutions sufficient to provide a skeleton on which the general development of Europe and its component states might be moulded, to give enough trees to show the conformation of the wood. An interpretation of the facts without those facts is apt to be nebulous, just as a superfluity of details without their interrelation is confusing.

The author's grateful thanks are due to Mr. Philip Grierson, Fellow of Gonville and Caius College, for his kind help in reading the proofs, in which it is so easy to overlook a blunder.

C. W. P. O.

August 1936

PUBLISHER'S NOTE
TO THIRD EDITION

The "Suggestions for Further Reading" at the ends of chapters have been brought up to date by Mrs. Janet Sondheimer, formerly of Girton College. Cambridge. Otherwise the text is unaltered.

1951

CONTENTS

vii

CONTENTS

MAPS

CHAPTER I

EUROPE AND ITS PEOPLES IN A.D. 1200

IT has been well said that, in addition to the obvious changes of civilization, languages, races, and religion, the centre of gravity of Europe also shifted between the beginning of the Dark Ages and the thirteenth century. Perhaps it may be claimed that there had now come into being two centres of gravity which were accompanied by the division of European civilization, or in other words of Christendom, into two divergent parts, the East and the West. In A.D. 400 Europe was a collection of lands and peoples clustered round the Mediterranean Sea which was both its centre and its main thoroughfare. It therefore included North Africa and the nearest Asia—Syria and Asia Minor; it was practically identical with the undivided Roman Empire, and the German, Celtic, and Slavonic tribes to the north were rather potential than actual members of it. There had long been apparent a fissure in this civilization: the Eastern half had taken a Greek and the Western a Roman impress; and the removal of the chief capital of the Empire to Constantinople, followed by the barbarian conquest of the West, had produced a definite dislocation, for the new Western populations were but faintly affected by the Romano-Greek East and formed more and more a barbaric civilization of their own. None the less, contact was not lost; the Mediterranean was still the central sea, and an ever-ready means of intercourse. It is conceivable that the whole of the West might at some time have come to be only the outer fringes of a Byzantine civilization, and that Europe might have found its centre in Constantinople.

This possibility was frustrated by the Arab conquest of the seventh and eighth centuries. Syria, and all North Africa, and even Spain ceased to be European and Christian; the Mediterranean from a centre became a frontier-line; and the fragile unity of Europe was broken. All-important divergences of race, language, intellectual development, and

[marginal note:] Division into East and West

1

material development had already divided East and West
Europe; now the two became strangers to one another,
uncomprehending and incomprehensible. What remained
of the East, compact round Constantinople, was still classic,
civilized in the narrower sense, the learned, if feebler, heir
of ancient culture. The West, which now included the
northern peoples beyond the domination of ancient Rome,
was barbaric and Germanized, endeavouring blindly to form
a new social structure out of the teeming wreckage of Antiquity and the originative capacity and pregnant traditions
of the barbarians. We ought not, perhaps, to speak of a
definite centre of gravity for it at all, so independent were
its parts, so rich and inspiring were the contributions of
each to the civilization they made, so diffused was their
initiative; but at least there is no doubt that the centre
of power lay to the north; the south might often teach,
combine, or devise, but the expansive peoples, and the
impetus of great movements, of new forms of society, of
dominant ideas came from the north. That the erstwhile
function of the Mediterranean was now provided by northern
rivers, seas, and roads implied an impoverishment in harmony
and universality, but also an enrichment in originality and
variety. The new civilization had all the more vigour and
creativeness from the abundance of its roots.

A feature of the centuries on either side of A.D. 1200
is the recovery by Italy of an equal share in the leadership
of Western Europe. The predominance of the Papacy,
localized in Rome, the reconquest of supremacy in the
Mediterranean, and the renewal of contact with the now
foreign East, in which the Crusades played their part, all
contributed to this result. For all that, the diffuse character
of Western Civilization, the independence and multiplicity
of its local sources remained the same; the great states of
Europe were still ultramontane.

The Europe of the end of the twelfth century fell then
into two main divisions, the East and the West, disparate in
civilization and traditions, but coming closer and closer into
contact as the Moslems lost their control of the Mediterranean.
Both, however, were far from homogeneous in language,
race, or government, and their geographical circumstances,
the configuration of the land, the means of communication,

EUROPE IN A.D. 1200

and the variations of climate, which still subsist, had then
an almost overwhelming influence on the development and
mutual relations of the several countries.   It will be well to
describe briefly this geographical setting and the political
formations that it framed, before narrating the events of the
period covered by this volume.

The Iberian
Peninsula   The outlying member of Europe to the west was the
Iberian peninsula, then still the battleground between Moslem
and Christian.   The fertile, sub-tropic Andalusia was held
by the Moors under the Moroccan dynasty of the Almohades.
The north with its tableland and mountains was divided
among several Christian states.   These kingdoms held a
comparatively isolated position in Europe.   By land they
were only connected with France, from which they were
separated by the continuous ridge of the Pyrenees, only to be
passed with ease along the coast at each end.   Under this
curb the strong French influences which filtered into Spain
were always transmuted there to local embodiments.   By sea
much the same insularity happened.   The Catalonian ports
were in touch but only in touch with all the Mediterranean,
the Portuguese with England and Aquitaine ; whatever they
borrowed rapidly took a regional form.   The country itself
was cut up by mountain ranges into distinct provinces, and
differences of language made for particularism.   The aberrant
Catalan dialect of Langue d'oc was spoken in Catalonia,
Spanish in the centre, Basque on the Bay of Biscay ; Portuguese was developing in the west.   But the kingdoms were
more the result of geographical than linguistic conditions.
The valley of the Ebro linked Aragon proper and Catalonia
in a kind of federal state ; little Navarre was Pyrenean ;
Castile and Leon shared the Cantabrian range and the barren
central uplands, and were inevitably drawn together ; while
Portugal held the rainy, fertile western slopes.   Thus the
Iberian peninsula as a whole was a meeting-place of diverse
influences from East and West, which when they reached it
became insulated and characteristic of the land.   In the same
way both through its provincial disunity, and its estranging
frontiers, the share of the peninsula in general European evolution tended to be spasmodic but most distinctive in character.

France   In complete contrast stand the kingdom and territory
of France.   In the first place, although so definitely bounded

by the Pyrenees and the sea on three sides, its eastern boundary was both ill-defined and permeable. The actual kingdom which owed allegiance to the monarch at Paris stopped at the Rhone, the Saône, and a wavering line at the foot of the Lorraine uplands and across the plain of the Netherlands. But the territories, where French dialects and French ethos predominated, reached up to the Alps and beyond the Jura and over the upper watersheds of the Meuse and the Moselle. And these linguistic frontiers were anything but barriers. Even the Alps were crossed by never-vacant routes. Whatever current of thought or trade or politics was astir would reach France; whatever arose in France would spread throughout Europe. It is no wonder that the great monastic movements arose along the vague border-line, that commerce found for a while its nodal point in the fairs of Champagne, that feudalism developed in France its typical forms, that Gothic architecture expanded from the lands of the Seine and Loire, that there scholasticism centred with the university of Paris as Western Europe's intellectual capital, that northern French, the Langue d'oïl, gave birth to the chief vernacular literature of the time and gave a ply to those of its neighbours.

The inner boundaries of France were no less open than her outer frontier. A vast fertile plain swept from the Rhine and Scheldt to the Pyrenees; the valley of the Rhone opened a wide way past the Cevennes Mountains to the lesser plain of the Midi. A succession of navigable rivers provided easier routes than the roads; and the possession of the city of Paris where the route from the Rhine to Bayonne crossed the Seine was an invaluable asset to the French monarchy. This accessibility was, however, quite compatible with provincial divergences, which both enriched the contribution of France to civilization and long delayed the completion of its unity. The first and principal of these divisions was that between North and South, which indeed in 1200 amounted to a separation of language and culture. Roughly speaking, the Midi, speaking Langue d'oc [1] (to which Catalan was allied), lay south of Lyons from the Alps to Bordeaux. It was the more Romanized part of

---

[1] So called from their different words for " yes " : oc (from Latin hoc) and oïl (modern oui, from Latin hoc illud). These groups of Romance dialects shaded off into one another, but they each clustered round one typical and eventually dominant literary form, which served as a cultural and linguistic centre.

Gaul, the *pays du droit écrit* (to use a later term) where Roman Law was the norm. Its poets were the troubadours, and their verse expressed a racial temperament as much akin to Italy as to Northern France. The North was definitely less Roman and more deeply penetrated by German settlers. It was the true France, a land of customary law, and its tongue, the Langue d'oïl, had a vogue and range which makes its rival seem transitory and provincial. To these main tongues must be added others of less significance : the unique Basque in Gascony, a backwater then and now ; Celtic Breton in Brittany, which might also be negligible had it not been one source for the imperishable Arthurian literature ; and Teutonic Flemish in Flanders which was steadily to draw its speakers out of the orbit of France.

The political divisions were even more variegated. At the accession of Philip Augustus in 1180 no monarch had less control of his great vassals than he. Dukes, counts, and great lords exercised in their fiefs all the ordinary functions of government. The king really ruled only over the royal " domain," i.e. the Île de France, where no count came between him and his petty vassals. There, however, his estates were large and his revenues, whether from tolls or lands, ample. Paris and Orleans were the strategic centre of France both for war and commerce. The greatest of the vassals was Henry II of England, whose possessions stretched from the Channel to the Pyrenees. But his control over parts of them was barely more efficient than that of his suzerain. The duchy of Normandy and the counties of Anjou, Touraine and Maine, were indeed well-knit states, but Brittany was really independent, and the greater part of the duchy of Aquitaine was in the hands of counts and barons. The lord of the Midi, the Count of Toulouse, was wealthy between Gascony and the Rhone, but he was rather the head of a bewildering feudal complex than the ruler of a state. Then there were the Counts of Champagne and Blois on either side of the royal domain, the Duke of French Burgundy on the Saône, and the Count of Flanders to the north-east, all little subordinate to the king, but far from unquestioned masters in their own territories.[1] Lesser potentates need not be mentioned here.

[1] The King of Aragon was a French vassal for part of Catalonia.

Across the Channel lay the British Isles, which require The British Isles notice for their international position, although their internal history is outside the scope of this volume. The kingdom of England was the most centralized of European monarchies. There was scarcely a great fief of the French type, and the king ruled the length and breadth of the land. Wales, however, was under vassal native princes or Anglo-Norman barons ; and Ireland was in the anarchy of a partial and neglected conquest ; it was hard for the English king to keep up a continuous effort there, drawn as he was to his French territories and hampered in any case by the difficulty of communications across the stormy Irish Sea. Lastly, the kingdom of Scotland was in the background to the north ; its king had but scant authority over his barons in the Lowlands, and practically none over the Highland clans beyond them. The insularity of the British Isles is a commonplace. They were cut off by the sea, and were at the end, not at the frequented junctions, of the trade-routes ; their evolution was exceptional. But their insularity was modified by circumstances and conditions, at least so far as Great Britain was concerned, which gave her a different lot in European history from that of the Spanish states. The narrow seas made intercourse easy and continuous with France and the Rhinelands, and the Norman Conquest, followed by the century-long political connexion with France, exercised a profound influence on both people and institutions. English feudalism was a variety of Norman feudalism, and the country responded and contributed to European thought and art with facility. In all but institutions, and those more in their later than in their earlier development, England was an integral part of Western Christendom.

East of France and covering Central Europe from the The Holy Roman Empire : (i) Germany North Sea to the Mediterranean were the lands of the Holy Roman Empire. Unlike the hereditary kingdom of France, the Empire was an elective monarchy, whereby the chosen of the German princes became King of the Romans, with a prescriptive right to be crowned Emperor at Rome. By the tradition universally accepted in the West the Empire, derived in reality from the Frankish monarchy of Charlemagne and refashioned by the German Otto the Great, was identical with the ancient Roman Empire and its Emperor

was the secular head of Christendom. It was composed
of three kingdoms, Germany and the two dependent realms
of Italy and Burgundy or Arles. To take Germany first,
this core of the Empire was mainly formed by the combination of some five or six tribal districts, each with
marked sub-national characteristics, which had once been
fairly united duchies, but, especially since the changes
effected by the Emperor Frederick Barbarossa, were now in
process of dissolution and division into many separate fiefs
of all sizes.

Upper Lorraine

On the upper waters of the Moselle were the wooded
highlands of the duchy of Upper Lorraine, of which the
duke still retained the greater part, although the three prince-
bishoprics of Metz, Toul, and Verdun subtracted much valuable territory. Despite his high title, he was not one of the
greatest princes, partly perhaps because of the French character of most of his land, partly because his lands were not
fertile, and therefore not populous.

Lower Lorraine

Lower Lorraine, on the other hand, had been practically
broken up. This territory, which extended from the lower
valley of the Moselle down both banks of the Rhine and over
all the lower Meuse as far as the Scheldt, was a variegated
land. It included the hills of the Eifel and the Ardennes
and the flats of the Low Countries, both the French-speaking
Walloons and High and Low Germans. Chief among its
potentates were the Archbishops of Cologne and Trèves,
the Bishop of Liége, and the Duke of Brabant. What most
distinguished it, together with the French county of Flanders
which geographically belonged to it, was its commerce. The
Rhineward towns thrived on the transit trade, those of the
Ardennes on their metal work, those of Flanders on their
cloth-manufacture as well. Here then was the native region
of free-towns, whether almost republics or more or less fettered
by the rights of Emperor or feudal lord.

Frisia, the coastland north of the Rhine, with its two
chief rulers, the Count of Holland and the Bishop of Utrecht,
may be passed over as the almost impregnable stronghold
of a race of fishermen, already but loosely connected with

Franconia and Swabia

the Empire. Franconia and Swabia, however, were the
Empire's heart, for in them lay the bulk of the imperial
demesne-lands and the family estates of the house of Hohen-

staufen which long had held the Empire. The dukedom of
Swabia was held by a Hohenstaufen, and that of Franconia was
mainly united to the Crown, while most of the great vassals
were loyal adherents to their ducal house. Swabia had for
its centre the uplands round the Black Forest, but reached
the Alps at Chur and the Vosges over the plain of Alsace ; the
Rhine route traversed it from Basel to near Hagenau, and
the route from the Splügen and the Septimer Passes through
Chur to Augsburg. Thus Swabia held a commanding position in the communications with the south. There was, however, one rival to the Hohenstaufen in the duchy, the Duke
of Zähringen, who not only held the Breisgau on the Rhine,
but was also rector of Burgundy, an anomalous title which
really gave him ducal powers between the Jura, the Alps,
and the Rhine (i.e. over most of modern Switzerland), where
he possessed considerable estates. Franconia consisted of
the hill country round the Main, the Neckar, and the Lahn,
with the Rhine valley from Swabia to Coblenz. It was a
land of great ecclesiastical princes, the Archbishop of Mainz,
chancellor of Germany, the Bishops of Spires, Worms, Würz-
burg, and Bamberg, and the Abbots of Fulda and Lorsch.
It was full of counts of the second rank, headed by a great
officer of the Empire, the Count Palatine of the Rhine.

The duchy of Bavaria, although curtailed, was perhaps Bavaria
along with Swabia the least splintered of the ancient tribes.
It stretched over the highlands of the upper Danube from
the Lech to the Böhmer Wald. Along its western boundary
lay a strip of Hohenstaufen and imperial domains, and the
house of Meran and the archbishopric of Salzburg cut it
short on the south, but the duke, now of the house of Wittelsbach, was firmly seated in the centre. Apart from its natural
resources, the importance of Bavaria was enhanced by its
command of the mouth of the chief and easiest pass to Italy,
the Brenner, as well as of the trade to Hungary down the
Danube.

The frontier provinces to the south-east, the duchies of Austria
Austria, Styria, and Carinthia, were extensions of Bavaria
which had been cut off from the parent tribe. Mountainous
frontier lands as they were, they lived a life apart, although
their iron and silver mines drew numbers of German colonists
among their half-Slav populations. Austria itself was under

the great house of Babenberg, and drew wealth and consequence as the guardian of the gate into Hungary and
the possessor of a long section of the Danube trade-route.

Saxony

To the north the wide lowland duchy of Saxony, never
very firmly held in hand by its dukes, save Henry the Lion,
was, since Frederick Barbarossa broke it up, in a state of
confusion, divided among quarrelling chieftains, too many to
list. The chief ecclesiastical princes were the Archbishops
of Bremen and Magdeburg, and the Bishop of Münster, as
well as the Archbishop of Cologne for his duchy of Westphalia, which he was endeavouring to make a reality. Among
lay princes were the still powerful Welfs, lords of Brunswick,
the counts of Holstein, who defended the Danish marches,
and the Ascanians, who held the March of Brandenburg on
both sides of the Elbe and the vain title of Duke of Saxony
with fragments of domain attached thereto. On its southern
border, but not within it, stretched the central districts of
Thuringia and Hessen under an ancient line of landgraves.

Saxony owed its weight in the Empire to the fighting
and trading qualities of its largely free and stubborn population, and from it Germany was spreading steadily at the
expense of the tribes of Wendish Slavs over the marshy or
wooded plains beyond the Elbe. The March of Brandenburg was still increasing; and the Margraves of Meissen
and Lusatia between it and the Erzgebirge of Bohemia had
long been among the greatest princes. The German movement eastward under these and other magnates was a pregnant fact of the time which made history while remaining
aloof from its main current.

These tribes and districts made up Germany, a unit in
spite of their particularism, which was increased by the
marked differences of dialect, grouped into the High German
to the south and the Low German to the north. As a whole
the land was more conservative than France. Feudalism,
though rapidly developing, had made far less progress; its
institutions and law still retained a savour of Carolingian
times; its vernacular literature, while borrowing much from
the French, was still mainly on native themes and expressed
the traditions of a society only just emerged from the primeval
forest which covered vast areas still. But Germany was rich
in men. Its conservatism and tribalism had for long given

it greater unity than France ; its kings held wide if scattered
domains, on which dwelt the numerous *ministeriales*, knights
in profession, serfs in status, the fighting force of the kingship ; prosperous cities sprang up not only on the Rhine
and the Danube but on the coasts of the North Sea and the
Baltic and on the routes between them. Germany was
open on the west and south to foreign influence, and was
itself the protagonist of Western culture towards the east.
Its association with the Empire made it the greatest European
state ; its possession of so many principal arteries of trade,
crossing its variegated territory and tribes from mountain
and valley and table-land to the heaths and marshes of the
north, made it receptive of all neighbouring influences. But
the needs and conditions of its varied inhabitants were so
different from one another that unity of aim or government
was almost impossible ; medieval Germany fell a victim not
only to the mirage of the Empire but to the hard facts of
its own internal geography.

The satellite kingdom of Burgundy or Arles between the (ii) Bur-
Rhone and Saône and the Alps was a collection of almost in- gundy or
dependent principalities, mostly French and south French in Arles
character. The land between the Rhine and the Jura, in part of
which its German population was settled, was, as we have
seen, under the Dukes of Zähringen. The flat land between the
Jura and the Saône formed the Free County (Franche Comté)
of Burgundy, very like the French duchy of Burgundy to
the west. Three other states require mention. The County
of Savoy was a road-land, controlling the three Alpine passes,
the Great and Little St. Bernard and the Mont Cenis. Its
princes showed an exceptional duality, for as Marquesses of
Italy they had a firm footing in Piedmont as well. The
Dauphins of Viennois were merely local rulers, although the
Mont Genèvre route passed through their lands. The Counts
of Provence, however, suzerains of the seaport-commune of
Marseilles, and themselves kinsmen of the Kings of Aragon,
had a far wider outlook, and their land was one of the chief
homes of the civilization of the Midi. But taken as a whole
the dislocated realm was a land which everyone passed
through, often apparently, as in the famous tale of St. Bernard,
without noticing the lake or mountain by which they rode.
Least of all medieval lands was its history recorded.

The Italian peninsula on the other hand was both a land of passage and a goal. It was the half-way house between east and west and the home of the Roman Curia. For a long time it had fallen into two main divisions of the north and of the south, one a land of local autonomy, the other a land of strong central government. The first consisted of the *Regnum Italicum*, one of the three kingdoms, however nominal, of the Holy Roman Empire; the second was the kingdom of Sicily, which extended over the island from which it took its name and Apulia or southern Italy. The *Regnum Italicum* again fell into well-marked natural subdivisions. The most northerly was that of Lombardy, i.e. the fertile watershed of the River Po and its tributaries between the encircling Alps and the Apennines. With the exception of a few fragmentary feudal states, chiefly in the hills, it was ruled by prosperous city-republics, the Lombard communes, which drew their fortunes from the transit-trade to the East and to Rome, and from indigenous manufactures. Chief among them was Milan at the converging point of most of the Alpine routes. Then there were Pavia, Piacenza, Cremona, Brescia, the university town Bologna, and others, each occupying its special coign of vantage at cross-road or ford. The incessant mutual hostilities of these cities were mainly due to questions of transit for commerce or fields for food supply. Two were specially fortunate in being seaports. Genoa, not in the Lombard plain but on the narrow southern slope of the Apennines, the Riviera, was in a first-rate position to reach both the east and west Mediterranean, the Levant and Ponent of the Italians. Venice, built in the impregnable lagoons at the mouths of the Rivers Adige and Brenta, was not within the Holy Roman Empire, and was even better placed than Genoa, once it had subdued the Dalmatian pirates, to become the chief port of the Mediterranean.

South and west of the Apennines came the amphitheatre of Tuscany. It, too, was happily astride of roads to Rome; it had its seaport in Pisa, Genoa's rival, and its manufacturing town in cloth-working Florence. There was an intellectual superiority in these Tuscans which compensated for natural resources less prodigal than those of Lombardy. Their communes, however, as a rule had been less independent than those of Lombardy. The Marquess of Tuscany, a nominated official, backed by imperial domains, had exercised a real government.

The other districts of the *Regnum Italicum* were the mountain lands of the Duchy of Spoleto (Umbria) and the March of Ancona and marshy Romagna, filled with restless little communes, all more or less in connexion with the eastern coast route to Rome, the Flaminian Way, all just escaping from the provincial control of imperial officials ; and finally the Patrimony of St. Peter under the unchallenged suzerainty of the Pope. Here were the malaria-haunted plains of the Campagna and Roman Tuscia and the enchanted city of Rome, the centre of Western Christendom, built upon a vision of prestige which counteracted her frequent anarchy under her commune and her material decay. *The Papal States*

To the south came the kingdom of Sicily, a fief of the Papacy, recently linked to the Empire in a personal union through its conquest by the Emperor Henry VI. Its Norman kings had welded it into a strongly centralized state, comparable to England. There was a considerable number of enfranchised towns, which were, however, kept in strict subordination to king or feudal lord ; but the main structure of society was feudal of the Norman type. The configuration of the sub-tropic land was much diversified, ranging from the fertile volcanic plain of the Terra di Lavoro and the similar Conca di Palermo to the rugged Apennines and the pastoral slopes of Apulia and the sun-baked hills of Sicily. The population and languages were as varied. There was a large Saracenic settlement in western Sicily, a decreasing number of Greek-speakers in eastern Sicily and Calabria, and the Italian-speakers of Sicily and the mainland. Language did not exhaust their divergences. The Campanians of the Terra di Lavoro, the Abruzzan highlanders, Apulians and Calabrians and stubborn Sicilians were strangers to one another, and over all were the Norman nobles, rebellious and resentful of the monarchy. In wealth and material civilization the kingdom took the first place in Italy. The land was not yet exhausted by taxation and misgovernment ; its favourable position on the trade-routes brought it commerce ; parts were very fertile. The half-Moslem traditions of the court and its connexions with Byzantium, Spain, and the East made its culture the highest in Western *The Kingdom of Sicily*

Europe. There Greek and Arabic could be translated, and
as in its central government so in its art it showed early
traces of the tendencies which later led to the Italian Renaissance. But there were fatal flaws in this brilliant fabric.
Homogeneity, unity, and common aims were alike lacking.

Scandinavia   East and north of the Holy Roman Empire we find
countries under conditions as a whole more primitive and
nations whose share in the general advance of European
civilization was less conspicuous. First among these were
the three Scandinavian peoples to the north. The kingdom
of Denmark consisted of lowland territories around the
entrance to the Baltic Sea, which it absolutely controlled
—the peninsula of Jutland, north of the River Eider, the
islands, and Scania on the opposite coast. Denmark was
by far the leading Scandinavian state. By reason of its
greater arable area it had the largest population ; the great
trade-route from the East through the Sound and the herring
fisheries off the Scanian coast gave it wealth, even if merchants and fishers mainly came from German ports ; and
its proximity to Germany made both royal power and
feudal organization more developed. The obvious policy of
the kings was to extend their rule over Holstein and to be
master of the Baltic ports. Norway and Sweden, lands of
mountain and forest, were more thinly peopled, and they
were farther from the new medieval civilization in whose
wake they slowly followed. Norway, facing west, had its
cod-fisheries and timber, but the vast viking emigration had
left the population lethargic ; it was enough to clear the
forests slowly and to live much the old life of warlike farmers
with a very gradual trend towards feudalism and monarchy.
Much the same may be said of Sweden ; only Sweden was
on the Baltic, and her kings looked to the eastern trade-route
and the conquest of Gotland with the wealthy German port
of Wisby which was its emporium.

Poland and   South of the Baltic, east of Germany, lay the vast plains,
Lithuania   partly marshy, partly heathy, partly forest, of the Vistula
watershed, reaching south to the Carpathians and east to
the swamps of the Pripet. The north-eastern part had been
so shrouded by marsh and forest that it was marvellously
primitive. The still-heathen Prussians on the coast and
Lithuanians inland lived a life almost prehistoric. Slavonic

Poland on the other hand was plunged since 1188 into eclipse and disaster. The practical break-up of the Polish kingdom into competing principalities under the house of Piast had fatally handicapped it. To begin with, the Wendish lands on the Oder had fallen to Germany as we have seen, and Pomerania on the Baltic, though not conquered, had become a German duchy. Then the chief Polish principality, Silesia, was likewise being attracted into a German orbit. In all German colonization was proceeding apace. The remaining principalities were in disorderly stagnation, but bound to the West and Rome by their allegiance to Western Christianity.

The Czech realm of Bohemia, vassal to Germany as it Bohemia was, retained, unlike Poland, a national prosperity within the circle of its mountains, the Erzgebirge and the Böhmer Wald. Its kings indeed pursued a policy of expansion, the defect of which was its uncertain aim—were they to assert themselves in Slavonic Poland, in alien Hungary, or in Germany? Their polity was that of a more advanced, better-organized Poland; but the cultural influences of the West were steadily gaining ground, and the penetration of German settlers, a welcome circumstance to the dynasty, had already begun. Bohemia, with its mines, had too its trade-route traversing the Moravian gap from the Adriatic to the Baltic.

Last of these western powers was Hungary and its depen- Hungary dencies. The dominant race, the Magyars, although they kept their Turanian language, were much changed from the wild horsemen of former times through continual intermixture with their subject-races. Slovaks on the southern slopes of the Carpathians and romance-speaking Vlachs in the Transylvanian mountains were their chief subjects; they themselves inhabited the rich alluvial plains of the Danube and the Theiss. In permanent alliance with Hungary was the Yugo-Slav kingdom of Croatia on the Save, but the possession of its coastal district of Dalmatia was fiercely disputed with Venice. In 1200 Croatia had the upper hand. Although Hungary commanded one of the main routes, that down the Danube and thence to Constantinople, it plays a curiously incidental part, as yet, in history. Occasional wars with all its neighbours had little permanent result; the towns were little more than villages, and the stirring influence of town-life was lacking. But the very large class of free landowners showed a strong political sense; while the official use of Latin and Hungary's membership of the Western Church decided with momentous after-effects to which division of Europe it belonged.

The Balkan peoples

We cross the Danube to East Europe, Byzantine in tradition, however barbaric in practice, Orthodox in religion, outside the real sphere of the Papacy, oriental and Greek in the descent of its culture. The Balkan mountain-lands might be called semi-barbaric. In the north-west was the newly founded Yugo-Slav monarchy of Serbia, but its extent kept changing and it was not a solid state. The greater part of the land between the Danube, Adrianople, and Skoplie was under the Tsars of Bulgaria, newly revolted from the Byzantine Empire. The main stock here was the Bulgarians, themselves a mixture of Slavs and Turks; and there were also the equally composite, but romance-speaking Vlachs, not to mention Yugo-Slavs. They were all wild and warlike, perpetually at odds with their neighbours and with one another. The Albanians occupied the Adriatic coast-land then as they do now. They were then unassimilated subjects of Byzantium.

The East Roman Empire

As we have seen, the Eastern or Byzantine Empire still continued the traditions of the Ancient World, of which in fact it was a surviving fragment. It was still the only real Roman Empire, its Emperor the true successor of Augustus. Although it has met with much unmerited depreciation, chiefly owing to the strong oriental element in its civilization, and although in 1200 there still remained in it a tenacious vitality, it can hardly be gainsaid that it was then exhibiting marked and perhaps irremediable signs of decay. Constantinople was still the world's emporium, the focus of eastern trade and manufacture; there was still good fighting material in the Empire, especially in Asia Minor. It retained a civilized bureaucratic government in spite of the semi-feudal tendencies of the great landed proprietors. But the administration was corrupt and out of gear, the dynasty of the Angeli incompetent, and the people decadent. In Europe the Empire covered the coasts of the Ægean Sea, true Greece, and Albania; in Asia it possessed the coasts and roughly the western third of Asia Minor, but the efforts of the Comnenian dynasty to recover the central tableland of Anatolia

and the safe frontier of the Taurus had finally failed in the
defeat of Myriocephalum in 1176. The army was too much
a collection of barbaric mercenaries, while the fleet, essential
for the safety of Constantinople, was non-existent. Thus the
carrying trade had become an Italian monopoly to the indignation of the Greeks; and the arrest and plunder of the
Venetians at Constantinople in 1171, followed by the massacre
of the Latin residents in 1182, had opened a bitter and fatal
feud. To make matters worse, the Emperor Manuel I had
indulged a misplaced and futile hope of recovering Italy, and
roused an enmity of the Western Empire only too much in
accordance with the national antipathy between Greeks and
Latins. A catastrophe was drawing near.

Over the plains to the north of the Black Sea, from the The
Danube to the Volga wandered the Turkish hordes of the Ukraine
Cumans, doubtless possessing many Slav, Vlach, and even and Russia
Gothic subjects. To the north of them again from Kiev to
Novgorod lay the Slav principalities of Russia under various
scions of the house of Rurik. Their civilization, like their
Christianity, was of Byzantine origin; but they were barbarous enough. Their wealth, like that of their Turkish
neighbours, the Great Bulgarians on the Upper Volga, was
due to their being on two oriental trade-routes, from the
Baltic to the Volga, and to Constantinople, to which they
contributed their native products of furs and corn. But
their importance for Europe, secluded as they were among
their frozen forests, was that of a buffer-land towards Asia.

Something should be said of Nearer Asia, occupied by Nearer Asia
fragments of the defunct empire of the Seljūk Turks. The
tableland of Asia Minor was in the hands of the Seljūks of
Rūm, whose dynasty, though not the people, was fortunately
for the Greeks in a state of decadence. The Taurus defiles
and the fertile coast of Cilicia with its ports were the seat
of the emigrant Christian kingdom of Little Armenia, held
by Armenian refugees from the Seljūk conquest. Over
Syria, Palestine, and wealthy Egypt ruled Saphadin, brother
and heir of the famous Saladin. Along the Syrian coast lay
the remains of Crusading principalities. Near by was the
Latin kingdom of Cyprus. Besides being the subject of
conflict between East and West, these, like Egypt, lay on
the main routes to the Indies and the East. With the

crusading impulse had been mingled the rivalry for the control of the Mediterranean, and these its Levantine outlets. Insignificant roadsteads and great seaports were alike the heads of caravan-routes stretching far into Asia, or in the case of Egypt of the land-crossing to the voyage of the Indian Ocean. Here was the " wealth of Ormuz and of Ind."

North Africa   Lastly, in this survey, come the Barbary States of North Africa. Tripoli was part of Saphadin's realm. The rest was under the decaying Berber dynasty of the Almohades. The Moors, whether Arab or Berber, were an energetic, but restlessly fickle people. They drove a thriving trade across both the Sahara and the Mediterranean. Their struggle with the Spaniards for Spain was still undecided, but at sea they had lost the dominion to Europe, while remaining an incessant plague as corsairs.

The Western Church and the Papacy   One cause of division which exacerbated the antipathy between East and West Europe was the difference of faith. The East was Orthodox, the West Roman and Catholic ; variations of creed and rite were not really so important as those of government, for the Western Church acknowledged the monarchical rule of the Papacy, and the East did not. It was, indeed, the Church and the Papacy, more than anything else, which bound Western Europe together. The Church was partitioned into a number of provinces, each under an archbishop who presided over the diocesan bishops, his suffragans, and these provinces were practically grouped in, or in some cases formed, Churches which for want of a better name we may call national, such as the Ecclesia Anglicana or Gallicana. But these local authorities and divisions were all subordinated to the Pope of Rome. The Pope's office and powers had received a glowing description from St. Bernard in his *De Consideratione* sixty years before 1200. He was the spiritual head of Christendom, the successor of St. Peter, prince of the Apostles, and Vicar of Christ. The sum of his authority was now often expressed by the term " *plenitudo potestatis*," " fullness of power." In strictly ecclesiastical matters, this may be roughly classed under three heads, judicial, legislative, and administrative.

The Pope's ecclesiastical powers   The Pope was the supreme court of appeal on all questions involving Canon Law, and the appeal to him might be made

per saltum, and not after recourse to bishop and archbishop.
Thus all causes belonging to the Courts Christian, which
included those where clergy were concerned as well as marriages, wills, and cases of conscience, were subject to his
intervention. This alone gave him enormous interpretative
and harmonizing power, but his direct legislative function
had few bounds. It was his prerogative to approve the
canons of Councils, and his continually multiplying decretals
on Canon Law were considered as binding on the Church.
Further, this fount of the law could override or suspend its
provisions. Thus he could allow the translation of a bishop,
otherwise forbidden, or a marriage of persons within the
forbidden degrees. These powers merge into the administrative. The Pope had proclaimed crusades; he could suspend or depose bishops, impose commands on all clergy,
intervene in any diocese. From time to time he would send
legates to the local churches, who, if *a latere,* acted in his
name as superior to all local authorities, and wielded large
part of his authority. To certain archbishoprics, like that
of Canterbury, was annexed the office of *legatus natus,* which
while conferring additional powers to those of a metropolitan,
also kept alive the continuous papal intervention in the provinces. It had even come to be held that no archbishop
could act as metropolitan until he had received papal recognition by the gift of the honorific vestment known as the
pallium from the Pope. Add to this that the Pope was
the fount of ecclesiastical privileges and exemptions within
the hierarchy—by his grant provinces were formed or dismembered, monastic rules confirmed, abbeys made exempt
from episcopal supervision and accountable only to the
Papacy; that in return for his protection he received a
revenue (*census*) from innumerable churches and monasteries;
that frequent councils, Roman or legatine, gathered together
the prelates, and with the bishops' visits to Rome *ad limina
apostolorum* brought them into touch with the Roman Curia;
that he could impose, without appeal, the still terrible penalties of excommunication and interdict [1]; and it will be seen
how vast the practical power and still more vast the theoretical claims of the Papacy could be. The claim, a century

[1] Excommunication was the exclusion of persons from Christian society
and the offices of the Church; interdict the suspension of all public worship.

later, that the Pope possessed all the power which resided in the Church as a whole, marked only a small advance on the doctrines of the " plenitude of power " held by Innocent III.

The Pope's secular authority
From this ecclesiastical authority branched off the quasi-secular authority of the Pope. According to the reigning allegory, the two swords in St. Peter's possession which Christ declared " sufficient " in the passage of St. Luke,[1] were the emblems of spiritual and temporal dominion ; the spiritual was to be used directly by the priesthood, the temporal at its instigation (*ad nutum*) by the secular rulers. And further, the Pope could intervene directly in secular affairs whenever the question of sin arose (*ratione peccati*). Since almost any act of state could raise the problem of right and wrong, the occasions for interference were almost unlimited in theory, and the lay powers, unconvinced by the doctrine of the inferiority of the temporal " sword," were hard put to it to answer the argument " *ratione peccati*." If the practice of papal superiority was far more halting and tethered than the theory, the lay rulers were in a way on the defensive and they were weakened by their own imperfect control of their dominions in the face of a resolute Pope who had his hands free at home.

Rivalry of Papacy and Empire
It was this freedom of action of the Papacy in Italy which made the relations of Papacy and Empire so uneasy. The difficulty the Pope had in ruling his city of Rome was formidable, but it could be thrust aside, for the interests of the Romans were local, and their affairs had little influence beyond central Italy. But the Empire was a mighty power ; its effective rule in Italy might bring the Papacy to a real subjection, and unlike other realms it had a theory and tradition of its own which made the Emperor the rival of the Pope for the theocratic rule of Christendom. From the time of Charlemagne onwards the Holy Roman Emperor had claimed to be the ruler of the City of God on earth as God's vice-gerent. The Romans had created their Empire by God's design to provide for the secular government of the world. As their ruler, as successor of Augustus and Constantine, the King of Germany, even before he was crowned Emperor at Rome by the Pope, was the head of all Chris-

[1] Luke xxii. 38.

tians by direct Divine commission ; the secular " sword "
was his free from papal control. The authority of his sacred
majesty interlocked inextricably with that of the Papacy
which his predecessors had at times reformed and guided.
The papal claim to omnipotence could never be realized in
face of a power almost as venerable which rallied the dissi-
dents to an incompatible scheme of world-government. Vain
and unreal as the doctrine of the Empire was, it provided
a theoretical embodiment for the tradition of the lay state,
governed by its own officers and owning no dependence on
a priestly hierarchy. By the side of the *sacerdotium* there
was set the *regnum* : one was never absorbed in the other.
While Papacy and Empire were concentrating on their
struggle, the more solid local kingdoms had time to grow
and to develop a system of state-independence more lasting
than the gorgeous phantom of the universal Empire.

The Empire had, however, missed its chance of becoming The Crusades
the effective secular head of Christendom in the great crusading movement of the twelfth century. That movement had
a diversity of causes. It was the last and most aggressive
stage of the reaction of Christendom against Islam, for it
completed the reconquest of the Mediterranean Sea. It was
part of the new expansion of the West European peoples,
the overflowing of their increasing population and surplus
energies, the growth of their commerce, wealth, and manufacture. It was also the warlike aspect of the religious revival
which came with reviving civilization, and it was the expression of the unity of that civilization, the sense, however
inefficient and alloyed, of the unity of Christendom. But
at the time of the Crusades' inception the Empire was paralysed by the decay of the imperial authority and the first
ill-omened feud with the Papacy. It was Pope Urban II
who read the signs of the times, placed himself at the head
of an enterprise he had half invented, and cemented its
natural religious connexion with the Papacy by the cut-and-
dried spiritual benefits he linked to the crusaders' expedition.
Those advantages were not lost by his successors. Amid
irremediable lay indiscipline and rivalry, the unified papal
authority, limited by no state-borders, remained supreme in
the crusading movement. Obedience, chequered indeed and
imperfect, was rendered by men to at least one central ruler

of all the West, and thereby that ruler was strengthened in things both ecclesiastical and lay. The Emperor perforce appeared as one secular agent among others. It was the Pope who proclaimed, urged on, and organized the joint effort of united Christendom in the Second and the Third as well as the First Crusade. It was the Papacy, already to men of the West the unquestioned head of the Christian Church, which in fact was chief of the only common secular enterprise of Christian lands.

But in this secular leadership, as indeed in its spiritual empire, there lay inevitable dangers for the Papacy. Like the enthusiasm of the Crusaders, it required substantial and lasting success for its continuance. How far in undertakings essentially warlike and political could an essentially unarmed and moral authority impart singleness of aim and unity of effort and command ? When it could not, when the conduct of war naturally fell to the warriors who waged it, when ignorance and indiscipline, racial hatreds, rivalry, and cupidity, striving under the enormous difficulties of campaigns in distant unfamiliar lands, in an alien and fatal climate, against formidable enemies, made the attempt to recover the Holy City in the Third Crusade fruitless, the limits of the papal achievement began to be shown. The Papacy could start a Crusade, but it could not control its course or determine its results. To give up the policy would be an evident confession of failure and a surrender of the ideal of converting strife among Christians into the Holy War against the infidel ; so the efforts of the Popes to maintain it continued long after Palestine was irrevocably lost. Underneath the old resounding phrases, the enthusiasm of Christendom had dwindled into fashion, and the Crusade became a burden and a diplomatic stock-in-trade to the Papacy itself. Meantime, in the twelfth century the Crusades had already played their part in immersing the Roman Curia in secular interests and in fostering its employment of secular means in a quasi-spiritual adventure, while at the same time they aroused by the contacts and rivalries they brought the nascent self-consciousness of nationalities, which were to ruin that unity of Christendom and of its chief embodiment, the medieval Church.

The unity of Western Christendom, indeed, if it was an

ecclesiastical fact, was never, save in the days of Charlemagne, more than a political theory.   The political reality of
Europe was an almost infinite subdivision which had come
into full existence with the dissolution of the Frankish
Empire.   There were kingdoms, it is true, and round the
kingship there remained a mingled tradition of immense
prestige, Roman, religious, Germanic, and feudal.   The king
in his land was heir to whatever traditions of Roman State
rule survived the Dark Ages, or were in course of revival
in the renovated civilization of the twelfth century.   He
was the guardian of peace, the enforcer of law and justice,
he was the source of public authority with a right to the
obedience of all subjects.   To this was added an ecclesiastical
religious sanction : he was the Lord's anointed by his sacring
and coronation, and ruled by God's will with the blessing
of the Church.   He was the feudal suzerain, direct or indirect,
of all the barons and lords of fiefs within his realm, however
wide their possessions or complete their authority within
them ; and within his realm he himself had no superior ;
his position was unique, and none of them but owed him
homage and service, and exercised a derivative power.
Whatever force lay in the feudal obligation—and all things
considered it was the strongest secular obligation of the
time—redounded to his advantage.   And lastly he was heir
to the tradition, shrouded and transmuted as it was, of the
Germanic chieftainship of the folk.   The ancient tribes of
Franks and the like had indeed long since dissolved or fused
with subject populations, but the sentiment which had held
them together had survived to find a new home in territorial,
embryo national feeling.   Community of habitat, of the race
formed there, of language, of moulding historical experience,
of habits and traditions was slowly forming not only a local
patriotism of near neighbours but also a wider sympathy
over the area of a kingdom.   As much as anything the
contact of men from different realms and of alien tongues
and mentality in the Crusades had tended to bring this
conscious sympathy about.   French, English, and Germans
conceived on new acquaintance a hearty dislike for one
another.   Each dimly realized that they were a nation, and
where there was a native hereditary kingship, a faint national
consciousness began to crystallize and give promise of be-

coming political round the person of the king. The emotion
was weak and elementary, and there were numberless hin-
drances to its development, in what we should later call
particularism, the earlier and stronger local attachments, in
indiscipline, in physical isolation, but combined with the
ideals the king stood for and the needs which, whenever
the chance was given, he could satisfy, it was bound to
grow.

Feudalism   This growth of the national kingship was, however, in
the year 1200 a thing of the future even in France and Spain.
In the lands of the Holy Roman Empire, what with the
strength of tribal particularism in Germany and the alien
character of the kings in Italy, and the dispersion of the
sovereigns' energies over too vast and incoherent a territory,
national feeling was never in the Middle Ages to take a
political shape. The reigning political system in Europe
was still feudalism, whether highly developed or retarded,
the autonomy of the local landowner, great and small. Its
origins and growth have been described in previous volumes,
and here need only be emphasized some of those conditions
and characteristics which ensured its vitality. In a world
of narrow horizons, still without good communications, still
too barbaric and illiterate to provide a professional centralized bureaucracy, still depending for its chief wealth on
the profits of land, the most feasible, in fact, the necessary
method of local government was to leave it in the hands of
the local noble who held the land and drew therefrom his
resources and his power. Again, when there were little or
no means of maintaining a disciplined army, the all-important
armed force for defence and aggression in a warlike age was
provided by the knight-service of these very nobles, who
held their fiefs in return for the quota of knights they owed
their suzerain. The elaborate fighting equipment, armour,
horse, and weapons, both by its costliness and the training
required to use it, was the monopoly of the landowner who
had leisure and means, and placed its possessor at an enormous
advantage over the unskilled, untrained, and miserably armed
peasant or bourgeois footmen. The castles which the nobles
had erected and could afford were both a necessity for
defence and control and only to be captured with the utmost
difficulty. The class of feudal lords were securely entrenched

in the domination of the countryside. Add to this, the immense weight of tradition, the whole existing legal and social system sanctioned by custom and antiquity, which made departure from it a slow and barely perceptible process. It was right that government and obedience should go by hereditary possession—and indeed, if hereditary right was lacking as it was to the Emperors, the want severely limited their appeal to the loyalty of their subjects. It was right and customary that the armed lord and knight should rule the unarmed peasants on the land they held by military service. It was not merely that, to give the most typical instance, France, the great tenants-in-chief of the Crown, the dukes and counts, practically exercised a royal authority over their fiefs, but their sub-tenants and the lesser barons of the royal domain possessed a full jurisdiction, *la haute justice*, and in turn were, to use a modern term, the executive over their lands, while even the lesser vassals ruled their manors with *la basse justice* and the customary monopolies (*banalités*) and powers of police. Complete dismemberment was prevented by the natural short-circuiting of this chain of feudal vassals. The king himself had no count with full powers under him in the royal domain of the Île de France. Not to mention his own manors,[1] lesser barons and plain knights there held their lands directly from him ; and the like situation existed within the great fiefs to the benefit of the dukes and counts. Thus the myriad of *seigneurs* were brigaded in feudal " States," and all through the twelfth century were submitting more and more to the governmental supervision of their superiors. The very complexity of feudal relationships, by which a man was often the vassal of several lords, ended in emphasizing this by the distinction of " liege homage " from simple homage. Liege vassalage meant that the lord to whom it was due had first claim on the vassal against any other of his lords. It was a pre-eminence of obligation. The monarchic principle was gaining ground at the expense of feudal anarchy.

Feudalism itself in its obligations was always weighted The feudal on the side of the suzerain if only he had power enough to contract

---

[1] In England these manors immediately in the king's possession formed the " royal demeane " ; in France, the " royal domain " included also lands under the king's immediate jurisdiction, similar to almost all England.

enforce his legal rights.   The vassal held his land and jurisdiction from his lord on condition of performing the strict
duties of the feudal contract.   He was bound to fidelity, aid,
and counsel, and these vague-sounding terms meant a number
of very precise things, the forty days' service in war, often
the temporary surrender of castles at need, the payment in
France of the four feudal " aids," [1] the attendance at the
suzerain's court (curia) to give him counsel in his affairs and
his justice.   As the fief was originally non-hereditary, on succession to it a " relief " had to be paid for the lord's consent.
Wardship of minors and the disposal of heiresses in marriage
were often the suzerain's right.   The vassal was subject to
his justice, and for lack of loyalty or other breach of the
feudal contract was liable to forfeiture of his fief.   In return
the suzerain was bound to respect his vassal's rights and to
give him protection ; if he broke the contract, the vassal
was released from his obligations and could appeal to the
superior lord, and could even wage war on the delinquent
suzerain.   But, if the king himself was the suzerain, the
right of revolt only remained, and this right, once formidable
and valuable, could lose most of its attractions when the
king had become far the more powerful of the two.

Homage
and fealty

The relationship of suzerain and vassal was entered into
by the composite ceremony of " homage " and " fealty."
The vassal became " the man " of his lord, i.e. did homage
by kneeling weaponless before him and placing his hands
within the hands of his lord ; then he swore " fealty " on
the Gospels, i.e. fidelity in feudal terms.   Lastly, the lord
" invested " him with the fief by some symbolic act.   The
bond thus created was at once legal and moral ; and in 1200
the moral tie was still strong enough to bind a conscientious
man to a different course of action after the ceremony than
before it ; it was a part of that loyalty which was the essence
of the ideal of knighthood.   A symbolic ceremony was to
the early Middle Ages, as to all primitive times, the necessary

Knighthood embodiment of a valid act.   Knighthood itself, the solemn
entrance into the class of noble warriors, was such an act.
It was derived from the public arming of the full-fledged
warrior, a kind of coming of age ; it had been adapted by

[1] On knighting the suzerain's eldest son, marriage of his eldest daughter,
his ransom from captivity, his departure for a crusade.

the Church with the object of Christianizing the character of valour and loyalty to kindred and lord which was expected of the initiate. The defence of women and the Church, courtesy, and honourable dealing were thus slowly added to an ideal of barbarous vigour. The times were still rude enough to make the full ideal of knightliness, even as then understood, attained by few ; yet it is a tribute to the growing civilization of the twelfth century that the level of the ideal and of ordinary behaviour steadily rose. It is easy to show how mediocre the practice was in the common run of men ; yet it was better than it had been, and the best acted by a higher standard than was known to their forbears of a century ago.

The reality of the life of the noble class in 1200 was indeed still barren and rude, violent and barbaric. Private war, the offspring of countless petty feuds, raged, springing up and dying down, over the greater part of the West ; public war, of greater moment if strongly similar in its causes, was almost as widespread. The intervals of stormy peace were filled with the mimic war of tournaments, which, grim in themselves, must have been an important influence, as were the Crusades, in diverting warlike energies from the senseless pillage of the countryside. The training in arms, hunting, and feasting provided occupation for more peaceful or darkling hours. Yet even so signs of a mellowing change were manifest. The fierce monotony of the *chansons de geste* of Charlemagne and his peers, themselves an awakening from the crass anarchy preceding them, was being variegated by the magic fancies of the suppler Arthurian lays and the quest of the Grail. In court and castle, even perhaps in country manor, men's thoughts took a wider range and a subtler insight, and *trouvère* and troubadour amused the leisure and caught the refinement of the ladies, less and less viragos, to whom they sang.

The life of the nobles

In the description of the fief and feudalism the lay vassal is the typical figure, but the ecclesiastical vassal is little less important for the picture. Every episcopal see in Western Europe was endowed with its lands on feudal or quasi-feudal terms, and offices and jurisdictions in the lay state were annexed to the bishopric. The bishop with his clerkly training and his non-hereditary office was in 1200 an indispensable

Episcopal Vassals

and invaluable vassal.   In France, for instance, the Archbishop of Rheims and the Bishop of Beauvais were counts
and pillars of the monarchy, the Archbishop of Rouen was
a leading Norman baron.   In Germany the possessions of
the bishops were so wide that the kingship largely depended
for its predominance on their loyal performance of their
duties as vassals of the Crown, and influence in their appointment was needful for the secure exercise of the king's authority.   They were princes of the Empire, whom both Emperor
and Pope endeavoured to control, the one as their secular,
the other as their spiritual superior.   The Concordat of Worms
in 1122 was an attempt to solve this difficult situation by a
compromise which in its nature was unstable.   The Concordat, indeed, expressed the dual subordination of the
prince-bishop to the Emperor as his suzerain and to the
Pope as head of the ecclesiastical hierarchy, but when the
interests of the two clashed whether over the Italian question
or over the interlocking relations of clerical and lay powers
in Germany, he would be compelled to choose which tie had
the greater hold upon him.   In France and elsewhere the
smaller secular jurisdictions and lands of the bishops, which
made them more dependent on the Crown and the Crown
less dependent upon them, and the comparative rarity of
major conflicts between Pope and king made the problem
less acute than in the Empire.   None the less the problem
was always there and was interwoven with the crises of the
thirteenth and fourteenth centuries.

The towns   To this feudal fabric of secular government the towns
formed a striking exception.   They depended on, and in
gross owed their origin to, another source of wealth and
power—buying and selling, manufacture, commerce—not on
land and the jurisdiction over it.   However much they might
be contaminated by their feudal ambient and assume or
submit to feudal obligations, they were essentially non-feudal.
Their ethos, their methods, their government, were of a
different cast.   Their organization was a system of association of partners, not of devolution from a superior.   Their
trading needs required a law and executive at once more
specialized and more elastic than the feudal, which was born
of the military levy and the agriculture of the countryside.
With these characteristics in common, however, at the end

of the twelfth century the towns displayed a wide range of degrees of autonomy, and still more varieties of internal organization that were to increase as time went on. Roughly they may be grouped in three main divisions ; first, the " commune " which possessed full local autonomy like a little republic. These were numerous, as we saw, in the *Regnum Italicum*, where indeed they acted as all but sovereign states. There were a certain number in Flanders and Lower Lorraine ; some too in France ; and they were soon to appear in Germany. Far more numerous was the second class, the " privileged town " self-administered under the control of its suzerain. Such were the English boroughs and a host of towns in France, Germany, South Italy, and Spain. Thirdly, there were the " rural towns," most commonly new chartered foundations (*villes neuves*), which were only endowed with certain functions and advantages by their lord. These were steadily increasing in number as a consequence of and as an incitement to the prosperity due to peace and trade.

The steady growth of peace and order, with the still more remarkable growth of population which accompanied it, was the main factor in the rise and increase of the towns. The townsmen could themselves carry on their undertakings more widely and securely ; the number and purchasing power of their customers were enlarged ; and their own power of production mounted in like manner as immigrants, runaway serfs and others, flowed in to the shelter of their walls. Indeed, an index of the movement is furnished by the new circles of walls built by the towns to contain their teeming inhabitants. While trade in some form was their *raison d'être*, the greatest towns were those which were engaged in " great commerce " of European extent. In Flanders, for instance, there was Bruges, which imported wool from England and exported it as cloth all over Europe. Venice, Pisa, and Genoa in Italy, Marseilles in Provence, Barcelona in Catalonia, were all engaged in the carrying trade of Oriental luxuries westward and of European raw materials and even cloth eastward. Hamburg, Lübeck, and Wisby were dominant in the carrying trade of the North Sea and the Baltic with its eastern outlet over Russia, as well as in the herring-fisheries of the Sound. Next to these and sometimes identical

Trade

with these came the manufacturing towns, great and small.
Cloth was woven, finished, and dyed for export in Bruges,
Ghent, and other Flemish centres, in Milan, Florence, and
many small Italian cities ; metal was worked in Liége,
Dinant, and Milan ; silk was woven at Palermo ; and smaller
industries, like the Gascon wine-trade, supplying wider or
narrower areas, found their home in numbers of smaller
towns, if the dispersion of their products was mainly, though
not wholly, due to the merchants of towns in " great commerce." Lastly, came the towns which merely supplied the
local market for their surrounding countryside. The " great
commerce " of the day in North Europe, however, was
largely transacted in periodic centres, the fairs, in which
the actual locality where they were held took only a subordinate part. The fairs were free from the severe restrictions
by which the towns sought to confine the profits of business
within them to their own inhabitants ; in them not mere
local regulations but the spontaneous " Law Merchant "
which had arisen over Western Europe by customary consent
decided disputes ; and thus the six fairs of Champagne,
which between them almost lasted out the year, situated
as they were at the point where the routes from all quarters
of the compass converged, became the chief market and
meeting-place of European commerce.

The mon-
asteries
Neither the ecclesiastical, the governmental, nor the
economic picture of twelfth-century Europe can be made
without reference to the monasteries. In town and country,
tilth, forest, and wilderness they thickly stud the map.
Ecclesiastically, their main divisions consisted of, first, those
under the old-fashioned Benedictine system (Black monks),
which implied the autonomy of each monastery under its
abbot. They were either under the supervision of the bishop
of the diocese or, if eminent and wealthy, were " exempt,"
i.e. subject to the Pope alone. Secondly, there was the
somewhat stricter Congregation of Cluny, offspring of the
early efforts at monastic reform in the tenth century. Local
autonomy in the Cluniacs gave way to the monarchic rule
of the Abbot of Cluny itself. The other 200 houses, even
if titular abbeys, were dependent priories subject to the
supreme abbot, who was only checked constitutionally by
the annual chapter of the priors. This was centralization

in the extreme, the antithesis of the normal Benedictine
ideal : they were all, however distant, supervised by the
one abbot, and as the Cluniacs were exempt, he was only
subject to the Pope. Thirdly, comes a real " Order " with
a Rule or " Customs " of its own, the Carthusians, whose
settlements, mainly in the wilderness, like the parent-house
of the Grande Chartreuse in Dauphiné, were sparse and
poor : they were a kind of collective hermitages, vowed
to silence, isolation, and great austerity. Their general
importance could be but small.

At the opposite pole in results, although curiously similar
in original motives and ultra-ascetic ideals, was the truly
cœnobitic Order of the Cistercians (White monks) with all
the power of its 700 federated abbeys and of its still growing
wealth. Several characteristics separated this Benedictine
offshoot from the older Benedictine Order. It had a federal
system of government of considerable ingenuity. The Order
was exempt and guided by General Chapters of its abbots.
Each house was ruled by its own abbot, and supervision
was effected by a kind of genealogical devolution. The
Abbot of Cîteaux, the original house, " visited " only the
four original colony-abbeys ; their abbots again " visited "
only their daughter houses ; and so on. Thus unity and
elasticity were combined. The ideal of the Cistercians had
originally been that of rigorous asceticism in the wilderness.
Their churches were to be bare and plain ; their monasteries
were built in the uninhabited forest or mountain-glen. But
in the enthusiasm for them inspired by the magnetic personality of St. Bernard, the twelfth-century saint *par excellence*, these very things became sources of art and wealth
and power. The sites they chose for wildness and solitude
were the homes of natural fascination. The churches became
marvels of beautiful, ungarnished form. The sheep which
fed on their clearings and valueless moors soon gave the
best wool supply in Europe. To ensure the banishment of
secular employees and their own freedom for the *opus Dei*
of prayer and meditation, they had fostered the older institution of lay-brethren (*conversi*) of inferior status for manual
labour, and the White Monks, like the Black, tended to
become lords among servants.

Only a word need be said of the Orders of Canons, Præ-

monstratensian and Augustinian, the first leaning more to
the Cistercian, the second to the Benedictine pattern.   Both
of them, being composed of clergy, whereas only selected
monks were ordained, were especially concerned with serving
the parish churches which formed a large part of their endowment, but by 1200 the Augustinians were already quitting
this field.

Beside the men's monasteries there existed the nunneries,
Benedictine, Cistercian, Præmonstratensian.   Some were
wealthy and therefore powerful ; practically all were, so to
say, preserves of the noble class.

One feature almost all these Orders and monasteries had
in common, devotion to the Papacy.   The protection they
gained from Rome, their universal character, their connexion with the Church reform of the eleventh century, all
encouraged this bent.   Indeed the monks had been the
natural allies of the Papacy since the time of Gregory the
Great.

The internal organization of each monastery was much
the same throughout the West.   They were little elective
monarchies under their head (abbot or abbess, prior, prioress,
provost), monarchies tempered by the chapter of the monks
and such external supervision as bishop, Pope, Abbot of
Cluny, or general chapter of their order, if it was federated
like the Cistercians, might afford.   Under the abbot were
the obedientiaries for the departments of administration.
The life of the professed monk, which has been described
in earlier volumes, was occupied in the first place by the
opus Dei, the round of prayer and divine service in the abbey
church ; the remainder of his waking hours was to be given
to private prayer and meditation, learning religious and
secular, and manual labour.   But whenever enthusiasm
diminished—and in 1200 it was generally on the wane—
and wealth from the stream of endowments grew, these
duties were frequently neglected ; the observance of the
Rule might be perfunctory ; manual labour was almost extinct ; the pursuit of comfort and indolence could replace
asceticism, the secular interests of large proprietors the abne-
gation of the world, a weak or worldly abbot could relax
discipline.   The novices, who were being trained for their
irrevocable profession as monks, were commonly received as

children or lads and might be little endowed with the monastic temperament.

The slack, and even the corrupt, monastery was to be found without difficulty in the thirteenth century. So was the wealthy house devoted to estate management and secular affairs, and the house whose indebtedness, due to mismanagement or improvident expenditure on sumptuous church and buildings, was the parent of disputes and disorder.

The lands with which the monasteries were endowed— for the vow of individual poverty did not exclude corporate wealth—made an abbot often a baron too, like a bishop, and in any case a feudal proprietor. Exempt from much feudal service he might be, holding in free alms, but he was not therefore denuded of feudal jurisdiction. Much of this, especially criminal jurisdiction, was commonly exercised in his name by a lay lord, the hereditary *advocatus* (in German *Vogt*), and this constituted a serious problem, for the *advocatus* would turn his functions as much as possible into an ordinary fief subtracted from the abbey's domain and control. Even with this diminution, however, an abbot of a wealthy monastery, like a bishop, who held a similar dual position, was a great potentate, secular as well as spiritual.

Wealth in lands, too, meant economic power and functions. The older Benedictine monasteries were places of call on the roads, entertaining the traveller. Little towns could, here and there, grow up round them, supplying their needs and benefiting by their situation and protection. Their demesne lands would be run on conservative lines with less capricious tyranny but with more unbending authority and more persistent maintenance of old rights than those of lay lords. Their tenants, serf or free, found it hard to improve their conditions in a changing world. Changes, indeed, the monasteries, especially the Cistercians, did make. They were inclined to consolidate their demesne lands, from the customary strips, in separate fields, a change beneficial to husbandry but which increased the numbers of landless peasants from whose strips the monastic fields were constructed. Whether in pastoral economy, agriculture, or the European trade in wool the monks therefore played an essential, and often a pioneering, rôle.

The monks had at one time been the intellectual leaders

of Western Europe, but by 1200 they were yielding this position to the young and growing institution of the Universities. Even that of Paris, indeed, was barely reaching its full embodiment, but, though immature, Paris and Bologna and Oxford were already capitals of European thought. Paris was the centre of scholasticism and its metaphysical theology, Bologna of the study of the Civil and the Canon Law. Soon most of the dignitaries and officials of Church and State received their mental training at the Universities ; they were frequented by clerks from all Western Christendom. While scholasticism belongs to the history of the mind and the Church, the Civil and the Canon Law were of high importance in secular life and government.   Canon Law, codified by Gratian and incessantly amplified by the Decretals of the Popes, regulated, we have seen, not only ecclesiastical persons and affairs but the conduct and morals of the laity as well ; sentence of excommunication was a formidable punishment and means of compulsion ; and the Christian man was under the jurisdiction of a complete hierarchy of ecclesiastical courts ascending to the Papacy, as well as under those of king and feudal lord. The Civil Law of Justinian and its doctors had no such effective validity, but they were constantly leavening the public and private customary law of the Latin countries. As societies grew more civilized they required a more civilized law, and could appreciate the principles and prescriptions of the Roman code. Moreover, it was constantly regarded as the ideal, even the rightful, law wherever the ancient Roman Empire had been, and its doctrines on royal and State authority were embraced and acted upon by the jurists who began to staff the royal bureaucracies and interpret feudal custom.

The language of Civil and Canon Law, of scholasticism, of learning, and the Church, was still Latin, changed somewhat but still essentially the same as classic Latin. While the vernaculars were still in growth and not well advanced beyond the expression of the concrete, the benefits of this use of a dead universal language far outweighed the disadvantages of expression in a medium foreign to all its users. It put men into touch with the works of antiquity and their civilizing influence ; it provided a fixed *lingua franca* for the speakers of a variety of tongues not yet standardized ;

it gave an exact terminology and rational sequence of thought in words, which so to say increased the faculty of precise rational thought in its users, and, not least, enabled them to develop unconsciously, it may be, the rationality and precision of their native tongues which were to replace it. This effect was already showing itself in the vernacular law-books which were beginning to arise.

Meantime, vernacular literature in the various and often unpolished dialects into which the languages of Europe were divided had attained a vigorous life and development. For certain things and in certain spheres it already easily sur-passed the acquired, imitative, and inevitably impoverished contemporary Latin. For the expression, truth, and variety of emotion, for the concrete realities of life and the world, for the charm of nature, and the poignancy of simple direct thought on daily experience, for the indescribable personal appeal of style vibrating like the tones of a voice, it was necessarily and triumphantly superior. We still read twelfth-century Latin mainly for the knowledge we get from it. We get knowledge of that distant past also from the ver-naculars, from Saga, romance, *chanson de geste,* and lay ; but we get too the pleasure and the vivid realization of living literature. That dead and silent world awakes to shadowy life. We hear the clank of weapons, the hoofs of galloping horses, the song at the feast, the babel of voices at the fair ; we see the miry streets of the town, the straggling train of pack-horses along the endless Roman road, the gaunt *donjon* on its rock, the forest green with leaves long ago fallen, and the ship of Leif Eriksson sailing westward to Vinland beneath a frosty moon.

The Ver-
naculars

SUGGESTIONS FOR READING ON CHAPTER I

A. GEOGRAPHY

East, W. G. : *An Historical Geography of Europe.* London, 1935.

Freeman, E. A. : *Historical Geography of Europe.* 2 vols. 3rd edn Bury, J. B. London, 1903.

Spruner-Menke : *Handatlas für die Geschichte des Mittelalters und der neueren Zeit.* Gotha, 1880.

B. POLITICS

Adams, G. B. : *Civilization during the Middle Ages.* 2nd edn. New York, 1914.

Baynes, N. H. : *The Byzantine Empire.* London, 1925.

Bloch, M. : *La société féodale.* 2 vols. Paris, 1939–40.

Bryce, J. : *The Holy Roman Empire.* London, 1906.

Calmette, J. : *La société féodale.* Paris, 1927.

Cambridge Medieval History, vol. iii, chapter xviii ; vol. v, chapter xx ; vol. vi, chapters xvi and xix.

Carlyle, R. W. and A. J. : *History of Mediæval Political Theory in the West.* 6 vols. London, 1903 ff.

Coulton, G. G. : *Five Centuries of Religion.* Vols. i–iii. Cambridge, 1923 ff.

Gibbon, E. : *History of the Decline and Fall of the Roman Empire.* 7 vols. Ed. Bury, J. B. London, 1909–14.

Gierke, O. : *Political Theories of the Middle Age.* Trans. Maitland, F. W. Cambridge, 1900.

Glotz, G. : *Histoire générale, Le Moyen Âge.* Vol. viii : La civilisation occidentale. Paris, 1933.

Hauck, A. : *Kirchengeschichte Deutschlands.* 5 vols. 3rd and 4th edns. Leipzig, 1904–20.

Lea, H. C. : *History of Sacerdotal Celibacy in the Christian Church.* 3rd edn. 2 vols. London, 1907.

Mitteis, H. : *Der Staat des hohen Mittelalters.* 3rd edn. Weimar, 1948.

Poole, R. L. : *Illustrations of the History of Medieval Thought and Learning.* 2nd edn. London, 1920.

Rashdall, H. : *The Universities of Europe in the Middle Ages.* Ed. Powicke, F. M., and Emden, A. B. 3 vols. Oxford, 1936.

Vinogradoff, P. : *Roman Law in Medieval Europe.* 2nd edn. Oxford, 1929.

C. For LITERATURE, see the suggestions for Chapters X and XX.

CHAPTER II

INNOCENT III AND THE PAPACY AT THE HEIGHT OF ITS POWER

THE sudden death of Henry VI, Emperor of the Romans and King of Sicily, on September 28, 1197, certainly brought about a lasting revolution in the state of the Empire, the Papacy, and Europe, but it may be questioned whether some such change would not have come about within the next twenty years even if Henry had lived them through. It is true that Germany was loyal, that the Lombard towns obeyed him, that central Italy was controlled by his lieutenants, that Sicily was submissive, that the Papacy had been outmanœuvred and daunted. But the bases of this power were not sound, and Henry was in course of overstraining them by his busy aggression, his vast schemes of world-dominion, and the wily rigour of the means he took to extend them. In Germany, the royal domains, though enlarged, were still comparatively too small to give the Emperor the whiphand of the princes ; the monarchy was elective, not hereditary, and this defect, besides depriving the German kings of loyalty in a custom-ruled age, opened the door to the rival ambitions of competing houses ; the Emperor Henry himself was not a national hero like his father Barbarossa ; there was an actively disaffected group headed by the Welfs in Saxony and Lower Lorraine, and many princes were willing to play with revolt. The Lombard cities were alarmed at the growth of his power in Italy ; the centre had been roused to a national hatred of the German officials and garrisons ; and the kingdom of Sicily was only kept down by terror. Pope Celestine III had shown a persevering if timid hostility to the power which threatened to enclose and dominate the Papacy, and he had taken every opportunity to thwart it.

The fact was that the Hohenstaufen policy of an effective dominion in Italy, a policy really inherent in the exist-

Death of the Emperor Henry VI

ence of the Holy Roman Empire, of which Henry VI was
almost an extreme exponent, ran counter to the natural
instincts and deep-seated interests of their subjects. Germany was essentially particularistic. The decay of the tribal
duchies, largely the consequence of imperial efforts, had
transferred this particularism to the smaller units, the princes
or tenants-in-chief of Germany ; and as feudalism made
progress at the expense of earlier tribalism, the princes,
individually weaker, became collectively stronger than the
dukes had been. They had no mind for a searching central
administration or an overwhelming royal power. They had
selfish shrewdness enough to see, and perhaps instinctive
particularism enough to feel, that the ancient customs, the
elective kingship, and the principle of regranting escheated
fiefs and not enriching the Crown with them,[1] were their
best safeguard. By manning the cathedral chapters with
their younger sons they were slowly making the German
Church, which had once thought imperially, an organ of
their power. It is no wonder that the Hohenstaufen turned
to their *ministeriales*, the serf-knights of their domains,[2] for
genuine support. And again, as we shall see, the living
interests of Germany turned north and east beyond the
Elbe, not to the unification of Italy under the Emperor.

In like manner, however disunited the Italians might be,
a deep aversion to the rule of alien Germans was common
to the whole peninsula. The benefits which might have
sprung from a single strong monarchy were not obvious.
In the north there existed the passionate desire for autonomy
in each city and town ; they wished to get the better of
one another, not to exist side by side under one impartial
rule, even Italian. In the kingdom of Sicily the feudal
nobles and the towns were always restive even under the
Norman dynasty, and their incoherent indiscipline was given
a kind of unity by racial hatred.

[1] That an escheated fief in Germany should be granted out again within
a year and a day was acknowledged by Frederick Barbarossa as part of the
price for the support of the princes in the overthrow of the Welf Henry the
Lion of Saxony.

[2] The continued existence of the class of serf-knights was a conservative
feature of Germany. They were serfs in status who held tenements rather
than fiefs on their lord's demesne for military service. They were far more
amenable to command than free vassals, and were often, like Markward of
Anweiler, entrusted with important office.

A wave of revolt rapidly passed over Italy at the news of Henry's death. His brother Philip, Duke of Swabia and Marquess of Tuscany, on his way to bring his nephew Frederick north, was forced to flee from Montefiascone back to Germany. The towns of the Duchy of Spoleto rose against the German duke, Conrad of Urslingen. Markward of Anweiler, the late Emperor's best general, experienced the same fate in the March of Ancona and County of Romagna. The Tuscan cities completed on November 11, 1197, at San Miniato dei Tedeschi a league long prepared for, directed against the Empire ; it soon broke up, but it marked Tuscany's emancipation. In Sicily, the Norman Empress Constance secured the person of her infant son Frederick and replaced German officials by natives, but the Germans and their troopers held fast to their strongholds on the mainland.

It was at this moment that the aged Pope Celestine III died, and was replaced the same day, January 8, 1198, by the Cardinal-deacon Lothar of the house of the Counts (Conti) of Segni as Innocent III. The change was one of persons, rather than of policy. In this favourable time for a bold forward policy the Cardinals [1] chose the youngest member of the College, a man of thirty-seven. Innocent III possessed an iron determination and a tireless industry. Sincerely but conventionally religious, he was of the stuff that rulers, not saints, are made. As a jurist his fame stands very high ; good sense and equity, insight into the essential point of a case, a grasp of general principles were all his. As a diplomatist, he was both subtle and supple ; he wrung the utmost out of circumstances. Daring in extremity, exacting in success, adroitly pliant and resourceful in adversity, he gambled with events, and in the long run rose a winner. Under him the medieval papacy reached its apogee. But we may doubt whether he did not sometimes buy success too dear and whether in his definitely political outlook he did not prepare the way for decline.

Innocent's first actions showed this political temper.

Accession of Innocent III

---

[1] For the College of Cardinals, see the preceding volume in this series. Once the leading local clergy of the Roman diocese, they had become an international council of the Pope, by whom they were nominated, and whom they elected. Since the Third Lateran Council of 1179 the election required a two-thirds majority of the Cardinals, and was valid directly that was obtained.

The Papal
States The Pope was nominal sovereign of the Patrimony of St. Peter, but in fact the disorderly commune of Rome and the little cities and the barons of the Campagna acted in independence. The cities of the Duchy of Spoleto, the March of Ancona, and the Romagna had indeed temporarily revolted from their imperial governors, but their internecine strife was a poor substitute. Innocent's remedy was to make his suzerainty effective in Rome and the Campagna, and, while the Empire was paralysed, on the strength of the Carolingian donations, not to mention that of Constantine, to extend that suzerainty over central Italy. Thus he would thrust back the dangerous Empire and divide it from Sicily, and give the Papacy a wide territorial basis, safe in which it could exercise its spiritual, and if need be temporal, control over Europe. In Rome itself he met with considerable success by dint of perseverance ; he ousted the Empire at once by insisting that the lord of Vico, the hereditary Prefect of the City, who exercised criminal justice, should become a liege vassal of the Papacy. The rule of the commune was in the hands of sometimes one, sometimes fifty-six Senators, elected annually ; Innocent assumed the right of appointing *mediani* who were to elect the new sole Senator. This brought no peace at first. Faction-fights between rival noble houses, between papalists and anti-papalists, were the order of the day for years : in 1203 the Pope had to quit Rome for fear of worse. Yet patient diplomacy, the adroit use of his family connexions, and the Romans' weariness of their own anarchy gave him the victory. After 1205 single Senators appointed by papal *mediani* peacefully ruled the City. Rome could not in fact throw off its economic dependence on the Papacy. The middle classes lived on the Curia and the prelates, litigants, and pilgrims who frequented it. If Rome was too anarchic or hostile for the Pope to remain there, the source of their prosperity dried up.

Annexation
of Spoleto
and Ancona The nominal annexation of the Duchy of Spoleto was an easier matter. Conrad of Urslingen retired from the contest with barely a struggle, and the towns accepted the Pope's suzerainty and the Rector he appointed without difficulty. But they intended to be independent republics, and Innocent had to be content with a show of control, and occasional obedience. Romagna, expelling Markward, escaped him al-

together, and, though the majority of the towns of the March of Ancona acknowledged papal overlordship, some did not, and all acted with untrammelled freedom. Innocent's last device, in 1212, the enfeofment of the March to the Marquess of Este, was quite fruitless; local independence and wars with one another were the primary instincts of these mountain towns.

Meanwhile in 1199 Markward, after a vain resistance, had retreated to the Regno,[1] to demand the regency. Here the Empress Constance, anti-German and trembling for her son, had bought the Pope's alliance on his own terms. She admitted the Pope's suzerainty, which Henry VI in his lifetime had never done, although on his death-bed he seems to have contemplated it, and surrendered perforce the extraordinary ecclesiastical privileges of the Sicilian Crown: henceforward appeals to Rome, the entrance of papal legates, the holding of synods, the review of episcopal elections were to be unhindered in the Regno as elsewhere. When on November 27, 1198, she died, she left her suzerain guardian of her son's kingdom. There followed a long struggle of not unequal forces amid growing anarchy. On the one side was the Pope, a faithful guardian who expected his share of the profits of success; on the other Markward and the other German captains, loyal in their fashion to the Hohenstaufen. Between these swayed Walter of Palear, Bishop of Troia and Chancellor, probably loyal and certainly greedy, and Innocent added to the competitors the Frenchman Walter of Brienne, son-in-law of King Tancred and suspect as a possible claimant of the kingdom. Strange to say, the young Frederick survived the wars of his would-be tutors and was well educated to boot. The most dangerous combatants died, Markward in 1202, Brienne in 1205; the Pope's support was steady and skilful; when Frederick was declared of age in 1208, the Regno, though disordered, was safely his.

In North Italy, however, Innocent had to be content with a not always effective spiritual authority. The Tuscan league soon dissolved into warring cities, Florence, Siena, and Lucca; Pisa had stoutly refused to join it. They all

The Kingdom of Sicily (the Regno)

North Italy

---

[1] To avoid the anachronisms of "The Two Sicilies" and "Naples" and the ambiguity of "Sicily" I shall, till the War of the Vespers, use the convenient Italian term of "the Regno" for the southern kingdom.

rebuffed the Pope's endeavour to make them his vassals. The Lombard towns seized the imperial domains, and pursued their mutual feuds almost without ceasing, but seemingly without doing permanent injury to their commercial prosperity.

Civil War in Germany

Behind all these events, as the condition of their happening, lay the disputed succession to the imperial throne and the civil war in Germany. That fateful civil war, the decisive crisis of German medieval history, drew its origin from a number of causes in past and present. First, there was the inveterate particularism which now found its embodiment in the princes, engrossed with local and family aims, stubbornly insubordinate, and fortified by the elective character of the kingship which itself had stunted the sentiment of instinctive loyalty to the monarch as chief of the State and people. Secondly, there was the especially wide fissure dividing the Low Germans, Saxons and Rhinelanders, from the High Germans, Swabians, Bavarians, and Franconians, which had been the bane of the Empire from the eleventh century and since the twelfth had coalesced with the family feud, typical of many others, between the houses of the Welfs and the Hohenstaufen. Then there were the complications of foreign alliances and the policies of foreign kings. It so happened that the chief of the Welfs in the later twelfth century, Henry the Lion, had married the daughter of Henry II of England, and his sons were nephews of Richard Cœur-de-lion, the reigning English king. Personal liking and family ties were perhaps enough to make Richard anxious to advance the Welfs, but there were further grounds of policy to influence him. England was in close trade relations with Cologne and Lower Lorraine ; Richard was at grips with his French suzerain, King Philip Augustus, and not only were Low German allies useful to him but also Philip Augustus was the ally of the Hohenstaufen. When Richard was captured by the Emperor Henry VI on his return from the Third Crusade, he had been compelled to desist from favouring his nephews in their disloyalty to the Emperor ; he had now a free hand to revert to his former policy and take his revenge.

Philip and Otto IV

The Emperor's death plunged this unsoldered Germany in the melting-pot. In spite of the efforts of his uncle

Philip of Swabia, it became clear that the princes, partly because of his age, partly from particularistic selfishness, would not keep the fealty they had sworn in 1196, to the child Frederick, when they had elected him " King of the Romans." [1] The Low German princes under the leadership of Albert, Archbishop of Cologne, began to seek a candidate from another dynasty. Then Philip himself came forward to save the crown for the Hohenstaufen and was elected King by his partisans on March 8, 1198. But the dissentients, consolidated by the bribes of Richard of England, now found a rival king in the second son of Henry the Lion, Otto Count of Poitou, and Otto was crowned at Aix-la-Chapelle on the throne of Charlemagne by the Archbishop of Cologne to whom the right of coronation belonged, while Philip was crowned indeed with the real royal insignia, but only by the Archbishop of Tarentaise at Mainz. The civil war had begun, and in its long devastating course brought about the temporary breakdown and the lasting weakness of the central power. The faithless and selfish princes changed from side to side, and in bribing them the rivals, more especially Philip, dissipated royal demesnes and revenues and helped to build up princely immunity from royal intervention in their fiefs.

The two kings were personally poor leaders. Otto was a stalwart knight, but stupid and blundering. Philip was honourable and clerkly ; he had not the gifts of inspiring devotion or overawing the disloyal. Otto, however, was much the weaker, and his main support, King Richard, died in 1199 ; and this gave the Pope his chance. Innocent maintained at first an attitude of neutrality, malevolent towards Philip, benevolent to Otto. An attempt to mediate made by the Archbishop of Mainz ended in smoke. In 1201 Otto was ready to accept the Pope's terms. Innocent's views of the situation and of his own powers, set forth in the secret *Deliberatio* of December 1200, and later in public The letters,[2] rested on two assumptions : first, that Pope Leo III *Deliberatio* in 800 had " transferred " the Empire from the Greeks to the Germans, and therefore the German princes elected the

---

[1] The title assumed by the Kings of Germany before their imperial coronation, to denote their rule over the whole Empire. Cf. above, p. 7.

[2] Such as the Decretal *Venerabilem* in 1201.

King of the Romans rather by papal permission than by
absolute right ; secondly, that the Pope created an Emperor
by crowning him, and therefore was judge of the fitness of
the candidate elected—he could not crown an infidel. On
these grounds, since there was a schism in the Empire,
Innocent rejected Philip and confirmed Otto IV. In return,
the fruit of much bargaining, Otto made the Promise of
Neuss on June 8, 1201. He was to cede to the Pope the
lands he claimed in Italy, the Duchy of Spoleto, the March
of Ancona, Romagna, the lands of Countess Matilda,[1] the
vassal kingdom of Sicily ; and in Germany he renounced
the ancient right to the *spolia*, the goods of deceased bishops,
which formed a useful part of the imperial income. It
amounted to a surrender of the imperial position in Italy.

Otto IV's Promise of Neuss

For a time Otto seemed to prosper and his adherents
increased. But he made no impression on South Germany,
and fell out with his own supporters. In 1204 his own elder
brother the Count Palatine, the Duke of Brabant, and Adolf
of Cologne went over to Philip : in 1205 Philip was crowned
at Aix-la-Chapelle ; and in 1207 the city of Cologne, attacked
for two years, at length surrendered. Otto, reduced to Brunswick, took refuge in England. Innocent III, meantime, had
long been haggling with the winning side, nor was his enemy
John of England's support of Otto IV likely to bind him
to the loser. Philip had to submit to be absolved from the
excommunication he had suffered before his accession from
Celestine III ; he admitted Innocent's deposition of the
turncoat Adolf of Cologne ; but he obtained in 1208 Innocent's recognition of his kingship and his rights over central
Italy. It is said that the Pope's nephew was to marry
Philip's daughter and receive Tuscany. Yet the decisive
fact was that Innocent had abandoned his protégé and
endured defeat.

Murder of King Philip

A crime—Innocent declared it a judgment of God—
annulled this surrender. On June 21, 1208, King Philip
was murdered by Otto of Wittelsbach, Count Palatine of
Bavaria, in revenge for a private grievance. His partisans
had no candidate, all were weary of civil war, and the sur-

---

[1] These lands in Tuscany and south Lombardy, left by Matilda to the
Papacy, had been in dispute throughout the twelfth century, but mostly
kept by the Emperors. See the preceding volume in this series.

viving Otto IV was re-elected king, promising to marry his
rival's daughter. The Pope was first delighted, then suspicious. In taking up the Hohenstaufen crown, Otto took
up, too, their policy. He must, of course, be crowned Emperor; he wished for their dominion in Italy. But the
coronation depended on the Pope, and Innocent bargained
once more, this time with a man who promised the more
largely because he had predetermined to break his faith.
At Spires on March 22, 1209, Otto IV renewed the conces- Otto IV's
sions of Neuss, and added concessions of still greater import. Concessions
He renounced now the royal right to the revenues of vacant German
bishoprics (*Regalia*) and the royal right, under the imperial Church at
interpretation of the Concordat of Worms (1122), to inter- Spires
vene in the election of prelates and to decide in cases of
discord; they were now to be only subject to Canon Law,
i.e. to the Pope's judgment. Lastly, the course of ecclesiastical appeals to the Pope was to be absolutely free, as it
was in France and England. In this way Otto gave up the
close control of the German Church as exercised by Barbarossa: the main pillar of the monarchy, established by
the Ottos, was sapped. In England and France, national
feeling, royal wealth, and a strong local royal administration
made this state of things of less moment, and royal influence
in the appointment of prelates was never set aside; in
Germany, where the kingship was relatively poor and particularistic feudalism was increasing day by day, it was a
fatal breach in the royal power.

Otto IV could now, to the growing alarm of the Pope, Otto IV's
make his Italian expedition at the head of a powerful army, breach with
and he was duly crowned Emperor on October 4, 1209. the Pope
But the Emperor, no longer styling himself " by the grace
of the Pope," was already showing his hand. He naturally
resumed all he could of the imperial domains in Lombardy
and Tuscany, which had been seized by the communes,
including the Matildine lands. But he also appointed a
Count of Romagna and a Duke of Spoleto, and like another
Henry VI, but without the shadow of a claim, prepared to
conquer the Regno from the Hohenstaufen Frederick, whose
German captains found him far too Sicilian. The fact was
that the impoverished German monarchy could less than
ever do without the wealth of the south. Despite papal

protests, the invasion began in 1210 and by March 1211 all
the mainland was conquered. A Pisan fleet prepared to
convey Otto into Sicily. Frederick, whose Germans deserted
him, was ready to fly to Africa.

Election of Frederick II

Innocent, deceived in all his calculations, could only
declare war, interdict, excommunication, and deposition
against his quondam protégé, but he had a powerful and
cool-headed ally in Philip Augustus of France, the inevitable
enemy of Otto and John of England. To that ally's policy
the Pope had now to bow, and in so doing take the risk of
a union of Sicily with the Empire, the prevention of which
had been one of his fixed principles of action. Otto with
his army was irresistible in Italy and the papal ban had only
a limited effect on the behaviour of the Italian communes.
But in Germany the powerful ecclesiastical princes were more
amenable, the old feuds were still awake, the name of the
Hohenstaufen had a charm, the princes were sullen at the
Emperor's determination to restore a central rule, and greedily
ready for the bribes that Philip Augustus could offer them.
Only one anti-Cæsar was possible, the Hohenstaufen heir,
Frederick of Sicily, himself, and Innocent resigned himself
at Philip of France's demand to promoting his candidature.
Money, self-interest, and religious dread soon bore fruit : in
September 1211 a number of the chief princes led by the
Ottonian Archbishop of Mainz elected Frederick II King of
the Romans, and the Pope himself urged the young King
of Sicily to accept the election. On Otto the rebellion had
all the desired effect. He could not allow Germany to slip
from him, and slowly moving north, reached the divided
realm in March 1212.

Meantime Frederick II had accepted the Pope's terms.
Ambition, and the natural desire to regain his rightful inheritance from his house's enemy, but above all self-preser-
vation urged him to this decision. Otto's garrisons still
held the mainland of the Regno, and if the German revolt
was allowed to die down, as it well might, destruction stood
very near him. But, as usual with Innocent, the bargain
was hard. Frederick was to repeat Otto's concessions, and
he was to abdicate the Sicilian throne in favour of his son
Henry, as soon as he was crowned Emperor, in order to
maintain the perpetual separation of the Empire and the

Regno. The baby Henry was, indeed, crowned co-regent ; the north of the Terra di Lavoro was delivered in pawn to the Pope and his relatives ; at Easter 1212 Frederick did personal homage to Innocent for Sicily. The feuds of the towns of Lombardy gave him a party there, and, eluding the Pisan fleet, he could safely land at Genoa. Thence with a small following he slipped across the Alps to Chur to woo the German princes to support him in the civil war.

Otto's power was still formidable, but his failure to prevent his rival entering Germany was his undoing. As Frederick moved down the Rhine, the Emperor could only retire to Saxony, for High Germany joined the Hohenstaufen, who was elected yet once more and then crowned for the first time at Mainz on December 9, 1212. It was not all due to papal influence or loyalty to his house ; the princes were dearly bought, and not even the early years of his uncle Philip were so destructive to the royal rights and domains. Money bribes were furnished by the King of France, with whose eldest son Louis Frederick contracted an alliance at Vaucouleurs on November 18. On his side Otto IV dispensed large English subsidies to his Low German supporters. In these circumstances the fighting was desultory and indecisive. The pressing question in Germany was whether to change sides ; and the critical battle took place outside the Empire in a foreign quarrel. John of England's subsidies were given so that his nephew should aid him to recover his lost French fiefs. While Otto at the head of his Low Battle of Germans attacked France through Flanders, John was to Bouvines march from the south towards the Loire. John failed ingloriously : Otto IV was routed by Philip Augustus in person in the pitched battle of Bouvines on July 27, 1214. It was one of the decisive battles of the world, for France, for England, for the civil war in Germany, and for the relative position of the Western nations : " Henceforward," wrote a Saxon chronicler, " sank the fame of the Germans among the Latins."

Desertions now went on apace throughout Lower Lor- Victory of raine, though Otto was safe in Cologne owing to the loyalty Frederick II of its citizens. But in 1215 Cologne, too, surrendered to Frederick, and the Emperor was left to hold out almost alone in his allodial lands round Brunswick. There he died

on May 19, 1218. His heirs were restricted to these Saxon
possessions, for the Palatinate of the Rhine had passed to
the Wittelsbach Duke of Bavaria. The great feud of Welf
and Hohenstaufen was over.

Golden Bull of Eger   But Frederick II paid dear for his victory. He did not
attempt, as Otto had done, to restore direct royal govern-
ment. He depended on the princes and the Pope. It was
absolutely necessary for him to placate Innocent and avoid
raising his suspicions. Accordingly, on July 12, 1213, he
issued the Golden Bull of Eger, which confirmed his own and
Otto IV's concessions to the Pope and the Church. Unlike
those former grants, which only emanated from the grantor,
and might be represented as invalid, the Golden Bull was
subscribed by the princes of the Empire, and was indubitable-
law. Innocent had gained the prize he had so long played
for ; and he adroitly made a further advance in doctrine
when the General Council of the Lateran confirmed the
deposition of Otto and the election of Frederick. This after
all expressed the fact : the Pope had disposed of the crowns
of Germany and the Empire. Meantime, further to win his
favour, Frederick had taken the cross on the occasion of his
second coronation at Aix-la-Chapelle in 1215. He might
hope also to secure a crusader's immunity from attack and
to divert the princes' thoughts abroad, but the Crusade was
to prove a long embarrassment to himself.

Doubtless, the long civil war and the reckless concessions
of the rival kings were the immediate causes of the decadence
of the German kingship, but they merely worked out tendencies now irresistible. That the German Church should be
wrenched from the old-fashioned legal tutelage of its kings
and placed under the unhindered control of the Pope was in
the long run inevitable in view of the actual development
of European thought and belief. Similarly, the deep-rooted
particularism of the Germans, and the selfish greed and
indiscipline of the princes which it both sanctioned and fostered, had long been gathering momentum, and were stronger
for the Emperors' attempts to check them. Personal gain
was the lodestar of the princes, and local feeling was with
them ; their relatives filled the chapters and elected the
bishops. How could the elective kingship, never adequately
endowed, hopelessly embroiled with the Papacy over its

Italian dominion, resist in perpetuity forces so strong and
interwoven, and build a lasting structure on these sapped
foundations ?

The " business of the Empire," of first importance as it Innocent III
was for Innocent's pontificate, was only one among the and the
Western
semi-political questions which absorbed the Pope's energies Kings
along with the incessant routine administration in the purely
ecclesiastical sphere. The Fourth Crusade and its sequels, and
the preparations for the Fifth, and the Crusade against the
Moors in Spain, are described in other chapters. His dealings with John of England can only be alluded to ; in them
Innocent's victory seemed complete, for he compelled the
King to admit (1213) his choice of Stephen Langton as Archbishop of Canterbury, which, in pursuance of the free course
of appeals to Rome admitted by Henry II in 1172, established the papal right of decision and provision in disputed
elections. England became by John's surrender a fief of
the Papacy. In addition to its theocratic claims the Papacy
was acquiring a purely temporal dominion over vassal kingdoms : Aragon in 1202, Portugal, and Hungary owed fealty
in some degree to the Roman Pontiff. In all this political
activity, Innocent met with open or concealed defeat in only
two instances. The open defeat was in Norway. In this
old-fashioned realm, the advances in Canon Law—free election of bishops, the restriction of lay patronage, the Courts
Christian, and clerical immunity—had only been introduced
in the second half of the twelfth century along with a law
which made succession to the throne depend on the bishops'
decision. But the old state of things was restored by the
mighty usurper Sverre, the champion of the lay state (1182–
1202). In vain the Pope excommunicated and deposed him,
and Innocent added interdict over all Norway to the measures
of his predecessors. The interdict was not observed, some
bishops held by their king, who even issued a pamphlet in
defence of the royal supremacy with arguments from Scripture and Gratian, and no invasion could be engineered from
Denmark or Sweden. It is true that Hakon III made a
compromise after Sverre's death, but this was itself conservative, and even in a later arrangement in 1247
the clergy still had to submit to the lay courts in secular
things.

The concealed defeat was over the mysterious case of Philip Augustus of France and his queen, Ingeborg. Philip had married this Danish princess in 1193, but scarcely had he married her than he put her away : an obedient synod annulled the marriage on a false reckoning of consanguinity. On Ingeborg's appeal Celestine III quashed the divorce, but Philip persisted, and even remarried, this time Agnes of the Bavarian house of Meran. Soon after his accession Innocent intervened to defend the persecuted wife, the law of the Church, and the authority of the Apostolic see : he demanded the restoration of Ingeborg and the dismissal of Agnes. When the King refused, north France was placed under interdict in 1200. It is significant that Philip was not excommunicated, and that most of his bishops sided with him. Still nine months of interdict had their effect : he nominally gave way, and the divorce case was reopened before papal legates. But he burked their judgment by suddenly pretending to take back Ingeborg, whom he then cruelly imprisoned for years. The Pope had won the legal point and defended his own supreme authority ; for Ingeborg he was content to protest, while legitimating the children of Agnes, now dead, and he even pointed out to Philip the admissions which, if Ingeborg could be persuaded to make them, would allow the divorce. The *impasse* continued till Philip, anxious to conciliate the Pope in view of his son's invasion of England, once more in 1213 gave up his demand for a divorce and finally reinstated Ingeborg as queen. Innocent had upheld the letter of the law rather than its spirit, and it is rather as the foe of corruption in the Courts Christian than as a moralist that he displayed here his courage and consistency.

In the routine course of affairs the influence of the Pope's appellate and direct jurisdiction and his constant supervision tended to a higher standard and wiser equity in times when justice was often blind and always harsh. It also tended to develop systematically the increasing centralization of the Church with results good and bad, of which the bad were to grow and to be more lasting. Innocent honestly fought abuses, but always by extending the use of his prerogative. The exercise of the " plenitude of power " lamed the local organization of the Church, and weakened the often misused power and initiative of the episcopate. The insistence on Clerical the exemption and superiority of ecclesiastics did much, in Immunity spite of failures, to thwart tyrannous aggression and lawless plunder, but it led Innocent to denounce the attempts of the Italian communes to tax the clergy like other citizens, and thus roused an anti-clerical indignation, which harmed the moral influence of the Church. If the papal right of provision to dignities, prebends, and parishes often produced Provisions better appointments, and also encouraged learning and merit, it also caused bitterness at the intrusion of strangers in order to endow members of the Roman Curia, and, although Innocent himself was sparing in the use of this prerogative, soon justified the accusation that the property of the local churches was being diverted to supply papal needs and subserve papal diplomacy. The venality of the Curia was notorious, its general fairness was less recognized. The wealth and pomp and power of the feudalized hierarchy, contrasting with the Gospel story, was made more glaring by the pre-eminence of its monarch and his court.

The estrangement of the ecclesiastical order from the Growth of common man was indeed a danger to the Church which Heresies might render nugatory its victories over kings and nobles. To some extent this estrangement was due to the continued universal belief that strict asceticism and poverty were the only true Christian life, and to the fact that the hierarchy and even the monks did not live up to this ideal. This had earlier led to the agitation of Arnold of Brescia for the complete poverty of the clergy ; it soon expanded into a desire among devout laity for evangelical perfection. Working alongside these ideals was that advance in civilization and mentality which is called the Twelfth-Century Renaissance. New ideas filtered in from the East. Men had a wider outlook, and thought and questioned and speculated. In ignorance and immaturity it was natural that the new beliefs and doubts should generally be quite uncritical in temper, and often less rational than the orthodoxy and organization they replaced. Orthodoxy attracted for the most part the best-equipped minds. The half-educated bourgeois and the lawless noble caught at novelty, and the more eagerly because it freed them from the duty of submission to a hierarchy, whose sins were patent and whose

exploitation of their privileges and wealth was a bitter
grievance. The movement for Church reform of the eleventh
and twelfth centuries, while it had brought about great
improvements and a higher standard, was limited and imperfect in its success, and very liable to relapse. In certain
strata of the clergy and in certain districts of Europe it had
either never made much way or had decayed. It is significant
that where the Church had the reputation of laxity and
corruption heresy flourished most.

Thus the twelfth century, besides being a period of the
development of the official Church, was also full of signs of
the limitations of its appeal and of rebellion from it. No-
where were they clearer than among the rapidly increasing
class of handworkers in the towns and of the peasantry of
the Mediterranean lands. The varieties of the movement
were numerous, but three main groups acquired a special
Humiliati   importance. One was the Humiliati of northern Italy, who
appeared first among the cloth-weavers of Lombardy. These
devout folk led austere lives of labour and prayer ; they
had all things in common ; that sections of them became
unorthodox was mainly due to their revolt from the extortionate, corrupt clergy, whose religious functions they proceeded to replace. Not dissimilar were the origin of the
Waldensians Waldensians and their subsequent revolt from the Church.
Peter Waldo, a merchant of Lyons, gave his wealth to the
poor, and in concert with his converts, the " Poor Men of
Lyons," devoted himself to preaching repentance and a strict
observance of the Gospel precepts. It was only when their
preaching was forbidden that they grew hostile and were
banned by Pope Lucius III. Even then there was a moderate
party, content with preaching and Bible reading in the
vernacular, but the majority, and especially their numerous
recruits in Lombardy and Germany, set aside the hierarchical
system. Their own *barbani*, vowed to poverty and austerity,
acted instead of the unworthy priesthood. A puritanic life
was incumbent on all Waldensians ; image-worship, saint-
worship, prayers for the dead were forbidden ; the Papacy
was for them the Babylonian harlot.

The Waldensians were dangerous rebels to the Church,
their narrow way of life was hardly favourable to advance
in civilization, but they only practised a rigid form of Christi-

anity. The Cathari or Albigensians [1] on the other hand held a different creed, founded on Manichæanism, which had slowly percolated from the East *via* the Bogomil sect in the Slavonic Balkans, and had found a new centre in Languedoc in the lands of the Count of Toulouse and his vassals. Thence Catharism spread on all sides, to North Italy, North France, and Germany. In contrast to Waldensianism, which was a belief of peasant and manual labourer, Albigensianism appealed to the more educated bourgeois and even to the nobles, at least in Languedoc and Italy. It provided an easy answer to the riddle of the universe, not less palatable because it justified the anti-clericalism provoked by the over-wealthy clergy. The Catharan belief was a dualism. There was the good God of the spiritual world, the God of the New Testament, and the evil God, creator of all matter, the God of the Old Testament. All acts that continued the material world were sinful, marriage and flesh-eating included, while the Catholic Church, with its rites and doctrines, propagated error. These tenets, which pushed the belief in asceticism common to the time to suicidal extremes, were, however, carried to their logical conclusions only by the elect of the Cathari, the *perfecti*, who had received the *consolamentum*, their only sacrament. The mass of believers (*credentes*) could live ordinary lives and receive the *consolamentum* on their death-bed. It was a system at war with life and nature, and cannot have promoted the health or progress of society ; but the *perfecti* were mostly of rigid virtue and compared favourably with too many of the Christian priesthood.

The condition of Languedoc, where this heresy had its stronghold and the wild baronage oppressed and exploited the Church, inevitably drew on a papal intervention. Innocent III, through his legates, persevered for some years in a mixed policy of reforming the clergy, converting the heretics, and inducing Raymond VI of Toulouse and other lords to expel the obstinate. It was in the attempt at conversion by argument that St. Dominic found his life-work. But no great success attended the legates' endeavours. Raymond and his fellows neither would nor could enforce orthodoxy on their subjects. At last the fiery legate, Pierre

[margin: Cathari or Albigensians]

---

[1] So called from Albi in Languedoc, one of their strongholds.

de Castelnau, inflicted excommunication on the count and interdict on his lands. Raymond submitted, but on January

The Albigensian Crusade

15, 1208, one of his squires murdered Castelnau. This finally decided the Pope to use force; he had already appealed to Philip Augustus of France, the count's suzerain, and the nobles of North France to crush the heretics and to receive in return the rewards of crusaders; he now proclaimed the Albigensian Crusade. The barons and knights of Langued'oïl, ardently orthodox and eager for plunder, gathered readily at the papal summons. It was of little use to the unhappy Raymond to do penance and himself take the cross. Languedoc was ravaged with fire and sword. Prosperous towns, Béziers (1209) and Carcassonne, were scenes of massacre. If most of the first crusaders departed, others took their place, and the crusade soon became a conquest of Languedoc for the benefit of north French adventurers, at their head an able general and statesman, the elder Simon de Montfort. Raymond was gradually forced into a hopeless contest, in which his lands were confiscated. His kinsman King Peter II of Aragon, who had rights of suzerainty in parts of Languedoc, came to aid his vassals only to fall in the crushing defeat of Muret (1213), and Simon de Montfort was elected Count of Toulouse. Pope Innocent had let loose a storm he could not control and which he only partially approved; at the Council of the Lateran in 1215 he was forced to confirm Simon's elevation.

Intervention of Louis of France

But after Innocent's death Raymond VI and his son returned to Languedoc and headed a desperate semi-national revolt against the hated northern plunderers. Simon de Montfort was killed in 1218 before Toulouse, which had rebelled and which he was besieging, and his son Amaury was quite unequal to the task of reconquest. Now, however, the French monarchy, the indubitable suzerain, which had held aloof in the earlier crusade, intervened. Louis, Philip Augustus's heir, in 1219, led one devastating army south which perpetrated an atrocious massacre at Marmande on the Garonne; in 1226, now become king, he made a new invasion. Amaury de Montfort had ceded his claims to the king, and Raymond VII of Toulouse, an undoubted Catholic, was now the leader of the Midi. His resistance was stubborn and lasted for nearly three years after the death of Louis VIII in 1226, but his lands were devastated and exhausted, and he was compelled to accept terms in 1229. The Papacy obtained the "Marquessata of Provence " in Burgundy, to be lost again in 1236 ; the French districts on the Rhone and Mediterranean were ceded to the Crown ; the count retained Toulouse proper, but on condition that his daughter should marry Alphonse, King Louis IX's brother, who was to be heir of the county. Vain revolts made no change in this arrangement, and Alphonse succeeded in 1249. The political results of these crusades were momentous. To France they brought the subjection of Languedoc to the north, the disappearance of its peculiar culture, and the extension of the Capetian monarchy to the Mediterranean. As to the Papacy, Innocent had used war to subdue a land, Christian in name, and very largely so in fact ; he had diverted the crusading impulse to the domestic quarrels of Europe with the effect of giving an unwilling blessing to rapine and greed. It was a precedent not lost on his successors.

A further result of the Albigensian wars was the permanent organization of large-scale persecution, and the establishment of the Inquisition to discover, cure, and punish heresy. Intermittent persecution of the crime of heresy, which was spiritual treason and endangered souls, had long existed, and while the severity of the punishment varied, burning alive was already thought appropriate for the obstinate. In the Albigensian Crusade it was frequent. But so far as there was a detective system and a judge it was the diocesan bishop until Innocent III gave his legates in Languedoc special powers. His successors bettered his example : Conrad of Marburg in Germany (1231-8) and Robert le Bougre in North France (1231-9) perpetrated indiscriminate horrors of savage injustice. Meantime, however, in 1233 Pope Gregory IX put the general papal Inquisition on a regular footing, and entrusted it to the orders of Friars, Dominicans and Franciscans. It ended in the second half of the century in Catholic Europe, at least the Latin countries, being mapped out under local tribunals of the Inquisition. Delation, the use of torture to extort confession, a procedure heavily weighted against the accused,[1] all made the Inquisition

The Papal Inquisition

---

[1] The accused was not told who were his accusers nor who were the witnesses against him. As evidence from any source, however polluted or

a thing of terror and warped by infection the far from
perfect lay systems of justice. The Inquisitors were indeed
anxious to convert the heretic rather than destroy him,
but the lesser punishments on the reconciled were cruelly
severe, and inflicted a ruinous stigma, while the death-
penalty of burning was all too frequent ; it was carried out
by the lay power, to whom the obstinate or offenders who
returned to heresy after submission were " relaxed " in
euphemistic phrase. The fact was that the Church stood
in dread of the increase of heresy and was fierce in the
intensity of its alarm. In Languedoc, where Catharism
had taken such strong root, the persecution was most
severe, and also most perverted, for it was mingled with
racial strife and private vengeance and the heartless use
of it by royal officials to crush particularist elements and
enlarge the royal domain by the confiscated property of the
condemned. After Count Raymond VII's last revolt its
action was intensified. It was successful and Catharism was
wiped out, but it is doubtful whether the acquiescence in
orthodoxy which was enforced was not a cynical indifference.

The Fourth
General
Council of
the Lateran
Innocent III summed up the triumphs of his pontificate
in the Fourth General Council of the Lateran, which he held
in 1215.   In its decrees and in numerous bulls he had issued
before it, he appears as a legislator for Europe, and much of
his legislation had enduring effects on later history. He it
was who first among the Popes taxed the clergy of Europe
by his own decree ; this was for the Crusade in 1199 ; and,
as we have seen, he denied the right of the lay powers to
do likewise, though they might receive a charitable gift.
He enforced not only the papal right of decision in disputed
elections but the new right of " devolution " by which a
vacant dignity after six months fell into the Pope's patronage. The lack of supervision which allowed decay among
the Benedictine monks was supplied by erecting associations
of monasteries in imitation of the Cistercians. Thus the
papal monarchy over the clergy in one way or another
became ever more complete as far as machinery could make

untrustworthy, was accepted from 1261 if hostile to the prisoner, and only
mortal enmity was esteemed to invalidate it (which, as he did not know
who accused him, he could only prove by chance), there was small likelihood,
and few cases, of complete acquittal.

it. But the formal control of the laity by the clergy was increased also. Henceforward every man was to confess his sins to the priest and communicate at least once a year. It was an attempt to raise the general morale, and the same effort is visible in two other directions. Innocent forbade the use of the primitive and superstitious ordeal, and thus forced the adoption of more rational methods of proof in the secular law. He also relaxed the absurd strictness of the law of consanguinity in marriage, which in scant and isolated communities was impossible of real observance and was only the parent of fraud and abuses, such as the affair of Ingeborg's divorce. Marriages were only to be invalid within the fourth, and no longer within the seventh degree. These reforms illustrate the best side of Innocent's pontificate : his endeavour to improve the human society of which he believed himself the autocrat as the successor to that St. Peter whom Christ had left " to govern not only the universal Church but all the secular world."

The great Pope died on July 16, 1216, but the system *Innocent* he had inherited and strengthened continued to grow with- *III's* out him. Even the mild and peaceful Honorius III (1216–27) *successors* advanced it by extending the papal right of provision so as to furnish salaries to the thronging Roman Curia. Gregory IX (1227–41) was a true kinsman of Innocent III, jurist and legislator, but without his dexterity and moderation. His passionate nature hurried him into blunders, but did not destroy his insight into the needs of the Church. This led him to the official codification of the constantly growing *The* Canon Law. By his command the Catalan Raymond of *Decretals of* Penyafort, a Dominican friar, digested into five books the *Gregory IX* Decretals and Canons which had been issued since Gratian's compilation, and this organized mass of legislation, reflecting the complexity and elaboration of actual conditions, was promulgated in 1234 as the law of the Church.

These reforms and organization of the Church, however, *St. Francis* under the immediate despotism of the Pope did not them- *of Assisi* selves reduce the estrangement of the common man from *and the* *Friars Minor* the hierarchy ; they rather increased it by unwelcome control and extortionate exactions. But here a new movement came to the rescue, that of the Mendicant Friars. In a way it allowed the orthodox to share and comply with the beliefs and aspirations of the malcontents; an orthodox satisfaction was given to the prevalent spiritual craving. This was mainly due to the enchanting personality of one man, St. Francis of Assisi. The most human of the saints was the gay and pleasure-loving son of a prosperous merchant of Assisi in Umbria, and thwarted in his boyish dreams of chivalry underwent a spiritual conversion, or more truly found himself in 1207. He gave his own originality to widespread ideas. Waldo had been a precisian and a critic; Francis loved and believed. With Pope Innocent's shrewd permission he founded his little society of Friars Minor. Utter renunciation and poverty and the literal imitation of the life of Christ amid the world and its doings, not the flight from the world and infinitely regulated asceticism of the ideal monk, were the discovery of St. Francis and the key to the heart of the people. His Lady Poverty was to him not a penance but a release from cares and fetters. A boundless sympathy and humility united him with life and nature. "More than a saint among saints, among sinners he was as one of themselves." And he imparted his unquestioning orthodoxy and reverence for the priesthood to a time that fretted under the splendid, rigid, legal hierarchy. The days of the free practice of his ideal were short, when he and his first friars wandered homeless, earning or begging their bread, preaching and praying through Italy; but for many years after, when the Friars had spread through Europe, they still amid much transformation retained the spirit of their founder. Everywhere they brought not merely a reconciliation of the time with the official Church, but also Christianity itself to peoples at heart pagan. Transformation, however, began early, partly from the large numbers of new friars which involved a rule and organization, partly from the intervention of the Papacy, which realized the immense human energy set free, and was resolved to discipline and guide it. The waterfall should turn a thousand Church wheels.

The first changes occurred while St. Francis was in the Levant, whither he had gone in the hope of converting the Moslems by persuasion—thereby reviving the missionary spirit in the Church. Not only did Cardinal Ugolino, the future Gregory IX, enforce monastic claustration on the

imitative order of the Poor Ladies (Clarisses) founded by
St. Francis's friend St. Clare but Francis's own lieutenants
enforced routine asceticism, and even began to build permanent residences. It was a practical measure, but not
St. Francis's nor of the first friars who were wandering with
startling success north of the Alps. On his return in 1220
some compromise had to be made between the dynamic
idealism of the saint and the need for organization and
discipline now urged by the harder-headed and more conventional zealots who thronged into the order. Francis himself obtained the appointment of Ugolino to be " Protector "
as a link with the Curia, and resigned the headship to a
Minister-General. A novitiate was prescribed by the Pope,
and a Rule was issued by St. Francis in 1223 which still
retained much of the original spirit though it introduced a
businesslike workaday organization very unlike the evan-
gelistic fervour of his first attempt. St. Francis died on
October 3, 1226, still regretting the change, but his " Testament " was declared not binding by Gregory IX, while he
canonized the saint for whom he had always felt admiration
and sympathy.

For the time the organizing party, to whom Elias the
Minister-General belonged, had the upper hand. A splendid
church was built at Assisi. Learning, which Francis had
disliked, and formal discipline were to be marks of the new
papal militia. Yet there were ups and downs in the internal
strife of principles, and it was not till the ministership of
St. Bonaventura (1257–74), " the Seraphic Doctor," that the
" Conventuals," as we may now call them,[1] definitely got
full control. The contest became centred on the question
of property : while keeping up relative poverty, the Conventuals by various subterfuges, such as ownership by the
Pope (1245) with use to the Friars, were content to be pro-
pertied ; the " Spirituals " demanded the literal observance
of St. Francis's ideal, which they followed with a pedantry
unknown to him—they tended to become recluse ascetics.
Even in the thirteenth century something like persecution
narrowed them and they had become deeply tinged with the
mystical speculations of Joachism. These had their origin
in the writings of a celebrated monk. Joachim, Abbot of

Formalization of the Order. Divisions among the Friars

Joachism

[1] The term is fourteenth-century.

Flora, was a Calabrian, who in his bilingual country was learned both in Greek and Latin. His fervent asceticism surpassed that of the early Cistercians, and he combined his essential orthodoxy with a mystical philosophy of history which led to a heretical dreamland. For Joachim, the history of mankind fell into three dispensations, that of God the Father or the Law of the Old Testament, that of the Son or the Gospel, and that of the Holy Ghost in the future, a millennium of mystical holiness no longer trammelled by partial laws and revelations. After his death in 1202, his attack on the exposition of the doctrine of the Trinity in Peter Lombard's *Sentences* had been condemned by the Lateran Council of 1215, but his speculations continued to appeal to fervent minds, uneasy in the hard institutional framework of the Church. Among the Spiritual Franciscans they were widely adopted and also perverted. St. Francis seemed to them to be the harbinger of the third perfect dispensation. An Introduction to Joachim's commentaries on Scripture was written in 1254 by Fra Gerardo da Borgo San Donnino, called "The Eternal Gospel," in which Joachim's works were represented as the inspired books of the reign of the Holy Ghost. The new era was to begin in 1260 led by a new mendicant Order; the partial revelation of the Gospel was to be completed, and the imperfect rule of the institutional Church was to end. This was rebellion, the fruit of dissatisfaction with the evils of the times and the cast-iron organization and hierarchic government of the official Church which was so deeply imbued with them. As rebellion it was treated—in 1257 the Spiritual Minister-General of the Order, John of Parma, was deposed—but in one form or another it proved hard to suppress. If its extravagance aided the Conventuals to secure the control of the Order and papal support, it appealed to widespread longings for a better world and gave a section of the Spirituals a hope to cling to. Meantime St. Bonaventura, the new Minister-General, famous as a scholastic philosopher, guided the Franciscans firmly on the path of organization and learning. In 1266 his expurgated official version of the life of St. Francis was adopted by the Order, and a vigorous attempt was made to suppress the genuine Lives of the Saint which betrayed too clearly how far the friars had journeyed from the unsophisticated holiness and unconventional ideals of their founder.

Yet the persecuting, formal Conventuals, engaged in papal political propaganda, were still heirs to St. Francis : they were the most moving preachers, the fullest of good works, the most unselfish of the Orders ; in learning they were only surpassed by the Dominicans. Their sordid struggles with the secular clergy over confessions and burials and the fees involved were after all a witness to their superiority as pastors and their hold on the impartial laity. But the memory of the real Francis and his brief revelation lived long in Italy ; it inspired the masterpiece of the *Fioretti*, and has never ceased to stir mankind.

Alongside of the Franciscans there worked another Order St. Dominic of Mendicant Friars, more specialized in its objects and more and the effective in the intellectual problems of the thirteenth century. Preachers The Dominicans or Friars Preachers owed their origin to the offensive against Albigensianism. In 1205 the Spanish Bishop of Osma, passing through Languedoc, struck out a new means of dealing with heretics : that trained missionaries, as poor and ascetic as the *perfecti*, should preach to them. He left behind a canon of his cathedral, Dominic, for the work. The serene and firm-willed St. Dominic, full of sound sense, presents a curious contrast to the effervescent, lovable St. Francis, but like him he gave what the Church needed. After ten years' labour among the heretics in Languedoc he obtained confirmation of his Order from Pope Honorius III in 1216. Because the Lateran Council had just forbidden new Orders, he adopted the elastic Rule of the Austin Canons to whom he belonged and added to it the " customs " of the Præmonstratensians : in 1219-20 he adopted the prohibition of property then the mark of the Franciscans, not for its own sake but for its popular appeal. In 1221 he died at Bologna. To combat heresy was the aim of the Friars Preachers. From the first they were a learned Order ; Paris was almost their capital ; and the greatest medieval schoolman, St. Thomas Aquinas, came from their ranks. As argumentative preachers and as thinkers they served their age well. But they were also naturally employed as the chief agents of the Inquisition, and were stern persecutors as well as devoted scholars. They, too, tended to acquire property as time went on; it was not such a breach with their founder's ideals as it was with the Franciscans. They developed constitutional government more successfully than other ecclesiastics. The Franciscans were governed from above; their general chapters were mainly composed of officials. The Dominican general chapter, during two years out of three, consisted of elected non-officials, and the general chapter, not the officials, decided important questions.

Effect of the Friars on the West There is only space to name the two imitative Orders of Friars, the Carmelites and the Augustinians, or the two female Orders attached to the Friars Minor and Preachers, the Clarisses and Dominican Sisters, soon only stricter nuns. But stress must be laid on the Franciscan Tertiaries, associations of devout laymen not unlike the Humiliati, for they typify the new roots the Church struck in the populations through the Mendicant Orders. Orthodox religion and Christianity itself entered with renewed vigour into European life. The distant, awe-inspiring pageant became a homely companion, and what hierarchic government, that did so much, could not do was done in some degree between 1200 and 1800 by comradeship and self-surrender.

SUGGESTIONS FOR READING ON CHAPTER II

A. SOURCES

(i) Documents

Innocent III : *Epistolæ* and *Registrum super negotio Romani Imperii.* Migne, *Patrologia Latina*, vols. 204–7.

Constitutiones et Acta Publica regum et imperatorum. Vol. ii. *Monumenta Germaniæ Historica.* Legum Sectio IV. 1896.

Huillard-Bréholles, J. L. A. : *Historia Diplomatica Friderici II.* 12 vols. Paris, 1852–61.

Gui, Bernard : *Manuel de l'Inquisition.* Ed. and trans. Mollat, G. (Classiques de l'histoire de France.) Paris, 1926–7.

(ii) Narrative

Otto de S. Blasio : *Chronica.* Ed. Hofmeister, A. Scriptores rerum Germanicarum in usum Scolarum. 1912.

Burchardus præpositus Urspergensis : *Chronicon.* Ed. Holder-Egger, O., and Simson, B. v. *Ibid.* 1916.

Annales Placentini Gibellini. Ed. Pertz, G. *Monumenta Germaniæ Historica.* Scriptores xviii.

Ryccardus de S. Germano : *Chronica.* Ed. Gaudenzi, A. (Soc. napol. di storia patria). Naples, 1888.

Chanson de la croisade contre les Albigeois. Ed. Meyer, P. 2 vols. Paris, 1875–9.

Thomas of Celano : *S. Francisci Assisiensis vita et miracula.* Ed. d'Alençon, E. Rome, 1906. Trans. Howell, A. G. F. London, 1908.

Speculum Perfectionis. Ed. Sabatier, P. 2 vols. London, 1928 ff. [Also English translations.]

I Fioretti del . . . Santo Francesco e de' suoi frati. Ed. Passerini, G. L. Florence, 1903. [Also English translations.]

Eccleston, Thomas : *De adventu Fratrum Minorum in Angliam.* Ed. Little, A. G. Paris, 1909. [Also English translations.]

Opuscula S.P. Francisci Assisiensis. Quaracchi, 1904.

Jordanes de Saxonia. *Vita S. Dominici.* Acta Sanctorum.   Aug. 4. Vol. i.

B. MODERN WORKS

Cambridge Medieval History, vol. vi, relevant chapters.

Coulton, G. G. : *Two Saints.* Cambridge, 1932.

Cuthbert, Father : *Life of St. Francis of Assisi.* 2nd edn. London, 1913.

Drane, A. T. : *History of St. Dominic.* London, 1891.

Essays in commemoration of St. Francis of Assisi. Ed. W. W. Seton. London, 1926.

Galbraith, G. R. : *The Constitution of the Dominican Order, 1216–1360.*

Glotz, G., ed. : *Histoire Générale. Le Moyen Âge.* Vol. iv, pts. 1 and 2. Paris, 1937–9.

Gregorovius, F. : *History of Rome in the Middle Ages.* Trans. Hamilton, A. Vol. v.

Guiraud, J. H. : *Histoire de l'Inquisition au Moyen Âge.* Paris, 1935.

Hampe, K. : *Deutsche Kaisergeschichte.* Leipzig, 1912.

Hauck, A. : *Kirchengeschichte Deutschlands,* vol. iv. Leipzig.

Lavisse, E., ed. : *Histoire de France,* vol. iii.

Lea, H. C. : *History of the Inquisition in the Middle Ages.* 3 vols. New York, 1887.

Luchaire, A. : *Innocent III.* 6 vols. Paris, 1907–8.

Mahn, J. B. : *L'Ordre cistercien et son Gouvernement des origines au milieu du treizième siècle,* 1098–1265. Bibliothèque des Ecoles françaises d'Athènes et de Rome, 1945.

Mandonnet, F. P. : *Saint Dominique, l'idée, l'homme et l'œuvre.* 2 vols. Paris, 1938.

Sabatier, P. : *Vie de St. François d'Assise.* Paris, 1894. And later editions.

CHAPTER III

THE EMPEROR FREDERICK II

Frederick II
and his Aims

IT had been the constant aim of the Hohenstaufen Emperors to translate the ideal of the Holy Roman Empire into fact, and this meant the endeavour to make of their triple realm a strong, solid, and united monarchy, and at its head to exercise the secular leadership of Europe. This tradition was the governing factor in the life of Frederick II, but from a mainly German he transmuted it to a mainly Italian embodiment. This was partly due to his parentage and upbringing. He was the heir of the Norman kings of Sicily as well as of the Hohenstaufen, and had been educated in the palace of Palermo in the culture and the habits of his Norman ancestors. But largely it was due to the changed circumstances of the Empire. The imperial authority and power had been so weakened in Germany by the civil war and its sequels and the new position of the Church that it would need the consistent hereditary labour of generations to restore them. Frederick Barbarossa and Henry VI could make Germany the basis of their schemes with Italy as an essential annex. With Frederick II the position was reversed. Sicily was the solid basis on which he hoped to build an effective monarchy over imperial Italy. To this he devoted his life. Germany was now the essential annex, the great source of man-power for his armies ; there, if they would only be loyal, he was content to maintain a limited direction over the semi-independent princes. Yet Frederick's ambition, pursued with immutable perseverance for over thirty years, was a chimera, for it ran counter to the strongest forces of the day. The North Italians desired their city autonomy above all things, not to be united under a monarchy ; and the Papacy looked on a revival of the Empire and the existence of a strong imperial or even native power in Italy as its worst danger. In spite of his material resources, it was only the marvellous personality of Frederick himself

64

which maintained the struggle and kept him undefeated to the end.

The natural gifts of Frederick II are not justly to be measured by the extent of his success in an undertaking which was in the circumstances impossible, and to which he was pledged by overwhelming tradition and by events of his youth in reality beyond his control. What universal talents could do, he did; and in the struggle this Samson cracked, if he could not break, the pillars of the edifice of the papal hierarchic dominion of Europe. He is not indeed a sympathetic hero of romance. With an intense appreciation of beauty and intellect, he seems almost heartless and pitiless of suffering; his faithlessness, if provoked by the Papacy, is in some degree ignoble; if he shared his sensuality with his Norman ancestors, the oriental harem which he inherited from them seems an undesirable exotic in the thirteenth century. He was open-minded in religion, and, it may be, incredulous; strange scoffs were reported of him; but this suspected sceptic was a bitter persecutor of heretics, either to conciliate opinion or in defence of the Christian society of which he was the secular head. In his talents he foreshadowed the " universal man " of the Italian renaissance. A respectable general, a remarkable legislator, an investigator in natural history, insatiably curious, a poet and a linguist, he was tireless in the personal rule of his kingdoms. To his own times he was the " wonder of the world."

For Frederick's plans the continued union of the Empire and the Regno was essential, and the peace-loving character of Pope Honorius III, intent on his spiritual authority, gave him the opportunity. *Election of Henry King of the Romans* His promise to abdicate the throne of Sicily in favour of the boy Henry would be of no advantage to the Papacy if Henry was elected co-regent of the Empire. To this election he bought the votes of the German prelates by the *Privilegium in favorem principum ecclesiasticorum* of April 26, 1220, which seriously reduced the Emperor's suzerain rights over the lands of the German Churches. Honorius, eager for the Crusade, gave way to the accomplished fact, and crowned Frederick Emperor in the same year without insisting on the promised abdication.

The first preoccupation of Frederick II was to reorganize

Organization of the Regno

the government of the Regno and to make it the model and most advanced State of the time. The nobles were out of hand, the royal domains and income much depleted, and the Moslems of Sicily in insurrection. Frederick thoroughly subdued the Moslems in 1222–3, and transported the greater part of them to the city of Lucera in Apulia. Isolated on the mainland and confirmed in the free practice of their religion, they became the Emperor's most loyal supporters, and furnished excellent foot-archers who were quite unaffected by papal denunciations. The Apulian nobles were tamed with the same vigour—four disloyal counts lost their lands—and the North Italian seaports, Pisa, Genoa, and Venice, were deprived of their privileged position in the Regno. In three great General Courts held at Capua (1220, 1223) and Messina (1221) Frederick restored the power of the Crown as it had existed at the death of William II in 1189 before the troublous times : all royal grants and alienations since then were annulled, " adulterine " castles [1] were destroyed, the royal revenue was reconstituted, the course of justice improved, the fleet was revived, and the wealth of the country, agricultural and commercial, successfully fostered. Characteristically, the Emperor took education under his especial care by founding the University of Naples.

The North Italian cities

The second preoccupation of Frederick was the cautious restoration of the imperial authority in North Italy, but the cities were refractory as of old. The five vicars whom he set up in 1220 could exercise little influence. Meantime, the cities, all growing in commercial prosperity, were engrossed in their own external and internal feuds. The great manufacturing and commercial town of Milan dominated the open country in the centre from the Po to the Alps. Brescia came second only to Milan. Asti and Alessandria flourished on the transit trade between Genoa, inner Lombardy, and the Alps. Verona held the chief exit from Lombardy and the Adriatic to the north-east. Bologna and Padua (from 1222) in addition to their trade did a thriving business as seats of universities. In Tuscany, a grouping took place, in which the imperialistic or Ghibelline [2] cities,

---

[1] I.e. castles built without royal licence.
[2] So called from a war-cry of the Hohenstaufen, taken from their castle of Waiblingen in Swabia.

Pisa, Siena, and others, stood opposed to the papal or Guelf [1]
towns, Florence, Lucca, and their allies.   The real causes of
dispute were commercial and territorial : the control of the
chief road to Rome and its trade was the apple of discord
between Lucca, Pisa, Siena, and Florence ; Pisa's hold on
the outlet of the manufactures of Florence by the Arno made
them bitter enemies ; each city wished to free its own trade
and to tax and hamper that of its neighbours.   In this conflict Pisa underwent its first serious defeat at Castello di
Bosco in 1222 at the hands of Lucca and Florence.   They
all, too, desired a larger territory and at least the control
of their own *contado*, the district of which they formed the
centre.   The food-supply was an important asset to a growing town, and both nobles and lesser citizens were landowners outside the walls as well as traders within them.
The links, personal and economic, between city and *contado*
were many and close, and the government of the *contado*
was a natural aim of the city.

Another common feature of the cities was that they were a Guelfs and
prey to internal discord.   This was of two kinds.   The noble Ghibellines
houses of each city were divided by old family feuds, which
in 1220 were in process of coalescing into one main feud of
two factions.   It was still a varying circumstance on what
principle the feud should be fought, but Frederick's reign
and his strife with the Papacy were to provide the combatants with such a principle : one faction in each Tuscan
city was to be Ghibelline and side with the Emperor, the
other Guelf and side with the Pope.   The second kind of
discord was definitely social.   As the cities grew in wealth Class
and population, the non-noble classes, the *popolani*, who were Divisions
becoming organized in gilds, were demanding a share in the
government of their communes, and this conflict blended
with the intestine strife among the *milites* or nobles.   These
troubles and wars were even more advanced in Lombardy.
There Milan was the rival of Cremona and Pavia, Verona
of Padua, while in 1221 the nobles of Milan departed from
the city to wage war on the plebeians with the help of her
enemies.   The alleviation of these broils which had come

[1] Called after the German house of the Welfs.   These names were first
applied in Tuscany during the contest of Frederick II with Otto IV.   They
spread later to Lombardy.

into vogue was the substitution of a single, mainly foreign, official, the *podestà*, as executive of a city for the board of native consuls—he would be impartial between the factions ; but there were already signs of another solution, the city despot.   Salinguerra and Azzo of Este had disputed for the mastery of Ferrara.

The Second Lombard League   It was partly with the view of restoring the imperial authority in Lombardy that Frederick proclaimed a general diet of the Empire to meet at Cremona at Easter 1226 ; the German princes headed by King Henry were to attend as well as Italians.   But the quarrelling cities at once took alarm, and sank their feuds in defence against the common enemy : on March 6, 1226, they formed the " second " Lombard League.   Even Verona joined Milan and Bologna, and they barred the exit of the Brenner into Italy.   The diet could not be held, and Frederick, who had just been flouting the Pope by claiming sovereignty in the Duchy of Spoleto, was obliged to accept papal mediation.   At this moment Gregory IX succeeded to the Papacy, and a new conflict began.

Frederick II's Crusade. Breach with Gregory IX   The pacific Honorius III had, ever since Frederick's coronation, been urging his vowed crusade.   Each date fixed, however, found Frederick still engaged in the Regno. Even his second marriage in 1225 with Yolande de Brienne, the heiress of Jerusalem, which was promoted by the Pope, proved an insufficient bribe.   But Gregory fiercely insisted, and in September 1227 the Emperor set sail, only to fall ill and land again.   Gregory in wrath excommunicated him, and when he really went next year, renewed the excommunication, since he had departed unabsolved.   The Pope's motives were indeed political.   Frederick's designs of subjugating North Italy and re-annexing the newly won papal territory were an obvious danger to the independence of the Papacy, by now thoroughly involved in secular policies, as Frederick himself declared in a fiery manifesto.   The Pope even levied a crusade against his vassal—a new degradation of the crusading ideal—and began to conquer the Regno by invading the Terra di Lavoro.   A revolt of discontented towns began.   But he had begun the duel prematurely. The German princes, ecclesiastical and lay, were unaffected by the ban on the Emperor.   When Frederick returned to

Italy in 1229—excommunicated again for that too—he easily
recovered and punished the towns he had lost, and peace Peace of S.
was made at San Germano (Ceprano) on July 23, 1230. Germano
Yet Frederick was forced to admit the immunities of the
clergy of the Regno. If Gregory had failed in his main
design, he had made some gains.

Frederick could now continue his organization of the Frederick's
Regno, as the first bureaucratic State, if we except the Reforms in
Papacy, of medieval Europe. He issued at Melfi in 1231 the Regno
the first medieval secular code of laws. It was compiled by
his minister Peter della Vigna and the Archbishop of Capua,
and fused and reformed the Norman-Sicilian legislation
and feudal and local custom. Its principles were inspired
by Justinian and the Canon Law. Frederick's own legislation, both in his code and in the supplementary *Novellæ*
which followed it, was directed to bureaucratic organization,
to better justice and order,[1] all under the personal direction
of an absolute monarch. At the same time he fostered the
kingdom's wealth by the encouragement and freeing of commerce—he reduced the export duties on corn—the improvement and extension of agriculture, and not least by the
reform of the coinage : he reintroduced (1231) a gold coinage
into the West by the issue of the augustal, his imitation of
the Byzantine bezant. He even summoned representatives
of the towns, which otherwise he kept in strict surveillance,
to his occasional general parliaments and to half-yearly local
assemblies. The flaw in this benevolent despotism was the
heavy expense it entailed ; Frederick made the Regno the
milch-cow for his Empire, and when the final struggle with
the Papacy drained his treasury the long process of exhaustion began which continued for many centuries. An
annual hearth-tax (*collecta*) was early instituted, grievous
State-monopolies damaged industry, and ruinous State debts
accumulated. He even on one occasion issued an augustal
of leather.

Frederick's relations with Pope Gregory, always uneasy, The Roman
were for some time alleviated by the Pope's difficulties with Commune
the restless commune of Rome. The Romans were wroth
at the favour shown by the Popes to the rival neigh-

---

[1] E.g. the abolition of the ordeal, the reservation of criminal justice for
the State, the organization of appeals.

bour cities of Viterbo and Perugia. Frederick's partisans
increased in the city, and on his excommunication Gregory
had been forced to take to flight. Returning, he was soon
in exile again, for the real object of the Romans was the
independent rule of the whole Campagna. These ambitions
were destroyed by Frederick's fatal opportunism. To gain
over the Pope, in October 1234 an imperial force overthrew
the Romans at Viterbo. They were compelled to submit,
although they were left their internal freedom. But peace
with the Pope had not brought peace with the Lombard
League, and the attempts at papal mediation all broke down,
Germany till in 1235 Frederick was obliged to revisit Germany. For
under King some years after 1220 Germany had been under the regency,
Henry first of Archbishop Engelbert of Cologne, who was murdered
by a family conspiracy in 1225, then of Lewis Duke of
Bavaria. The archbishop had kept order, which was one
reason for his death, and in his time King Waldemar of Denmark had been thrust back beyond the Eider [1]; Lewis had
allowed the rapid growth of feuds between the princes; but
both had represented the interests of the princely class. The
young King Henry took over the government in 1228, and
reversed this policy; he relied on the imperial *ministeriales*,
and favoured the desires of the townsmen for autonomy
against their immediate lords, largely the bishops. As a
policy, it was doubtless in the interests of the German monarchy, which was losing power to the princes, and the towns,
which already in 1226 had formed a soon forbidden league
on the middle Rhine, were an advancing power and a valuable ally. But on the one hand it estranged the princes, on
whom Frederick relied, and on the other King Henry, head-
strong and wavering, had no capacity to pursue it successfully. In 1230 he confirmed a league of towns mostly in
the prince-bishopric of Liége. In 1231 the indignant princes
compelled him to issue not only a prohibition of all town-
Constitutio leagues but also the *Constitutio in favorem principum*, a
in favorem concession to the lay princes similar to that of his father
principum to the prelates in 1220 : the direct action of the Crown was
excluded from the princely domains. The two edicts together made the German princes the little hampered rulers
of their lands, *domini terræ* as they were called.

[1] See below, Chap. VIII, p. 160.

Henry's mismanagement of affairs, then and subsequently, estranged him from his father, and the mysterious murder of Duke Lewis of Bavaria added to the unrest in Germany. The Emperor, at the Diet of Aquileia (Cividale), whither the princes could come in 1232 in spite of the Lombard League, was compelled to confirm the *Constitutio* : he fulminated against the communal governments and unauthorized institutions of the episcopal towns, and accepted Henry's submission only on promise of good behaviour and co-operation with the princes. Henry, however, did not improve. He fell out once more and fiercely with the lay princes, and feuds increased. A better side of his policy was shown in allaying the furious bout of heretic hunting (1231-3) which took place under Conrad of Marburg. The Papacy was Conrad of organizing the Inquisition at the time, and undoubtedly the Marburg's Waldensians and Catharans were spreading in Germany. persecution of heretics But as in North France under Robert le Bougre, this situation gave an opportunity to the insane fanaticism of an inquisitor. The merciless Conrad of Marburg did not ask for proof : he burnt all the accused. The nobles themselves did not escape. It ended in the bishops and the king opposing Conrad, who, too, was murdered himself. In 1234 a royal Constitution prescribed a more just procedure, and the persecution died down, but the unfortunate Henry thereby offended the politic Emperor, who was anxious to satisfy Revolt of the Pope. Then at last in 1234 Henry openly rebelled and King Henry allied with the Lombard League against his father.

Frederick knew he had little to fear, and entered Ger-Frederick II many in 1235 from the south-east in full state with a mere in Germany. bodyguard. The princes hastened to join him, the towns Conrad IV submitted, and the wretched Henry was deposed and im-as King of prisoned in Apulia, where he died in 1242. The Emperor the Romans replaced him by the election (1237) of his second son, the boy Conrad IV, as King of the Romans, while he himself married (1235) as his third wife Isabella, the sister of the English Henry III, a match which secured him the important English influence in the Rhineland. Meantime he made belated efforts to strengthen the monarchy. He effected a final reconciliation with the Welfs by erecting (1235) their Saxon lands into the duchy of Brunswick-Lüneburg. Among other acquisitions he put the refractory Duke Frederick of

Austria and Styria to the ban of the Empire, and vainly
endeavoured to conquer his duchies for the imperial domain.
He began to favour the towns by charters of privilege, given
not only to imperial cities but also, with the bishops' consent,
to episcopal towns, and in the great peace (*Landfriede*) of
Mainz in 1235, the first imperial law drafted in German,
he attempted to restore order, and created a central court
of justice. All this, however, was subsidiary to his Italian
schemes, for which he utilized his popularity among the
princes.

Frederick's War with the Lombard Cities

Owing to the Austrian war, the Emperor's first invasion
of Lombardy from the north in 1236 produced little effect
beyond the reduction of the Veneto, but it was marked by
two manifestos, the prelude to the struggle with the Papacy.
Frederick declared that he would make Italy re-enter the
unity of the Empire and resume the lands ceded to the un-
grateful Popes ; Gregory IX replied by insisting on the
papal supremacy in things spiritual and temporal and reiterat-
ing the Donation of Constantine and the fable of the " translation " of the Empire from the Greeks to the Germans by
the papal fiat. Frederick by now had the gate of Lombardy
open to him by the adhesion of Verona to his cause under
the influence of its grim tyrant, Ezzelin da Romano, who
in 1232 had become its *de facto* ruler and five years later
subjected Padua to his ferocious domination. In 1237,
leaving the boy Conrad and Archbishop Siegfried of Mainz
to represent him in Germany, Frederick renewed the campaign
and crushed the Milanese and their allies in the battle of

Battle of Cortenuova

Cortenuova near the River Oglio (November 27). The
Milanese *podestà* and *carroccio* were captured on the field.
The cities submitted one after another, when Frederick made
his fatal mistake of demanding the unconditional surrender
of Milan. This nerved the remaining rebels to resist to the
last, and the failure of the siege of Brescia in the autumn of
1238 marked the end of his good fortune.

Renewed Struggle of Papacy and Empire

Gregory IX decided to throw down the gauntlet. He
had been recently irritated by Frederick's creation of his
bastard son Enzo as King of Sardinia, following his marriage
to the heiress of one of its provinces,[1] for the Papacy claimed
Sardinia as a fief and had recently received the homage of

[1] There were four provinces of Sardinia under hereditary " judges."

its rulers. But the true cause was the same as formerly : the Pope could not endure to see Italy united under the Emperor by the conquest of the Lombard cities and the annexation, at least in part, of the Papal States. On March 20, 1239, he excommunicated Frederick, adding to his griev- ances the charge of heresy, to which the Emperor's free- thinking utterances gave occasion. Thus began the death- struggle between the Empire and the Papacy, while as yet other powers stood neutral. In armed force Frederick, with his Germans and Saracens and Italian allies, seemed much the stronger ; against him Gregory could only pit the forces of a number of Lombard cities. But the contest was also one of wealth : Frederick's over-taxed kingdom of Sicily was a poor match for the European resources of the Church and the ever-growing wealth of the Italian trading cities. Further, the Papacy still had the greater hold on European public opinion : the clergy were at its command ; the friars were the best of propagandists ; men feared its judgments even when they disapproved them. And Frederick's weak- ness was in Germany. The prelates were likely, however unwilling, to desert him under papal pressure, and the lay princes, popular as he was with them, were as ready as ever to rebel for their private ambition or profit. In 1239 the King of Bohemia and the Duke of Bavaria had joined Fred- erick of Austria in his revolt, if next year all three were reconciled to the Emperor. At best they rather suffered the monarchy to exist than gave it loyal obedience.

The campaign of 1239 in Lombardy was unfavourable to the Emperor : he vainly besieged Milan, and lost Ferrara and Ravenna in the Romagna, both important for his com- munications and supplies. But the rivals of Milan—Cremona, Pavia, and Parma—were for him, and he secured the great road, Via Francigena, in Tuscany, and won ground in the Papal State. Rome, the key position, however, held this time firmly by the Pope, and Gregory could confidently make his most dangerous move—the summons of a General Council at Rome in 1241. It would mean the array of the Church against Frederick and his deposition, and regardless of the scandal the Pisan and Sicilian fleets under King Enzo attacked the Genoese convoy on May 3 at the island of Giglio ; they carried captive a hundred prelates with two cardinals. Not long after, in August, the unbending centenarian Pope breathed his last. It may be questioned whether in his fear and distrust of Frederick he had not made a worse bargain for the spiritual interests of the Papacy than the patient Honorius III. His successor, Celestine IV, lived only a few days, and in the long vacancy which followed, the war languished. The Senator Matteo Rosso, head of the great Roman house of Orsini, held Rome firmly for the Guelfs against the Emperor's repeated attacks, but the greater part of Umbria and the March of Ancona submitted to Frederick. Then on June 23, 1243, under pressure from Frederick himself was elected a celebrated canon lawyer, the Genoese

Cardinal Sinibaldo Fieschi, as Pope Innocent IV. No more formidable choice could have been made. The cold and crafty Innocent was a man of iron resolution and the most adroit of statesmen. He made it the end of his policy to uproot the Hohenstaufen dynasty, and employed without scruple all the means at his command. The entire armoury and prerogative of the Papacy were turned to secular uses. Provisions, dispensations, appointments, depositions, taxation, excommunication, interdict, crusade were made consistently weapons of diplomacy and war. The spiritual functions of the Papacy and the Church were degraded by bold misuse, and the medieval ecclesiastical system never recovered from the decay induced by his pontificate. He exacerbated every existing tendency to decline. In spite of shortcomings the Papacy had hitherto appeared as a force for reform and the raising of the standards of life; now more and more men doubted its zeal for righteousness, and resented the unconscionable exercise of the religious authority in which they believed.

To satisfy the general wish for peace and to gain time for his plans Innocent played with his adversary's offers. There seemed to be nothing that Frederick would not yield under pressure save the dominion of Lombardy. Even the treacherous recapture of Viterbo by the papal legate did not prevent his envoys accepting in 1244 the most submissive

terms, including the evacuation of the Papal State. But the Lombard question remained insoluble and the Emperor became more obdurate: he began to encourage his partisans in Rome. Then to his amazement, in June 1244, Innocent fled in disguise to his native Genoa, and eventually took his way to the city of Lyons, where he was still nominally in the Empire and yet had France near him as a safe refuge. Almost immediately thereafter he called a General Council to Lyons for June 24, 1245. Frederick's petitions and the intercession of St. Louis were unavailing; the assembled prelates were unanimous in defence of the claims of Pope and Church, and on July 17 he was deposed and banned, like Otto IV before him, for sacrilege and heresy.

The First General Council of Lyons

Deposition of Frederick II

With the Council's authority at his back and the enormous influence he could now wield over clergy and laity, Innocent IV developed his attack. Circumstances in Germany were favourable. In 1241 the three Rhineland Archbishops, of Mainz, Cologne, and Trèves had deserted Frederick in a body, and the new legate, the scrupleless Philip, Bishop-elect of Ferrara, used any and every means to bribe and coerce clergy and laity. In 1246 the papal bishops elected Henry Raspe, Landgrave of Thuringia, anti-Cæsar. Only towns such as Worms, Ratisbon, and Erfurt heartily supported King Conrad and now received the full favour of the Emperor. If the princes showed little zeal to recognize either Henry Raspe or on his death in 1247 his successor as anti-Cæsar, William Count of Holland, they gave little aid to the Hohenstaufen. The Margrave of Meissen accepted indeed from the Emperor the inheritance of Thuringia due to him; Otto, Duke of Bavaria, married his daughter to King Conrad; and the death (1246) of Frederick of Austria without male heirs allowed the young king to establish a much-contested rule in his two vacant duchies; on the other hand William secured the Lower Rhine; but the war of the rival kings merely brought to Germany the ineffectual anarchy of a stalemate.

Civil War in Germany

Henry Raspe, anti-Cæsar

William of Holland, anti-Cæsar

In Italy the impression of the Emperor's excommunication, which was incessantly fanned by Innocent's best propagandists, the Mendicant Friars, combined with the discontent simmering in the tax-drained Regno to produce a dangerous conspiracy among high officials aiming at Frederick's life, but it was discovered in time (in February 1246) and put down with ferocious cruelty. The remnant of the Saracens in Sicily, who had risen in revolt, were subdued, and transplanted among their kinsfolk in Lucera. In Lombardy and

The War in Italy

the North and in the Papal State Frederick gained ground rather than otherwise, while the cities on his side were held firmly in leash by the *podestàs* he appointed and his General Vicar, King Enzo. His ally, rather than subject, the tyrant Ezzelin da Romano, had established a reign of terror over Verona, Padua, and Vicenza. The papal legate, Gregory of Montelongo, though far from overcome, did not do more than keep up a tenacious resistance. Then in 1247 Frederick resolved to put pressure on the Pope by an advance on Lyons through Savoy, whose Count, Amadeus IV, was now his adherent. He hoped to reach Germany, and was ready, while St. Louis of France mediated in the interests of the Crusade, to make great concessions. But as he advanced, news came that Parma behind him had revolted on June 16 to the papal side. It was the key to his communications with Tuscany and the south, for Genoa, Piacenza, and Bologna were steadily papalist. Frederick was obliged to gather all his forces to reduce the rebellious city.

Battle of Victoria

The siege ended in disaster. While Frederick was away hunting, the papalists, who had gathered in Parma, fell upon his camp, misnamed Victoria, on February 18, 1248, dispersed his army, and captured his treasure. His trusted minister, Taddeo of Sessa, was among the slain. A papal legate meanwhile was recovering the March of Ancona and invading the Regno. Frederick vainly made fresh offers of submission, but the Pope insisted on his renouncing the Empire. Another plot against the Emperor's life was discovered in 1249, and on suspicion of his complicity Peter della Vigna, the pillar of the imperial court, was blinded, and then committed suicide to escape worse. To crown all,

Capture of King Enzo

Frederick's favourite and capable bastard son, King Enzo, was defeated on May 26, 1249, by the Bolognese at La Fossalta and led into lifelong captivity. Yet the balance swayed back again. Ezzelin extended his dominion ; the legate was defeated in the March of Ancona ; Piacenza became imperialist in hatred of Parma, and Parma itself was recaptured in 1250 ; progress was made in Romagna.

Death of Frederick II

Frederick was hopefully preparing a new campaign when he died on December 13, 1250, at Fiorentino in Apulia, professing, as he had done all along, his devotion to the Church, but leaving Empire and Regno to his son Conrad IV. A bastard son, Manfred, was to be regent of the Regno till Conrad's arrival.

However much in his organized bureaucratic government and his intellectual comprehensiveness and receptivity Frederick forecast the Renaissance, he was the last true ruler of the Holy Roman Empire in the old sense, of the universal Christian secular State, and under him, although his personal authority and partial success in the unification of Italy, of which he was the only native Emperor, might conceal the fact, the Holy Roman Empire crumbled steadily. He only held Germany, its basis, by ceasing to govern it in any effective fashion, and in the struggle with the Papacy the Empire was fatally undermined. Of the two chiefs of Christendom, spiritual and secular, neither could endure the independent supremacy of the other, and when Frederick openly bid for the absolute rule of Italy, the Papacy bent all its strength to his utter overthrow. That overthrow was delayed by Frederick's personal genius, but it would have needed more than one man's life to resist successfully the monarch of the Western Church, entrenched in its organization, armed with spiritual terrors, and attended with a reverence and devotion, which it needed many years of misuse, perversion, and disillusion even to impair. In the decline of the medieval Papacy, besides the faults of Popes and prelates, Frederick played his part. Whatever truth might lie in the danger to papal independence involved in a unified, monarchic Italy, men saw the Popes using every spiritual weapon for a secular policy they scarcely ventured to avow. Was the Vicar of God only to be able to work for men's salvation by incessant war against Christians, by artful diplomacy, by bribes, by jobbery, and by exactions ? Frederick's manifestos, his championship of the secular State, were only premature in so far as they awaited proofs from the actions, long enough repeated, of the Popes themselves. What he could not do was to be done by the monarchs of the national States, already arising in his day. They could count on a national solidarity and organization unknown in Germany and Italy. Their monarchs in the thirteenth century acquired a dominion over their subjects ecclesiastical and lay, such as Frederick, save in Sicily, never exercised, and they had a shrewd fellow-feeling for one another which

Decay of the Holy Roman Empire under him

,they could not feel for the universal Emperor. They viewed a Papacy tarnished by its conflicts. But the Holy Roman Empire expressed an ideal of the past, and rested on ancient, weak, and now disrupted foundations ; for all their endeavours the Hohenstaufen could not renovate them. That Empire, the creation of Charlemagne and Otto the Great, fell with Frederick.

SUGGESTIONS FOR READING ON CHAPTER III

A. Sources

(i) Documents

Böhmer : *Regesta Imperii . . . 1198–1272.* Ed. Ficker, J., and Winkelmann, E. Innsbruck, 1881–1901. ⌐Indispensable classified index of facts from the sources.]

Huillard-Bréholles, J. L. A. : *Historia diplomatica Friderici Secundi.* 12 vols. Paris, 1852–61.

Potthast, A. : *Regesta Pontificum Romanorum, 1198–1304.* Berlin, 1874–5.

Constitutiones et Acta Publica regum et imperatorum. Vol. ii. *Mon. Germ. Hist.* Legum Sectio IV. Hanover, 1896.

(ii) Chronicles

(a) Italian :

Annales Ianuenses Cafari et continuatorum. Vols. ii, iii. Ed. Belgrano and Imperiale di S. Angelo. Fonti per la storia d'Italia. Rome, 1901–23.

Annales Placentini Gibellini. Ed. Pertz. *Mon. Germ. Hist.* XVIII. Hanover, 1863.

Carbio, N. de : *Vita Innocentii IV papae.* Ed. Pagnotti. Archivio storico della r. Società Romana di storia patria. XXI. 1898. [Also in Muratori, *Rerum Ital. Script.* III (1st ed.).]

Chronicon Marchiae Tarvisinae et Lombardiae (Annales S. Iustinae Patavini). Ed. Botteghi. Muratori, *Rer. Ital. Script.* New edn. VIII. 1916.

Dandolo, A. : *Chronicon Venetum.* Muratori, *Rer. Ital. Script.* XII (1st edn.).

Jamsilla, N. de : *Historia de rebus gestis Friderici II.* Del Re, *Cronisti e scrittori sincroni napoletani.* Vol. ii.

Malaspina, S. : *Rerum Sicularum libri vi.* Del Re, *op. cit.*

Matthew Paris : *Chronica majora.* Ed. Luard. Rolls Series. 1872–83.

Rolandinus Patavinus : *Chronica.* Ed. Bonardi. Muratori, *Rer. Ital. Script.* (new edn.). VIII. 1905 ff.

Ryccardus de S. Germano : *Chronica.* First version. Ed. Gaudenzi with *Ignoti monachi Cist.S. Mariae de Ferraria.* Soc. Napol. di storia patria. Naples, 1888.

Salimbene : *Cronica.* Ed. Holder-Egger. *Mon. Germ. Hist. Script.* XXXI. Hanover, 1903.

Villani, G. : *Historie florentine.* Muratori, *Rer. Ital. Script.* XIII (1st edn.).

Vita Gregorii IX. Ibid. III (1st edn.).

(*b*) German :

Burchardus praepositus Urspurgensis. *Chronicon.* Ed. Holder-Egger and Simson. Scriptores rerum Germanicarum in usum Scholarum. Hanover, 1916.

Chronica regia Coloniensis. Ed. Waitz. *Ibid.* 1880.

Monumenta Erphesfurtensia. Ed. Holder-Egger. *Ibid.* 1899.

B. MODERN WORKS

Barraclough, G. : *The Origins of Modern Germany* 2nd edn. 1947

Brown, H. : *Venice.* 1895.

Butler, W. F. : *The Lombard Communes.* 1906.

Cambridge Medieval History. Vol. vi (relevant chapters). 1929.

Davidsohn, R. : *Geschichte Florenz.* Vol. ii, pt. i. [Monumental, authoritative, immense detail.]

Fisher, H. A. L. : *The Medieval Empire.* 1908.

Gregorovius, F. : *History of the City of Rome in the Middle Ages.* Trans. Hamilton. Vol. v.

Glotz, G. : *Histoire Générale, Le Moyen Âge,* vol. iv, pt. i, *L'Allemagne et l'Italie au douzième et treizième siècles.* Paris, 1939.

Hampe, K. : *Deutsche Kaisergeschichte im Zeitalter der Salier und Staufer.* Leipzig, 1912.

Hauck, A. : *Kirchengeschichte Deutschlands.* Vol. iv. Leipzig, 1913.

Huillard-Bréholles, A. : *Op. cit.* (A. i). Introduction in vol. xii.

Jordan, E. : *Les origines de la domination angevine en Italie.* Paris, 1909.

Kington (-Oliphant), T. L. : *History of Frederick II.* 1862.

Sedgwick, H. D. : *Italy in the Thirteenth Century.* 1913.

CHAPTER IV

THE PAPACY AND ITALY, 1250–c. 1300

Italy at the
Death of
Frederick II

THE death of Frederick II deprived his partisans in Italy of their unity of direction. His illegitimate son Manfred, the Prince of Taranto, himself dubiously loyal to his half-brother Conrad IV, was hampered by the suspicions of the German troops under Margrave Berthold of Hohenburg and of the chief officials. There was deep discontent and dislike of the Germans in the over-taxed Regno, and it was not long before the Terra di Lavoro (the ancient Campania), led by Naples and Capua, was in revolt. In North Italy, Ezzelin held his cities in the " March of Treviso," and Marquess Oberto Pelavicini, the vicar of Central Lombardy, a great noble of the north slope of the Apennines, held Cremona, but they acted as independent potentates. In Tuscany, just before Frederick's death a revolution had occurred in Florence which set up the constitution of the *Primo Popolo* (" the first people "). It was an instance of the new arrangements by which the non-nobles were obtaining a larger or even a chief share of power. Besides the older councils of the " commune " in which the nobles were predominant and their official chief, the *podestà*, there were set up councils of the " people " with a " captain of the people " at their head, and based on membership of the more important gilds. In Florence the revolution was followed in January 1251 by the return of the exiled Guelf nobles and soon after by the exile of the Ghibellines, and the city became under its vigorous new government the leading state in Tuscany. Some years later a parallel movement took place in Genoa, where the traders of the gilds had grown restive under the domination of the feudal nobles who owned and sailed the ships and monopolized the government. In a revolution of 1257 they put in a kind of dictator, the merchant Guglielmo Boccanegra, as captain of the people. But the war with Genoa's rival, Venice, in the

Levant went badly, and the nobles who fought it were
able in 1262 to bring about a reaction and a restoration
of the older constitution, equally unstable, for a few
years.

Innocent IV hailed the new era with excessive confidence. Innocent
He prepared at once to return to Italy and to conquer, as IV's Return
he hoped, the Regno. In the spring he held a Lombard and Schemes
congress at Genoa and journeyed slowly through Lombardy
to Perugia, which he reached in November 1251. But his
gains, though real in West Lombardy and the Papal States,
were small. The cities were intent on their own policies
and quarrels ; his means were exhausted, and negotiations
with Manfred and Berthold were fruitless. In 1252 Conrad IV
came from Germany to secure his kingdom and recruit his
finances. He quickly thrust aside Manfred, and with some
difficulty subdued the rebels in the Terra di Lavoro. Even
Rome, where the Pope dared not reside, was in his favour.
The Ghibelline Colonna and the middle class had called in
(1252) an able Bolognese, Brancaleone Andalò, as sole
Senator, who reduced the city to unwonted order. Innocent
gained time by repeated negotiations with Conrad, which all
split on the rock of the union of Sicily with the Empire ;
but before the end of 1252 he had already decided on a
new scheme : to obtain a foreign champion, who should
drive out the Hohenstaufen and be King of Sicily. Richard,
Earl of Cornwall, brother of Henry III of England, and
Charles, Count of Anjou, brother of Louis IX of France,
both refused the bait, one through his own prudence, the
other owing to the aversion of St. Louis for the enterprise.
But, when the young Henry of Hohenstaufen, Empress
Isabella's son, died in 1253, and snapped the link between
his house and the Plantagenets, Henry III, injudicious as
ever, was fired with the prospect of making his second son,
Edmund, King of Sicily. The effect of the treaty he accepted
was a paradox : he was to find the money, the Pope was to
attempt to carry out the conquest. Meantime, however,
Conrad, whose heart was in Germany, had replenished his
treasure from the Regno, and was preparing to march across Death of
the Alps when he died of fever on May 21, 1254, leaving in Conrad IV
Bavaria an infant son, Conrad II or Conradin, to succeed
him as King of Sicily. Thus the precarious union of the

Empire with Sicily, which had been so full of momentous consequences, came to an end.

How black the outlook appeared to Conrad IV on his death-bed was shown by his will, which made the German Berthold regent to the exclusion of the popular Manfred, and the deadly enemy of the Hohenstaufen, Pope Innocent, guardian of his heir. Berthold was disliked and quickly resigned in favour of Manfred, while the Pope demanded immediate possession of the Regno. When Innocent, with the help of Henry III's credit, sent an army across the frontier and followed it himself, Manfred, who could not depend on the German troopers, gave way. Conradin's rights were to be adjudicated on when he came of age; Manfred was to be vicar of the southern mainland; the Pope was to rule. But Innocent's faithlessness ruined his victory; he was cheating Henry III; he now broke the treaty with Manfred, and set about annexing Sicily and Calabria to the Papal State. At the same time Manfred killed a baron among his personal enemies in a rencontre, and fled for his life to the Saracen colony of Lucera, sure

foes of papal dominion. In November 1254 he seized the royal treasure there and revolted. Now, too, even if Berthold remained dubiously papalist, the Germans and most of the kingdom, loyal to Conradin, were willing to take his side, for the Pope's policy was unveiled. A victory over a detachment of Berthold's troops was sufficient to send the hastily levied papal army, which was entering Apulia, and the incompetent papal nephew in command of it, flying

north in panic. The news found Innocent sick to death at Naples. On December 7 he closed his eventful pontificate, according to the Friars, whom he had aggrieved, in remorse and gloom. His personal influence on the history of his time was epoch-making. He had defeated the Empire and ruined it; he had definitely begun the degeneracy of the medieval Papacy, secularizing its aims and methods and abusing its spiritual authority.

The next pontificate by a natural reaction showed a spiritually-minded Pope entangled irresistibly in the policy of a Curia now largely manned by ecclesiastical statesmen and lawyers who differed little in life and methods from their secular counterparts. The genial Alexander IV (1254–61),

the last Pope of the house of Conti, was unable to make
head against his adversary. He raised money by finally
investing Edmund of England with the Regno, while his
mercenary army under Cardinal Octavian Ubaldini once more
marched to Apulia to join up with the disloyal towns. But
the legate, possibly as a result of Berthold's double-dealing,
was surrounded and starved to surrender at Foggia in September 1255. Although Alexander cancelled the not unfavourable treaty which acknowledged Conradin, he was
obliged to look on while Manfred first established his rule **Manfred**
over all the Regno and then, after spreading a false report **becomes**
of his nephew's death, was crowned king in Palermo in **King of**
August 1258. **Sicily**

With Manfred the desire to be predominant in North **His Policy**
Italy became a Sicilian, not an imperial, ambition. It was **in North**
partly a defensive tendency against the irreconcilable Papacy, **Italy**
and it always wears the appearance of a foreign policy. · He
allied with the mighty Lombard Ghibelline chief, Pelavicini, who, based on Cremona, held the middle Po ; he invaded central Italy ; and he sent his German troopers to
Tuscany to aid Siena and the Ghibelline Florentine exiles
to win the famous victory of Montaperti in 1260, which
placed Florence once more under the rule of its Ghibelline
faction and drove out the Guelf nobles. But the foundations
of Manfred's power were sandy : by his usurpation he had
lost the safeguard of legitimate succession which appealed to
St. Louis of France ; the mainland of the Regno was never
devoted to his dynasty ; centralization and taxation were
still a bitter grievance ; the king himself, brilliant, amiable,
and brave, had a streak of indolence in his character, and
preferred diplomacy to strenuous war. Lombardy was ruled **Rise of**
now mainly by independent city-tyrants. In general, the **Tyrants in**
party of the *popolo* were unable to maintain peace and order **Lombardy**
under a republican government ; they gave a faction-chief
supreme power as holder of one of the chief offices, preferen-
tially that of captain of the people, for a term of years. His
powers would be increased by successive enactments, ending
in his appointment for life and in the grant of the *arbitrium
generale*, i.e. emancipation from the law, and of legislative
functions. The legal development of the tyrant was a
gradual process, but his real despotism, which the *arbitrium*

generale signified in formal law, existed very soon in his career. Of such men the Guelf Martin della Torre was tyrant of Milan (since 1258), Azzo, Marquess of Este, practically hereditary tyrant of Ferrara. But the ferocious Ghibelline Ezzelin da Romano held his tyranny with no official title in his cities, of which Verona was the chief. His abnormal cruelty and blood-lust had at last, however, awakened resistance in Padua. The pious Alexander IV proclaimed a crusade against the favourer of the Patarine heretics ; his unclerical legate, Philip, fierce and unscrupulous as any tyrant, who had been Innocent's agent in Germany and was now Archbishop-elect of Ravenna, collected with the aid of Venice a ruffianly army, and in 1256 seized Padua and held it. Ezzelin was still strong enough to seize Brescia, but in doing so he fell out with Pelavicini, whom he cheated of his share, and Pelavicini headed a league of all the neighbour states against him. He ended his career by suicide in 1259, after his capture in the battle of Cassano.

Pope Urban IV

To the weak Alexander there succeeded the dominating Urban IV (1261–4), who in his brief pontificate resumed the aggressive policy of Innocent IV. He was a Frenchman, the son of a shoemaker of Troyes, and naturally looked to France and had influence there. Among the fourteen cardinals he created six were French, and from this time a powerful French party existed in the Curia. He was resolved to seek a champion in France to conquer Sicily. The unhelpful Henry III was left, with the debts he had contracted, to face his baronage. The recovery of Constantinople by the Greeks in 1261 [1] was itself a diplomatic advantage, for St. Louis was persuaded that Manfred, in spite of his proffers to attack Palaeologus, stood in the way of the Crusade thither and to the Holy Land. Long negotiations were diplomatically begun with Manfred and duly failed ; then the crown of Sicily was offered again to Charles of Anjou in 1263, this time with St. Louis' approval. No better choice of a champion could have been made : the dour, rabidly ambitious count was a general and an organizing autocrat. In 1246 he had obtained by marriage with a daughter of Count Raymond-Berengar IV the county of Provence in the Arelate and had there suppressed local autonomy under his

Charles of Anjou

[1] See below, Chap. VI, p. 128.

efficient sway.   By skilful intervention he had formed a new
state round Cuneo in the neighbouring parts of West Lombardy, named for some eighty years the county of Piedmont.[1]   He thus possessed an excellent base for the invasion
of Italy.   Now chosen by the Pope, he haggled long and
successfully for better terms.   The fact that the Guelfs had
obtained the preponderance in Rome after Brancaleone's
death in 1259 proved an advantage, as did the successes of
Manfred's arms in the Papal States, for the Romans elected
Charles Senator and received his deputy, and Urban had to
sanction the dangerous appointment as a temporary measure.
The treaty was in a fair way to conclusion when Urban died
in October 1264.

One achievement of Urban IV, who " did what he willed," *Urban IV's*
had been the subjection of the North Italian banking inter- *Control*
ests to the policy of the Papacy.   In the great development *of the*
of the papal revenues from beyond the Alps during the first *Florentine*
half of the thirteenth century, the Italian traders, and espe- *Bankers*
cially the Tuscans, had played a foremost part.   They had
transmitted revenue in the form of goods, they had lent
large sums in anticipation of it and thereby reaped high
profits.   But the Papacy by excommunication and the like
held the whip-hand over its bankers and creditors.   Urban IV
insisted on Guelfic politics ;   one by one the Ghibelline
bankers of Florence were converted to Guelfism, while their
rivals of Ghibelline Siena, for instance, were ousted from the
English trade for their recalcitrance.   Urban IV left the
bankers the Papacy's firm allies, and the Church with
enlarged powers of raising credits for the war.

When after a four-months' vacancy a successor was at *Pope*
last elected, the choice of the cardinals could not have been *Clement IV*
more favourable to Charles.   Guy Foulquois, now Pope
Clement IV (1265-8), was a Frenchman of Languedoc devoted
to the house of Capet, whose minister he had long been.   In
April 1265 the treaty with Charles was made : the Sicilian
tribute to the Pope was to be raised to 8,000 ounces of gold ;
the new king was to surrender the senatorship of Rome
within three years, and to hold no other dominion in central
or   northern Italy, Piedmont excepted.   His campaign

[1] This county is distinct from the later principality of Piedmont acquired
by the house of Savoy.

should be a crusade, and the clergy of France and the Arelate were to pay a tenth of their incomes towards his expenses, while Clement and Charles strained their credit to raise further supplies. Fortune favoured the allies. Charles in May successfully evaded Manfred's fleet and entered Rome to be solemnly invested with the Regno. It was a daring move which contrasted with Manfred's slack proceedings. In February Philip della Torre, the new tyrant of Milan, had formed a fresh Guelfic league with Obizzo of Este and Ferrara, which gained over city after city. In November the crusading army could assemble in Charles's city of Alba in Piedmont and pursue its march past the helpless Pelavicini to Rome. Manfred was now preparing for the war and assembling all his forces, but the mainland barons and towns were already meditating revolt. The two armies met on February 26, 1266, close to Benevento on the main road to Apulia. There the treacherous barons fled and Manfred fell fighting in the lost battle. The Regno at once submitted to the conqueror. The battle of Benevento did more than change the dynasty which ruled the Regno. It put an end to the primacy of the southern Sicilian civilization in Italy. That brilliant compound of West and East, Norman, Byzantine, and Moslem, never recovered from the uncongenial north French rule of Charles of Anjou. Vernacular Italian literature, which had its birth in the court of Frederick II, and art, with the new creative tendencies he had fostered, henceforth found their chief homes in the northern cities. Nor was it less a triumph of the Papacy over its ancient dread, and sometime defender, the Norman realm of Sicily, and a triumph of French knights over German that marked the rise of France to the first place in Europe.

Though the Guelfic factions, however, were momentarily triumphant over Italy, and Pelavicini was deprived of the remnant of his dominion, the situation was far from stable. Charles's government in the Regno, with his debts to pay and great schemes in prospect, was even more extortionate and absolute than that of the Hohenstaufens had been. The chief posts were naturally given to his foreign followers, and the inhabitants soon began to turn to the rightful heir in Germany, King Conradin, now a boy of fifteen. Meanwhile,

Charles of Anjou's Invasion

Battle of Benevento

Charles' Rule (a) in the Regno

the Tuscan towns were going their own way, and the Pope, to curb them, appointed Charles *Paciarius* or " Peacemaker " in Tuscany in spite of his own treaty.   In 1267 Charles was there fighting the Ghibellines and reorganizing the city of Florence.   Thence the Ghibellines fled, and Charles was *(b) in* elected *Signore* or lord of the town.   His new constitution *Tuscany* placed the Guelf nobles and bankers in power : the *popolo*, just revived, was again abolished, and the faction organization, the *Parte Guelfa*, was endowed with vast confiscated Ghibelline property to secure its own predominance.   But a counter-movement was maturing in favour of the boy Conradin.   Pisa and Siena were strongly Ghibelline.   Rome, after the victory of Benevento, had been placed by Clement IV under an adventurous prince, Don Henry of Castile, who showed the same sympathies.   In the island of Sicily, always more loyal to the native claimant, a formidable revolt broke out in August 1267.

Conradin, gallant and sanguine, had resolved to strike *Conradin's* for his inheritance and join his supporters.   With a German *Invasion* army, disregarding the papal anathema, he reached the ever-Ghibelline Pavia in January 1268, for the tyrant of Verona, Mastino della Scala, had opened the way to him through the Alpine defiles.   Charles meantime was called south by the rebellion of the Saracens of Lucera, and Conradin could make his adventure, skilfully enough, across the Apennines at Cento Croci Pass, by sea to Pisa, by land to Rome and Don Henry, and thence towards the Abruzzi to trace a northern circuit to Lucera.   But his rival was a resolute veteran.   Breaking up the siege of Lucera, leaving Apulia to revolt behind him, Charles met the Hohenstaufen at Albe *Battle of* not far from the frontier on the road to Tagliacozzo.   On *Tagliacozzo* August 23, 1268, the invaders were routed by his general-*(Albe)* ship and the valour of his French knights.   He could triumphantly invite the Pope to " arise and eat of his son's venison."   One of his first victims was Conradin himself, who was captured in his flight, and tried and executed along with another boy, Frederick of Baden, claimant of Austria, at Naples in October.   The legitimate Hohenstaufen were extinguished in his person, perishing fitly in swift tragedy, not in impotent festering decay.

King Charles could now have his will of his enemies.

Charles at
the Height
of his Power

Ruthless executions marked the subjection of captive or obstinate rebels. Lucera surrendered in 1269, and Sicily was subdued in 1270. The conquest of the Regno entailed a French immigration of nobles endowed with confiscated fiefs, and their retainers, who acted as a garrison for the dynasty. Naples, never loyal to the Hohenstaufen, on the mainland became his capital in place of Palermo. Farther north, he recovered the senatorship of Rome for ten years, and was named " Imperial " Vicar of Tuscany indefinitely by the Pope's appointment. Siena and Pisa were obliged to submit to his authority. Not the least part of his good fortune was the opportune death of Clement IV in November 1268, which was followed by a prolonged vacancy of the Holy See, and left his hands free for ambitious schemes not likely to meet with full papal approval. Charles aimed, in fact, at diverting at least for a time the crusading efforts of Christendom from the Holy Land to the reconquest of Constantinople from the schismatic Greeks. He had already seized on Corfu, the dowry of Manfred's widow ; he had contracted an alliance with Baldwin II, the expelled Latin Emperor of Constantinople, and married his son Philip to the heiress of the principality of Achaia (Morea), which became a vassal state of the Angevins. A vast dominion in the East was the goal of his ambitions. But his preparations were delayed by the insistence of his brother St. Louis on a fresh crusade against the infidel. It was perhaps largely due to Charles's influence that the preliminary object of this crusade was made the conversion or the conquest of Tunis, the former ally of Manfred and tributary of Sicily. When St. Louis died in his fever-stricken camp at Carthage in August 1270, it was Charles who reaped the fruit of the enterprise by renewing and doubling the Tunisian tribute. His immediate gains, however, were snatched from his grasp by a storm which destroyed the returning fleet at Trapani on the Sicilian coast ; and the Grecian war was perforce deferred.

His Eastern
Schemes

St. Louis'
Crusade and
Death

Decline of
Charles's
Power in
North Italy

The decline in the fortunes of Charles of Anjou now began. In 1270 a revolution took place in Genoa : the Guelf nobles, headed by the Fieschi and Grimaldi, lost their predominance, and the city came under the joint sway of the two Ghibelline chiefs, Oberto Doria and Oberto Spinola,

whose dictatorial government, as their title of captains of
the people indicated, rested on an alliance with the *popolo*,
i.e. the merchants and traders whose goods the nobles carried in their ships.   After Charles had vainly besieged Genoa
in 1273, the Genoese allowed a Spanish force sent by Alfonso X
of Castile, claimant of the Empire, to enter Lombardy and
support the Ghibellines.   Soon after, in 1275, Marquess
Thomas of Saluzzo defeated Charles's troops at Roccavione,
and for the time being Charles's county of Piedmont disappeared.   More important was the change in the Papacy,
which had created the Angevin greatness and inevitably
exercised a control over its creature.   In spite of Charles's
endeavours to obtain the election of a French pope, the
wary majority of the cardinals finally, in September 1271,
chose a moderate Lombard Guelf, Tedaldo Visconti of Pope
Piacenza, who took the style of Gregory X.   The new pon- Gregory X.
tiff, who had spent the best years of his life in the Holy His Policy
Land, provides a happy contrast to his belligerent predecessors.   Zealous for peace and reconcilement and unity among
Christians, he was still more zealous for a real crusade to win
back Jerusalem.   To this end he bent his disinterested
statesmanship.   There should be once again an Emperor,
no longer dangerous to the Popes in Italy.   There Charles
should be a favoured vassal, but no more.   Charles's very
ambitions should be used as a lever to induce the Greeks
to abandon their schism for fear of invasion.   If they submitted, Charles could not stir, and the way to a crusade
was plain.   So Gregory obtained the election of Rudolf of
Habsburg as King of the Romans, received his renunciation
of all claims over the Papal States, enforced the withdrawal
of Alfonso of Castile and the departure of his Spanish troopers
from Lombardy, and endeavoured to reconcile Rudolf with
Charles, whom he had foiled in his attempt to promote his
nephew, Philip III of France, to the Empire.   Meantime the
Pope had held the second General Council of Lyons in 1274, The Second
and there had nominally healed the schism of East and General
West.   The Greek Emperor gave way in return for protec- Council
of Lyons.
tion from Charles.   Gregory X seemed in the full tide of Reunion
success when he died in January 1276.   Yet the Empire he with the
had restored was perhaps only less unreal than the Union Greek
Church
of the Churches.

Three ephemeral Popes swiftly succeeded one another while Charles's influence ebbed among the cardinals, till in November 1277 John Gaetan of the great Roman house of **Pope Nicholas III** the Orsini was elected as Nicholas III (1277-80). Under his capable but thoroughly worldly guidance the Papacy and the Church became once more immersed in political and essentially Italian schemes. He made nepotism, the exaltation of his Orsini kinsmen, a leading aim of his pontificate, which earned him Dante's condemnation to the Inferno. He even thought of making one relative king of the *Regnum Italicum,* while Rudolf was to be compensated by the hereditary rule of Germany and Charles by a kingdom of the Arelate. This was a vision. But in the narrow sphere of politics which he preferred Nicholas was effective. He finally secured the real cession of Romagna by the Empire, thus completing the structure of the Papal States ; he deprived Charles of Rome and Tuscany ; his legate, Cardinal Latino Malabranca, repatriated the Ghibellines of Florence, and reorganized the constitution, so that the *popolo* once more secured a growing share of power.

Pope Martin IV The death of Nicholas, however, threw the game into Charles's hands.   He forced through the election of a French Pope, Simon de Brie, who became Martin IV (1281-5). This pontiff was first and foremost a Frenchman and partisan of the house of Anjou ; the captivity to French interests, deferred by Gregory X and Nicholas III, loomed ever nearer. Martin at once restored his patron to the rule of Rome, and governed the Papal States by means of Angevin officials. What was more important, he fell in with Charles's plan of conquering the schismatic Greeks of Constantinople. He **End of the Union with the Greek Church** denounced the hollow Union of Gregory X in 1281. This was the indispensable preliminary for war, and Charles gained the adhesion of Venice to his anti-Greek league. But there were weak spots in the Angevin's armour, a discontented people and a dangerous competitor, and these Michael Palaeologus, who was not lacking in wealth and diplomacy, exploited to the full to ward off the threatened invasion. **Discontent of Sicily** Charles and the French had earned the hatred of a large part of the subjects of the Regno. His government had been autocratic, harsh, and extortionate, exaggerating the worse features of Hohenstaufen rule without its intelligent

ITALY *c.* A.D. 1300

care for the people's welfare or its sympathetic culture. The
hated *collectæ* had been levied yearly and increased in incidence
to provide for Charles's vast schemes; the parliaments, which
could have expressed popular grievances, were no longer
summoned ; the king was a grim North French noble out of
touch with his subjects.   Meantime, the new French nobility
were oppressive, bred as they were in the less controlled
feudalism north of the Alps, and the French troopers were
intolerably insolent.   In the island of Sicily, now become a
subsidiary province, these grievances were most severe and
unalloyed hatred of the French most rampant.

On his conquest of the Regno Charles had placed Manfred's helpless children in perpetual imprisonment, but the
eldest daughter, Constance, was safe from him, for she had

Peter of Aragon's Schemes

been married to Peter the Great, the heir of Aragon, and
Peter was resolved to claim his wife's inheritance.   He was
now King of Aragon, and in the ships of seafaring Catalonia
possessed one of the strongest fleets of the Mediterranean,
not to mention the formidable army of knights and of light
infantry, the *almugàvers*, of his country.   Curiously enough,
his admiral, the best of the day, was a Calabrian exile, Roger
Lauria or Loria.   Another exile, John of Procida, acted as
go-between with Michael and the Sicilians, and wove the
web of the conspiracy.   There was a certain irony in Peter's
proceedings : he proclaimed a crusade to Barbary, and
demanded papal aid.

The Sicilian Vespers

Before he set sail, however, revolt had broken out inde-
pendently of his plans.   On Easter Monday (March 30) 1282,
provoked by an outrage by a French soldier, the Palermitans
had risen and massacred the foreigners and were imitated
throughout the island.   This was the Sicilian Vespers, in
which over 3,000 irrespective of sex or age perished.   Charles
at once diverted his Grecian armament to the siege of Messina,
and the danger forced the rebels, who had at first thought

Peter becomes King of Sicily

of a republican league of towns, to offer the crown to Peter,
now in Barbary.   He landed on August 30 and soon compelled the retreat of Charles to the mainland.   The separation, thus casually effected, of the Regno into the island
kingdom of Sicily and the titular kingdom of Sicily, or
Naples, on the mainland was never reversed till the nineteenth century.

The war of the Vespers, however, dragged on for twenty years. Neither would the Angevins abandon their conquest nor would the Papacy admit defeat in its tenacious policy without using every effort. The treasures and the authority of Rome, the arms and alliances of the house of Anjou were all to be exhausted in the cause. Pope Martin IV declared the kingdom of Aragon forfeit and conferred it on Charles, Count of Valois, the younger son of Philip III of France, who led a huge crusade to conquer it. Charles of Anjou strained every nerve for an invincible invasion of Sicily, while he and Peter arranged, neither sincerely, for a chivalrous combat at Bordeaux over their rights. But the decisive part was played by the Sicilian and Catalan fleet under Loria. One victory on June 5, 1284, in the Bay of Naples resulted in the capture of Charles's heir, Charles the Lame ; another off Gerona, which Philip III was besieging, wrecked the French fleet and the crusade together : Philip drew off his diseased and starving army to die himself at Perpignan in October 1285. Peter the Great only survived till November, when one son Alfonso III succeeded to Aragon, the second, James, to Sicily. Charles of Anjou, who had revolutionized Italy and made the Papacy his instrument, died disappointed of his ambitions at Foggia on January 7, 1285. He was followed to the grave in March by the Pope who had been his tool.

None of these deaths, however, deflected the stubborn policy of the Roman Curia, now wedded to the reconquest of Sicily. Alfonso III of Aragon, whose subjects had little interest in the strife, was induced to buy himself out of it in the treaty of Canfranc by the surrender of his captive, King Charles the Lame, and the abandonment of his brother James. But it was all that the new King of Naples could do to defend Calabria and the coast from Sicilian attacks until in 1291 the childless death of Alfonso called James to the throne of Aragon and the defence of Aragonese interests. Meantime two insignificant Popes, Honorius IV and Nicholas IV, were followed from 1292 to 1294 by another prolonged vacancy of the Apostolic See. The nepotism and local entanglements of recent pontiffs had resulted in the College of Cardinals, much reduced in numbers, being divided into the two factions of Orsini and Colonna. In the city

of Rome these two great families now outdistanced all competitors ; they were bitterly hostile to one another in true
Italian fashion, and their scions carried the feud into the
Curia, of which they were powerful members. As was
natural, they found rival policies over which to contend
The Ghibelline Colonna adopted the wiser course of recognizing accomplished facts and accepting the separation of
Sicily from Naples ; the Guelf Orsini were for reconquest
and the Angevin alliance. Neither had the necessary two-
thirds majority to elect a Pope. At last Cardinal Latino
Malabranca had the inspiration of proposing the famous
hermit Peter of Morrone in the Abruzzi. In view of the
harm the Church was receiving from political Popes and
secular preoccupations, it might well occur to the pious
Latino, the author of the hymn *Dies iræ*, to find a way out
by means of the election of a thoroughly unworldly ascetic
But Celestine V, though he accepted the call, was miserable
in his new position, and had no capacity for directing the
greatest bureaucracy in the world nor any grasp of the
problems of the Church. He settled not at Rome but at
Naples, completely under the influence of Charles II. In a
few months, with growing agony of conscience, he had reduced the administration of the Curia to chaos ; according
to rumour his mind was made up to abdicate by a pseudo-
angelic voice which was really that of Cardinal Benedict
Gaetani heard through a speaking-tube. It was, however,
very dubious whether a Pope could divorce himself from
his see, and Celestine issued a solemn pronouncement that
it was legitimate to do so before he resigned the tiara on
December 13, 1294, making the *gran rifiuto* that Dante
scorned. In ten days Gaetani became Pope Boniface VIII.

The choice would not, perhaps, have been made had the
Papacy seemed a desirable ambition in its perplexities and
with the dubious legitimacy after an abdication. Boniface
was of dauntless courage and autocratic temper, a first-rate
administrator and a jurist of distinction ; but he was insolent and overbearing to excess, of an ungovernable temper
aggravated by his physical sufferings from the stone, so rash
in his utterances as to rouse suspicions of his orthodoxy
and filled with a passionate nepotism beyond precedent. He
was an extreme instance of the worldly prelate bred by the

Marginal notes:

Pope Celestine V

His Abdication

Pope Boniface VIII

world-dominion, the wars and territorial politics of the Papacy. His management, however, of the Sicilian war showed his capacity. By using the danger of further foreign invasion and the discontent in Aragon at the long dynastic war, he induced James to surrender Sicily and become the ally of Charles II in 1295. After some years of pressure James even brought the invincible Catalan fleet under Roger Loria to assist the Angevin in another attack in 1299. Meantime, the deserted Sicilians under James's younger brother Frederick II, whom they had made their king in 1295, were carrying on a vigorous offensive in Calabria. James, however, won a great sea-battle over his brother off Cape Orlando in July 1299, and Neapolitan armies were landed in east and west Sicily, while James, who had performed his contract, sailed back to Spain. Robert, the heir of Naples, took Catania and besieged Messina ; his brother Philip of Taranto landed at Trapani and marched inland. But Philip was met **Battle of** on December 1, 1299, by King Frederick at the head of the **Falconaria** Sicilians and his Catalan mercenaries in the plain of Falconaria. There by a device already used in Tuscany and distantly resembling the tactics of Hannibal at Cannæ, Frederick enclosed the enemies' mailed horse pressing on his centre by his left wing on their flank, and drove them in rout, capturing Philip. It was in some degree a victory of professional foot, the *almugàvers*, over the Angevin knights. But the Angevins, under Loria, retained the command of the sea with a victory at Ponza in 1300, although no real progress was made on land. At last the Pope, enraged with his helpless protégés, called in a French champion once more. This time it was Charles of Valois, the ex-pretender to Aragon, who was hired to lead the crusade against Sicily, and promised subsequent aid for his pretensions to Constantinople. He turned out to be a bad choice. Landed in Sicily in May 1302, he crossed the island to besiege Sciacca in the south in the heat of summer while disease raged among horses and men. At the end of August he was glad to make the peace **Peace of** of Caltabellotta, which was a surrender. Frederick II was **Caltabellotta** to be King of island Sicily or Trinacria for life ; he was to marry Charles II's daughter. Boniface resisted and bargained, but he was already at odds with France, and he ended by assenting to the treaty on May 21, 1303, stipulating for the vassalage and tribute of Frederick to the Papacy and the style of King of Trinacria. The War of the Vespers thus ended in the defeat of the Papacy after the unstinting sacrifice of blood and treasure and the concentrated diplomacy of twenty years.

State of Sicily

The obstinate national resistance of the Sicilians, isolated against such great forces, had been accompanied by an effort to secure reforms in the government and some limitation in the autocracy of the Crown. The parliament, under Aragonese influence, had developed into the three " *Braccia* " of the barons, the prelates, and the royal towns, and the " statutes of King James " legislated against abuses and for the rights of the subjects. But the island was now become a small and poor State ; its European importance had been lost ; the nobles, who had won the war, were all-powerful, and as the intervals in the recrudescent conflict with Naples grew longer during the fourteenth century, they became absorbed in profitless feuds. Sicily kept her independence, but her civilization steadily declined.

The North Italian Cities

While in South Italy the liquidation of the ruin of the Hohenstaufen had led to a decadent feudal regression, in the North and Centre the final dissolution of imperial rule had meant the liberation of the forces which had made the city-state to pursue an unfettered development according to the natural strength of each in the various communes. The same growth of trade and industry which had produced first the " commune " and then the " *popolo* " led in Lombardy

The Lombard Tyrants

to the emergence of the tyranny, and then to the formation under the tyrants of larger territories composed of several cities. It was an obvious advantage to enlarge the economic range and control of each State both for freedom of transit and trade-outlets and for the more solid development of its commercial structure. But this need was countered by the passionate desire for city-autonomy which permeated the North Italians and by their inability to create a lasting *modus vivendi* or federation based on mutual concessions, which was shown, too, in the inner life of each commune. Thus the effort to form larger States meant the subjection of the weaker to the stronger by war, and war was the opportunity of the would-be tyrant, already created by the internecine factions and class-warfare in the several cities

Armed forces were imperatively necessary, and to be efficient they must mainly be either fighting nobles or professional mercenaries. Such would follow the leader who would give them victory in war and secure employment in peace. Even the amateurish citizen levies, who were more and more out-classed in the field, needed, unless the bourgeois were exceptionally numerous and well organized, a leader to enable them to be victorious and enforce the internal peace they desired in the street conflicts where their effectiveness lay. The bourgeois struggle to tame and rule the riotous, faction-ridden nobles, and the virulence of faction and class hatred which banished the defeated side in a civil conflict placed each city in a permanent state of war. The exiles held out in their fortresses in the countryside (*contado*) and leagued with their city's rivals, waiting for an opportunity for forcible re-entry and the infliction of reprisals on their opponents. Thus confusion was endemic, and tended steadily to produce the tyrant who would keep order, quell or utterly ruin the factions, satisfy the traders, and subjugate or at least hold at bay rival cities.

A feature of central Lombardy was the numbers and landed wealth of the noble class which rendered it excep-tionally strong in spite of the rival prosperity of manufacture and commerce. With the growth of industry, too, the solidarity of rich and poor plebeians, of employers and employed, had become weaker. None the less, while the Empire was still dangerous, the Guelf plebeians of Milan had remained tolerably united against the Ghibelline majority of the nobles. Yet the conflict within and without gave rise to tyranny under the noble Guelf house of Della Torre. Then the tendency for the formation of larger States in the open Lombard plain became manifest. The Della Torre obtained the rule of neighbour cities : Vercelli, Novara, Lodi, Bergamo. But they were beginners at tyranny : their rule was oppressive to the bourgeois and the nobles were irreconcilably hostile ; as Gregory X's pressure on Alfonso of Castile dissociated the Ghibellines from foreign interference, it was the Della Torre with their German guard sent by Rudolf of Habsburg who incurred odium. Soon the nobles rose under the Archbishop of Milan, Ottone Visconti, and Napoleon della Torre was defeated and captured at

The Della Torre of Milan

The Visconti of Milan Desio in January 1278. The archbishop now founded a Ghibelline tyranny. Insecure at first when he had to share power with Marquess William of Montferrat, his reconciling policy won over the Milanese. He, too, ruled a group of towns, and left his State to his colleague and great-nephew Matteo in 1295.

Other Tyrants Ezzelin da Romano had left Verona incapable of self-government and its nobles on the way to extermination. Here the Ghibelline tyranny of the Della Scala rested on the merchants and plebeians only; otherwise they were Visconti on a smaller scale. But the State of William of Montferrat was of another type. In West Lombardy the ancient feudal dynasties were still strong. It was as a useful armed princeling that William acquired an uncertain dominion over many cities. He was, however, always an alien, and easily expelled by the citizens, finally dying a captive in an iron cage at Alessandria. His neighbours of the House of Savoy were more securely based in their feudal principality beyond the Alps in Burgundy; their reacquisition of Turin in 1280 proved permanent, the true beginning of their progress in Italy.

Surviving Communes Yet tyranny, however inevitable and efficient, and however much endowed with its powers by legal forms, was repellent to Italians, and where circumstances were less unfavourable republicanism made a prolonged fight for its life. The two great university towns, where the lawyer class was strong, Padua and Bologna, both retained it into the fourteenth century. Padua succumbed at last when her power **Bologna** was broken by the Della Scala; Bologna, less exposed to attack and guided by the wealthy gilds of lawyers and merchants, was formidable to her neighbours in spite of the furious factions of her nobles and the class-war which was involved with them. In 1274 the Ghibellines, locally called Lambertazzi, went into exile, whence they did not really return till 1299. But the *popolo* kept a tight hand over the victorious Guelfs, or Geremei, with whom they sided. Political power was restricted to the Societies of Gilds and Arms in which only Guelfs who practised their profession or trade could vote, and these plebeian bodies were reinforced by the Company of Justice to maintain order. Under the influence of a famous jurist, Rolandino Passeggeri, by the ordinances called *sacrati et sacratissimi*, the nobles were placed under laws of exception and made subject to especially harsh punishment for any delinquency against a *popolano*. Yet by crushing the nobles Bologna broke her own military power, while war raged with the exiles and rival cities in Romagna. Nor was internal peace secured. The fact was that thirteenth-century civilization was too immature, too much the prey of violent passions, the inheritance of slowly yielding barbarism, to practise the necessary concessions, the give-and-take, of free government. Absolute victory, satiety of revenge were dominant desires, and the sober and moderate wreaked on the lawless a hatred like their own.

The new dominion of the Papacy in Romagna, won by Gregory X and Nicholas III, had proved rather a fresh disturbing element than an effective check on city autonomy. The reconciliation of Bolognese factions in 1299, which was due to Boniface VIII, led to a brief interlude of moderate government, but this was overthrown by the extreme Guelfs in 1306 in alliance with Florence, and exile and proscription became once more the order of the day. In Tuscany, however, papal influence had a more lasting effect. The constitution of Nicholas III's nephew Cardinal Latino Malabranca was indeed singularly transitory in Florence, but it Florence revived the power of the gilds as opposed to that of the Parte Guelfa. The more substantial *popolani*, members of the seven greater gilds, soon took advantage of the situation, and from 1282 the true government of Florence resided in the two-monthly board of Priors of the Gilds, to whom the *Podestà* and the revived Captain of the People were in fact subordinate. A social conflict rapidly appeared : the nobles, whether of ancient standing or risen more recently to knighthood by banking and merchandise, were odious to their inferiors through their feuds and riotous insolence and their engrossing of authority in the State. As at Bologna, but with more consistency and success, the *popolani* took legislative action against them, culminating in the Ordinances The of Justice carried through in 1293 under the influence of the Ordinances democrat, Giano della Bella, who almost immediately was of Justice forced into exile by the jealousies of the gildsmen and their natural fear of tyranny. As a result a list of magnate houses, the Grandi, was made, whose members were excluded from office and placed under severe laws of exception to secure their good behaviour. Punishments for offences against *popolani* were made heavier for them and they were obliged to give security for their good conduct. This still left them their social influence in the government, for they were closely connected with the leading *popolani* and often themselves pillars of Florentine commerce. Florence paid a price for bourgeois supremacy in the continued class and faction feuds which worked within the formal constitution and distorted it. But at the cost of much injustice the city escaped tyranny ; and this was due not only to the shrewdness and political sense of the *popolani* but also to their exceptional prosperity and numbers. They were able to control the nobles above and the workmen below them. Florence was industrial as well as commercial : the greater gilds, who dealt in banking and manufactured on a large scale for export, themselves a numerous body, were backed by the fourteen lesser gilds of " small masters " and provisioners whose wares were sold in the city. With a skilful if complicated organization, guided by ruthless men of business and capitalists, they weathered storm after storm by a policy in which finance and politics were inseparable. They could even exploit the greatest diplomatic force of the day, their ally and debtor, the Papacy.

Florentine Plutocracy

The Tuscan League

One of the most advantageous of the achievements of the Florentines was the reformation of the Tuscan Guelf League, to which almost all Tuscan towns were forced to belong. Toll-freedom for the goods of each member was peculiarly favourable to manufacturing Florence, and the 500 mercenary troopers maintained by the League were a safeguard against the nobles' predominance, if they also outclassed and hastened the decadence of the citizen militia. The battle of Campaldino in 1289 against Arezzo and the Ghibellines, in which Dante fought, was the last in which the Florentine nobles were the deciding factor.

The Seapowers

Republicanism retained its vitality also in the three great sea-powers of Italy : Pisa, Genoa, and Venice. The carrying trade furnished a broader basis, all classes of the population were linked together in a single interest, not separated in discordant gilds, and the comparative unity of effort

necessary in the joint voyages over the pirate-ridden sea
produced in varying degrees a habit of joint action at home.
Pisa indeed was near her fall.   Overstrained by her Tuscan Pisa
enmities with Florence and Lucca, made the more exhaust-
ing by her open *contado*, she was engaged in deadly rivalry
with Genoa over the sea-trade of the Mediterranean and the
profitable control of Sardinia.   In 1284 she underwent a
crushing defeat in the sea-battle of Meloria at the hands of Her Fall
the Genoese.   Though she maintained a heroic resistance
against her banded foes, she was compelled in 1293 to enter
the Tuscan League, and henceforth as the Arno slowly silted
up her port she declined steadily to the rank of a third-rate
power.

Genoa was more fortunate than Pisa in her geographical Genoa
situation, for the Apennines protected her narrow coastland
from the Lombard communes to the north, but her nobles,
who, like the Pisan, were all sea-captains as well as feudal
landowners, were as torn by faction as those of any city.
The joint dictatorship of Doria and Spinola avoided the
tyrannis, but implied the suppression or exile of the Guelf
Fieschi and Grimaldi.   There was always the tendency, too,
towards further division in the dominant families.   The Doria
and the Spinola fell out after the victory over Pisa, and
while their Guelf rivals were active in attempts to overthrow them, the claims of the trading *popolani*, who were
taking a greater share in the government, were increasing
still.   There ceased to be stability in Genoa after 1290.
Externally, the commune was involved in war with Venice Rivalry with
in the fierce competition for the Levantine commerce.   The Venice
Genoese had the worse in a long war from 1257 to 1271, in
which they were temporarily driven from the Christian
Syrian ports, but by the treaty of Nymphæum in 1261 with
Michael Palaeologus they obtained a privileged position in
the revived Byzantine Empire, which included a settlement
at Galata by Constantinople, and the bulk of the Black Sea
trade.   The fall of Acre and the Latin kingdom of Jerusalem
in 1291 renewed the war between the two republics.   Genoa,
under her great admiral, Lamba Doria, won a complete victory in the battle of Curzola (1298) off the Dalmatian coast, Battle of
and the peace which followed in 1299 left her almost a Curzola
monopoly of the Black Sea, while Venice concentrated more

on the Alexandrine commerce with Egypt. There was in
fact more than enough for both in the Levant had they
been contented to live and let live, a course which ran
contrary to their instincts rather than their interests.

Venice   It was Venice which successfully solved the problem of
developing republican institutions which would work with a
minimum of friction and deal out a reasonable satisfaction
to the interests of the various classes of her inhabitants.
She had had the immense advantage of security from land-
ward attack on her islands amid the lagoons and the consequent freedom from conquest by the Lombards and the
introduction of feudal habits and the pernicious blood-feud.
The shipping trade was supreme, and all classes—the ship-
owners and merchants, in Venice a single class, who formed
the nobility, the handicraft gilds, and the sailors and workmen of the arsenal—were dependent on it and united in it.
Thus faction of the fierce mainland type had little room for
growth, and the ship-owners, who naturally took and jealously
kept the lead, dared not, if they wished, disregard the welfare of the seamen on whose valour and skill they counted.

Aristocratic   None the less, the thirteenth century saw the exclusion of
Government the plebeians from all share in the government and finally
the closing of the aristocracy against fresh recruits. Jealousy
of new men was doubtless one reason, but the fear of their
individual ambition and the desire to prevent the excessive
power of popular and land-owning families played an important part. First, the popular assembly, the *arengo*, went out
of use, and was succeeded by a Great Council of notables.
Then, the monarchic power of the elected life-Doge, inherited

The *Serrata* from Byzantine times, was severely limited. Lastly, by a
del Gran   series of laws, among which the " *Serrata* (closing) of the
Consiglio   Great Council " in 1297 was conspicuous, the right to sit in
the Great Council was restricted to those families who already
had seats in it, and was extended by further enactments to
all legitimate adult males of those families. The *Serrata* was
not a violently restrictive measure, for the number of newly-
risen families included was considerable, but it stereotyped
and organized the nobility who ruled the State and prevented
fresh accessions. The Great Council became a large, electoral,
sovran body. Councils and boards of officials, so elected as
to ban individual or family predominance, governed the State

under the Doge's presidency.   Those citizen-families who had
not secured seats in the Great Council were compensated by
a monopoly of the " Civil Service " ; the gilds and the seamen were carefully fostered ; and the Venetians excelled all
contemporaries in their devotion to the State and in the
general content with its government.   Had there been more
grievances, no sufficient armed force was at the call of the
ambitious and disaffected in the horseless island city.

By the year 1300 the evolution of Italy had turned away Italy in 1300
from national unity.   The particularistic instinct was too
strong, and the utmost that geographical and material influences could enforce was regionalism.   The city-states of
the north were tending to form larger, regional units, and
this was accompanied by the failure of republican institutions.
In favourable circumstances the communes maintained themselves, but almost always with a maimed life.   The single
true exception was Venice, which had, we might perhaps say,
survived from the Ancient World.

SUGGESTIONS FOR READING ON CHAPTER IV

A. SOURCES
(i) Documents

Böhmer, Potthast, as for Chapter III.
Constitutiones (see Chapter III), Vols. ii, iii.
Acta Aragonensia. Ed. Finke. Berlin, 1908 ff. [Selection in *Aus den
Tagen Bonifaz VIII*, see below B.]

(ii) Chronicles, etc.

Annales Ianuenses (see Chapter III), Vols. iii–v.
Annales Placentini Gibellini, Carbio, *Chron. Marchiae Tarvisinae*, Dan-
dolo, Jamsilla, Malaspina, Matthew Paris, Rolandinus, Salimbene, Villani,
as for Chapter III.
Dino Compagni : *Cronica.* Eng. trans. 1906.
Martin da Canal : *La cronique des Veniciens.* Ed. Polidori. Archivio
Storico Italiano. Vol. viii. 1845.
Muntaner, R. : *Cronica catalana.* Trans. Goodenough. London, 1920–1.
Neocastro, B. de : *Historia Sicula.* Ed. Paladino. Muratori (new edn.),
Rer. Ital. Script. XIII.
Tholomeus Lucensis : *Annales.* Ed. Schmeidler. *Mon. Germ. Hist*
Script. Rer. Germ. Hanover, 1930.

B. MODERN WORKS

Amari, M. : *La guerra del Vespro Siciliano.* 9th edn. Milan, 1886.
Boase, T. S. R. : *Boniface VIII.* 1933.
Caggese, R. : *Firenze.* Florence, 1912 ff.

Cambridge Medieval History. Vols. vi, vii (relevant chapters). 1929, 1932.

Caro, G. : *Genua und die Mächte am Mittelmeer.* Halle-a.-S., 1899.

Finke, H. : *Aus den Tagen Bonifaz VIII.* Münster-i.-W., 1902.

Foligno, C. : *The Story of Padua.* 1910.

Gardner, E. : *The Story of Florence.* 4th edn. London, 1903.

Gregorovius, vol. v ; Hauck, vol. iv ; Jordan, Davidsohn, Butler, Sedgwick, Brown, as for Chapter III.

Luchaire, J. : *Les démocraties italiennes.* Paris, 1915.

Salzer, E. : *Ueber die Anfänge der Signorie in Oberitalien.* Berlin, 1900.

Schevill, A. : *History of Florence.* London, 1937.

Schevill, F. : *Siena.* 1909.

Villari, P. : *Mediaeval Italy from Charlemagne to Henry VII.* Trans. Hulton. 1910.

Villari, P. : *The First Two Centuries of Florentine History.* Eng. trans. 1901.

CHAPTER V

FRANCE, 1198–1270

THE thirteenth century is the period during which Character the kingdom of France ceased to be a geographical and Achieve- expression and became the greatest and most solid ment of Philip State of Europe. This remarkable change was in part the Augustus consequence of a long evolution, the product of the institutions and events of preceding centuries ; it was also due to the personal qualities and long reign of Philip II, surnamed Augustus " *quia augebat regnum*," [1] who reigned at Paris from 1180 to 1223. His character had not the stamp of genius which would have gained for him the title of " the Great," but he was richly endowed with just those gifts which were most aptly fitted to exploit to the full the situation he inherited, to respond to the currents of the time, and to use every turn of events to accomplish his persistent aims. Passionate and impulsive as he might seem on occasion, he was guided in his policy by a frosty light of reason, remote from enthusiasm or ideals. Clear-sighted and matter-of-fact to a degree, he had no temptation to depart from the conventional ideas of his age, but was marvellously equipped for dealing with men and the practical problems before him. He could with genial adroitness win friendship when and while he wished. He could calculate forces and motives, and make brisk, shrewd decisions. Cautious, aggressive, and persevering, a warrior at need, a diplomat and statesman always, he transmuted the French monarchy from something like a theory into a fact.

In the second place Philip's inheritance was better than Assets of the it perhaps appeared. If he did not rule the largest terri- Monarchy tory in France, it was, as we have seen, the best situated and probably the wealthiest for its extent. Further, he had the immense advantage of being king without a suzerain. To the moral prestige and appeal of the kingship,[2] which

[1] " Because he increased the realm." [2] See above, Chap. I, p. 23.

105

had grown steadily during the twelfth century, he added the moral authority of the feudal superior of all France, and the recognized feudal powers which feudal law inculcated. All the advances which the great vassals of the Crown had made in controlling their vassals and enforcing peace and feudal law redounded in opinion to the king's profit, for he was the undoubted source of his vassals' powers, and they could not disregard his rights without encouraging contempt of their own. They were always, by their own theory of government, which they were unable to replace, at a legal and moral disadvantage in their relations with him. Their strength against him lay in the strong instinct of particularism, and this very particularism made it impossible for them to combine heartily to oppose him : they were unsympathetic rivals to one another as well as recalcitrant to him. Whatever instinct of State-unity or embryo national cohesion existed in the true France of the north worked in favour of the king, with his traditional leadership and his unquestioned rights as the supreme feudal suzerain.

Aims of Philip Augustus

Three main objects governed the policy of Philip Augustus : the enlargement of the royal domain, more feasible in France than in Germany, for there was no custom established in France that escheated fiefs should be granted to new holders ; the abasement and, if possible, the ruin of the great vassal house of Anjou, whose vast collection of fiefs overshadowed the Capetian domain ; and the assertion of the royal rights over vassals great and small. It is obvious that these aims were complementary to one another and could hardly be pursued apart.

Acquisition of the Somme Valley

The first enlargement of the domain was made in the north and was the result of a complicated feud in which the disunion of the great vassals and the skilful manœuvring of the king were made evident. Philip married first Isabella, daughter of Baldwin V, Count of Hainault, and niece of Philip, Count of Flanders. He fell out with both counts, and Philip of Flanders formed a league with the Counts of Champagne and Blois, the king's maternal uncles. This was an unstable coalition, incapable of concerted action. The king countered by winning the support of Henry II, the Angevin King of England, and when his uncles were reconciled to him, he gained over Baldwin V and in 1185 forced

the Count of Flanders to buy peace by cessions. Amiens and
its neighbourhood were ceded to the king with the expecta-
tion of Vermandois, which fell in to the Crown in 1192.
By this acquisition the royal domain was enlarged over the
valley of the Somme to the Channel, and the great vassals
of the north were taught a lesson. Philip could now turn
to the more formidable house of Anjou. He had two advan- Attack on
tages, each invaluable to him and used without scruple. the Angevins
One was that the French dominions of Henry II were composed of at least three discordant portions, Normandy,
Anjou-Touraine, and Aquitaine, of which Aquitaine was in
perpetual feudal anarchy of the ancient sort. The other
was the insensate rivalries and disloyalty of Henry II's sons
which tore to pieces their inharmonious lands, and played
into the hands of the astute suzerain. Greed, disunion, and
blind impulse were unequally matched against foresight and
a steady purpose.

It was by utilizing the desire for the whole Angevin
inheritance of Richard Cœur-de-lion, Henry's eldest surviving son, in a fever of suspicion at Henry's schemes to provide
for his youngest and favourite son, John Lackland, that
Philip was able at last to bring Henry to his knees at the
treaty of Colombières in 1189. Philip's chief gain was the
immediate suzerainty of the county of Auvergne, thus de-
tached from Aquitaine. Against Richard, once his fervent
friend, now his hereditary enemy, Philip still had John to
use, and did so remorselessly. But Richard, if no statesman,
was the best soldier of the day. In spite of Philip's intrigues
and his own misfortunes, he routed Philip in the field, maintained alliances with Flanders and Toulouse and his nephew,
Otto of Brunswick, and fortified the Norman frontier with
Château Gaillard, his new fortress, as the key of the defences.
Yet it is noticeable that Richard was waging a defensive
war against his suzerain—the Île de France was practically
untouched—and the growing authority of Philip was shown
by the " protections " which Norman monasteries found it
in their interest to obtain from him.

It was the death of Richard Cœur-de-lion on April 6, Accession of
1199, which gave Philip his opportunity. To begin with, John of
there was a disputed succession. Aquitaine and Normandy, England
like England, partly under the influence of Henry II's widow,

Eleanor of Aquitaine, accepted John, her youngest son;
Anjou, Touraine, and Maine preferred Arthur, Duke of Brittany, the son of John's dead elder brother Geoffrey.   There
was as yet no fixed rule of the representation of a deceased
elder brother by his children, and provincial preferences and
personal antipathies could have free course.   Philip, as
suzerain, declared for John, and was paid for his adhesion
by the treaty of Le Goulet in May 1200, which pushed his
frontier northwards by the acquisition of the Norman Vexin
and Évreux.   But his greatest gain was the character of
the candidate he favoured.   John had the temperament of
an able criminal.   A prey to his passions, of greed, revenge,
or voluptuousness, without faith or gratitude, he could never
be counted on, either in his fits of energy or in those of lassi-
tude, and the personal aversion he inspired lamed the execution of his best-considered schemes.   He almost immediately
gave Philip a legal excuse and alienated feudal opinion by
marrying Isabelle, the heiress of his vassal the Count of
Angoulême.   She was the betrothed of another vassal of
John, the Poitevin Hugh IX of Lusignan, Count of La
Marche.   The marriage was thus a breach of the feudal
contract, fighting followed with the Lusignans, and Hugh
eventually appealed to the supreme suzerain, King Philip.
John refused to appear in Philip's court to answer the charge,

**Philip's
Annexation
of Nor-
mandy and
Anjou**

and was condemned to forfeiture of all his fiefs for con-
tumacy.   The war began in May 1202.   Philip made immediate use of the rival in John's own house.   He invaded
Normandy himself, but invested Arthur with the rest of the
Angevin fiefs.   Arthur, however, was defeated, and disappeared next year, indubitably by murder, in his uncle's
dungeons.   This atrocity aroused universal odium, and Philip
in 1203 was able to annex Anjou, Maine, and Touraine to the
Crown by consent, while the Bretons accepted Arthur's stepfather Guy of Thouars as their rightful ruler.   Meanwhile,
the Norman barons were deserting to Philip, as the ducal
castles fell one after another.   John seemed paralysed and
retreated to England.   With the surrender of Rouen, the
capital, and Château Gaillard, the strongest fortress, the
conquest was completed in 1204.   The war continued in
Aquitaine with less success for Philip, for the barons of that
duchy still revelled in their shifting anarchy.   But none the

less, the King of France secured the direct suzerainty of La Marche and the Limousin. Thus the great achievement of Philip's reign was really consummated. The royal domain, governed by the king and not by great vassals, was more than trebled; the estates of the Crown (in English terminology, the " royal demesne ") were enormously increased both by the Angevin estates and the confiscated lands of Norman barons who held by John and their English possessions. Henceforward, no great vassal in France could at all vie with the Crown in wealth and territory. The swift submission and continuous loyalty of the Normans to their new ruler seem strange enough after their centuries of autonomy, but on the one hand Philip maintained their law and administration with the minimum of change, and on the other John was in fact more alien to the duchy than the king, and the material advantages of the change could be seen at once—there ceased to be an uneasy frontier between Rouen and Paris, and Normandy was no longer sucked dry by the defensive exactions of her imperilled dukes. The same considerations apply equally to Anjou and the lands north of the Loire.

John, however, was by no means at the end of his John's resources or inclined to surrender his inheritance. In spite League of his excommunication by the Pope over the Canterbury election,[1] he had for the time a firm hold over England, and he used his English resources to weave alliances on Philip's eastern frontier. A collection of Low German princes headed by his nephew, Otto of Brunswick, one of the rival Kings of the Romans, were in his pay; so were some of Philip's discontented vassals, including the new Count of Flanders, Ferrand of Portugal, who had been cheated by Philip over towns in Artois, and the changeable Renaud of Dammartin, Count of Boulogne. Philip, in alarm, prepared to strike at England. In 1213 he was ready, in the Pope's name, to lead the crusade from Gravelines, when John suddenly surrendered and became the Pope's vassal. The crusade was over before it was begun, and Philip turned his preparations against Flanders. A defeat of his fleet on the Zwin, the little river that led to Bruges, prevented indeed a conquest, but the war went on. Meanwhile, John was planning his

[1] See above, Chap. II, p. 49.

critical campaign. The Emperor Otto IV was now at grips
with the Pope and Frederick II of Hohenstaufen, and Philip,
like John, was busily subsidizing these allies of his. The
key to the German war lay in France. Otto, at the head
of a great confederacy, should invade north-eastern France ;
John from Aquitaine should reconquer Anjou. The campaign of 1214 was decisive. John, partly from his personal
unpopularity, partly from the strength of his rival's defence,
failed hopelessly in his attack on the Loire before Louis,
the heir to France ; Otto IV and his host were utterly over-

**Battle of
Bouvines
1214**

thrown by Philip in person in the battle of Bouvines (July
27), Ferrand and Renaud being captured. John had no
choice but to make the truce of Chinon which preserved the
status quo ante, and Philip returned to Paris to enjoy a
national triumph. New as well as old subjects rejoiced at
the victory of the King of France.

**Philip and
Languedoc**

Philip's attitude to the Albigensian Crusade showed both
his astuteness and his prudence. He consistently maintained
his rights as suzerain, but refused to be diverted by the
Pope's appeals from the struggle with the Angevins. The
Crusade might be recruited from his lands ; that was an
advantage. He was well aware of the profit the Crown was
likely to gain from the crushing of Languedoc, and watched
the process with wary patience.[1] Not unlike was his action
or inaction over his son's invasion of England in 1216 at
the invitation of the English barons. He allowed it, he
refused to admit the Pope's claim to forbid it, but he saw
it fail with philosophy. His own task had been performed.

**Adminis-
tration :
Institution
of *baillis***

Philip Augustus not only insisted on and increased by
definition his legal rights over his vassals, even the once-
unfettered great vassals, like the Count of Champagne, but
he also gave the administration of the royal domain a new
bureaucratic consistency. He followed in fact the example
long set in Normandy and England. Hitherto, petty pro-
vosts had administered the Capetian estates ; Philip divided
the whole domain into districts under nominated *baillis*,[2] who
corresponded to the English sheriffs and controlled both the
royal estates and the vassals of their bailiwicks. These *baillis*
were strictly subordinated to the royal Curia, that varying

---

[1] Cf. above, Chap. II, p. 54.
[2] *Baillis* are, however, found occasionally earlier.

assemblage of vassals and household officials, which assisted
the king in all his functions. A system of records, intro- Records
duced by Philip, made this central control continuous and
effective, and promoted the growing specialization which
was to issue in departments of state. The lawyers and
clerks of the royal household formed a new bureaucratic
class imbued with Roman ideas of the royal supremacy, of
which they were the most active propagandists.

The process was aided by the changes which were taking Impoverish-
place in the population. Round about the year 1200 the ment of the
nobles of France were as a class poorer than formerly. Their Nobles
extravagant mode of life—crusade, tournament, war, and
display—exhausted their resources. While they retained
and abused their feudal jurisdiction and control of their
serfs, the system of *corvées*—labour-dues by the latter—had
grown unremunerative and was falling into disuse, being
replaced by fixed rents. Thus the nobles themselves became
more eager to serve the king for a livelihood, and their
extortions and brigand-like endeavours to increase their
receipts impelled the peaceable classes to ardent support of
the king who could protect them. Clergy and monks were Clergy and
on the king's side and submitted grumbling to his orderly *pariage*
exactions ; they admitted him as co-*seigneur* of their lands
by agreements of *pariage* which gave him in practice the
direct control of their local government. The peasants looked
to the king for peace and justice. In like manner the bourgeois of the towns looked to the king as their patron. If The Towns
the autonomous commune was only favoured by him outside the royal domain, the self-administering town was
encouraged and multiplied by him. He was a large granter
of charters, sometimes even to mere villages. He maintained his authority even over Paris, but the merchant in
fair and town had no better friend than the king throughout
France.

The reign of the capable and colourless Louis VIII is a Louis VIII
mere epilogue to his father's, yet it was marked by two
achievements and an important innovation. The conquest
of Languedoc for the Crown, in which he played a decisive
part, brought the royal domain to the Rhone and the Mediterranean.[1] In his father's lifetime he had made two incon-

[1] See above, Chap. II, pp. 54–55.

clusive crusades against the Albigenses in 1215 and 1219, which at least served to give the monarchy the lead in the movement. In 1226, when Amaury de Montfort had definitely withdrawn from Simon's conquest and Raymond VII was banned and deposed in the Council of Bourges, Louis VIII led his full force to the South determined on annexation.

Royal Domain in Languedoc

The city of Avignon in the imperial kingdom of Burgundy was stormed. If Raymond still held out in Toulouse, there was general submission, and a royal domain could be constituted round Beaucaire and Carcassonne. The *seneschal* here was the counterpart of the northern *bailli*. This conquest not only meant the acquisition of rich domains for the monarchy. It was of first importance for the welding together of North and South France in a single national monarchy, and it gave that monarchy a share in the shores and the trade of the Mediterranean. Henceforward France had a coast on two seas.

Conquest of Poitou

The second achievement of Louis VIII's reign, the conquest of Poitou in 1224 during the minority of Henry III of England, in like manner brought the royal domain to the Atlantic, and reduced the Angevin lands still further. The innovation which Louis introduced lay in the provisions of his will when he died in 1226. Instead of the small endowments of earlier times, he erected new great fiefs as appanages for his

The Appanages

younger sons—Robert was made Count of Artois, Alphonse Count of Poitou and Auvergne, and Charles Count of Anjou and Maine. The policy had much to recommend it. The new counts were kept in far greater subjection than the older great vassals ; their fiefs were to return to the Crown on the extinction of heirs male ; and their supervised rule made a convenient concession to particularism on the way to direct royal government. But the princes of the *fleurs-de-lys* were given a dangerous power by these rich local endowments, and their ambitions were naturally shown in rivalries for influence with their royal kinsman which later brought feudal irresponsibility back to the court and administration.

Regency of Queen Blanche

The death of Louis VIII in 1226 and the succession of his twelve-years-old son Louis IX was the signal of an attempt of the great vassals to restore the old state of affairs by resisting the regency of the Queen-mother Blanche

of Castille. But Blanche was a stern, resolute character,
and more than a match for her opponents in statecraft.
The discontented barons, Philip Hurepel, a son of Philip Revolts of
Augustus and Count of Boulogne, Peter Mauclerc Duke of the Great
Brittany, the poet Theobald IV Count of Champagne, Hugh Vassals
Count of La Marche, none of them men of much note, showed
the old incapacity for concerted action and more than the
old reluctance to defy the king completely. Their more
stubborn allies, Raymond VII of Toulouse and Henry III
of England, lacked the one resources, the other any military
ability, while Theobald of Champagne soon changed sides.
In 1227 the barons failed to capture the king and his mother
at Montlhéry, where, a significant fact, they were saved by
the people of Paris in arms. Toulouse was ravaged by a
crusading army, and in 1229 Raymond made submission in
the treaty of Paris and was allowed to keep for his life his
diminished fief. Peter Mauclerc lost his castle of Bellême.
In 1230 Henry III made a fiasco of his expedition from Brittany to Bordeaux ; Theobald, the chief victim of his allies,
who did not dread turning their arms against a fellow
vassal, surrendered his suzerainty of Blois to the Crown.
Peter Mauclerc, the only resolute rebel, was subdued in 1234,
and not long after surrendered Brittany to his son and ward
Duke John. Meantime, Louis IX attained his majority in
1234, and met the last feudal outbreak in person. In 1242
Henry III came to the aid of his stepfather, the once more
rebelling Count of La Marche, and for the reconquest of
Poitou. It was a war of the South against the North, for the
Count of Toulouse joined in the coalition, helped by the
hatred of the Inquisition and the tyrannous royal *seneschals* in
Languedoc. But Henry III was easily routed by Louis at
Taillebourg in Saintonge, Hugh of La Marche submitted Battle of
humbly, and the treaty of Lorris in 1243 sealed the conquest Taillebourg
of Languedoc and the final subjection of Raymond, who
was gently treated on his promise to be a persecutor. On
Raymond VII's death in 1249 his son-in-law Alphonse of
Poitou succeeded to Toulouse, and gave its government a
North French complexion. For the rest of the reign feudal
resistance to the king vanished, and obedience to the
monarchy became a habit of France.

That devotion to the Crown was largely due to Louis IX.

St. Louis IX, In his own person he was the ideal of the medieval knight
Character   and king. For the first time in the Middle Ages a king in
active secular life was an indubitable saint. St. Louis was
neither weak nor a recluse, but he ruled his kingdom as a
religious duty. His justice, his love of peace, and his goodness
made him enforce equally the rights of the vassals and the
Crown, so that opposition to him seemed mere selfishness
Increase of and unrighteousness. All the more effective, then, were the
the Royal   insistence on and the increase of the royal prerogative in
Power   his reign. He forbade the barbaric ordeal by battle in the
royal courts ; in 1258 he prohibited the ancient custom of
private war. But he respected the feudal courts of his
barons, while maintaining his own. Appeals to the Curia
Regis from the barons' courts multiplied even from the
greatest fiefs, but under feudal rules. So did the cases of
" prevention " in which the royal justice was invoked in the
first instance, and the *cas royaux* in which the " majesty "
of the state was involved, and which consequently were dealt
with by the Curia. It was obviously just that the royal
coinage should be current over all France, the baronial
money used only in certain districts ; but this meant that
the one triumphed over the other. The surveillance of the
fiefs by the neighbouring *bailli* was natural, but it ended in
subjection.

The *Curia*   It was under St. Louis that the specialization of the work
Regis   of the Curia Regis began to take clearer shape. The Curia
was manned by the " chevaliers " and " clercs du roi." The
judicial sessions were entrusted in the main to a body of
trained lawyers, who became the high court of the realm,
soon to be known as the Parlement de Paris. The financial
officials similarly gathered, with routine and record, in what
was later known as the Chambre des Comptes. The hardest
matter, however, was to correct the manifold oppressions
and abuses of the local agents of the Crown. For this, in
January 1247, before he started on his first crusade, St.
The   Louis devised a new remedy. He sent out Franciscan Friars
Enquêteurs as *enquêteurs* to receive and redress complaints against the
baillis and their subordinates. The system became permanent, and a secular element was introduced among the
enquêteurs. While St. Louis lived, a genuine check was
exercised on official tyranny, and the popularity of the

monarchy enhanced in the same degree as its effectiveness.

St. Louis favoured the towns of set purpose, for he saw The Towns
in them one of the strongest supports of the monarchy.
But he had no intention of relaxing his authority over them,
and their state invited interference in their government.
There was a steady trend towards oligarchy among them,
as the general increase of trade magnified the differences of
wealth within them. The oligarchs misused their power in
unfairly burdening the lesser folk, who were dependent on
them, and the royal taxes were in any case heavy. The
financial administration of the towns was inefficient and
corrupt. In 1268 the king intervened by ordering the town
accounts to be inspected annually at Paris. Supervision
thus began and was never abated. The decline of town self-
administration had set in.

Nor with all his piety and veneration for the Church was The Clergy
the king inclined to yield the rights of the kingship over
the clergy. He maintained firmly his rights of jurisdiction ;
he refused to confiscate for them the goods of the excommunicated ; and on occasion he was ready to rebuke his
prelates for their un-Christian behaviour. He protested
solemnly against the Pope's taxation of the French clergy
in his war with Frederick II. A strong king who surrendered
the tithes acquired by his ancestors, whose Church appointments were impeccable, whose respect for the Canon Law
was unalterable, and whose chief interest was in religion,
was easily master of his clergy.

The same firm good sense, coupled with conscientious Treaty of
uprightness, was shown by St. Louis in the most difficult Corbeil, 1258
questions of foreign policy. There was a delicate situation
in Languedoc. The King of Aragon, James I, was vassal
of the French Crown for the County of Barcelona beyond
the Pyrenees [1] ; he also had claims as intermediate suzerain
of Languedoc, claims which had been defeated at Muret in
1213, but never abandoned, and which had made Catalonia
the haunt of Languedoc refugees and a sally-port for rebellion. St. Louis ended the tension by the Treaty of Corbeil
(May 11, 1258). He renounced his suzerainty of Barcelona,
while James I abandoned his claims in Languedoc, retaining

[1] Cf. above, Chap. I, p. 6, n. 1 and below, Chap. VIII, p. 158.

only the direct fief of Montpellier which he had always possessed.   Thus the southern boundary of France was fixed at the natural frontier of the Pyrenees, and a dangerous source of friction and entanglements was done away.

A similar course, but over an incurable conflict of interests, was followed by St. Louis with regard to the English possessions in Aquitaine or Guienne.   In spite of truces the situation created by the forfeiture of John's lands had never found a solution.   Henry III still ruled as Duke of Guienne ; he had never done homage to the King of France, and he claimed all his hereditary fiefs.   St. Louis took advantage of his cousin's embroilments with the English barons to

Treaty of Paris, 1258-9
force on him a generous settlement.   By the treaty of Paris of May 1258 and December 1259, Henry surrendered his claims to Normandy, Anjou and its appendages, and Poitou ; he acknowledged his vassalage for Guienne.   In return, Louis retroceded to him the demesne and the intermediate suzerainty of fiefs in Limousin, Quercy, and Périgueux, with an undertaking to do the same in Agenais and south Saintonge when Alphonse of Poitou, who held them, should die.   The

Its Results
war was thus ended with large prospective gains to Henry, but Guienne was recovered for French suzerainty with all that it implied.   Henceforward the duchy was open to appeals to the Parlement of Paris and to royal intervention of the now normal kind.   It was as good an arrangement as could justly be made, but the situation—a great fief held by a powerful foreign monarch—was exactly what Louis had abolished in his treaty with the King of Aragon.   The friction and divergent aims which were inevitable when St. Louis was dead were the main cause of the Hundred Years' War.

Attitude to Frederick II
The same ruling desire for justice and peace and the same political moderation marked Louis' conduct towards the Empire.   His devotion to the Church was combined with a strong belief in the rights of secular rulers, of whom the Emperor was in his eyes the representative.   He declined to take sides with the Popes against the Emperor Frederick ; he would not allow his brother Robert of Artois to be elected anti-Cæsar in Germany, while he secured the release of the French prelates captured in 1241 by Frederick ; when Innocent IV fled from Rome, he refused him a refuge in France,

and only prepared to protect him when Frederick II planned
a direct attack on Lyons. The sentence of deposition on
the Emperor decreed by the Council of Lyons in 1245 was
in his eyes invalid—it had been passed against his wishes—
and he maintained friendly relations with the Emperor to
the last. It was only after Manfred's usurpation of the
crown of Sicily that he began to feel at liberty to change
his attitude, and under the influence of the French Pope,
Urban IV, gave his permission, essential for success, to his
brother Charles of Anjou, who had become by marriage Count
of Provence in the kingdom of Burgundy, to lead a crusade
against the illegitimate King of Sicily.

None the less, the dissolution of the Empire and the con- Greatness of
solidation of France made the Capetian monarchy the chief France
power in Europe, and this position was fortified and extended
by St. Louis' personal virtues. Known to be just, disinterested, and impartial, he was chosen arbiter by other
potentates, whether his vassals or not. In the "Dit à
Péronne" he settled the thorny question of the succession
to Flanders and Hainault.[1] The most remarkable instance
of his prestige was when Henry III and the English barons
appealed to him in 1263 to pronounce on their dispute.
The "Mise of Amiens" published by St. Louis was indeed
a failure, for he could not declare for the diminution of
an anointed king's freedom in choosing his ministers or in
his exercise of his legal authority. Yet it did not decrease
his prestige or the trust men reposed in him.

One reason for his influence and success was the fact that St. Louis
the king was so thoroughly at home in his times. Without and Heresy
a particle of originality, he accepted the current ideas whole-
heartedly and without question. He zealously supported the
Inquisition in its fierce war against heresy, with the result
that it worked with greater freedom and with greater success
in France than elsewhere in Europe. One of the most
frantic of persecutions, curiously paralleled in Germany,
was that carried out in north-west France from 1233 to 1239
by the converted Albigensian, Robert le Bougre (i.e. the
Catharan). He was reckless if the orthodox perished with
the heretic, and at last, after he had burnt 183 accused in
one holocaust in Champagne, he was removed from office,

[1] See below, Chap. VII, pp. 188-89.

and imprisoned. It was in Louis' reign and under his pious
patronage that the native nobility of Languedoc was rooted
out by a persecution at once fanatical and unscrupulous,
which subserved private greed and revenge and inflicted
misery on both Catholic and heretic in the native population.

His Crusades The exception to his love of peace was his ardour for the
Holy War against the Infidel. To that end he directed his
foreign policy and wasted his own best energies and the
resources of his kingdom. His first Crusade (1249–54),
which, as it reached the East, will be told in another chapter,[1]
was a disastrous failure, but he was in no way disillusioned
or discouraged. To lead another was still his chief aim, and
the design was largely responsible for his decision to allow
Charles of Anjou to attack Manfred, who seemed an obstacle
to it. At last in 1270 his preparations were ready ; the
Crusade was to be directed against Egypt which ruled Palestine, but a preliminary objective was introduced at the last
moment. St. Louis in his unconquerable idealism was induced to believe that the Moslem Emir of Tunis was ready
for conversion to Christianity and only needed the argument
of an invasion ; and Tunis would be a fine base of operations
against Egypt. It is evident what his brother Charles, now
King of Sicily, would advise, for Charles was on friendly
terms with Egypt, was an enemy of Tunis, whose tribute he
claimed, and was really desirous of conquering the Greeks
of Constantinople, not the Holy Land. In any case, Louis
sailed from Aigues Mortes, the new seaport he had built on
the Gulf of Lyons, already sick to death. The Crusaders
landed in Tunis to find the Emir prepared to fight and
His Death themselves to fall victims to pestilence. On August 25,
1270, Louis himself died, and the Crusade broke up. Charles
made a good bargain with the Emir and returned to Sicily
for his mundane schemes ; Edward of England proceeded
to the Holy Land ; Philip III of France went home, while
the greater part of the crusading fleet was sunk in a storm
off Trapani. The politics of Europe seemed to descend to
a lower plane with the death of the royal saint, yet the
effect of his reign, however unintended by himself, was to

---

[1] See below, Chap. VI. The news of his captivity, and his long stay in
the East produced in 1251 the strange popular movement of the Pastoureaux,
a curious combination of fanaticism and lawlessness ; cf. below, Chap. XX.

shape the history of France for many generations. Henceforward Frenchmen looked to the king for justice, for reform, and for safety.

SUGGESTIONS FOR READING ON CHAPTER V

A. SOURCES
(i) Documents

Innocent III : *Epistolae* (as for Chapter II).
Delisle, L. : *Catalogue des Actes de Philippe Auguste.* Paris, 1856.

(ii) Chronicles, etc.

Rigord, monk of St. Denis : *Gesta Philippi Augusti.* Ed. Delaborde, H. F. Société de l'histoire de France. Paris, 1882.
William le Breton : (1) *Gesta Philippi regis.* (2) *Philippis.* Ed. Delaborde, H. F. Société de l'histoire de France. 2 vols. Paris, 1882, 1885.
Roger of Wendover : *Flores historiarum.* [Contained with additions in Matthew Paris ; see next entry.]
Matthew Paris : *Chronica Majora.* Ed. Luard, H. R. Rolls Series. 6 vols. London, 1876–80. [Adds to and after 1235 continues Roger of Wendover. Many documents.]
Jehan, Sire de Joinville : *Mémoires.* Ed. Wailly, N. de. Paris, 1874. [On St. Louis. Several English translations.]
William of St. Pathus : *Vie de St. Louis.* Ed. Delaborde, H. F. Collection de textes pour servir à l'étude et à l'enseignement de l'histoire. Paris, 1899.
Guilhem Pelhisso : *Chronicon.* Ed. Douais, C. Paris, 1881. [For the Midi and heresy.]

B. MODERN WORKS

Belperron, J. : *La Croisade contre les Albigeois et l'Union du Languedoc à la France.* Paris, 1945.
Berger, E. : *Blanche de Castille.* Paris, 1895.
Cartellieri, A. : *Philipp II August, König von Frankreich.* 4 vols. Leipzig, 1899–1922.
Cambridge Medieval History, Vol. vi, relevant chapters.
Glotz, ed. : *Histoire Générale, Le Moyen Âge.* Vol. iv, Pt. II. L'Essor des États d'Occident. Paris, 1937.
Lavisse, E. ed. : *Histoire de France.* Vol. iii (by Luchaire, A., and Langlois, C. V.). Paris, 1901.
Luchaire, A. : *Innocent III* (as for Chapter II).
Perry, F. : *St. Louis* (Heroes of the Nations).
Petit-Dutaillis, C. : *Étude sur la vie et le règne de Louis VIII.* Paris, 1894.
Petit-Dutaillis, C. : *La monarchie féodale en France et en Angleterre.* Paris, 1933. [English translation, 1936.]
Pirenne, H. : *Histoire de Belgique.* Vol. i. Brussels, 1909.
Powicke, F. M. : *The Loss of Normandy.* Manchester, 1913.
Wallon, H. : *St. Louis et son temps.* 2 vols. Paris, 1875.

CHAPTER VI

THE EMPIRE OF THE EAST AND THE CRUSADES,
1198–1291

The Latin
States in
Syria, 1197

THE arrangement between Richard Cœur-de-lion and Saladin in 1192 had only been intended as a truce until either combatant was able to make a fresh effort, and hostilities were resumed by the German crusaders sent by Henry VI in 1197 with some success. If Jaffa was lost to Saphadin, Beyrout and Sidon were recovered for the Christians. If King Henry of Champagne died, his widow Isabelle brought the kingship of Jerusalem to her fourth husband Amaury II de Lusignan, the King of Cyprus, and thus the resources of the Latins were consolidated for a time. The other two Latin states, the county of Tripoli and the principality of Antioch, held their own, and in 1201 were united under Bohemond IV. All these were the hybrid results of the conquests of the twelfth-century crusaders. On a native population of Moslems and Greek or Monophysite Christians were superimposed the Latin or Frankish settlers, led by barons under ultra-feudal institutions. But these were not the only western element. In each coast town of Syria there were privileged merchant quarters of the Italian traders, Venetians, Genoese, and Pisans, all enjoying a degree of self-government, and all bitter rivals. Further, there were the Military Orders of Knights, the Templars and Hospitallers, under monastic vows, recruited and endowed with lands in the West, who formed the best fighting force of the Latins but seldom acted in unison. Their castles, such as Crac-des-Chevaliers in Lebanon, were the strongest fortifications of the day, impregnable to direct assault. Last of these eastern states was the kingdom of Little Armenia under Leo II (1185–1219), which was linked with the West by a hollow ecclesiastical reconciliation, and both fended off the Seljūk Turks of Rūm to the north and warred with Antioch to the south.

Meantime, however, the death of Henry VI in 1197 put The Fourth Crusade, Origins an end to the German crusade, and left the propaganda for a new expedition to the Papacy and the ambitious minor princes of Europe. Thus the Fourth Crusade resembles the First in being led by a group of barons, who, if not more ambitious and self-seeking than the kings of the Third Crusade and Henry VI, were inferior in statesmanship if only owing to the multiplicity of the interests they were planning to satisfy and their lack of resources for the task : the crusade is an adventure led by adventurers.

The movement began in 1199 in North France under the leadership of Count Theobald III of Champagne and Count Baldwin IX of Flanders and Hainault, and it met with the fervent approval of Innocent III. Taught by the experience of the Third Crusade, the leaders at once chose the sea-route to Palestine, and negotiations were begun with Venice for the hire of transport. In April 1201 the terms were arranged which already showed the political and strategic spirit which ruled in the Crusade. The attack was to be made on Egypt, the centre of the Moslem power, the conquest of which would not only provide an incomparable base for the recovery of Palestine but would reward the crusaders with wealth and territory incalculable in Western eyes. Venice, who Bargain with Venice was obtaining valuable privileges in Egypt and can hardly have desired this objective, became a partner in the crusade : she was to provide transport for 4,500 knights, 5,000 squires, and 20,000 sergeants, and provisions for nine months ; in return she made a good bargain, 85,000 silver marks in cash and half of the prospective conquests. At this moment Theobald of Champagne, the elected chief, died and was succeeded by Boniface, Marquess of Montferrat, whose brother Conrad had been for a month King of Jerusalem in the Third Crusade. The expedition was to begin in June 1202.

But, while these hard terms were being settled, another The Eastern Empire. Deposition of Isaac II Angelus train of events was on foot which was eventually to alter the course of the enterprise. The reign of the Emperor Isaac II Angelus of Constantinople had been an uninterrupted succession of disasters, in which his incompetence had been glaring. At last, in 1195 he had been dethroned and blinded by his own brother Alexius III, but his son, also named Alexius, escaped and betook himself (1202) to the court of

his brother-in-law Philip of Swabia, the cousin of Boniface.
From that time a scheme existed to combine the crusade
with the restoration of Isaac II and the submission of the
Greek Church to the Western, and when the crusading
leaders were at Venice in 1202 it was made known to them
and to the Pope.   But another factor appeared at the same

The
Diversion
to Zara

time : the crusaders' numbers were much below the estimate,
and they were unable to make full payment of their debt
to Venice; 36,000 marks were left owing.   The Venetians,
guided by their Doge, the blind and old but masterful
Enrico Dandolo, offered a respite if the crusaders would
recapture for them the Dalmatian city of Zara, which was
of first importance for their control of the Adriatic and had
been taken from them by the King of Hungary.   It was a
scandalous perversion of the expedition to use crusading
forces to besiege a Christian city, but the crusaders, marooned
at Venice, had little choice and consented.   The Doge thereupon took the cross and became one of the chiefs of the
Crusade.   In November Zara surrendered with the inevitable
result of causing a breach with Innocent III, who very honour-
ably excommunicated the culprits, though but for a short
period.

The
Diversion to
Constanti-
nople

The mass of the crusaders had thus become mercenaries,
and were more open than ever to the solicitations of Philip
of Swabia and the exiled Alexius, backed by Dandolo—for
Venice had a long score to settle with the Eastern Empire
—and Boniface of Montferrat.   When they reached Corfù a
treaty was signed in May 1203.   The first task of the Crusade
was to be the restoration of Isaac Angelus.   In return the
young Alexius promised to subject the Greek Church to the
Papacy, to pay 200,000 silver marks, to join the Crusade,
and to maintain 500 knights in the Holy Land.   Innocent
forbade the new diversion, but took no further action.   Certain honest crusaders, led by Simon de Montfort, indignantly
separated from the fleet and went vainly to Palestine.   The

The
Crusaders
at Con-
stantinople.
Restoration
of Isaac II
and
Alexius IV

vast majority set sail for Constantinople.

It was now seen what a fatal flaw had been created in
the defences of city and Empire when the command of the
sea, perhaps inevitably, had been allowed to slip into the
hands of the Italians in the twelfth century.   The Venetian
fleet dominated the Straits, once the guarantee of Constanti-

nople's safety; it forced the entrance to the harbour of the Golden Horn on July 7, 1203. Ten days later a general assault terrified the craven Alexius III into flight, and Isaac was at once restored along with his son Alexius IV to the throne. But Alexius IV could perform only a part of his promises, and the crusaders stayed on outside the city to exact a full acquittance. This sojourn made a new outbreak of hostilities almost inevitable. Amid mutual grievances the impatient anger of the Greeks produced a revolution in February 1204. Isaac and Alexius IV were murdered, **Alexius V** and Alexius V Ducas, nicknamed Mourtzouphlos, " of the **Ducas** bushy eyebrows," was made Emperor to lead the resistance. Now Doge Dandolo and the grasping barons, with the wealthiest of cities before their eyes, had their chance. It was agreed to conquer the Empire and divide the spoil, Venice securing as usual the best of the bargain, including the right to nominate the new Latin patriarch of Constantinople. On April 12 the victorious assault, followed by the flight **Capture** of Mourtzouphlos, took place and the treasures and civiliza- **of Constantinople** tion of the Eastern Empire fell to the valiant brigands of **by the** the West. The horrors of the long sack obliterated much **Crusaders** of the art, the literature, and the culture which had survived in Constantinople as the salvage of the Ancient World.

The so-called Latin Empire was now set up by the con- **The Latin** querors. It was a congeries of feudal states under the **Empire of** nominal suzerainty of an Emperor. Baldwin of Flanders **Constantinople** became Emperor, Boniface of Montferrat King of Thessalonica; a principality of Achaia was conquered in the Morea, and there were lesser fiefs, but the lion's share fell to Venice. Three-eighths of the capital, key towns on the coasts, Crete and many islands in the Ægean Sea protected her commercial supremacy. Innocent III, at first horrified by the sack, was gained over by the compulsory subjection of the Greeks to the Papacy; he looked on it as providential, and a step to the recovery of the Holy Land. At a later age it appears as an irreparable disaster to civilization, and the destruction of the surest bulwark of Europe against its Eastern enemies.

The Latin Empire, however, tottered from the first. **Its Weak-** Not only was it a collection of jangling feudal states imposed **ness and** on alien and hostile populations, but it was surrounded by **Foes**

The
Byzantine
Fragments

dangerous foes. In the first place, the hardier Byzantines held out on the fringes of the Empire : an Angelus became Despot of the mountain districts of Epirus and Albania on the Adriatic ; a Comnenus established the Empire of Trebizond on the Black Sea ; most important of all, Theodore I Lascaris, son-in-law of Alexius III, revived the Greek Empire

Empire of
Nicæa

at Nicæa in Asia Minor. Theodore rallied round him the best elements of the Empire both in civilization and in war, and he was aided by the embarrassments of his Latin enemies in Europe. In 1204–5 he met with two severe defeats from the Frankish armies ; north-west Asia Minor was lost. But the invaders were recalled to fight the Bulgarians, and the same thing happened in 1206–7. Theodore could be crowned by a newly elected Greek Patriarch. Meantime he repulsed attacks from his rivals of Trebizond. In 1210 he slew and defeated the Seljūk Sultan Kai-Khusrū I at Antioch on the Mæander, and captured the ex-Emperor Alexius III, whom the Turk was endeavouring to restore to the throne. Next year, indeed, he was defeated by the Latin Emperor Henry, and in the peace which followed was obliged to cede the coast districts of the Sea of Marmora. But he died in 1222 the ruler of a solid State.

Bulgaria

More immediately formidable to the Latin Empire than the Nicæans was Kalojan or Johannitsa, Tsar of the Bulgarians and Vlachs north of the Hæmus range. Called in by the Greeks of Thrace, who loathed their schismatic oppressors, he defeated and captured the Emperor Baldwin at Adrianople in 1205 and defeated and killed King Boniface in 1207, only himself to be assassinated at the siege of Thessalonica in the same year. He had already alienated the Greeks by indiscriminate massacres. Baldwin's disappearance after his defeat at Adrianople—he was probably murdered in cap-

The Latin
Emperor
Henry

tivity—had meantime proved a benefit to the Latin Empire, for it brought to the throne his brother Henry, a really able general and statesman, who in his short reign (1206–16) gave some reality to his imperial title. He acted as real suzerain of Thessalonica and of the Latin states of Achaia and Athens. He was tolerant to the Greeks and compelled the new Latin clergy to fulfil their obligations to the State. Besides his victory over Theodore Lascaris, he won a battle against Tsar Boril, who had usurped the Bulgarian throne

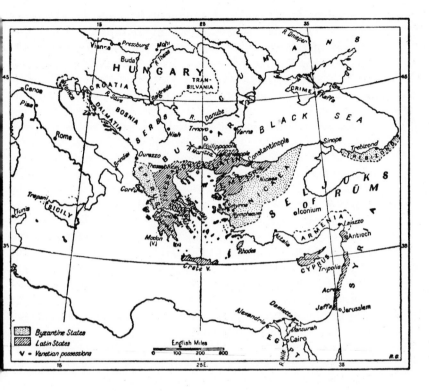

English Miles
0   100   200   800

THE EASTERN EMPIRE AND THE LEVANT c. A.D. 1220

(1207–18), and married his daughter in an advantageous peace. After his death decline began apace. Peter and Robert of Courtenay, his brother-in-law and nephew (1216–28), were incapable of making head against their enemies, who pressed on all sides. The Despot of Epirus, Theodore Ducas Angelus, in 1222 conquered Thessalonica from its Frankish king, Demetrius of Montferrat, and took the title of Emperor, a permanent loss to the Latins even if it accentuated the rivalry between the Epirotes and Nicæans for the heirship to the Byzantine Empire. Now, however, Bulgaria re-entered the contest. John Asên II, the son of Johannitsa, had recovered the Bulgarian throne from the usurper Boril with Russian aid, and, more civilized and statesmanlike than his fierce predecessors, made Bulgaria a leading power. While conciliatory to his Greek subjects, he revived the Bulgarian Patriarchate of Trnovo in 1235 with the consent of Nicæa. In 1230 he routed and captured Theodore Ducas Angelus at Klokotinitza, and annexed Macedonia, leaving only Thessalonica and Thessaly to the new Emperor Manuel, who also lost Epirus (1236) to another kinsman, the Despot Michael.

Advance of Bulgaria and Epirus

More stable were the victories of Nicæa. John III Vatatzes, Theodore's son-in-law and successor (1222–54), was the last of the great rulers of the Eastern Empire. He showed an unusual thoroughness in promoting the economic prosperity of his fertile share of Asia Minor, but in war and diplomacy he was equally successful. He began by recovering through the victory of Pœmanenum most of the small Latin possessions to the east of the Sea of Marmora in 1225, and in 1233 foiled the Emperor-regent, the adventurer John of Brienne (1229–37), in the last Latin attempt at conquest. He could now invade Europe with the assistance of the Latins' other foe, John Asên II. A joint attack subdued Thrace, the Greek share extending to the River Maritza; in 1236 they besieged Constantinople. But the Italian cities united for once to send their fleets, the Prince of Achaia brought reinforcements, and the attempt failed. John Asên, become alive to the danger of a strong Byzantine Empire, then turned against his ally, and gave passage to a horde of Cumans, who fought on the Latin side. None the less Vatatzes had gained a footing in Europe, and soon was able

John Vatatzes of Nicæa

to advance. In 1242 he forced John of Thessalonica to abandon the title of Emperor for that of Despot; in 1246 he conquered Macedonia from the now-declining Bulgarians, and at last annexed Thessalonica. The remnant of the Latin possessions in Asia was already his. The Mongol invasion and the defeat of the Seljūks of Rūm [1] proved beneficial to the Greeks, for the Seljūks were glad of Vatatzes' alliance against the dreaded enemy, and the Mongols turned to other wars. At his death Vatatzes left his Empire doubled in extent, well-governed, and strong. His successor was his highly educated, neurasthenic son Theodore II Lascaris (1254-8), a capable but uncertain ruler. Theodore had to face the revenge of the Bulgarians. Tsar Kaliman I (1241-6) had been Vatatzes' ally, Tsar Michael Asên (1254-57) his victim, losing about half his territory to the Greeks. On Vatatzes' death Michael Asên recovered easily part of his losses and threatened to regain the rest. In two brilliant campaigns Theodore defeated the Tsar, in spite of his Cuman allies and restored his father's frontier. Michael Asên was promptly murdered for his ill-success, and his dynasty was extinguished in the same year by the slaughter of the usurper Kaliman II. The new Tsar who was then elected, Constantine Asên (1255-77), who had a rival Mytzês to quell, was glad to make an alliance and marry Theodore II's daughter, who through her mother was a descendant of Johannitsa. Against the Despot Michael II of Epirus Theodore was less successful. He knavishly extorted the cession of the town of Durazzo, the Epirote seaport, by detaining the Despot's wife when she made a state visit to him. Michael II in his turn took advantage of the Emperor's ill-health and preoccupation with Seljūk and Mongol to invade and conquer most of Macedonia. This was the situation when Theodore died, just after an abdication which his failing brain made necessary.

Theodore had long been racked with suspicions of one of his best generals, Michael Palæologus, a noble of old descent, with the blood of the Comneni and Angeli in his veins. Exiled and threatened and restored, Palæologus soon justified these suspicions, when Theodore's child son John IV succeeded him. He at once contrived the murder in a riot

Theodore II Lascaris of Nicæa

Michael VIII Palæologus of Nicæa

[1] See below, Chap. VIII, p. 165.

of the low-born regent Muzalon whom Theodore had appointed, and took over the regency himself. On January 1, 1259, he was crowned co-Emperor as Michael VIII. Within two years he blinded and imprisoned his unhappy ward. There was no doubt that the ablest competitor had become Emperor ; it was unfortunate for the Empire that he was a slippery, unprincipled scoundrel. He first dealt with the Epirote war. His brother John met the forces of the Despot Michael and his ally Prince William of Achaia at Pelagonia in 1259. The Despot decamped, and William was routed by the Byzantine archers and captured as well. Though the Despot won a battle next year, he lost Macedonia in his peace with his namesake.

The Latin Emperor Baldwin II
    The Latin Empire under Baldwin II of Courtenay (1237–61) counted for very little in these struggles, restricted as it was to a small territory round Constantinople, and vainly mendicant for help from the West. When the Nicæan throne was usurped by a capable general and intriguer and Achaia, its best ally, was crippled by the defeat of Pelagonia, its doom was near. The furious mutual hostility of Genoa and Venice gave Michael VIII the opportunity of gaining a Western ally. The Genoese, who were getting the worst of their conflict with Venice on the Syrian coast, indemnified themselves by wrecking their rival's trade pre-eminence in the Black Sea. On March 13, 1261, they signed the alliance with Michael VIII at Nymphæum. They were to enjoy free trade and almost a monopoly in the Eastern Empire and the Black Sea in return for their naval assistance to the schismatic Emperor. But before the promised squadron arrived, a surprise attack by Michael's general, Alexius Stratego-poulos, gave Constantinople once more to the Eastern Empire on July 25, 1261. Baldwin II fled ; the Venetians, who had been absent on an expedition in the Black Sea, were only able to rescue their non-combatants; and the Latin Empire, though not its fiefs in Greece and the Ægean Sea, came to an unhonoured end.

Treaty of Nymphæum

Constantinople recaptured. Fall of the Latin Empire

The New Byzantine Empire
    The Byzantine Empire, however, as restored by Palæologus was a very different state from that left by the Comneni in the twelfth century, and even from that left by the warlike Lascaris forty years earlier. Subjugation, plunder, and exhaustion had left fatal marks on the Byzantines. Byzan-

tium under Michael VIII ceased to be a military power.
Nicæa itself had largely depended on mercenaries, even
Franks; now the peasant militia of Asia Minor was dissolved by Michael in fear for his throne from the deposed
and blinded John IV. It is true that he extorted (1262)
from his captive, the Prince of Achaia, the cession of the
south-eastern corner of the Morea, and that his fleet won
back a number of the Greek islands. But these were his
last acquisitions. He devoted himself to the defences of
Constantinople, and trusted to diplomatic alliances. It was
this that led to the transitory union of the Churches. Charles Schemes of
of Anjou was, as we have seen, possessed with Eastern Charles of
ambitions. He concluded in 1267 with the exiled Baldwin Anjou
II the treaty of Viterbo, by which he became suzerain of
Achaia and the father-in-law of Baldwin's heir. In 1271 his
second son was married to the heiress of Achaia. To ward
off the threatened invasion by the conqueror of Sicily Michael
grasped at the readiest means—submission to the Pope, who
alone could curb Charles of Anjou, the creation of the Papacy.
And there was once more a Pope to appeal to who had an
ecumenic outlook. Gregory X (1271–6)[1] bartered his protection in exchange for Union, to which Michael submitted Temporary
at the Council of Lyons in 1274. This checkmated Charles, of the
but left Michael in difficulties with his own subjects. The Churches
Byzantines, who seemed to be losing all interest in the State
and its welfare, were more addicted than ever to religion
on its doctrinal and indeed superstitious side: national
repugnance found its expression in religious hatred. The
Union, at first dissimulated, could only be enforced by
persecution, and that ineffectually. As its unreality became
clear to the West, it was denounced by the Angevin partisan,
Pope Martin IV, in 1280, and Charles, who had become
Prince of Achaia by treaty in 1278, prepared for invasion.
It was the Sicilian Vespers of 1282, to the origins of which
Michael was a contributor, which saved the Byzantine
Empire.

Michael died in the same year, leaving the Balkans almost The Latins
as divided as he found them. The most prosperous parts, of Greece
perhaps, were the principality of Achaia and the duchy of
Athens under their French rulers, and the islands under

[1] See above, Chap. IV, p. 89.

their Venetian dynasties. In 1204 King Boniface of Thessalonica had achieved the conquest of Thessaly for himself

Athens and of Attica and Bœotia for his vassal Othon de la Roche,
who became Sire or Duke of Athens. Thence Boniface dispatched a small force under William de Champlitte and
Geoffrey de Villehardouin to subdue the Morea. One victory,
at Koundoura in Messenia, made Champlitte lord of the

Achaia land as Prince of Achaia ; Venice was content with the
south-west corner round the port of Modon and in the north
with the suzerainty of the lords of the island of Negropont.
Venetian adventurers founded little states, like the duchy of
the Archipelago, in the Ægean. Thus Greece was partitioned
among the Franks. A change of dynasty almost immediately took place in Achaia. Champlitte died in 1209 on a
journey to France, and his unfaithful vicegerent, Geoffrey de
Villehardouin, succeeded in delaying the formal claim of the
heir until the due legal period for its assertion had elapsed.
He was then elected prince himself, as his eminent ability
suggested. His reign (1210–18) was one of organization and
rounding off the principality. His son Geoffrey II (1218–46)
ruled prosperously for twenty-eight years, and was succeeded
by a warrior brother William II (1246–78), who defeated
(1258) the vassal Duke Guy I of Athens, but was himself
made a Byzantine captive at the disaster of Pelagonia. As
almost all his barons were killed or taken, his ransom—the
cession of south-east Morea to Michael VIII—was agreed
to by the " Ladies' Parliament " of wives and widows at
Nikli, and from that time war with the Byzantine province
of Mistra was almost permanent, to the damage of Achaia's
prosperity. Prince William's remedy was to ally himself
with the ambitious Charles of Anjou. He became his vassal ;
the succession was guaranteed to Charles, who obtained it
in 1278, and Achaia was thenceforth an Angevin dependency.
The duchy of Athens, although vassal, was better off under
the line of de la Roche.

Latin These Frankish States were organized on feudal principles
Government borrowed from the kingdom of Cyprus. The *Assizes of*
in Greece *Jerusalem,* under which Cyprus was governed, were adapted
as the *Customs of the Empire of Romania.* In Athens great
barons were almost absent ; in Achaia they were many and
powerful, and ruled their fiefs from their strongholds. The

Latin Church was endowed and favoured. Although the Greeks were mere subjects and their Orthodox bishops in exile, the Frankish lords were tolerant of native religion and custom. Only the peasant serfs were almost rightless, if not grievously ill-used. Splendid and chivalrous courts were kept up at Andravida in Achaia and at Thebes, the two capitals. In the secure times before 1262 in Achaia and before 1311 in Athens, there was busy trade in fruit, wine, and oil, and in the silk of Thebes. In short, alien and feudal as they were, the Franks governed well, and in their later days they were cultured. It is noticeable that the best medieval translator of Aristotle, William of Moerbeke, was Latin Archbishop of Corinth.

Although most of his subjects were turbulent Albanian Epirus clansmen, the Despot Michael II of Epirus maintained Greek rule in his dominions. When he died in 1271, his son Nicephorus I only succeeded to Epirus from the gulf of Corinth northwards ; his bastard son John, called the Duke of Neopatras from his capital, secured Thessaly with its hybrid population of Vlachs and Greeks. With the aid of Duke John of Athens he defeated the Emperor Michael VIII's attempt to conquer him, and pursued a tacking policy between Greeks and Franks.

Against Bulgaria, too, the cause of the Greeks prospered. Decline of Constantine Asên had to meet a Hungarian invasion, which Bulgaria for a time bid fair to conquer the country. Delivered from this, he attacked Michael VIII with the aid of the Tartars of the Golden Horde, who devastated Thrace. The faithless Michael made peace by marrying his niece Maria to Constantine, who was a widower, and then withheld the towns which he had promised as her dowry. Maria, however, turned a patriotic Bulgarian ; the war was renewed. Michael thereupon bought another ally by giving his natural daughter to the Tartar chief Nogai Khan, whose hordes ravaged Bulgaria. The Tsaritsa Maria was occupied in grasping power, by assassination, for the Tsar was crippled and incapacitated, and Bulgaria was temporarily rescued by the victories of a popular leader, the swineherd Ivailo, who slew Constantine Asên in 1277. He became Tsar and married Maria, but rapidly fell before attacks from both Greeks and Tartars. Yet Bulgaria, through all these turmoils, preserved its independence and with it the ineradicable divisions of the Balkans.

The Yugo-Slavs

The same vitality was shown in the north-west by the Serbs with even less union, perhaps, between the various districts inhabited by the race. The Croats had long been Catholic and linked with Hungary. The Bosnians, a natural object of Hungarian ambition, were under native *bans*. Besides these the chief districts were Hum (Herzegovina),

Serbia

the Zeta (Montenegro), and Rascia. It was Stephen Nemanya who first in the twelfth century united Rascia, the Zeta, and Hum, together with North Albania, into a Serbian State. In 1196 he retired to a monastery, leaving his sons to struggle for the position of suzerain prince. Another son, the ecclesiastic St. Sava, contrived to reconcile his brothers. Stephen II (1196–1228) used his supremacy and an opportune acceptance of Catholicism to obtain the title of king in 1217 from Pope Honorius III. Then under St. Sava's influence he reverted to the Orthodox Church, and was crowned again in 1222 by his brother, who secured from the Patriarch of Constantinople recognition of the autonomy of the Serbian Church and became himself first " Archbishop of the Serbian lands." This was a good beginning, and Stephen Urosh I (1243–76) ruled in peace and prosperity his somewhat free-booting subjects until he was dethroned by his unnatural son Stephen Dragutin. Bosnia and Hum, meantime, continued under local princes with intervals of Hungarian domination. All, like the Bulgarians, were not far removed from uncultured barbarism, which they took long to throw off. The urgent need of the Balkans in the future was to be union for defence against the Turks, and this their sturdy barbarians and their civilized weaklings were alike incapable of achieving.

The Fifth Crusade

During all this period the policy of the Popes and the fashion rather than the zeal of the West were directed to the genuine crusades and the maintenance of the Latin dominion in Syria. It soon became clear that the erection of the Latin Empire of Constantinople had been completely fruitless for this purpose, and Innocent III reverted to the scheme of the direct crusade which had now so many rivals in Europe. The Lateran Council of 1215 solemnly proclaimed the new effort, in which Frederick II was to take part. The secular leader ended in being the French adventurer, John de Brienne, the King-consort of Jerusalem, now separated from Cyprus, but more power was possessed by the Cardinal-legate Pelagius to the general detriment. It was resolved to resume the plan of attacking Egypt, and the port of Damietta was captured in May 1218. The death of Saphadin with the disorders it entailed in Egypt was of great advantage to the Christians, but the crusaders came and went in batches and Frederick II, though he sent large contingents, never arrived. The legate's fanatic folly refused the cession of the whole kingdom of Jerusalem by the alarmed Sultan Kāmil, and insisted in 1221 on an advance on Cairo. This was fatal. The Christians were blockaded at Mansūrah amid the branches of the Nile, and bought their retreat by the surrender of Damietta. The Fifth Crusade had proved a complete fiasco.

The lesson was not lost on the Emperor Frederick II, who, married to John de Brienne's daughter Yolande, had in his turn become King of Jerusalem, when he at last set forth on his long-delayed crusade in 1228. Excommunicated as he was, with small forces, with the Templars and Hospitallers sullenly hostile, he made use of Sultan Kāmil's feuds with the rival princes of his house in Syria, and the fact that Jerusalem was now by Kāmil's own act in the Fifth Crusade unwalled and poverty-stricken, to arrange a treaty in 1229 by which the Holy City, Nazareth, and the road from Jaffa were ceded to him on condition of tolerating the Moslems, who kept the Mosque of Omar on the temple-site at Jerusalem. North Syria was left excluded from the peace, which was only recognized by the Pope some years later. Thus the banned Emperor, no enthusiastic crusader, accomplished what the great armies of the Third and Fifth Crusades had failed to do—the recovery of Jerusalem and the Holy Places. *Frederick II's Recovery of Jerusalem*

But the absentee rule of Frederick and of his son Conrad, who became king by descent in 1243, lacked most of the elements of success. The royal vicegerents, the Military Orders, the native nobility, the Lusignans of Cyprus, the Italian sea-powers, were all at odds with one another, and the situation was made more often worse than better by the fitful energy of sporadic semi-crusades. The feuds of the numerous descendants of Saphadin, each beset in his own *Final Loss of Jerusalem by the Christians*

principality, and grasping at the rest, were the Latins' best
safeguard.   In 1239 Jerusalem, in the course of these wars,
fell before Nāsir of Kerak.   Restored ₁.ext year by a treaty
with Egypt bought by Richard, Earl of Cornwall, the brother
of the English Henry III, it remained precariously Christian
till 1244.   Then against the Christians and Sālih Ismāīl of
Damascus the Egyptian Sultan Sālih Ayyūb allied with the
Turkish horde of the Khwārazmians, who had been driven
west from the Oxus by the Mongol invasion.   Jerusalem was
sacked and lost to Christendom, and the Franks and Syrian
Moslems received a crushing defeat at Gaza.

**St. Louis'
First
Crusade**
    It was to retrieve this disaster that St. Louis of France
made his first Crusade.   It was a curious replica of the
Fifth.   St. Louis, too, captured Damietta in 1249 ; he, too,
untaught by the experience of his predecessors, marched on
Cairo by their route and was held up at Mansūrah, where
a fruitless battle was fought.   When, too late, he retreated,
he was surrounded, and captured amid the slaughter of his
army in April 1250 by Sultan Tūrān Shāh.   He only regained
his liberty by the surrender of Damietta.

**The
Mamlūks
of Egypt**
    In the next few years a change took place in the govern-
ment of Egypt.   The Sultans had recently depended more
on the kernel of their army, their trained military guard of
Turkish slaves or Mamlūks.   In 1250 the Mamlūks set up
one of themselves as Sultan, and henceforth a succession of
slave-kings ruled Egypt.   Their reigns were seldom long,
but they showed a competitive vigour and they disposed of
a magnificent fighting force in the constantly recruited
Mamlūks.   These transitory prætorians proved to be the
survival of the fittest in an age of war.   Their advent
to power, indeed, was only just in time to check the
advance to the Mediterranean of the civilization-destroying
Mongol invasion.[1]   In 1258 Hūlāgū, grandson of Jenghiz
Khan, who ruled Persia, captured Baghdad and put an
end to the Abbasid Caliphate.   Syria was his next conquest, but he was fortunately called east by the wars following the death of the Great Khan Mangū.   His general,
**The Repulse
of the
Mongols
from Syria**
Ketbughā, was met on September 3, 1260, by Kutuz the
Mamlūk Sultan at Ain-Jālūt at the foot of Mount Gilboa in
Palestine.   It was the first time that the Mongols were

[1] See below, Chap. VIII, p. 166.

decisively worsted in a pitched battle, and the victory set, as it turned out, permanent bounds to the Mongol conquest. Kutuz secured the rule or suzerainty of Syria as far as the Euphrates, only to be murdered and succeeded by his best general, Baibars Bundukdārī, the bitter foe of the Latin States in the Levant.

Meanwhile, disunion and civil war were wrecking all chances of a successful Christian resistance. The throne, after the death of the nominal king, Conradin of Swabia, in 1268, was disputed between Hugh III of Cyprus and Mary of Antioch, who eventually in 1277 sold her claims to Charles of Anjou. Templars, Hospitallers, and barons were in internecine war. As deadly were the rivalries of the Italian cities. In 1257 war broke out between Venice and Genoa over their Levantine trade and settlements : the Venetians were driven from Tyre, the Genoese in 1258 from Acre, and the fighting continued with little remission until a truce in 1270. Baibars, who kept the Mongols of Persia at bay by an alliance with the rival Mongols of the Golden Horde to the north, could begin a systematic attack on the Latin coastland. After preliminary campaigns he made an end of the principality of Antioch in 1268, and took the great Hospitaller fortress, Crac-des-Chevaliers, in 1271. As we have seen, St. Louis' second Crusade never reached the East, and Edward I's in 1271 had small effect. The terrible Assassins, long the dread of both sides, were cleared out of their fortresses by the Mamlūks. A new Sultan, Kalāūn, continued Baibars' policy. He gave the Persian Mongols their final defeat at Hims in 1281, and then attacked the Latins piecemeal. Tripoli fell in 1289, and next year Kalāūn ordered the siege of Acre. The town, where each faction conducted its own defence, was by now the sink of Christendom, but its fractions resisted bravely the assaults of Kalāūn's successor Khalīl. None the less it was stormed on May 18, 1291. Soon after, the few remaining coast-towns surrendered. The Latin kingdom of Jerusalem thus disappeared. There were only left to the Christians the kingdom of Cyprus and Little Armenia in the Taurus Mountains. Both in a way gained by the fall of the Latin States of Syria, for they became outposts and centres of trade of the Latins in the Levant. Cyprus was an ultra-feudal monarchy under the dynasty of Lusignan.

The Mamlūk Conquest of the Latins in Syria

Fall of Acre

Cyprus and Armenia

There the so-called *Assizes of Jerusalem,* the most feudal of
legal codes, were compiled from older law and custom and
applied.   Little Armenia was in constant strife with the
Seljūks of Rūm and the Syrian Moslems.   The Armenians
fought most bravely, but when the Mamlūks conquered
Syria they suffered severely in their self-defence.   Their best
friends were the heathen Mongols, to whom in 1244 King
Hethum I (1226–70) became a vassal.   This meant a powerful
ally but no respite from war and invasion.

The Effect
of the
Crusades on
Europe

No serious efforts were ever made to retrieve the disaster
of the fall of Acre, for subsequent crusades were directed to
Europe's second line of defence on the sea and on the coasts
of the Ægean.   The main results of the whole movement
have been dealt with in the previous volume.   Here may
be stressed the enormous loss of life and treasure by Western
Europe in the movement.   The Crusades had indeed acted
as a safety-valve to the anarchic fighting spirit and ambitions
of the Western nobles, and had so far aided the introduction
of some kind of order in the West ; they had enabled the
Italian sea-towns, and to a less extent those of Provence
and Spain, to complete their command of the Mediterranean,
and an enormous increment, which the Mamlūk victories did
not cancel, was thus added to the wealth of Europe by the
profits of the Eastern trade.   If the twelfth-century renaissance drew most of its recovery of Greek learning through
the channels of Moorish Spain and Sicily, yet the translations
of Aristotle direct from the Greek seem mainly due to the
close connexion established with Byzantium.   But reaching
wider and deeper was the influence of the alien and higher
material civilization of the Byzantines and the Moslems.
It was not only actual borrowings and imitations, it was the
stimulus given to native growth, the extended and freer
outlook, which as the horizon receded came to the West,
and quickened its maturity.   Nobles and merchants whose
experience extended from Syria and Constantinople to Spain
and England and the Baltic were less fettered by their own
past and more capable of developing their inheritance.   It
was no mere coincidence which made Italy, the land most
in contact with Byzantium and the Levant, the earliest
country of the West to evolve a new spirit in art and a new
outlook on life.

SUGGESTIONS FOR READING ON CHAPTER VI

A. SOURCES

(i) Documents

Innocent III's *Epistolae*, as for Chapter II.
Epistolae ad quartum bellum sacrum pertinentes. Migne, *Patrologia Latina,* ccix, ccxiii.

(ii) Chronicles

Acropolites, G. : Χρονικὴ συγγραφή. Ed. Heisenberg. Leipzig, 1903.
Clari, R. de : *La prise de Constantinople.* Ed. Lauer. Paris, 1924. [Also English translation.]
Ernoul and Bernard the Treasurer : *Chronique d'Outremer.* Ed. Mas-Latrie. Paris, 1871. [For Jerusalem, etc.]
Joinville, J. de : *Histoire de St. Louis.* Ed. Wailly. Paris, 1874 (and in translations).
Livre d'Éraclès : Recueil des historiens des croisades. Vol. ii. Paris, 1859. [For Jerusalem, etc.]
Nicetas Akominatos : *Historia.* Ed. Bekker. Corpus Scriptorum Historiae Byzantinae. Bonn, 1835.
The Chronicle of the Morea. Ed. Schmitt. Byzantine Texts. 1904.
Villehardouin, G. de : *La conquête de Constantinople.* Ed. Wailly. Paris, 1874. [Trans. Marzials. Everyman's Library.]

B. MODERN WORKS

Baynes, N. H. : *The Byzantine Empire.* 1925.
Bréhier, L. : *L'Église et l'Orient au moyen âge. Les Croisades.* Paris, 1907.
Bréhier, L. : *Le Monde Byzantin.* 3 vols. Paris, 1947.
Cambridge Medieval History, vols. iv and v, relevant chapters.
Coulton, G. G. : *Crusades, Commerce and Adventure.* 1930.
Diehl, C. : *Byzance : grandeur et décadence.* Paris, 1919.
Finlay, G. : *History of Greece.* Ed. Tozer. 1877.
Gardner, A. : *The Lascarids of Nicæa.* 1912.
Gibbon, E. : *History of the Decline and Fall of the Roman Empire.* Ed. Bury. 1909–14.
Grousset, R. : *Histoire des Croisades et du royaume de Jérusalem.* 3 vols. Paris, 1934–36.
Heyd, W. : *Histoire du Levant au Moyen Âge.* 2 vols. Leipzig, 1923.
Hill, G. : *A History of Cyprus.* Vol. ii. Cambridge, 1948.
Jorga, N. : *The Byzantine Empire.* 1907.
La Monte, J. L. : *Feudal Monarchy in the Latin Kingdom of Jerusalem, 1100–1291.* Cambridge, Mass., 1932.
Lane-Poole, S. : *History of Egypt. The Middle Ages.* 1901.
Luchaire, A. : *Innocent III,* as for Chapter II.
Miller, W. : *The Latins in the Levant.* 1908.
Miller, W. : *Essays on the Latin Orient.* 1921.
Miller, W. : *Trebizond.* 1926.
Runciman, S. : *Byzantine Civilization.* 1933.
Temperley, H. : *History of Serbia.* 1917.

CHAPTER VII

GERMANY IN ANARCHY, 1250–1313

The Dis-
solution of
the German
Kingdom

THE process of dissolution which the German kingdom had been undergoing ever since the fatal Civil War between Philip of Swabia and Otto IV, and which had been accentuated by the policy and absenteeism of Frederick II, was immensely accelerated and in a sense completed by the deposition of Frederick at the Council of Lyons in 1245 and the civil war and anarchy which were its consequence. The lay princes might in general be loyal to the Emperor, but the ecclesiastics, willingly or unwillingly, were obliged to follow the commands of the Pope who controlled their appointment by relentless use of his prerogative rather than those of the Emperor who had practically exempted them from State interference. The crusade against Frederick was preached by the Friars; excommunication and interdict, liberally employed, disorganized religious life; and the ineffective campaigns of the rivals, if they did little to decide the issue, combined with the abeyance of the central government to let loose private war between princes and nobles and violence, robbery, and insecurity in the whole country. The Great Interregnum, which is reckoned from Frederick's death in 1250, really began when the Papacy inflamed this civil war.

The Great
Interregnum

William, Count of Holland, the second anti-Cæsar raised up by Innocent IV, was, at the time of Frederick's death in 1250, only really recognized along the lower Rhine, the erstwhile duchy of Lower Lorraine, and even so the care of his patrimonial interests engrossed much of his resources. The Netherlands were already showing signs of forming a new country, separate in circumstances and instincts from both Germany and France. There William was engaged in extending his county of Holland over Friesland, and prosecuting his feud with Margaret Countess of Flanders, whose territories and claims interlocked with his own in Zealand at the mouths of the Rhine, and who was at war with her own son, by her first marriage of very dubious validity, John of Avesnes, over the succession to Flanders and Hainault. John was King William's brother-in-law, and Louis IX of France was suzerain of Flanders. When after William's death the war ended by St. Louis' arbitration in 1256, John was indeed given Hainault, but not Flanders or its imperial annexes. A Netherlands dispute had been settled irrespective of the Empire.

Meanwhile, King William was gaining ground at the expense of his rival King Conrad IV of Hohenstaufen, who had left Germany to secure his inheritance of Sicily. A new election in which two of the north German lay " electors " shared improved his legal position, and the death of Conrad in 1254 left him without a rival until his own death against his enemies in Friesland on January 28, 1256. Yet it is with justice that the whole period of German history from 1250 to the election of Rudolf of Habsburg is called the Great Interregnum. Neither William nor the shadowy claimants after him exercised any universal or real authority. The princes saw their opportunity and grasped it. Without a king or with a puppet king they could fortify their virtual autonomy in their own lands, increase it and their revenues by royal grants from the claimants, and prosecute their private feuds. With not less selfishness and with more anti-social violence the lesser lords and the " Knights of the Empire," who were the ancient *ministeriales* of the royal demesne, could make themselves supreme in their little, often tiny, fiefs, and plunder peaceful neighbours and merchants with all but impunity. The " robber baron " became a characteristic of south-west Germany.

The greater princes meantime were becoming both more powerful and less effective in using their power at the same moment. Only the Slav King of Bohemia ruled a solid state which he was occupied in increasing by the conquest of the inheritance of the extinct Babenbergs, the south-eastern duchies of Austria, Styria, and other districts.[1] The Wittelsbachs held both the duchy of Bavaria and the Rhenish Palatinate ; the Ascanians were Dukes of Saxony and Margraves of Brandenburg, and were extending Brandenburg

The Princes of Germany : sub-division of their lands

[1] See below, Chap. VIII, pp. 171-78.

to the Oder by conquest from the Wendish Slavs ; on the extinction of the Landgraves of Thuringia with Henry Raspe's death, a long private war for his dominions ended in 1263 with the acquisition of Thuringia proper by the Margrave of Meissen and of Hessen by a scion of the Dukes of Brabant. But this strength was partly paralysed by the absence of primogeniture. The male heirs had always shared up landed estates in Germany, more particularly the old-fashioned " allods " which were held in full possession not in fief ; but offices, such as Count and Duke had been indivisible—thus Henry the Lion had been the only Duke of Bavaria while his uncle Welf VI took the Swabian estates of the Welfs— and this tended to maintain a kind of unity in direction of a great house. Now, since the reign of Frederick II, the male heirs took over the full rights of Duke or Count with their share of lands and superiorities. There were two, and soon to be four and more Dukes of Bavaria, one of whom was Elector Palatine. The Ascanians were still more sub-divided, and the same rule held good in other houses. Thus Germany as a whole became ever more split up among prince-lings, strong in their legal position and almost invulnerable collectively, but incapable of concerted action for any national or even provincial purpose, and forming an insuperable obstacle to a central government. When we consider that these disunited princelings were themselves struggling with insubordinate vassal nobles and towns to set up an effective government in their principalities, that they were divided by family feuds and ambitions, that the ecclesiastical prin-cipalities, to which their clerical kinsmen were the electors, were continually the object of their schemes, now that papal interference had diminished while the evil policy of Innocent IV in allowing laymen and men in minor orders to hold sees as " bishops elect " had affected the character of the episco-pate, it will be realized into what chaos Germany fell.

The Seven Electors   The Imperial Diets of tenants-in-chief provided no remedy. Their membership, to which imperial free towns were added from the time of William of Holland, varied—it depended on the summons of the monarch. While their assent was necessary to the promulgation of laws and to taxation, they acted like a collection of individuals ; they were a congress rather than a corporate assembly. Yet one central and inefficient institution was growing in these years of disorder. By custom the King of the Romans had been elected by the Princes, i.e. the immediate vassals, of the Empire. In the mid-thirteenth century it became, with a mysterious swiftness, the doctrine that only seven had the right to elect. Three were ecclesiastical, the Rhenish Archbishops of Mainz, Cologne, and Trèves ; four were lay, the Count Palatine of the Rhine, the Duke of Saxony, the Margrave of Brandenburg, and an uncertain fourth. The King of Bohemia claimed the office as Cupbearer of the Empire, for the lay electorates depended on ceremonial court offices ; but the Duke of Bavaria was a rival and might have been successful had not he been for long identical with the Count Palatine. This institution was to make for order in the future, but not immediately. There was no majority rule in Germany ; equally or unequally divided, the Electors might maintain rival candidates. Secondly, it was uncertain who had the right to vote. Not only was there the Bohemo-Bavarian dispute, but in the lack of primogeniture it was not clear which Duke of Saxony or Margrave of Brandenburg or whether all jointly possessed the electoral power. For over a century Germany suffered from disputed elections to the kingship and the consequent civil wars and national paralysis.

The death of King William brought out both the lack of unanimity of the Electors and their united preference for a monarch who could not exercise any real power. No strong prince of the Empire, such as Ottokar II of Bohemia, could obtain support, and the leading candidates were foreigners : Richard, Earl of Cornwall, brother of the English Henry III, and Alfonso the Learned, King of Castile. Richard was wealthy and Alfonso willing to intervene in Italy : they had no other fitness. Richard's bribes gained him the votes of three Electors, Mainz, Cologne, and the Count Palatine, and the dubious adhesion of Bohemia in January 1257 ; Alfonso was elected in April by four, Trèves, Saxony, Brandenburg, and the double-dealing Ottokar. Both rivals negotiated long and vainly for a papal recognition and coronation. In the use of their position Alfonso showed activity in Italy only,[1] but King Richard tried to be a real king. He was crowned in Aix-la-Chapelle, and made in all

Double Election of Richard of Cornwall and Alfonso X of Castile

[1] See above, Chap. IV, p. 89.

four visits to Germany, pouring out money and privileges on princes and towns. But he was little recognized outside the Rhineland, and even there was only a figure-head. In April 1272 he died, and left the way free for new measures.

The Leagues and the Free Towns

So far as there was any attempt to stem the prevailing anarchy in this period, it was made by the ancient device of *Landfrieden,* i.e. local leagues to keep and enforce the peace for a certain number of years. In this movement the towns took a leading part, whether they were directly under the Empire or subjects of one of the princes. Under the influence of the general advance of trade in the thirteenth century the German towns situated on the great trade routes from the Alps, on the Rhine, and on the north sea-coasts had developed rapidly. They followed in the wake of the earlier twelfth-century advance of towns in France and the Netherlands, and did so in face of steady opposition. Frederick II was the enemy of civic independence, and the princes, ecclesiastical and lay, hated town autonomy and feared the extension of town dominion by the gift of citizenship to *Pfahlbürgers,* that is residents in the countryside round a town. None the less, towns all over Germany prospered and acquired self-government. Their crying need was peace and safety on the trade-routes and the repression of extortionate and illegal tolls, and for this purpose and for self-defence against princes and nobles they began to form town leagues of a sporadic character even under Frederick II. In 1254 in the anarchy of the Great Interregnum a really wide League was formed by all the Rhine towns from Basel to Cologne. It was patronized by William of Holland, but the inclusion of princes and nobles within it for the peace lamed its effectiveness and it soon broke up. Other smaller leagues, however, succeeded the Rhine League on the middle Rhine, in Westphalia, and most important of all on the Baltic coast. There

The Origins of the Hansa League

in 1259 the " Wendish " towns of Lübeck, Rostock, and Wismar formed an alliance which developed into the famous Hansa League.[1] The Interregnum closed with a crowd of autonomous towns in Germany, whose representatives even appeared occasionally in the amorphous Diets or imperial

---

[1] See below, Chap. IX, p. 186. These towns were in the territory conquered from the Wends and Germanized in the twelfth century.

assemblies of princes, prelates, and nobles held by the shadow kings like the ruling Emperors before them.

By the time of King Richard's death even the princes were weary of the Interregnum, and as it happened the vacancy in the Papacy, which had given a free hand to the anti-imperial policy of Charles of Anjou, had just come to an end with the enthronement of Pope Gregory X summoned from the Holy Land. The new Pope no longer dreaded the Empire ; he needed it for the Crusade on which he had set his heart and to counterbalance the prepotency of the overgrown papal protégé, Charles, in Italy. Accordingly he spurred on the willing Electors. There were obvious difficulties. First of all, Electors and princes dreaded too strong a king ; secondly, they were anxious to secure their usurpations of imperial demesne and dues ; thirdly, there were powerful candidates, Ottokar II of Bohemia and the foreign Philip III of France, eager for the imperial title. These difficulties were met by the election of Rudolf, Count of Habsburg, as King of the Romans on October 1 and his coronation at Aix-la-Chapelle on October 24, 1273. Rudolf I had many recommendations : he was genial, prudent, and strong and universally respected as a faithful adherent of the Hohenstaufen ; he had wide lands in Swabia—in Alsace and Breisgau and south of the Rhine round his castle of Habsburg in what is now German Switzerland [1] ; but he had no royal blood or imperial traditions, and was not too powerful, not even a prince of the Empire.[2] He might be relied on to pursue a cautious German policy, and, while reclaiming imperial possessions and rights—the popular cry —to deal tenderly with some of the chief usurpers of them, the Electors and their friends. Only Ottokar II, disappointed of the crown and threatened with reclamation of his conquests, Austria, etc., stood out. His right to vote was denied, he being a " foreigner," and that of Bavaria admitted instead, and Rudolf was authorized to reclaim all imperial demesne alienated since Frederick II's " deposition " in 1245. The

Pope Gregory X

Election of Rudolf of Habsburg

---

[1] Here he had inherited some of the lands of the extinct house of the Dukes of Zähringen ; see below, Chap. XV, pp. 318–19.

[2] At this time the lay princes consisted only of those lay tenants-in-chief of the Empire who were at least counts and did not also hold fiefs of another lay tenant-in-chief. Thus a number of powerful counts were excluded from the number of princes, though not from the Diet of the Empire.

Pope still had to walk warily in view of the opposition of France and Charles, but Rudolf smoothed his path by asking for his approbation of the election, and in September 1274 this was at last solemnly given. Even Alfonso of Castile was induced by the Pope to renounce his claims. The Empire, at least as regards its German kingdom, had been revived, in peaceful accord with the Papacy.

Overthrow of Ottokar II of Bohemia   There was still the recalcitrant Ottokar to deal with, and here Rudolf was backed not only by the Bohemian's jealous neighbours, the Wittelsbachs of Bavaria and the Counts of Tyrol, but by discontented Austrians and disloyal Czech nobles. At Vienna in November 1276 Ottokar was compelled to surrender all his conquests and accept the investiture of Bohemia and Moravia from his rival. When, having neutralized the Wittelsbachs, he revolted again, Rudolf gained the support of Ladislas IV of Hungary and with his aid defeated on the Marchfeld the Bohemian king, who was slain in his flight (1278).

Rudolf I and the Empire   In this way the danger, so far as it really existed, of a great Slav State dominating the Empire, was removed. Wenceslas II of Bohemia, on coming of age, turned his real ambitions eastward. It remained to be seen how Rudolf would use his victory. He did so by utilizing his conquests for dynastic aggrandisement, thereby setting an example for all his successors on the imperial throne. It was not a deliberate abandonment of the interests of the German kingship. Rudolf strove earnestly to retain the kingship in his house. He almost secured the election of his younger son Rudolf as co-regent, and when the prince's death in 1290 frustrated this scheme, continued his vain endeavours to obtain the election of his eldest son Albert until his own death. If the Habsburg house was strong and reigned, the imperial power in their hands might recover. But to advance the imperial power in its own right and give it independent strength Rudolf renounced. He left untouched the autonomy and usually the wars of the princes; he reclaimed imperial demesne but partially—the wealthiest part of it, the Free Towns of the Empire, he left to self-government fortified by his costly charters, and wisely enough permitted them to form their leagues and policies unhindered. His chief service to the Empire was the encouragement he consistently gave to *Landfrieden*. In his designs for his house, however, the custom of the Empire, by which escheated fiefs had to be granted out again, gave him his opportunity. In 1282 he induced the Electors, whose consent was now by law necessary, to agree to the enfeoffment of his sons Albert and Rudolf with the vacant duchies of Austria and Styria. The terms of the grant showed how acutely Rudolf diagnosed the evils of the practice of equal inheritance which was laming the Princes of the Empire. Although Albert and Rudolf and all their male descendants in the male line were to be dukes, the actual rule of the two duchies was confined to Albert and the senior of his successive heirs. Thus, so far as law could do it, the power of the house of Habsburg was assured. Rudolf had succeeded in establishing his secondary family as one of the greatest houses of Germany in a territory which his descendants retained until our own day.

Grant of Austria to the Habsburgs

The conferment of this solid block of territory in the south-east on the Habsburgs confirmed and furthered a new transference of the centre of gravity of Germany. Situated in Saxony under the Ottos, this had moved south under the Salians, and rested in Swabia under the Hohenstaufen. As the north and its fractions tended to remain in particularist isolation, and the centre and west broke up into petty dominions of nobles and towns, the comparatively wide territories of the south-east, Bavaria, Austria, and the like, acquired a greater weight. Their rulers could control some of the wealth of the expanding transit trade. They formed the mightier active factors of imperial politics till the Reformation.

Leadership of South-East Germany

The conduct of his subjects gave Rudolf every excuse for his policy. His attempts at central administration and taxation were met with resistance and disaffection. His attempt to revive the duchy of Swabia for one of his sons was checkmated by the resistance of the nobles headed by the Count of Wurtemberg ; they were now accustomed to their independence. In the Netherlands the contest for the succession to the duchy of Limburg was fought out without him. The Duke of Brabant defeated and captured the Archbishop of Cologne and other Rhenish nobles in 1288 at Worringen, and secured the prize. North-east Germany ignored the king. In Thuringia indeed, he intervened in the domestic war between the Landgrave Albert and his sons, and

Rudolf I and North Germany

The Papacy enforced a *Landfriede*. Further, he seriously endeavoured to obtain the imperial crown at Rome and to defend the rights of the Empire over its border countries. He dearly bought the favour of Pope Nicholas III by the final and complete cession of the Romagna and central Italy to the Papacy, but some obstacle always prevented his Roman coronation : he, like many of his successors, remained King **France and** only of the Romans. Nearer to his interests lay the main- **the Arelate** tenance of the western frontier against aggressive France. The Arelate was under French influence. A French prince was Count of Provence ; the Dauphin and the Count of Savoy were Francophil ; Franche Comté was openly rebel- lious. Farther north the frontier princes inclined to France. Rudolf at one time was willing to make an Angevin King of Arles in return for an alliance ; later he thought of so en- dowing his son Rudolf. In 1289 he extorted the homage of the Count of Franche Comté by force of arms. At least he retained his formal suzerainty intact. In the east he even attempted to assert a suzerainty over Hungary with a view to conferring the kingdom on his son Albert, but this proved utterly vain.

Significance The reign of Rudolf I marks an epoch in German history. **of Rudolf I's** While it ensured the continuance of the Holy Roman Empire **Reign** and the German kingdom united with it, it also proved that the Empire was little more than a disorderly federation. His imperial and royal title gave dignity to the prince chosen by the Electors, but little revenue and less domains. The monarchy was bankrupt of resources. Yet its prerogatives gave advantages to its holder against the rival princes who were his vassals, and immense opportunities to an able ruler to increase the power and lands of his own family. This was the main aim of future Emperors. That it was so, was really due to the multitudinous princes, all of them engaged in a similar design, whose innermost aversion was to the restoration of a central government to Germany.

King Adolf When Rudolf I died on July 15, 1291, it was the fear **of Nassau** of a strong monarch which decided the choice of the Electors. Duke Albert of Austria was the most powerful and the richest prince ; he was besides a soldier and ruler of great talent, harsh and unpopular. So the Electors, even Wenceslas II of Bohemia, Albert's brother-in-law, now restored by Rudolf to his electoral vote, turned in May 1292 to another minor count, the poor and valiant Adolf of Nassau in the Rhineland. But Adolf laboured under two burdens : his promises to the Electors, which were too large to be fulfilled, and the enmity of Austria. He tried to play the great game, to endow his family by seizing Meissen and Thuringia, to defend the Empire from French aggression in alliance with Edward I of England. In 1291 Frederick Tuto, Margrave of Meissen, of the house of Wettin, died childless, and his lands were taken over by his brother's sons, Frederick and Diezmann of Thuringia. But Meissen could be claimed as a lapsed fief. So Adolf declared it, while he bought outright Thuringia itself from Albert the landgrave, who had been long at feud with his sons. For the necessary conquest King Adolf used with little scruple the subsidy he had obtained for the French war from Edward I. But the transient success brought with it the distrust of the princes : the frontier potentates preferred France, and the alarmed Electors deserted a too ambitious and faithless king. In 1298 Duke Albert marched with a half-foreign army of Czechs and Hungarians to Strasbourg, while a Diet at Mainz deposed King Adolf and elected the rebel. On July 2 the rivals met in battle at Göllheim near Worms, and Adolf was slain.

While Albert was resolved to assert his power over his nominal subjects, his first business was to placate them. On the one hand he supported the princes against the towns territorially, on the other he reduced the imperial tolls. Yet no powerful king could retain the loyalty of the Electors, especially when suggestions of an hereditary monarchy were made. Albert fortified himself by an alliance in September 1299 with Philip the Fair of France. This practically gave up the Arelate to French encroachment, but also left Albert free to intervene in the succession to the vacant county of Holland, which had been seized by John, Count of Hainault, on the extinction of the native dynasty. The alliance, however, embroiled Albert with Philip's enemy, Pope Boniface VIII, who had never recognized his election and now summoned him to defend himself from the guilt of rebellion and of King Adolf's death, while forbidding the princes to obey him. King Albert was able to subdue an insurrection of the four Rhenish Electors in 1301, but flinched before the resist-

Albert I of Austria

ance of Count John of Hainault, another step in the slow
separation of the Netherlands from Germany. Boniface's
struggle with Philip the Fair, meanwhile, lowered the Pope's
terms, which had once included the cession of Tuscany to
the Papal States. Yet his terms were high; the superiority
of the Papacy over the Empire, the right to approve or
quash the Electors' choice, a feudal oath of obedience from
the chosen king. No former Emperor had admitted as much.
Albert submitted to all (1303), and further broke off his
alliance with the French king.

The king's own preoccupations by this time were eastern.
The acquisition of Poland by Wenceslas II of Bohemia in
1800 and his attempt to make his heir King of Hungary in
1301 raised the spectre of a vast confederate State on the
Empire's borders.[1] Albert went to war to prevent the
danger. If none too successful, his invasion of Bohemia led
to the abandonment of Hungary to the rival claimant, Charles
Robert of Anjou, and the death of Wenceslas II in 1305
induced the young Wenceslas III to a peace, which ceded
Meissen, since King Adolf's time a bone of contention between him and the heirs of the house of Wettin, to the
King of the Romans. Wenceslas III's own murder next
year opened a new prospect, for with him the Přemyslids
became extinct. King Albert, by force and bribes, succeeded
in obtaining the election of his eldest son Rudolf as King
of Bohemia, thus anticipating, as Ottokar II had done, the
later structure of the Habsburg monarchy. But it was
only for a moment. Rudolf died childless in 1307, and the
throne of Bohemia was filled by Henry, Duke of Carinthia
and Count of Tyrol, the son-in-law of Wenceslas II, while
Frederick the Handsome, Albert's second son, maintained
himself in Moravia. War to conquer Bohemia and Carinthia,
as well as Meissen and Thuringia, where the Wettins sturdily
held out, filled the last months of Albert's reign until his murder on May 1, 1308 by his nephew John Parricida, from whom
he had withheld his due share of the Habsburg inheritance.
Hard and grasping as his rule had been, he had seemed well
on the way to dominate the Empire. He had even recovered
some of the imperial demesne from its princely usurpers.

The Electors were well aware of the danger they had run,

**Gain and
Loss of
Bohemia**

[1] Cf. below, Chap. VIII, p. 172.

and from the outset no powerful German prince had a chance Henry VII
for the crown, least of all Frederick the Handsome. But of Luxem-
Germany was threatened once more with a foreign king, for burg
Philip the Fair of France, whose influence was potent on
the Rhine, pressed for the candidature of his brother, Charles,
Count of Valois. He was unsuccessful; Pope Clement V,
galled in his " Babylonish captivity " by the French yoke,
gave outward support and secret resistance. In these circumstances the Rhenish archbishops found a way of compromise. Henry, Count of Luxemburg, brother of the
Elector of Trèves, was a minor prince, ruling a half French
territory, brought up in the French court, speaking French,
and of little power. Withal he was a knight without reproach, amiable and high-spirited, in the prime of life. He
promised to abandon once more the imperial possessions
recovered by King Albert to the Electors with compensation
for their temporary confiscation, and he was chosen King
of the Romans on November 27, 1308. Pope Clement hastened to approve, although Henry VII reverted to the
formula of King Rudolf instead of that submitted to by
Albert I; and Philip could only grumble.

Henry VII's heart was set on the revival of the Empire Acquisition
in Italy and the hastening of his imperial coronation at of Bohemia
Rome. In this he was, so to say, a reactionary; in Germany
he belonged to the new era. The monarchy in his hands
was devoted to dynastic aggrandisement; imperial interests
went by the board in concert with the Electors. By a lucky
chance Henry was given the opportunity to endow his family.
King Henry of Carinthia was unpopular in Bohemia, Frederick
of Habsburg had resigned his claims, and there was still one
unmarried daughter, Elizabeth, of Wenceslas II. The Czech
malcontents begged and obtained the deprivation of their
monarch, and the vacant kingdom was conferred in 1310 on
Henry VII's son John, together with the hand of Elizabeth.
The deposed King Henry withdrew after a short contest to
his county of Tyrol, his ally Frederick of the house of Wettin
was pacified by the peaceful possession of his long-contested
inheritance of Meissen and Thuringia, and Henry VII could
depart on his famous Italian expedition, during which he
died in 1313.[1]

[1] See below, Chap. XVI, pp. 330-33.

Rise of
Habsburgs
and Luxem-
burgs

Thus in the forty years from 1273 the Electors and princes of Germany had succeeded in avoiding the real revival of the kingship and a central government, but their choices had resulted in raising two new houses, the Habsburgs and the Luxemburgers, to be the strongest in the Empire. Along with the Wittelsbachs of Bavaria and the Palatinate, who were tending to subdivision, they possessed the south-east, and they derived further importance by their guardianship of the frontier against Hungary and Poland. In the north the Welfs were already weakened by partitions, the Wettins were occupied in recovering themselves in Meissen and Thuringia, the Ascanians of Brandenburg and Saxony were too subdivided for strength, the Netherlands were slipping away from the Empire. In the west Philip of France had already shifted the frontier to his advantage. Yet this period saw the continuance of German expansion eastward. Prussia on the Baltic was Germanized by the Teutonic Order ; Brandenburg reached its full dimensions ; Pomerania and Silesia became German duchies in essentials ; German colonists spread into Bohemia, Poland, and Hungary. The insubordinate enterprise which kept Germany divided and feud-ridden inspired noble, merchant, and peasant in this vigorous expansion. Most wide-reaching of all, the amorphous league of Hansa towns was on its way to supremacy in the sea-borne trade of the north. The place of Germany in Europe was not to be measured by its inefficiency as an organized State.

SUGGESTIONS FOR READING ON CHAPTER VII

A. SOURCES

(i) Documents

Constitutiones et acta publica imperatorum et regum. Vols. ii, iii, iv. *Monumenta Germaniae Historica.* Legum Sectio IV. 1896 ff.

Epistolae saeculi XIII e regestis pontificum Romanorum selectae. Ed. Rodenburg, C. *Mon. Germ. Hist.* 1883–94.

Bonaini, F.: *Acta Henrici VII imperatoris et monumenta quaedam alia suorum temporum historiam illustrantia.* 2 vols. Florence, 1877.

Kotzschke, R.: *Quellen zur Geschichte der ostdeutschen Kolonisation im 12–14 Jahrhundert.* Leipzig, 1912.

Krammer, M.: *Quellen zur Geschichte der deutschen Königswahl und des Kurfürstenkollegs.* 2 vols. Leipzig, 1912.

(ii) Chronicles, etc.

Hermannus Altahensis : *Annales.* Ed. Jaffé, P. *Monumenta Germaniae Historica.* Scriptores. Vol. xvii (continuatio in vol. xxiv).

Johannes Victoriensis : *Liber certarum historiarum.* Ed. Schneider, F. Scriptores rerum Germanicarum in usum Scholarum. Hanover, 1909.

Matthias von Neuenburg : *Chronica.* Ed. Hofmeister, A. *Mon. Germ. Hist.,* new series, vol. iv. 1924 ff.

B. Modern Works

Cambridge Medieval History, vols. vi and vii, relevant chapters.

Fisher, H. A. L. : *The Mediaeval Empire.* 2 vols. London, 1898.

Hampe, K. : *Deutsche Kaisergeschichte in der Zeit der Salier und Staufer.* Leipzig, 1923.

Hauck, A. : *Kirchengeschichte Deutschlands.* Vols. iv, v. Leipzig, 1904–20.

Huillard-Bréholles, J. L. A. : *Historia diplomatica Friderici II.* 12 vols, introduction, in vol. xii. Paris, 1852–61.

Kington(-Oliphant), T. L. : *History of Frederick II, Emperor of the Romans.* 2 vols. London, 1862.

Lindner, T. : *Deutsche Geschichte unter den Habsburgen und Luxemburgern.* 2 vols. Stuttgart, 1888–93.

Redlich, O. : *Rudolf von Habsburg.* Innsbruck, 1903.

Schirmacher, F. W. : *Die letzten Hohenstaufen.* Göttingen, 1871.

Barraclough, Glotz, as for Chapter III.

CHAPTER VIII

THE OUTSKIRTS OF EUROPE IN THE THIRTEENTH
CENTURY

The Iberian
Peninsula

WHILE the three central countries, Germany, Italy, and France, provide the main currents of medieval history and give the direction to medieval culture, the outlying lands of Europe both exercised an important influence on that culture and history and are of high interest in themselves : they form an integral part of Europe and are indispensable elements of its fortunes and civilization. The most active and influential of these outskirts was the Iberian peninsula.

The
Almohades

At the beginning of the thirteenth century the peninsula was still debatable ground between East and West. The Berber Moslem sect of the Almohades had in the previous century established an empire over all North Africa as far as the Egyptian frontier, and in the meantime had conquered Moorish Spain. A stubborn war began with the Christian states of the north, and in 1196 seemed to be renewing the Moorish predominance when the army of the Almohade Yakūb routed Alfonso VIII, King of Castile, at Alarcos. But the Spanish Christians only made greater efforts in what was now an official crusade. Finally, on July 16, 1212, the

Battle of
Las Navas
de Tolosa

fate of the peninsula was decided at the battle of Las Navas de Tolosa to the south of the dividing range of the Sierra Morena. There Alfonso VIII, assisted for once by all the Christian kings, save his namesake of Leon, inflicted a crushing defeat on the Almohade Mohammed in person. The tables were turned and a renewed Christian advance could begin. The kingdom of Leon, in 1228, reached the River Guadiana at Badajoz, while Portugal did the same at Elvas. The Almohade dominion, too, after the death of Yūsuf in 1223 began to break up both in Spain and Africa, and the quarrels of rival Moorish potentates offered the best opportunity for Spanish reconquest.

For a time, however, the Christian kingdoms were hampered by their own dissensions. Peter II of Aragon and Catalonia (1196–1213) was more concerned with his interests in Languedoc than with the Moors. He disputed the suzerainty of a large territory with the Count of Toulouse, and possessed directly in right of his wife the lordship of Montpellier. Here arose a difficulty : Peter and the Catalans were orthodox ; his vassals and partisans north of the Pyrenees were largely Albigensian heretics. Peter placated Pope Innocent III, so far as he was personally concerned, by a pilgrimage in 1204 to Rome, where he accepted Aragon and Catalonia as fiefs of the Papacy, but this angered his nobles, who denounced the act as invalid, and it did not eventually prevent the Albigensian Crusade. The Catholic Peter at last took arms to defend his feudal vassals, and met his death in the defeat of Muret in 1213. His son James I the Conqueror (1213–76) was then a minor in the hands of Simon de Montfort, and it was only Innocent III's pressure which secured his release. His lands were in the power of indisciplined nobles ; not for some years was he old enough to assert himself, and after a struggle in which his shrewdness and courage were conspicuous he became in 1227 master of his States. In 1247 he was able to issue at the Cortes of Huesca a written code of law for Aragon, the *Fueros de Huesca*, which were influenced by the Roman Civil Law, and formed the basis of subsequent legislation. Even in Catalonia, which held fast to the ancient code of the *Usatges*, new laws were affected by the Roman jurisprudence.

In Castile, the deaths of Alfonso VIII in 1214 and of his son Henry I, still a minor, in 1217 left another father and son rivals for the throne. Ferdinand III (1217–52) was the son of Alfonso VIII's daughter Berenguela by Alfonso IX, King of Leon (1188–1230), but this marriage had been annulled, and Alfonso IX claimed the Castilian crown himself as heir male. In the civil war St. Ferdinand gained, however, the upper hand, and in 1230 he inherited Leon from his father. Thus the two kingdoms of Castile and Leon were finally united, and central Spain could exert its full strength against the Moslems.

The war had already begun in 1225. Ferdinand was even the ally of the Almohade ruler, now confined to Morocco.

Conquests
from the
Moors

The Spanish Moors were split into three or more discordant kingdoms. In 1236 Ferdinand captured the ancient Moorish capital of Cordova. The King of Murcia, Ibn Hud, was assassinated and his subjects rather than submit to their rivals of Granada acknowledged Castilian suzerainty (1241). In 1246 Granada, too, became a vassal-state, ceding Jaen by the treaty, and the conquest of Seville in 1248 brought Ferdinand's frontier to the sea at Cadiz. Estremadura had already been annexed by Alfonso IX, and as the Kings of Portugal were pressing south at the same time (1238-40), finally conquering the Algarve in 1250, the Moors of Andalusia were expelled from the south-west. Meantime, James of Aragon conquered Majorca and the other Balearic Islands in 1229-35, an acquisition which strengthened the Catalan sea-power, and gave Christendom a completer hold on the western Mediterranean. Then he turned south and between 1233 and 1245 subdued the Moors of Valencia, which he made a third kingdom of the Aragonese and Catalan federation. The respective limits of Castile and Aragon were fixed in 1244 by treaty. When a revolt of Murcia caused its annexation by Alfonso X of Castile with James's help in 1266, only Granada was left to Moorish rule in Spain.

Granada

The kingdom of Granada had been put together by Mohammed I Ibn-al-Ahmar (1232-73), the founder of the Nasrid dynasty, from fragments of the Almohade realm. Entrenched in the Alpujarras Mountains, with the coastland of Málaga and the fertile valley of the Xenil, it was hard to conquer, and in its isolation little dangerous. There for over two centuries, Moorish civilization lasted with little change, centred round the palace of Alhambra which Mohammed I founded. In spite of intestine strife its prosperity and culture formed a vivid contrast to the more primitive life and turbulent poverty of Christian Castile.

Alfonso X
the Learned

The internal history of the Iberian kingdoms, after the cessation of the great conquests from the Moors, was marked by internecine wars between them, with little lasting results, and by baronial turbulence, without, save in Aragon, the development of feudal organization and without any consistent trend of constitutional progress. Alfonso X the Learned of Castile (1252-85) deserved his sobriquet, but was not the man to cope with a warlike aristocracy, richly endowed with Moorish lands, and the scarcely less turbulent townsmen. His services to Spanish jurisprudence by the issue of his code, *Las Partidas*, were great, he was a historian and a poet, and he wisely endeavoured to keep peace with his immediate neighbours; but his learned vanity led him to waste his energies on pursuing the mirage of the Holy Roman Empire during the Great Interregnum, and he was unfortunate in the death of his eldest son Ferdinand (1275). As a legist, he supported the succession of his grandson, in accordance with the then barely established doctrine of " representation " of the dead heir, while his second son, Sancho, demanded the inheritance. Hence came a series of civil wars. At first Alfonso gave way to the general wish of his subjects, disregarded his legal views, and declared Sancho his heir. But the " Infantes de la Cerda," the The Infantes children of the dead Ferdinand, maintained their rights, de la Cerda supported by their maternal kinsman, the King of France, and Alfonso proposed to buy them off by creating a vassal kingdom of Jaen for the eldest of them. Meanwhile, the wars with Granada led to one reverse after another and to need of money, which the king, denied fresh taxes, endeavoured to supply by debasing the coinage. Sancho, determined to yield nothing to his nephews, allied himself with Mohammed II of Granada, and in 1282 summoned a Cortes at Valladolid, which appointed him regent with full powers. Alfonso replied by declaring Ferdinand de la Cerda his heir and by obtaining somewhat incongruous allies for himself: Pope Martin IV placed Sancho and his supporters under interdict and excommunication; the Sultan of Morocco, the enemy of Granada, sent an army for a while. Alfonso's younger sons, Don John and Don James, now returned to his side from their brother's, and, when he died worn out in April 1284, he left them the vassal kingdoms of Murcia and Badajoz. Sancho IV, however, secured general recognition, Sancho IV but, as he disregarded the cessions to his brothers in his father's will and was himself treacherous, his reign was troubled with war within and without, from the Infantes de la Cerda, his neighbours of Morocco and Aragon, and his nobles.

The history of little Navarre, penned up in the Pyrenees Navarre and inherited in 1234 by a French dynasty in the person of

Theobald of Champagne, may be passed over; that of Portugal is a variant of Castile's, but here the struggle with the over-wealthy and over-powerful Church was in the forefront.

Portugal

Sancho I

This began in the reign of Sancho I the Populator (1185–1211), who, if he did not notably enlarge his kingdom in the Moorish wars, fortified the frontier along the Tagus and colonized the deserted borderland. Sancho fell out with the Bishops of Oporto and Coimbra, but was quelled on his deathbed by the redoubtable Innocent III by means of an interdict. Portugal was admitted to be tributary to the Papacy. The contest had been marked by a composition of Julian the Portuguese Chancellor, maintaining the doctrine of the complete poverty of the clergy advanced fifty years earlier by Arnold of Brescia. Sancho's son Afonso II (1211–23) paid the arrears of tribute and admitted the Canon Law as superior to and overriding secular enactments. He shared in the victory of Las Navas de Tolosa, which gained him the support of Alfonso VIII of Castile, when civil war broke out and Alfonso IX of Leon assisted the rebels. The ground of dispute was Afonso II's claim that Crown lands could not be alienated, which he alleged as his reason for not carrying out his father's grants to his brothers. Afonso weathered the first outbreak, but about 1220 he enraged both clergy and nobles together. The first were angered because the king endeavoured to enforce a law of mortmain, decreed in 1211 against further acquisitions of land by the exempt Church; the second by his inquest into the titles to fiefs. The general hostility involved brought the king to submission. This meant that an unhealthy condition of affairs continued, and his son Sancho II (1223–48), although the interdict imposed by Pope Honorius III was removed and he won fresh territory from the Moors, was too weak a ruler to prevent matters growing worse between the greed of the clergy and the turbulence of the nobles. On one occasion Sancho fully submitted to the Church, but the anarchy increased. The prelates and other malcontents appealed to Pope Innocent IV, who took action in 1245. As suzerain of Portugal he deprived the childless king, for obdurate incompetence, of his royal functions, and appointed his brother Afonso, Count of Boulogne, curator of the realm. It was a remarkable precedent, for Innocent distinguished

Afonso II

Constitutional and Ecclesiastical Conflicts

Sancho II

the royal office from its holder with legal clearness and advanced the doctrine of the State. Sancho vainly resisted and died in exile.

As king on Sancho's death, however, Afonso III (1248–79) Afonso III continued his predecessor's offences against the Church and its immunities. He was of sterner metal than his brother, patient and determined, with a policy. When the Algarve was conquered from the Moors he disputed its possession with Alfonso the Learned of Castile. In 1253 he secured it by marrying Alfonso's natural daughter in his own wife's lifetime, and actually years after obtained the legitimation of the offspring of this match from Pope Urban IV. In 1267 by a treaty of Badajoz the Algarve was finally ceded to Portugal and the frontier with Castile fixed for centuries. Meantime Afonso III had gained the firm support of the townsmen, the natural favourers of a strong monarch. They appeared in the Cortes from 1254 onwards. Taxes and dues were to be paid in money and not in kind. In 1261 the pernicious royal right of debasing the coinage every seven years was commuted for a lump sum payable in each reign, while new taxes could only be granted by the Cortes. As the result of an Inquest in 1258 a resumption of alienated Crown lands, which had either been sold or left uncultivated by the grantees, was ordered in 1265 with compensation to the buyers. The rich Military Orders, a feature of Portuguese, as of Castilian, history, were made subject to taxation. The bishops were up in arms, and appealed to the Pope. Afonso, however, had the people behind him. He persecuted the clergy in return. When the Pope excommunicated and deposed him in 1277, and laid Portugal under interdict, nothing happened. Afonso, indeed, made a death-bed repentance, but his son Dinis (1279–1325) followed Dinis his footsteps with less violence. At last in 1289 he succeeded in arranging a Concordat with the Papacy, which Concordat maintained some part of what the kings had striven for, with the especially the prohibition of the cession of still more land Church to the Church.

Unlike the other Iberian states, the composite monarchy Aragon of Aragon, with its Mediterranean coastline, took a continuous part in general European history. The rule of James I was, indeed, marked by a retreat from France, James I

and an alienation from the Languedoc lands. In 1258 by
the treaty of Corbeil northern Catalonia, as we saw,[1] was
freed from French suzerainty, but James only retained
Montpellier of his French lands to the north of the Pyrenees.
Already in 1245 by the death of his cousin Raymond Berengar
IV the county of Provence had passed from the Aragonese
house to the Capetians by the succession of Charles of Anjou.
But under James the trade relations across the sea grew in
volume, and he married his heir, Peter, significantly to
Constance, daughter of Manfred of Sicily. Unhappily he
gave his youngest son James II an appanage in the kingdom of Majorca, along with Roussillon and Montpellier,
which for long was a source of civil war and of weakness
to the elder line of Aragon.   Peter III the Great (1276–85),
a warrior and statesman, aimed at a west Mediterranean
realm by the conquest of Sicily in right of his wife Constance,
and withstood successfully the Papacy and France combined
in the War of the Vespers.[2]   The light-armed professional
soldiers of his country (*almugàvers*) became famous. Yet
he diminished the royal power.   Inland Aragon proper disliked the war and its sacrifices, and he was compelled to
grant the *Privilegio General* in 1283, which established the
liberties of nobles and towns.   His weaker son Alfonso III
the Liberal (1285–91), when making the abortive peace of
Canfranc (1288) with France, the Papacy, and Naples, was
obliged to submit to further tutelage from his Aragonese
subjects by the *Privilegio de la Unión*, granted to the league
of nobles and towns. James II, the King of Sicily, who
succeeded Alfonso (1291–1327), inherited these restrictions,
and as we have seen abandoned Sicily in 1295. But at
least he gained the friendship of the Pope, and conjured the
French danger. He even in the end maintained his influence
in the Mediterranean, for his brother Frederick II after all
kept Sicily and he himself was granted the kingdom of
Sardinia to conquer if he could. Meantime the Catalan fleet
and the *almugàvers* as well as the heavy armed Catalan
troopers remained redoubted everywhere. The Grand Catalan Company in the Balkans and the Catalans in Italy under
Diego de la Rat made history, however unhappily for those
lands.

Treaty of
Corbeil

Kingdom of
Majorca

Peter III
the Great

*Privilegio
General*

Alfonso III

*Privilegio
de la Unión*

James II

[1] See above, Chap. V, pp. 115–116.   [2] See above, Chap. IV, pp. 92–93.

The social characteristics of the Iberian kingdoms were determined partly by their isolation from the rest of Europe, remote save Catalonia from the consequences of the spread of Frankish institutions, and partly by the fact of recon- quest from the Moors. Feudalism proper, with its jurisdic- tions, never took root among them, with the exception of Catalonia. The peasants were largely serfs, but mixed with a large proportion of free farmers—Moors, Christian Mozarabs, and settlers in waste lands ; and the towns early obtained a warlike independence. Even in Catalonia, where full serf- dom flourished, the middle class of townsmen and farmers was exceptionally and early strong. Yet anarchic, warlike conditions produced throughout the peninsula a quasi-feudal nobility, strong in lands and privileges, and the wealthy Church possessed the familiar immunities. Hence local and class independence tethered the monarchy as much as in any really feudal state. Central assemblies of the powerful classes grew up in the several kingdoms earlier than else- where in Europe under the name of Cortes. For the first time they met as " Estates " of the realm, separated by class and vocation, rather than by the conditions of tenure. The three divisions of the Cortes, nobles, clergy, and towns, claimed a share in the government and taxation and an in- fluence on royal law-making. In the triple state of Aragon the three separate Cortes, and occasionally their joint meet- ing, enjoyed a special degree of power. In Aragon proper the monarchy was at times almost in leading strings : about 1300 the dignitary called Justicia Mayor, named by the king but closely connected with the Cortes, supervised the royal courts ; the lesser nobles added a fourth branch to the usual three " houses " of prelates, barons, and townsmen, and the Cortes shared in legislation after Peter III's time and watched by means of a permanent committee, the Diputación, over the royal administration. In feudal Catalonia, where there were only the three houses of the Cortes,[1] they shared in legislation and supervised finance. If in all the Iberian kingdoms, Castile and Leon, Navarre, and Portugal, the monarchy was checked by its turbulent subjects, in the Aragonese complex it was definitely limited at the beginning

[1] Representatives of the towns sat in the Catalan Cortes from 1218, a later date than in Castile.

of the fourteenth century. To sum up, as in the rest of
Spanish medieval history, the usual ingredients of medieval
society were all present, but subject to unusual influences
and blended in exceptional proportions. Spain was more
advanced and more primitive at one and the same time.

Scandinavia, on the other hand, in the extreme north
is rather in the nature of a backwater, responding slowly
and imperfectly to the common currents and tides of the
medieval sea. Denmark, indeed, appeared for a brief period
once more as a great power. Counselled by the great Archbishop Absalon of Lund, King Canute VI (1182–1202) made
the semi-Slavonic southern coast of the Baltic, Mecklenburg
and Pomerania, subject to Denmark, and had conquered the
German county of Holstein, while even the free sea-towns
of Lübeck and Hamburg submitted to him. His brother
Waldemar II the Victorious (1202–41) conquered heathen
Esthonia and part of Livonia to the east in alliance with
the crusading Knights of the Sword, and dominated the
Baltic Sea. But the king's capture during a hunting-party
in 1223 by the German Count Henry of Schwerin, whom he
had expelled from his lands, broke up his dominion. The
Danish regent and then the liberated Waldemar himself
received two crushing defeats at the hands of the Saxons
at Mölln in 1225 and Bornhöved in 1227, and the southern
frontier of Denmark was fixed at the ancient limit of the
River Eider. In 1238 the king lost his share of Livonia
to the Teutonic Knights.

These wars hastened the internal development of Denmark. The kings needed mounted knights, and rewarded
them with fiscal rights and jurisdiction, i.e. with fiefs. The
leidang or levy of freeholders for war became converted into
a composition tax, and the new feudal nobility, little to be
distinguished from their German neighbours, became the
chief power in the diets and the land, while the peasants
fell into serfdom. The rising towns on the royal demesne
were no make-weight, and the Church was concerned with
its own privileges. Troubles began with the death of Waldemar the Victorious. There were five sons to be provided
for in Denmark, and the younger took up arms against the
eldest, Eric Ploughpenny (1241–50), with the aid of the
Counts of Holstein and the Swedes. Family ties were not

Scandinavia

Denmark

Internal
Develop-
ment

strong in Scandinavia. Eric earned his name by a new tax on ploughs, much needed by the impoverished monarchy and very unpopular. When Eric was murdered, his brother Abel (1250–2), who may have caused his death, was elected king, only to fall in battle with the Frisians,[1] from whom he attempted to exact the ploughpenny. The next brother to be elected, Christopher I (1252–9), began a violent struggle with the clergy which long outlasted his reign. The king demanded the *leidang* from the Church lands; the Archbishop Jacob Erlandson of Lund (1254–74) not only resisted the tax, but claimed the full independence, indeed the superiority of the Church. When Christopher, who laid hands on the prelates, died, perhaps by poison, he was excommunicate and Denmark under interdict. His son, Eric Clipping, " the Blinker " (1259–86), lost the day to clergy and nobles. In 1282 he was forced to issue a general charter, the first in Danish history. General parliaments were to meet once a year; punishments were only to be inflicted after legal trial. This freedom was only for the nobles and the Church, for the peasants sank into serfdom. Eric himself was soon after murdered by his nobles, and left a debilitated monarchy to his son Eric Menved (1286–1319). *Restriction of the Monarchy*

In Norway the progress of feudalism was slower but perceptible. King Sverre succeeded in replacing the local chieftains by his own sheriffs. After Sverre, the remnants of the old nobles of pre-monarchic origin coalesced with the king's vassals to whom he granted land for military service, and formed a new powerful class, but the peasants retained their freedom. The question of Church privilege remained the chief source of dispute[2] in spite of a temporary settlement under his son Hakon (1217–63), who had a hard fight for the crown in his first five years and did not overthrow his last rival till 1240. He gained over the Pope and was crowned by a papal legate in 1247 in derogation of the claims of the Archbishop of Nidaros. At the same time a compromise was effected with the clergy, by which free election and clerical immunity were guaranteed to the Church and the bishops' right of electing the king on the failure of a direct heir was abandoned, while the competence of the secular courts in secular matters was admitted. Hakon *Norway. The New Nobility*

---

[1] In modern Schleswig.   [2] Cf. above, Chap. II, p. 49.

obtained the submission of the Norse colonies of Iceland
and Greenland to his crown (1261-2), but he died in the
midst of an unsuccessful war with Scotland over the Hebrides.
His son Magnus the Lawmender (1263-80) made peace by
the cession (1266) of these islands to the Scots. With the
Church, too, he bought a temporary peace, when the Archbishop of Nidaros renewed his claims, by economic concessions. Against these surrenders may be set his creation in
1276 of a uniform law for the whole of Norway. His son
Eric the Priest-hater (1280-99), under the influence of the
nobles, renewed the conflict with the Church. The archbishop was exiled, and in the final compromise of 1290 the
concessions wrung from King Magnus were revoked. Meantime, in spite of its apparent power, the vassal nobles were
already overawing the kingship. As in Denmark, the efforts
of the Church to tame the barbaric violence of the kings
and nobles were partly frustrated by its own greed, and also
undermined the strength of the monarchy, in which lay the
best hope of advance.

Sweden   In Sweden, much the same results were reached through
the strife of the rival houses of Sverker and St. Eric for the
crown. They both became extinct with the deaths of John I
Sverkersson (1216-22) and Eric XI Ericsson (1222-9, 1234-
50), but the real rulers for some time had been the " earls "
The   of the powerful house of Folkung from the province of Öster-
Folkungs   götland, who held a position not unlike the earlier Frankish
mayors of the palace. In 1250 Earl Birger Magnusson had
long been in control ; his wife was the sister of Eric XI,
and their son Waldemar (1250-75) was elected king under
his father's regency. Earl Birger was an active legislator,
civilizing to some extent the traditional law. He sternly
repressed his fellow nobles ; he was conqueror of west Finland across the Gulf of Bothnia ; he encouraged the settlement of German merchants. What he could not alter was
the turbulent individualism of the nobles, who each fought
for his own hand. On his death (1266), Waldemar was
soon involved in disputes with his brothers, which, aggravated by his own vices, led to his deposition. His brother
King Magnus Barnlock (1275-90), while he renewed the
good order of Earl Birger, gave legal privilege to nobility
by declaring the mounted knights to be tax-free. As the

greater nobility existed already, and the Church was guaranteed the customary immunities, Sweden too approximated to the political conditions of feudal Europe. But, whereas Norway acquired Iceland only and lost the Hebrides to Scotland, Sweden was expanding by the conquest of the alien Finns to the north and east, if it failed in Russia at the defeat of the Neva in 1240. Its iron mines and foreign trade developed. It thus drew ahead as the second Scandinavian power.

While the Scandinavian kingdoms were remote and conservative in their development, they yet belonged, in their civilization and their fortunes, wholly to Western Europe. In contrast, the Slavs to the south of the Baltic Sea and the Magyars of Hungary, if through the influence of the Church and their western neighbours they too belonged to the West, were linked as well by race and geographical situation to Eastern Europe, to Russia and Byzantium, in the history of which they bore a part ; and the history of Russia was more profoundly affected by the true East, by Asia and its peoples, than any other part of Europe. All of them endured the Mongol invasion, and their thirteenth-century history can hardly be told consecutively without first recounting the rise and progress of the last great movement of peoples similar to those in which the West Roman Empire foundered in the fifth century and the states of Western Asia were transformed in the eleventh. *Eastern Europe*

From time immemorial the plains and mountains of Central Asia from the Volga River—one might say the Black Sea—to the Pacific Ocean had been inhabited by nomad tribes of Ural-Altaian or Turanian stock, the many-named peoples of Turks, Huns, Avars, Patzinaks, Bulgars, and others. They were marked off from their neighbours by language, and by habits of life. Their physique displayed the wiry strength, the smooth cheeks, the straight hair, and the " Mongolian fold " at the eyes, of the yellow race ; their languages in their many forms were agglutinative, totally distinct from the Indo-European tongues. In their way of life they were pastoral and hunting nomads, always on horseback, and moving periodically to and fro to summer and winter quarters on the steppes of Asia. Their organization was in families, grouped in " camps " and linked into clans *The Nomads of Central Asia* and wider tribes. Their native religion was a mixture of spirit and ancestor worship. In war their extraordinarily mobile bands of archer-horsemen of dauntless courage were almost irresistible in their combination of elusive tactics and enveloping charges. Few armies could successfully counter this natural generalship of the unwearied nomads. Unhappily, when they emerged from the steppes, they were the deadly foes of all higher civilization, of which they were by their ancestral specialized life, their savagery and reckless greed, incapable. They destroyed and abased the peoples and cultures they conquered. Long mixture of race and acclimatization among their victims did indeed modify their physique and characteristics ; even so, however, their rule had a sterilizing effect. In nearer Asia under their sway civilization fell to a lower level, and proved for many centuries incapable of recovery and advance.

Over-population, the temporary rise of a conquering chief, and the expulsion of defeated tribes in internecine warfare seem to have been the main causes of their occasional over-flow to agricultural and civilized lands ; and, the more they were known to the Turanians, the attraction of those countries of wealth and plenty to the nomads of the barren steppes was the more potent. Once a wave of conquest was set going, it spread wider and wider till its own extension en-feebled it and made the checks then received a final limit to its progress. Such a wave was the world-changing Mongol Empire of the thirteenth century.

The Mongols. Jenghiz Khan

The Mongols in the twelfth century were a well-defined collection of Altaian tribes inhabiting the territory round about the Rivers Onon and Kerulen to the north of China. Among them arose the insatiable conqueror, Temujin, later known as Jenghiz Khan, " the Inflexible Lord " or Autocrat. His earlier years were passed in incessant fighting with his neighbours. It was not till 1203 that he united under his rule the tribes to the north of the Gobi desert by the con-quest of the Kerait Turks, whose Christian king gave rise to the Western legend of Prester John. His rule now spread on all sides, absorbing the nomad tribes of Turks, who began to form the bulk of his armies. Among his Turkish subjects were the Tatars, whose name, punned as Tartars, " the hellish," became the term under which the Mongols and their allies were known to Europe. Temujin adopted the ancient Turkish capital of Karakorum as his residence, and in 1206 assumed the imperial style of Jenghiz Khan. He now aimed at two objectives : the conquest of the ancient civilized land of China, and the conquest of the West. The Chinese war was long to outlast his reign. There were then two empires in China : that of the South under the native dynasty of Sung, and that of the North under the Tungus dynasty of Kin, "the Golden," themselves of nomad race. Jenghiz began the conquest of the Kin; it was completed under his successor Ogodai in 1234. War then was begun with the Sung; and ended in the subjugation of all China by Khubilai by 1279 : Khubilai, already Great Khan of the Mongols, became Emperor of China as the first of the Yuen dynasty. *Conquest of China*

The second objective of the Mongols was the West. There the recently established Turkish kingdom of the kings of Khwārazm (Khiva) was swiftly overthrown from 1219 to 1221. This meant the annexation of Transoxiana and Northern Persia, while the remnant of the Khwārazmians were driven westwards and eventually, as we have seen,[1] made an end of the Latin possession of Jerusalem, the first repercussion of the Mongol Empire on Europe. *Overthrow of the Khwārazmians*

In the midst of his victories Jenghiz Khan died on August 18, 1227. He was the most ruthless of conquerors, the "Scourge of God" to the unhappy peoples he massacred. But, besides his obvious military ability, he was a man of imperial ideas. Within the Mongol frontiers there should be peace and trade; all religions were protected; he had a respect for the learning and civilization he harmed so greatly. The government he established was a kind of federation of groups of tribes ruled by his descendants under the suzerainty of one of them, the Great Khan. On his death his son Ogodai (1229–41) ruled as Great Khan at Karakorum, Juji took the lands from the Aral sea westwards, Chagatai Transoxiana and Eastern Turkestan. Meanwhile the empire kept expanding. By 1233 all Persia was subjugated. In 1243 the Seljūks of Rūm were crushed at Kuza-Dagh and became vassals of the Mongols; they never recovered from this defeat, and by the end of the century *The Mongol Empire* *Conquest of Persia and Rūm*

[1] See above, Chap. VI, p. 134.

Rūm was broken up among petty emirs.   In 1244 the Chris-

End of the
Abbasid
Caliphate
tian King of Little Armenia submitted.   At last, in February 1258 Hūlāgū, grandson of Jenghiz Khan and Il-Khan of the new Mongol state of Persia, captured Baghdad ; he slaughtered the last regnant Abbasid Caliph and devastated Irak beyond recovery.   The richest, most fertile tract of Asia became a desolate land of waste and swamp.   He then

Defeat of
the Mongols
in Syria
attacked Syria, but here the Mongols were at last checked by the Mamlūk victory of Ain-Jālūt : [1] save for the vassal states of Little Armenia and Rūm, their frontiers never reached the Mediterranean.   Nearer Asia, however, had received a blow from which it never revived.   Henceforward, the Christians of Europe rapidly gained upon and surpassed the Moslem East in civilization.   There was, indeed, a rem- nant of the older vigour left at Cairo under the Mamlūks, who set up a shadowy, merely spiritual Abbasid Caliphate, but the power to advance was confined to Europe.

Russia
All the more fateful, therefore, was the event of the Mongol invasion of Europe.   Russia, at the beginning of the thirteenth century, was broken up into a number of principalities under different branches of the house of Rurik. The chief was the Great Prince of Vladímir to the north in Great Russia, the wealthiest the Prince of Galicia in the south-west.   But endless subdivision among the male agnates of the house of Rurik weakened the Russians in spite of the increase of population, and the Cuman Turks held all the steppes to the north of the Black Sea.   It was in Jenghiz

Mongol
Conquest of
the Ukraine
Khan's lifetime that the first Tartar attack on the lands west of the River Volga was made.   Two generals, Jebe and Subutai, crossed the Caucasus from the south and overthrew first the Cumans and their Caucasian neighbours, and then their Russian allies at the battle of the River Kalka near the Sea of Azov in 1223.   The Cumans submitted ; but the death of Jenghiz Khan prevented for a while a second cam- paign.   In 1237, however, Ogodai took up the plan.   He dispatched his nephew Batu " the good-natured," son and heir of Juji, as nominal head of an army which was really under the command of Subutai, the greatest of the Mongol generals.   First, the trading tribe of the Bulgars on the upper Volga were crushed.   Then came the turn of the Russians ;

[1] See above, Chap. VI, p. 134.

town after town was taken and sacked with an atrocity new **Conquest**
to Europe, till in 1240 Kiev, the ancient capital, was also **of Russia**
destroyed. Only Novgorod, the commercial principality in
the north, escaped owing to thé swamps which surround it.
Subutai now devised a plan of campaign, which showed how
superior in strategy and in its efficient execution the Mongols
were to feudal Europe. One Tartar army was to make a
diversion north of the Carpathians and occupy the Polish
and German princes, while the main army under Subutai
himself was to conquer Hungary. In 1241 the northern
army victoriously rode through Poland, sacking Cracow, and
defeated Poles and Germans together under Duke Henry II
of Silesia at Liegnitz on April 9. Then it turned, unmolested **Battle of**
by the Bohemian king, through the Moravian gap to rejoin **Liegnitz**
Subutai in Hungary. Meanwhile, Subutai had crossed the
Carpathians. On April 11 he annihilated the Hungarian
forces under King Béla IV at Mohi on the River Sajó, and **Battle of**
Hungary was delivered to devastation. It seemed as if the **Mohi**
Magyars would form a Mongol province. The West was
alive to its danger, yet appeared paralysed. Pope Gregory
IX had proclaimed one of the many crusades ; the Emperor
Frederick II called Europe to arms in fervid circulars ; but
each was engrossed in their own contest, and defence was
left to the unruly German princes. The Tartars had reached
the Adriatic and Austria when the news of the death of
Ogodai called them to Asia, to the election of a new Great
Khan. They departed ravaging the northern Balkans in **Retreat of**
1242, and they never came back. It took time for the **the Mongols**
emulous descendants of Temujin to elect a new Great Khan,
Guyuk (1246–8) ; the Mongol energies were diverted to
China ; and Batu was no conqueror—he settled down as
Khan of the Golden Horde with his capital at Serai on the **The Golden**
Volga, content to rule from the mouth of the Danube east- **Horde**
wards in the steppes and to be suzerain of the Russian
princes. The danger which Europe escaped was immense,
the sufferings of Asia enormous, yet some good came of the
Mongol rule. For nearly a century the roads, however long,
were open between the Crimea, Syria, and China within the
Mongol federation. The Popes began to hope for the Tartars' conversion ; traders, like the Polo, followed missionary
friars ; much wealth and some knowledge journeyed west-

ward in the wake of the incredible horrors of the Mongol conquests.

Russia under the "Tartar Yoke" To Russia the centuries of the "Tartar Yoke" were an unmitigated disaster. After the devastation of the first conquest, the various principalities existed as Tartar vassals, paying a heavy tribute through Tartar collectors, and growing ever more numerous, as the sons of each prince divided his inheritance. Intrigue and bribery to obtain the necessary Tartar investiture were incessant. None the less there still remained a Great Prince of Vladimir appointed from among the princes by the Great Khan, and the rule of the princes in their principalities grew more despotic; there was a tendency, too, for the lesser princes to become vassals of the greater like the ordinary boyars or nobles. Now that the steppe-land of the nomads was increasing on the South, and Kiev was a border town, the Metropolitan of the Russian Church moved north and in 1300 Vladimir became his see. He was invested by the Tartars, and the Russian Church thus exchanged its former Byzantine dependence on the prince for an autonomous partnership. Meantime the already decaying trade-route from Constantinople to Kiev and the North, which had civilized Russia, was severed, and the land vegetated in isolated barbarism.

The "Tartar Yoke," by practically destroying the unity of Russia, accelerated the formation of all but separate sub-nationalities. **Galicia** The Red Russians of Galicia and the Ukraine for a time flourished till a Tartar raid in 1282 desolated the land, and left it to fall under the sway of its western and **Lithuania** northern neighbours, Poland and Lithuania. The White Russians of the Upper Dnieper fell under the rule of the princes of the heathen Lithuanians. This Balt people, the most primitive in language and manners of all the Indo-European speaking races, were protected behind their marshes and forests from the Mongol raids. In the thirteenth century, under Mindovg (Mindaugas) (1219–63) they became aggressive: they not only conquered White Russia, and resisted the Teutonic Knights, but also raided Poland.

Novgorod The north part of Great Russia formed the wide state of Novgorod, wealthy as the terminus of the Hansa and other western traders in the Baltic, to whom it supplied the furs and other raw products of the north. Novgorod only paid tribute to the Tartars through the Great Prince of Vladimir, whom it generally elected its own prince, for it never became a hereditary principality. It was in reality a republic ruled by trading nobles and a general assembly. Here were won the only Russian victories of the century. In 1240 Prince Alexander Nevski defeated the invading Swedes on the River Neva; in 1242 he overthrew the Teutonic Knights on the frozen Lake of Peipus. Thus the westernization of Russia was repulsed for centuries. When he became Great Prince of Vladimir (1246–63), St. Alexander Nevski looked eastward : he conciliated his Tartar suzerains, to lighten their extortionate dominion; he was the champion of Russia and the Orthodox Church against the encroaching West. His youngest son Daniel (*ob.* 1303) founded the small central principality of Moscow, which was to grow. St. Alexander Nevski

The West Slav country of Poland suffered as much as Russia from the Mongol hordes, but retained its independence. Unlike Russia, by dint of their Latin Christianity and their neighbourhood to Germany, the Poles took part in Western history. They were divided into several principalities under members of the house of Piast, who fought for the dignity of Great Prince at the capital of Cracow. Of these the princes or dukes of the westernmost province of Silesia were already half German when the Tartar invasion broke on the land in 1241. Still worse damage was inflicted in 1259 and later years, so that the divided but unsubdued land was ruined and depopulated. One result was that Silesia became definitely German under its Piast dukes. German settlers poured into town and country; they kept their own law and brought their own more advanced civilization, and spread beyond Silesia eastwards. Przemyslav II of Greater Poland did indeed try to reunite the Poles and was crowned King at Gnesen in 1295; but a foreign competitor, King Wenceslas II of Bohemia, who represented German as well as Czech interests, conquered most of the country and became King (1300–5). On his death the internecine wars and the German infiltration continued. Poland German Immigration

Germany's expansion eastward, however, was most signally manifested in the conquests of the Teutonic Order. Here missionary and crusading ardour combined with the spirit of adventure, the hunger for land and wealth of the The Teutonic Order teeming knights, peasants, and townsmen of Germany. Heathendom still reigned among the Baltic Prussians, Lithuanians, and Letts, and the Finnish Ests of the eastern coast of the Baltic. It was the churchman Albert, a canon of Bremen, who with support from Pope Innocent III and in alliance with Canute VI of Denmark led the first crusade. He founded in 1201 the bishopric and colony of Riga, and instituted the Order of the Knights of the Sword to conquer Livonia, while his Danish ally seized on the Esthonian coast. Slowly they penetrated inland, christianizing and settling in the country in spite of the resistance of the natives, mostly reduced to serfs, and their Russian allies. At last, in 1236 the Order was nearly annihilated by the Semigallians, and turned for rescue to union with the Teutonic Knights in 1237. The Teutonic Order had been founded in 1197, in imitation of the Hospitallers, to defend the Holy Land ; but an eminent Grand Master, the statesman Herman of Salza (1211–39), realized the little scope that the Levant offered.

Conquest of Prussia After a transitory episode in Transylvania, he accepted an offer of Kulm from the Polish Prince Conrad of Mazovia, in return for waging war against the fierce Prussians who had been tormenting their Christian neighbours by their raids. In 1229 the Teutonic Knights took up the struggle. Poles, Pomeranians, and German princes joined in the crusade, which was systematically organized by land and sea. By 1241 Prussia between the Vistula and the Pregel was conquered and fortified by the Knights as a fief held from Pope and Emperor. In Livonia and Kurland, meanwhile, the advance was resumed, but the defeat of Liegnitz in 1241 at the hands of the Mongols, in which the Teutonic Knights and Poles shared, encouraged the Prussians and the endangered Slavs to resist. St. Alexander Nevski, as we saw, put a bound to the Order's Russian expansion in the battle of Lake Peipus. Sventopelk of Pomerella roused the newly-won Prussia to a general massacre of Germans. Yet the Order held out, and in 1254 a fresh crusade, led by Ottokar II of Bohemia, subdued the land to the Memel, and founded the new town of Königsberg in the king's honour.

The aggression of the Order on Samogitia, the Lithuanian land between the Memel and Kurland, however, brought about a new conflict, in which Mindovg of Lithuania was

the chief foe and the Prussians, once more in revolt, shared.
The Knights were defeated at Durben in 1260, but retrieved
the disaster. The war, which lasted twenty-three years,
was one of extermination and large parts of Prussia became
void of inhabitants. It ended by 1283 in the consolidation
of the land under the Teutonic Knights. The Grand Master
himself took up his residence at Marienburg in 1309, a sign
that the Levantine mission of the Order was finally abandoned. Pomerella meantime, between the Vistula and
Pomerania, had been annexed by 1310. Thus a new State
was added to Europe, the culmination of the German expansion eastward which had begun under Otto the Great.
It was governed by an oligarchy of professed Knights, and Government
drew much of its resources from the endowments of the of the Order
Order in Germany. Below the Knights was a numerous
aristocracy of immigrant German nobles. In Prussia the
peasantry, too, were mainly immigrants from populous Germany attracted by unusually free and favourable conditions
of tenure ; but in Livonia the peasants were ill-used Lettish
serfs. The trading towns were prosperous German settlements, members of the Hansa league. In all this prosperity,
however, there were two dangers : the persistent war with
Lithuania, threatened in its existence, and the growing
enmity of Poland, once the Order's ally, but now cheated
of their common gains and cut off from the Baltic by the
annexation of Pomerella.

While the history of the Teutonic Order shows the forcible Bohemia
expansion of Germany eastward, that of Bohemia displays
the successful maintenance of a Slav State, which yet was
in close connexion with Germany and was strongly affected
by German cultural influences and by ambitions of its own
tending alternately in German and Slav directions. Most
of all the princes of the Empire the ruler of Bohemia profited
by the civil war between Philip of Swabia and Otto IV.
Duke Ottokar I (1197–1230) finally secured the title of king
in 1198, and obtained in 1212 a Golden Bull from the Emperor Frederick II, by which his feudal duties were reduced
to a minimum and the bishoprics of Bohemia were recognized
as held from him. His grandson Ottokar II (1253–78) Ottokar II
aimed at being the greatest German prince. On the extinction of his kinsmen, the Babenberg Dukes of Austria, he

claimed and eventually conquered their lands of Austria and
Styria ; Carinthia and Carniola fell to him in 1269 ; in these
years of the Great Interregnum he was reputed to be one of
the seven Electors to the imperial crown, in virtue of his
office of Chief Butler of the Empire.[1] With dominions which
forecast those of the later house of Habsburg, his aims too
resembled theirs and he hoped for election as King of the
Romans. But Rudolf of Habsburg secured the prize, and
on Ottokar's resistance attacked him with the full support
of the jealous German princes. A first war in 1276 resulted
in the loss of all Ottokar's conquests ; a second, when Hungary also attacked him, ended in his defeat and death on
the Marchfeld by the Danube on August 26, 1278. The
real strength of Bohemia with its dependent margravate of
Moravia was, however, little affected. Ottokar's son Wenceslas II (1278–1305) could aspire to eastern ambitions ; he
became Duke of Silesia ; in 1300 he was crowned King of
Poland ; next year he set up his son Wenceslas as claimant
King of Hungary. This meant war with the alarmed King
of the Romans, Albert, as well as in Hungary, but Wenceslas
II died in the midst of it and his son Wenceslas III, who
abandoned Hungary, was murdered while preparing a
campaign in Poland in 1306. With him the house of
Přemysl, which had ruled Bohemia for centuries, became
extinct.

Government of Bohemia

The rule of the Přemyslids in the thirteenth century
had been marked by the steady feudalizing and Germanizing
of Bohemia. From a patriarchal Slav monarchy it became
a Western State. The Church attained its independence in
spiritual jurisdiction. First the Church and then the greater
landowners acquired feudal jurisdiction over their estates.
The peasantry fell under the sway of private lords, but
largely owing to the influence of favoured German immigrants were preserved as yet from true serfdom. The towns,
especially in Moravia on the trade-route from the Mediterranean to the Baltic, were largely the strongholds of privileged
German burghers, and the court itself was as much German
as Czech. Yet the kingdom retained its national identity.
The judicial and political assemblies of the nobles were
becoming national diets, and the Crown, wealthy with the

[1] See above, Chap. VII, p. 141.

silver-mines of Kutná Hora (Kuttenberg), in spite of feudalism developed a central administration.

Last of these outlying members of Europe comes the **Hungary**
anomalous kingdom of Hungary. Here there was a medley
of races surpassing any other in Europe—the Magyars in the
central plain, subject Slavs and Vlachs on the mountainous
fringes and in the south, German and other immigrants
already filtering in. These had been held together by two
institutions : the monarchy of the house of Árpád, supported
by its prestige and enormous landed possessions, and the
ancient Magyar clan system. But by 1200 both were already
in decay. The monarchy was impoverished by prodigal
grants to the Church and the great nobles ; the clan tie was
weakening, and a social cleft had arisen between the over-
mighty barons and the lesser nobles or knightly class ; the
plain freeman was gravitating towards serfdom. Under the
weak rule of Andrew II (1203–35) this decay led to new
developments. The lesser nobles banded together in county-
assemblies, one for each administrative county of the realm,
and in 1222 the king was forced to promulgate the Golden **The Golden**
Bull—a kind of fundamental law—which safeguarded the **Bull**
rights of the nobility as a whole and the status of the knightly
class. The king was to summon the diet of nobles—prelates,
magnates, and knights—every year ; they were to be tax-
free, they were only to be tried before the independent court
of the " Count Palatine " ; they had the right of rebellion
if the Golden Bull was infringed. On the other hand, the
" counts " of the counties were not to be hereditary, but
nominated royal officials like the English sheriffs—a provision
as much in the interests of the lesser nobles as of the Crown.
This limited monarchy, however, was not sufficient to conjure
the growing anarchy produced by the decay of the older
system and the rise of new powers. King Béla IV (1235–70)
struggled valiantly. He introduced in 1239 fresh colonists
and confusion in granting lands to the nomad heathen
Cumans, fleeing from the Black Sea steppes to escape the
Mongols. But the terrible Tartar invasion of 1241 [1] and its
devastations wrecked his efforts, and under his infant grandson Ladislas IV (1272–90), half a Cuman and half a heathen,
anarchy prevailed. Civil war followed his death between

[1] See above, p. 167.

the male heir, Andrew III (1290–1301), and the next of kin,
Charles Martel, the son of Charles the Lame of Naples.
Although, or perhaps because, his rival was upheld by the
Papacy, Andrew III was the victor.   Real power, however,
had fallen into the hands of a few magnates ruling over vast
tracts of the kingdom in practical independence.   It was at
the same time the last predominance of the clan system and
the result of the unchecked growth of a class of over-mighty
landed barons.   With the extinction of the house of Árpád
in Andrew's person, a disputed succession added to the
anarchy of these local potentates.

The feud-
alizing of
East Central
Europe

A common characteristic of all these frontier lands of
Europe, save Russia, is the testimony they provide to the
continued expansion of Western Christendom in the thirteenth
century with its secular framework of feudal civilization.
In Spain it was an advance of Romance Europe against the
Moors, in Prussia an advance of Germany against non-
Teutonic heathen, which completed the formation of a new
Germany beyond the Elbe, and thus it was a movement of
epoch-making importance for modern times.   But the steady
reception of Western feudalism by the Slavs and Magyars
in Bohemia, Poland, and Hungary was no less significant.
Though seemingly disintegrating, it was to give these countries a solid, elaborate framework of institutions, which was
capable of civilizing advance, in exchange for more primitive
arrangements which were decaying, and it rendered them
able both to maintain their independence and to take an
effective part in the future development of Europe.   The
feudalizing of east Central Europe was not indeed all gain.
It came later and departed later after its creative power
had ceased : it was never a refuge from worse disorder as
it had been in the West, but only a system suited for a more
elaborate civilized life and a coming national competition ;
their crumbling substance was baked hard in that fire.

Growth of
Constitu-
tionalism

Perhaps the fact of the later reception of the influences
of full-blown feudalism partly accounts for the earliness and
vigour of the constitutionalism of these States.   The conviction of the rights of feudal vassals coalesced in Spain
with the claims of bands of fellow-conquerors and in Central
Europe with a not-yet-forgotten tradition of tribal assemblies.
However this may be, the earliest and most effective system

of Estates, in which the king's Great Council is divided into
" houses " corresponding to the main classes of his vassals,
appears in Spain in the thirteenth century, still limited, it
is to be noted, to barons, prelates, and town-representatives
who were in direct dependence on the Crown.   So, too, the
clearest limitation of the Crown's powers by such an assembly
appears in Aragon, its imitator Sicily, and Hungary.   In
all, no doubt, a moving cause was the need the kings experienced for their subjects' support, but some stress must also
be laid on the instinct, born of frontier war and surviving
earlier tribalism, which impelled the subjects to respond to
the kings' initiative in so political a fashion.

The effects of this expansion on European trade and Emigration
culture are the subject of later chapters, but here should from the
be noted its importance, like that of the Crusades, as a safety- West
valve for the superfluous energies of the West.   Ambitious
prince, adventurous knight, discontented peasant could all
find an outlet there.   It made more possible the advance in
order and government at home in combination of course
with many other causes.   In Germany it helped to hide
political decadence.   When the expansion ceased later, an
era of increased internal and external strife, of problems
without solution, of difficulties to which there seemed to be
no exit, dawned for Europe.

SUGGESTIONS FOR READING ON CHAPTER VIII

I. THE IBERIAN PENINSULA

A. Sources

Three vernacular Catalan chronicles have been translated into English :
James I, The Chronicle of. Trans. Forster, J.   2 vols.   1883.
Muntaner, R., The Chronicle of. Trans. Goodenough, Lady.   2 vols.
Hakluyt Soc.   1920–1.
Desclot, B. : *Chronicle of King Pedro III of Aragon.*   Trans. Critchlow,
F. L.   2 vols.   Princeton, 1928, 1934.

B. Modern Works

Altamira, R. : *Historia de España.*   3rd edn.   Barcelona, 1913–14.
Altamira, R. : *History of Spanish Civilization.*   London, 1930.
Altamira, R. : *Magna Carta and Medieval Spanish Jurisprudence.*   In
Magna Carta Commemorative Essays.   Royal Historical Soc.   London, 1917.
Burke, U. R. : *History of Spain.*   2 vols.   Ed. Hume, M. A.   London,
1900.
Cambridge Medieval History, vols. vi and viii, relevant chapters.

Chaytor, H. J. : *History of Aragon and Catalonia.* London, 1933.

Glotz, ed.: *Histoire Générale, Le Moyen Âge.* Vol. iv, Pt. II. L'Essor des États d'Occident. Paris, 1937.

Lane-Poole, S. : *The Moors in Spain.* Story of the Nations. London, 1889.

Merriman, R. B. : *The Rise of the Spanish Empire.* Vol. i. New York, 1918.

Morse Stephens, H. : *Portugal.* Story of the Nations. London, 1891.

Prestage, E. : *The Royal Power and the Cortes in Portugal.* Watford, 1927.

II. SCANDINAVIA

MODERN WORKS

Allen, C. F. : *Histoire de Danemark.* French trans. Beauvois, E. 2 vols. Copenhagen, 1878.

Cambridge Medieval History, vol. vi, chapter xi.

Gjerset, K. : *History of the Norwegian People.* New York, 1915.

Hallendorf, C., and Schück, A. : *History of Sweden.* Stockholm, 1929.

III. THE MONGOLS

MODERN WORKS

Cahun, L. : *Introduction à l'histoire de l'Asie, Turcs et Mongols.* Paris, 1896.

Cambridge Medieval History, vol. iv, chapter xx.

Curtin, J. : *The Mongols in Russia.* London, 1908.

Grousset, R. : *Histoire de l'Extrême Orient.* 2 vols. Paris, 1929.

Olschki, L. : *Marco Polo's Predecessors.* Baltimore, 1943.

Parker, E. : *A Thousand Years of the Tartars.* 1895.

IV. RUSSIA

MODERN WORKS

Cambridge Medieval History, vol. vii, chapter xxi.

Eck, A. : *Le moyen âge russe.* Paris, 1933.

Kluchevsky, V. O. : *History of Russia.* Vol. i. Trans. Hogarth, C. J. London, 1911.

Pares, Sir B. : *History of Russia.* London, 1926.

Rambaud, A. : *Histoire de Russie.* 5th edn. Paris, 1900.

V. POLAND, LITHUANIA, AND THE TEUTONIC KNIGHTS

MODERN WORKS

Cambridge Medieval History, vol. vi, chapter xiii (B), and vol. vii, chapter ix.

Cambridge History of Poland, vol. i. 1950.

VI. BOHEMIA

MODERN WORKS

Cambridge Medieval History, vol. vi, chapter xiii (A).

Lutzow, Count F. : *Bohemia.* Everyman's Library. London, 1909.

VII. HUNGARY

MODERN WORKS

Cambridge Medieval History, vol. vi, chapter xiii (C) ; vol. viii, chapter xix.

Eckhart, F. : *Introduction à l'histoire hongroise.* Paris, 1928.

Temperley, H. W. V. : The Earlier History of Hungary (in Marczali, H. : *Hungary in the Eighteenth Century.* Cambridge, 1910).

Vambéry, A. : *Hungary.* Story of the Nations. London, 1887.

CHAPTER IX

TOWNSMEN AND PEASANTS, 1200–1382

URING the greater part of the period covered by Increase of Population and Security this volume there was a steady growth in the prosperity, the population, and the organization of the towns of Western Europe. The two main causes of this progress were the steady increase of the population on the land, to which we shall recur, and the steady increase of security which, however imperfect it may seem to-day, had been slowly effected by the continuous efforts of kings and greater potentates and Church, and indeed in some degree by townsman and peasant themselves, during the centuries since A.D. 1000. This meant the multiplication both of the consumers themselves and of their powers of spending, and therefore the increase of their needs beyond the rude productions of a purely self-sufficing community.

This was the mainspring of town prosperity. It is true Growth of Towns that most towns had an agricultural side to their life, and that a market or even a fair could exist for the exchange or purchase of commodities in a mere village. But the normal town manufactured or passed on for an area of the countryside round it the products of specialized labour, and received in turn most or part of the foodstuffs necessary for its own subsistence. The normal town was indeed a small place ; even the great town did not number many thousands of inhabitants, as a rule, in the fourteenth century.

Towns of these centuries may be classified politically or The Free Towns economically, and the classifications in part coincide. As we have seen,[1] there was the town politically free, although the import of this freedom differed : in Italy the free commune was in practice an independent republic ; in Germany, the imperial free city, like Lübeck or Nuremberg, was by 1300 in the same position, along with other towns under bishop or prince which in practice enjoyed the same privi-

[1] Cf. Chap. I, p. 29.

leges ; in France some 200 towns, under the name of *commune* (in the north) or *consulat* (in the south) were in much the same relation to the Crown as was a feudal *seigneur*. It was among these towns, although not by any means in all, that " great " commerce flourished.

Self-Ad-ministrating Towns

The next political grade was formed by the towns possessing by charter some measure, in varying degrees, of self-administration, analogous to the English boroughs although usually inferior in privilege. In these king or feudal lord was always supreme, however he might have limited his power. Below these, as the thirteenth century wore on, *Villes neuves* were the very numerous fresh foundations, *villes neuves* or *bastides* in France, where the rights of self-administration were more restricted, but where the inhabitants were personally free and could sell or leave by will their property. These might be mainly agricultural.

Typical Townsmen. The Craft-gilds

The typical townsman of the typical town was a member of a craft-gild (*métier, arte, Bruderschaft, Zunft*, etc.) ; the butchers, the bakers, the smiths, vintners, carpenters, leather-workers, and the like, each formed little corporations for the regulation and benefit of their craft, for the maintenance of the monopoly of its members in its wares and the prevention of underselling or undue absorption of custom by any single craftsman. Associated with or within each gild was its appropriate charitable and religious confraternity for mutual assistance and devotion. In such a craft-gild there was little essential distinction between employer and employed. The gild was composed of the " masters," each independent in his business, and assisted in it by apprentices (boys bound to him to learn the craft), and perhaps by journeymen (fully trained craftsmen who had not yet set up for themselves as masters). The number of apprentices and journeymen a master might employ was limited, they lived with him on a domestic footing, the entry into the ranks of the master was not too difficult, and the whole régime was that of a small domestic industry, monopolistic and stable, where the ruling conception was that each crafts-man should be able to live according to his status. The raw material of the trade was stinted, at least in theory, to its members, quality and price of goods, hours of work and methods were prescribed and supervised by the gild officials, and in the known market of a limited area something like the " just price " of medieval theologians, which should apportion to each his fair remuneration, was possible to fix. That countless evasions and delinquencies should exist in practice was natural enough, but in the ordinary small town the system, unfavourable to initiative and improvement and vexatiously inquisitive and hidebound as it was, roused little discontent. The craft-gild defended and disciplined its members, who to other crafts were consumers. It was suitable to a society whose methods and ideals changed but slowly.

The government and institutions of the towns were almost infinitely varied, but here, too, a rough grouping may be observed and certain general tendencies. The lowest grade, the *villes neuves*, were by the nature of the case equalitarian : their limited privileges and functions were shared by all the inhabitants. The privileged towns and the towns politically free were at the beginning of the thirteenth century still usually in name a kind of democracy of the bourgeois, but in most of them some kind of oligarchy Oligarchic was the real practice, which tended in the subsequent decades Government to be defined by law. Sometimes the ownership of real property within the town was the qualification, sometimes membership of the merchant gild, both always resulting in the political monopoly of the wealthier burgesses. In the Low Countries and Germany there arose from these a privileged caste of hereditary governors (*lignages, Geschlechter,* etc.), who have received the convenient modern name of patricians. They retained power by the narrowest system of co-optation, and their administration, at first marked by considerable public spirit and efficiency, degenerated as the thirteenth century wore on, into a narrow class selfishness and corruption, which led to bitter discontent among their subjects and to riot and revolt. St. Louis was obliged to intervene in the French communes to check tyranny and disorder and to remedy financial waste and insolvency.

These troubles were specially characteristic of the great European towns, whose commerce was European and which were the Commerce seat of the great exporting industries, and for their explanation it is necessary to examine again the growth of the trade of Western Europe which gave occasion for them.[1]

[1] Cf. Chap. I, pp. 28–30.

First, there was the distant commerce in commodities from Eastern or African lands which had been enormously stimulated, but by no means created, by the Crusades and Christian dominance in the Mediterranean. From the Levant, Constantinople, and Barbary came the pepper, sugar, spices, dye-woods, ivory, silks, muslin, linen, jewels, which were spread over the West by the Mediterranean traders. Venice, Pisa, and Genoa, not to mention other towns in Italy, Barcelona in Spain, Marseilles in Provence, are examples of towns, whose prosperity was based on their shipping and furthered by the land ventures of their merchants to the fairs of the north, of which the great fairs of Champagne formed the central junction of commerce. A similar function, of a narrower and more northern range was performed by the merchant gilds of the Flemish towns and the " Wendish " towns headed by Lübeck which engrossed the Baltic and North Sea trade in fish, hemp, furs, skins, and wood, all objects of primary necessity. The " Hanse of London " formed by the Flemish coast-towns, the " Hanse of Seventeen Towns " of the Netherlands, connected with the fairs of Champagne, gained wealth by this commerce. The staple of their trade was wool, which was more and more drawn from England, and this wool-trade brought about the larger part of the growth of " great " manufacture for export, that of cloth, although iron and timber were likewise sent by Europe to the Levant.

The manufacture of rough cloth had begun, and continued throughout the Middle Ages, as a domestic industry used for local needs ; the housewife spun and wove for her family. But it soon became, too, a trade of a more expert kind, and although in its ruder forms widely spread, found its special home in certain districts in the Netherlands and North Italy. The main current of the trade flowed through Flanders. The Flemish merchants of Bruges, Ghent, Ypres, and other towns bought the raw English wool and wove it into various kinds of cloth. A large proportion of this cloth was exported to Italy, where by further dressing and dyeing it was made into the finest cloth available—this was, for instance, the chief occupation of the Florentine Arte di Calimala. Further, the Italians also imported the raw wool, to be made into cloth by their cloth-gilds like the Arte della Lana of Florence.

Marginal notes:

Import and Export. The East and the North

The Fairs of Champagne

Cloth Trade

Now this cloth-manufacture, depending on the importation of large quantities of raw material and on export to most foreign countries, was naturally under the control of the wealthy, experienced, and travelled merchants who started and maintained it. Unlike the trade of the normal gild of " small masters," which has been described above, it displayed a primitive form of capitalism, i.e. it was financed and managed by groups of employers, to whom the spinner, weaver, fuller, dyer, and the like, who carried out the actual process of manufacture by their manual labour, were merely wage-earners. The latter were not employed in factories ; they did their work in their own homes ; but they were none the less employees, and in their lower grades a mere proletariat, the " blue-nails " of Flanders, the *Ciompi* of Florence. The concentration of the trade produced, too, an exceptional concentration of population—the cloth-making towns were the largest of the time, and in them the cloth-making wage-earners formed the majority of the inhabitants. This prosperity brought new ills as well. Such a trade in distant markets brought uncertainty and occasional bad times, and therefore unemployment, deficiency in supply, slump in demand, whether from war or famine or trade-cycles. Then, too, the employers misused their advantages in good times. They were oligarchic rulers, landlords of their workmen, organized in an exclusive gild, and they controlled supply of raw material and sale of the finished product ; they ruthlessly stinted their employees' wages, used the truck-system in payments, and kept the proletariat in stern subjection. In the latter half of the thirteenth century, the Flemish towns were seething with discontent. The degeneracy and misgovernment of the narrow ruling patriciate at that time disgusted also the gilds of small masters in the non-capitalistic trades and even those members of the merchant gild who were not in the hereditary ring of town-rulers. By the year 1300 everything was ripe in Flanders for an explosion.

When that explosion came, however, partly social and economic and partly " nationalistic," it brought no wide-reaching remedy, although it did bring some diminution of oppression. For one thing, the ethos of the townsmen remained incurably narrow and sectional ; the different

(marginal note: Employers and Employees)

(marginal note: Failure of Revolution)

groups of the cloth-workers each sought only their own dominance ; so did their allies and rivals, the small masters of the retail gilds. For another thing, all together could not understand the conditions of a world-export trade and injured it by a blind belief in local monopoly, protection, and restriction. A century of revolution and mistakes left them disappointed in decaying towns.

The Italian Bankers   In Italy, and more especially in Tuscany, where the same trouble between employer and employee was brewing, though, as we shall see, it burst out later than in Flanders, the position of the great mercantile and manufacturing gilds was fortified by their activity as money-changers, bankers, and usurers for Western Christendom. The twelfth century, and still more the thirteenth, were marked by the rapid growth of a money-economy and by the use of coins themselves. Nothing is more striking in the records of taxation, commerce, and warfare than the large quantities of silver coins from a hundred mints current in the West. They flowed from town to country, from land to land, from taxpayer and customer to ruler and merchant. But their immense variety in value and weight made exchange difficult ; it was the travelled Italian merchants in the thirteenth century, as it was the international Jews in the twelfth, who knew and could exchange their varieties and pay in one country a debt contracted in another, and who with their local partners and agents over the West could largely avoid the actual transfer of specie over the great distances involved. Two factors worked together in this banking, money-changing business : the importation of rough cloth and wool into Italy and the vast increase of the revenues of the Papacy and of the members of the Curia derived from Western Europe by way of taxation, judicial fees, and the income of benefices. The merchants of Florence and Siena could transmit those revenues largely in the form of wool and cloth, and credit the Papacy with the values.

The Florin   In 1252 Florence gave a further strength to this banking business. Hitherto, the gold coin of the Mediterranean had been the bezant of Constantinople. Its rival, the augustal of Frederick II, had been handicapped by his wars. Now Florence minted the gold florin, which, kept of unvarying fineness, became both the standard of value of the West and the easiest way of making large payments in cash. It was one of the most effective means that could have been devised to secure a banking and commercial supremacy, and by a striking coincidence true bills of exchange appear in Genoese transactions at nearly the same date. Merchants with these facilities could control the money-market and the course of trade in Europe.

The ubiquity of these Italians, and their formation of great firms with partners or agents strewn over Europe, dealt a final blow to the eminence of the Jews in money-lending and finance and deprived them of their main usefulness to their Christian neighbours. Time had been, at the close of the twelfth century, when the Jews with their widely spread connexions and addiction to costly, far-come commerce were the chief holders of stored-up specie, and being unaffected by the prohibitions of usury were able to furnish the loans needed to the church builder and castle builder, the crusader, and the tax-payer. They were protected and exploited by the kings and potentates, who by special taxation of them shared in their gains. But quite early in the thirteenth century this quasi-monopoly was broken down by Italian and South French merchants and money-changers. Usury, the reception of interest for a secured loan, was indeed a mortal sin for Christians, but it was not only frankly practised by them almost under the ægis of the Church whose collectors and creditors they were in the vast financial operations of the Roman Curia, it was also evaded, as a commercial necessity, by various subterfuges. The sleeping partnership with full risk could develop into a fully secured loan ; fictitious sale and repurchase, the acknowledgement of a loan in excess of the amount received, and most of all the legal exaction of interest as compensation after an impossibly short term for repayment of the principal, could all allow for both the anticipation of revenue, the provision of the sudden needs of smaller folk, the extravagance of monasteries, and the adventures of the merchant. Veiled or open, the employment of capital at interest was by 1300 the commonplace of the Italian financiers and their imitators. The Jews were thereby fatally weakened and exposed to the full force of the religious and racial hatred of their neighbours and debtors. It was in 1290 that Edward I, whose creditors

The Decline of the Jews

Usury and its Disguises

Persecution of the Jews

were Italians, expelled the Jews from England; in 1806 Philip the Fair of France confiscated the French Jews' property, expelled them from his realm, and exacted debts due to them for the profit of the Crown. Violent persecution of them spread in the fourteenth century. It was a strange result of the necessary evolution of commerce and loans for interest in an advancing society. So necessary was the evolution and so conscience-struck its effecters at their sin of usury that a fourteenth-century Florentine banking firm regularly devoted part of its profits to charitable purposes as the share of " *Domeneddio* [1]," thus made the accomplice in its unlawful gains.

Trade-routes   The routes of great commerce began in the East. Across Turkestan and the Volga to Kaffa, the Genoese port in the Crimea, the Central Asia fabrics came to join up with the grain of the Ukraine, already a source of supply for Italy. Across Persia the same wares met Persian stuffs and spices and divided, going to Trebizond and the Black Sea, to Mosul and Baghdad and the Levantine ports. A third stream came by way of the Indian Ocean to Egypt and Alexandria. The events of the thirteenth century changed in some degree the Levantine outlets of this trade. The Mamlūk conquest of Syria and Palestine tended to concentrate the southern routes in Laiazzo in Little Armenia and above all in Alexandria, the chief resort of the Venetians. Constantinople remained an emporium of the first rank, but the establishment of the Latin Empire gave the superiority to Venice, and in 1261 the recovery of their capital by the Greeks gave the Genoese the preponderance there and in the Black Sea trade. Most important for a while was the erection of the Mongol empire. This opened anew for the first time for many centuries the direct trans-Asiatic routes to China both by land and sea. The Mongol Great Khans were beneficent **The Direct** at least in this. The land route débouched at Kaffa, Trebi-
Route to zond, and Laiazzo, the circumnavigating route in the Red
China Sea and Alexandria. It was not long before the new opportunity was seized. First, from 1245 came Franciscan missionaries, eager to convert the yet heathen Tartars to the Faith; they reached the Mongol capital of Karakorum. Then in 1260 came the merchants. The Venetian brothers

[1] " The Lord God."

Polo, journeying to the Volga, were forced by the wars of the Hordes to penetrate farther to Bokhara and then across the Pamirs to Kubla Khan at his capital of Peking. In a second expedition in 1271 they took with them their nephew, the famous Marco Polo, who remained seventeen years in China and finally returned in 1295 by the sea-route. By 1315 the route from Kaffa to Peking was established and merchants were bringing to Europe at known prices and under known conditions the damasks of Cathay.

Two contemporaneous circumstances, however, closed Its Closing once more the routes of the Far East to Europeans for many generations. One was the overthrow of the Mongol dynasty in China by the native, anti-Christian Ming dynasty in 1368; the other, in 1369, was the accession to power in Turkestan of the fervent Musulman and ferocious conqueror, Tamerlane. The Christian missions were practically destroyed, and amid wars and massacres Christian merchants could no longer venture beyond the Volga. The Far East retreated once more into legend.

From the Levantine ports and those of North Africa the Routes across Europe Venetian and Genoese trading fleets, officially organized, escorted, and led for fear of pirates and one another—for they were deadly rivals—sailed to their home ports. Thence the oriental imports divided. A small, but costly, portion went by sea to England and Flanders; much was spread over Italy; a part went north from Venice, some over the Brenner Pass to Augsburg and Nuremberg, and thence either to the Rhine or to Magdeburg on the Elbe and Hamburg, some north-easterly to the Danube and through the Moravian "gap" to Poland. Other portions went north from Milan, either over the St. Gothard to Zurich and Constance or over the Great St. Bernard to Basel; yet another crossed the Mont Cenis Pass to Lyons and joined the other streams in the fairs of Champagne. Then there was the partly direct and separate, partly transit from Italy, trade through Marseilles and Barcelona to France and to Spain. By all these routes back to Italy and the East travelled the wool, cloth, metals, and the like of England, Flanders, and the North.

The Northern trade formed a separate sphere. From The Northern Trade Novgorod came the Russian trade—furs, skins, hemp, and some Oriental products—to Wisby in the island of Gotland,

and thence to Lübeck, the " Wendish towns," and Hamburg. It was joined by the Swedish exports, and the Norwegian timber, and the North Sea fish-supply, and was fortified, like that of Venice in the Mediterranean, by the salt from Lüneburg and the mouth of the River Loire. From the German ports it was spread to Flanders, Champagne, and England and over the German routes leading south. This trade was in the hands of the formless league of Imperial, chiefly German towns, which grew from the league of " Wendish towns " in the late thirteenth century, and was denomi-

The Hansa League nated the Hansa *par excellence*. The main outlet was Bruges, but the centre of the League was Lübeck. The weakness of the Scandinavian kings, slowly succumbing in their struggle with selfish nobles, and of the Russians under the " Tartar Yoke " allowed the Hansa to establish a kind of monopoly, which it maintained by commercial boycott and blockade and on pressing occasion by war.

Reduction of Norway and Flanders by Boycott The use of a commercial blockade extorted the confirmation of the Hanseatic towns' privileges in Norway by the treaty of Tönsberg with King Eric II the Priest-hater in 1294. The same method in 1388–92 brought Novgorod to heel. Only a boycott could be resorted to against the protectionist town of Bruges in 1356 ; the staple of the Hansa was moved to Dordrecht in Holland, and no Hanseatic wares were sent to Flanders ; and in 1360 Flanders and Bruges were forced to surrender and even to increase the exemptions of the Hansa.

Reduction of Denmark by War War, on the other hand, was needed with Denmark, which not only controlled the main artery of Hanseatic trade by its possession of both shores of the Sound and was anxious to draw a large revenue from the transit dues, but was also ambitious of subduing and absorbing the wealthy " Wendish towns " themselves. King Eric VI Menved (1286–1319) made them his vassals, although internal strife in Denmark cancelled this subjection after his death. King Waldemar III Atterdag (1340–75) increased the dues and threatened the Scanian fisheries. Not only that, he took and destroyed Wisby (1360), which never recovered its importance. In a first war, he won the battle of Helsingborg (1362), and enforced a disadvantageous truce. But his exactions roused the Hansa to extend their league. In the " Confederation of Cologne " 77 towns of the Hansa, called

" hens " by the warlike king, allied against him, and they were joined by neighbouring princes. War began in 1368. While Waldemar was seeking help in Germany, the Hansa defeated his forces and conquered Scania. This and a commercial blockade wrung the Peace of Stralsund from the Danish government in 1369, which Waldemar himself was compelled to ratify. The treaty gave the Hansa League complete freedom of trade and even the right, later revoked, to share in the election of Danish kings. At this moment the Hansa stood at the height of its power with a complete commercial monopoly in Scandinavia and the Baltic.

No confederation was ever looser than the Hansa. Some 200 towns and districts at one time or another belonged to it, but the actual membership was variable and seemingly not known to the towns themselves. The general assemblies or *Hansetage* were rare and poorly attended. Central organization there was little or none. Yet members could be expelled and decrees made. The League was divided into " Thirds," and the foreign settlements, called Kontors, like that at Bruges, were really organized. Yet, however amorphous, the League was a great power and dominated the northern seas. Internally, the towns were usually governed by a narrow hereditary oligarchy of commercial or landed plutocrats, the *Geschlechter*. Below them were often discontented craft-gilds, and in some towns also a real proletariat. In the fourteenth century we already find attempts at revolution : in Cologne in 1371 over 1800 weavers were expelled by the oligarchs ; outside the Hanse's sphere, in Nuremberg in 1348 the craft-gilds seized power for a year. But prosperity depended on the commercial families, and they maintained in general their control. *Government of the League and its Towns*

While the towns and their activities were perhaps the most dynamic factor of medieval life, the most dissolvent of old conditions and creative of new and of a new mentality, yet the basis of the whole structure was the land and its cultivators. Of the four layers of society as envisaged in the Middle Ages, the chivalrous class, the clergy, the bourgeois, and the peasant, the last formed the bulk of the population, it provided the food-supply of all, and made possible the advancing activities of the age. *The Peasants*

The agriculture and rural life of the thirteenth century

in Western Europe were susceptible to an almost measure-
less degree of local variation, due to geography, climate, and
an infinity of historical happenings. Nevertheless, in an
outline it may be divided, roughly enough and with borders
as vague and melting as those of the colours of a spectrum,
into certain vast types of village organization, each with its
history, its reactions to feudalism, and its characteristic, yet
kindred, developments in the evolution of a more prosperous

Rapid Increase of Population and densely settled society. The basic fact of that evolution
is that Europe began in the Dark Ages with a sparse popula-
tion amid the waste and the dense woodland. In the year
1200 this population had long been in rapid increase, not
only furnishing the growing towns with their inhabitants
but also invading waste and forest and marsh and tilling
and peopling the rural solitudes. How much this was due
to the slowly won security, partial as it was, has already
been said, but clearly there were other factors. The rate
of infant mortality must, for reasons that are obscure, have
been comparatively low in these centuries. Whether the
terrible conditions of the Dark Ages had resulted in the
survival of only the toughest stocks, or whether certain
infantile epidemics were then going through a cycle of a less
deadly phase, it is clear that large families not only were
born but survived and bred. Statistics are naturally not
available, but it can be seen from the genealogy of some
Italian family-clans how fast the population could grow. A
Cavalcante of c. 1200 could have eighty male descendants
of his name of full age in 1300 ; similar multiplication can
be seen in the Genoese Doria. We can infer the same
phenomenon from the fortunes of countless villages. Life
remained short, but the population was continually replenished by fresh generations. The resulting numbers were
indeed still scanty compared with the millions of to-day,
but none the less far exceeded their predecessors.

Types of Agriculture. The Northern Type   Of the four chief types of village life and agriculture,
the best known extended over the plain of North Europe.
France north of the Loire, south-east and central England,
the German levels and Denmark, were its natural home. It
was characterized by the heavy, wheeled plough (itself a
northern invention) and the elongated strip field (the English
furlong), which diminished the number of times the clumsy

plough and its team of oxen had to turn.   Three kinds of
cultivation were practised.   The most primitive and least
widespread was that of the *infield*, always cropped, round
the village, and the *outfield* from which a crop might be
taken sporadically for two or three years, and its site abandoned once more.   In the second kind, the two-field system,
there were two great cultivated " common " fields, each
divided into many strips among the villagers.   One of these
fields in turn was left fallow every year to refresh the soil.
In the third kind, the three-field system, there were three
" common " fields, of which one was left fallow in turn every
year, while the two others were sown with a different cereal
—the winter and the spring sowing.   Certain features were
common to all three ; the cottages with their little plot for
herbs, the common meadow for hay, perhaps the pea or
bean field, and outside the fields the stretch of waste and
woodland, where the villagers fed their beasts and pigs and
gathered their wood.   The life of the village was marked
by its communal, customary character.   In the scattered
strips in the common fields the same routine had perforce
to be followed, the draught oxen clubbed to draw the few
ploughs ; the use of waste and meadow was a matter of
common right and custom.

The second type of village organization was characteristic of the West Mediterranean, south France, Italy, and
Spain.   Here the two-field system was in vogue, but the
two fields were divided in irregular squares among the villagers and were ploughed by the light, wheelless plough of
Roman origin, which required little turning space.   It was
compatible with much more individual farming, but required
equally with the strip system common pasture, meadow, and
waste.   The pastoral and the close types ought perhaps to
be regarded as special modifications of the other two.   In
mountainous or infertile lands, thinly peopled by consequence,
the common pasturage and waste were all-important and the
tilth likely to be managed on the infield and outfield system.
In lands of special crops, vine, olive, and the like, the closed
field managed by its proprietor was in vogue for those
products from ancient times.

In the year 1200 the peasants who pursued these different
methods of cultivation were still predominantly hereditary

The Southern Type

The Pastoral and the Closed Field Types

serfs, bound to the rule of the lord of the village or fief, owing him service and rendering heavy dues, tribute in kind, the payment of a poll-tax, a payment on marriage, the best beast and the like on death, tallageable at his need, justiciable in his manor court. At the same time, they possessed by custom a hereditary right in their shares of the village land, and their dues, though heavy, tended to be fixed by custom also. A growing minority, indeed, were freemen, but none the less subject to much of the peasant burdens. There was, too, no such thing as equality of wealth among them; the shares in the common fields varied from large holdings to almost nothing. The subjection to the lord was expressed in the village economy. Each serf family owed a certain amount of days of labour on the home-farm of the lord, which might be separate or scattered in the common fields; a free man owed some service ("boon-work" in England), but far less. The peasant was bound to the lord's monopolies, his mill, his bakery, his sale of wine. The dues and services varied greatly over Europe, but the principle was the same. The land was ultimately the feudal lord's; so were the bodies of his serfs; he took his rent and his profit of his own, and gave justice and protection.

But equally in the year 1200 this oppressive state of things was changing steadily in favour of the peasant. With the growth of population there was a continual growth of the area of cultivation by "assarts" from the waste and forest, whether by additions of separate fields round the common fields of existing villages or by the foundation of new villages or *villes neuves* in the vacant spaces. In the Netherlands the marshy coastlands were won from the sea and made fertile as "polders." In Spain the waste lands between Christian and Moslem were settled as the frontier was pushed by conquest farther south. To the east of the Elbe, in the new-won lands of Germany, in the conquests of the Teutonic Order, in Poland and Hungary by the invitation of native rulers, German and Netherlander peasants flocked through the thirteenth century in the hope of new, freely held farms—the great eastward colonizing movement of the Middle Ages. The result was the uplift of the peasant. The lords profited by new revenue, the market of the sterile towns made a vent for their and the peasants' food-stuffs, the risk of flight of serfs and emigration could not be faced. Hence came the alleviation of serf conditions in old land ; assart or *ville neuve* were held under free, milder terms ; the lords' rights diminished.   The market brought in a money economy, in which the fixed payment or valuation alleviated the services due.   It became more profitable to employ wage labour instead of an unwilling *corvée*.

In certain countries this process was speedier and more effectual.   The villagers of pastoral lands had always owed Pastoral little labour service, and indeed serfdom was rarer among Lands them.   In North Italy, with the rise of the city communes North Italy and the weakness and over-multiplication and consequent impoverishment of the feudal lords, the peasants had for some time the whip-hand.   Special terms for the much-needed and profitable closes of vine and olive had led the way.   Simple default in dues and services followed.   The fortification of the country towns (*castelli*) in the earlier middle ages resulted in the free ownership of houses in them, even if the owner was personally unfree.   Besides, in the open country a peasant might well own some land which was not his lord's property.   If he emigrated to the city and prospered, he retained his country possessions and added to them by purchase if he could.   The village community, itself of old date, grew in that land of association into the rural commune.   Only rents, largely in the shape of the *mezzadria* (half and half sharing of the produce), and the profits of justice remained to the lords.   Large numbers of the lords were city-dwellers and citizens, preoccupied with the city's food-supply and therefore more yielding.   North Italy was the home of the autonomous village, and the system of separate farming.

In France, speedier and more completely in the south, France slower and more piecemeal in the north, something of the same process was seen in the thirteenth century.   The labour-services withered to nothing ; the home-farms became small or disappeared ; France was becoming a land of peasant proprietors and tenants, with a needy class of nobles, eagerly exploiting their judicial, pastoral, and woodland rights.   In central Germany the peasants, or rather a class Germany of them, rose to the position of hereditary money-paying tenants.   All of them, with the increased value and quantity of their products, and the fixed money value of their commuted services, were far more prosperous.

Increase of Freedom

In the same process came the diminution of serfdom. The freeman was a more profitable subject. Here North Italy led the way, for the opportunities of emigration were greatest there, numbers of the peasants in the thirteenth century were becoming citizens and acquiring freedom, and the city communes found the free peasant more taxable, more utilizable, more justiciable. By the year 1300 serfdom there was on the way to extinction. In France, too, the freemen increased by the foundation of the *villes neuves* and by emancipation, a matter of bargain and sale, which exchanged decadent, unprofitable rights for an opportune sum at need. To raise a large sum of ready money, for the many occasions of expense, was always the problem, and loans from Lombard or Jew, which after all had to be repaid, were but stop-gaps.

Decay of Peasant Prosperity

Thus the thirteenth century saw the general rise in prosperity of the peasant who held land, yet partly through the other effects of the same causes, partly through untoward events, this prospect was soon over-cast. The multiplication of the landed peasants brought about the subdivision of their holdings, and therefore poverty. There had, too, always existed the mere cottager who had scarcely any land or none. He was the earliest to be freed, but he became as the landless wage-earner an element of instability, an often wretched rural proletariat. Events concurred in this fourteenth-century depression. In Germany, as the Empire dissolved, the unchecked feudal lords who ruled the countryside used their jurisdictions to revive old services. This happened, too, in Flanders, where an attempt to revive serfdom among the free coast-dwellers brought about in 1322–8 a ferocious peasant revolt, which there warded off the innovation. In North Italy, the town-dwelling landlord, often a merchant purchaser, backed now by the city-commune, reduced the rural commune to a nullity and kept his peasant tenants and labourers in hard subordination to his own and his city's interests. In France, the Hundred Years' War with England, which broke out in 1337, proved the ruin of peasant prosperity. The raids of the English armies and still more the continuous plundering of the mercenary Free

Companies on both sides gradually rendered half France a desert ; the starving remnants of the peasantry were in terrible contrast to their fathers, whose rich fields and pastures had gone to wrack in this inhuman warfare and under its breed of harpies.

In the midst of this retrogression came the famous plague The Black of the Black Death. The bubonic plague, endemic in parts Death of Asia, made its appearance in Europe in 1346 in the grain port of Kaffa in the Crimea. It travelled with the merchant ships to Constantinople, to Sicily, and Genoa in 1348 ; thence it spread through France to England ; it had traversed Germany and Scandinavia by 1350, and—a speaking commentary on the bar to commerce in Southern Russia— reached Poland by this circuitous route from the West. Where it passed it may have destroyed a third of the population. This first and worst attack produced a natural demoralization. Superstition grew, typified by the frenzy of the Flagellants, who wandered in Germany scourging themselves in mad penance and became a peril to society ; the Jews were attacked on the charge of poisoning the wells to cause the plague. A decadence in the standards of conduct was observable everywhere. Yet it was not this sudden visitation but the recurrence of the plague every ten years that had the severest consequences. It put a stop to the increase of population, which, much diminished, remained stationary for over a century. Thence came shortage of labour, higher wages, and dearer food. In a time of fixed dues, of partial serfdom, of remaining labour services, of distress and war, and of no economic knowledge or foresight, it produced a painful strain on the existing system. The lord or peasant proprietor endeavoured to force the wages of the free labourer back to the old level. However vain in the long run, this attempt produced long resentment and discord. In Germany it stimulated the recrudescence of serfdom and oppression, which prepared the way for the frequent and fruitless peasant revolts of the fifteenth century. In France it joined with war and pillage to provoke the Peasant Jacquerie of 1358 and the widespread revolts of 1382. In Revolts Florence, as we shall see, it had its share in the revolts of the town proletariat, the Ciompi, in 1378. Thus over Europe the fourteenth century drew to its close in a spirit of discontent, of blind adherence to and blind revolt against the survivals, the degenerations, and the achievements of the ancient order.

SUGGESTIONS FOR READING ON CHAPTER IX

A. SOURCES

Much light is thrown by literary works, such as Chaucer's and *Piers Plowman* ; Boccaccio in the *Decameron*, Sacchetti in his *Novelle* ; Montaiglon, A. de, and Raynaud, G., *Receuil général et complet des fabliaux des xiii et xiv siècles.* 6 vols. Paris, 1872–88. Also from certain chroniclers, such as Froissart and Villani, and travellers, such as (to the East) Marco Polo (ed. Yule, H. 2 vols. London, 1920) and Guillaume de Rubruquis (ed. Rockhill, W. W., Hakluyt Soc., London, 1900). Admirable selections from all sources are in Coulton, G. G., *Life in the Middle Ages*, 2nd edn., 4 vols. Cambridge, 1928–30, and *Social Life in Britain from the Conquest to the Reformation*, Cambridge, 1918. A merchant's handbook is Pegolotti, F. B., *La pratica della mercatura*, ed. Evans, A., Cambridge, Mass., 1936.

B. MODERN WORKS

I. TOWNS

Boissonnade, P. : *Life and Labour in the Middle Ages.* Trans. Power, E. E. London, 1927.
Cambridge Medieval History, vol. vi, chapter xiv.
Clarke, M. V. : *The Medieval City State.* London, 1926.
Cunningham, W. : *The Growth of English Industry and Commerce.* Vol. i. 5th edn. Cambridge, 1910.
Davidsohn, R. : *Geschichte Florenz.* Vol. iv. Berlin, 1922–7.
Glotz, G., ed. : *Histoire Générale, Le Moyen Âge.* Vol. viii. La civilisation occidentale. Paris, 1933.
Lavisse, E. : *Histoire de France.* Vols. iii and iv, relevant chapters.
Lipson, E. : *Economic History of England. The Middle Ages.* London, 1915.
Luchaire, A. : *Les communes françaises à l'époque des Capétiens directs.* Paris, 1911.
Molmenti, P. : *Venice. The Middle Ages.* Trans. Brown, H. 2 vols. London, 1908.
Pirenne, H. : *Early Belgian Democracy.* Trans. Saunders, J. V. Manchester, 1915.
Renard, G. : *Histoire de travail à Florence.* 2 vols. Paris, 1913–14.
Salzman, L. F. : *English Industries of the Middle Ages.* Oxford, 1923.

II. COMMERCE

Cambridge Medieval History, vol. vi, chapter xiv ; vol. vii, chapters viii, xxii.
Cunningham, W. : *Essay on Western Civilization in its Economic Aspect.* Vol. ii. Cambridge, 1898.
Doehard, R. : *L'Expansion économique belge au Moyen Âge.* Brussels, 1947.
Glotz, G. : ed., *Histoire Générale*, as above.
Heyd, W. : *Histoire du commerce du Levant au Moyen Âge.* 2 vols. Leipzig, 1923.
Hill, G. F. : *Coins and Medals.* Helps for Students of History. London, 1920.

Sayous, A. E. : *Le commerce des Européens à Tunis.* Paris, 1929.

Schaube, A. : *Handelsgeschichte der romanischen Völker des Mittelmeers-gebiet bis zum Ende der Kreuzzüge.* Munich, 1906.

Usher, A. P. : *Early History of Deposit Banking in Europe.* Harvard University Press, 1943.

Zimmern, H. : *The Hansa Towns.* Story of the Nations. London, 1889.

[Also other works in I]

III. PEASANTS AND AGRICULTURE

Bloch, M. : *Les caractères originaux de l'histoire rurale française.* Oslo, 1931.

Boutruche, R. : *La Crise d'une Société. Seigneurs et Paysans du Bordelais pendant la Guerre de Cent Ans.* Paris, 1947.

Caggese, R. : *La proprietà fondiaria e le classi rurali nel medio evo italiano.* 2 vols. Florence, 1907–8.

Cambridge Economic History of Europe, vol. i. 1941.

Cambridge Medieval History, vol. vii, chapter xxiv.

Coulton, G. G. : *The Medieval Village.* Cambridge, 1925.

Glotz, G., ed. : *Histoire Générale,* as above.

Klein, J. : *The Mesta. A Study in Spanish Economic History, 1273–1836.* Cambridge, Mass., 1920.

Niccolini di Camugliano, G. : *The Chronicles of a Florentine Family, 1200–1470.* London, 1933.

Plesner, J. : *L'émigration de la campagne à la ville libre de Florence au XIII⁰ siècle.* Copenhagen, 1934.

Sée, H. : *Les classes rurales et le régime domanial en France au moyen âge.* Paris, 1901.

Thompson, J. W. : *Feudal Germany.* Chicago, 1928.

[Also other works in I]

IV. THE BLACK DEATH

Coulton, G. G. : *The Black Death.* London, 1929.

Creighton, C. : *History of Epidemics in Britain.* Vol. i. London, 1891.

Saltmarsh, J. : *Plague and Economic Decline in England.* In *Cambridge Historical Journal,* vol. vii. 1941.

CHAPTER X

INTELLECTUAL LIFE, LITERATURE, AND ART

Literacy and Latin

THE mental training and the thought of the Middle Ages were indissociable from a knowledge of Latin, in which the remnants of their classical heritage were written, and in which as the language of the Church and of learning and as a kind of scholars' *lingua franca* the original philosophy, science, law, and ambitious literature of the time were composed. From the thirteenth century onwards this somewhat elementary but sound knowledge of Latin was mainly imparted in the grammar schools existing in towns and often connected with the cathedral churches, and in them the numerous class of " clerks," which included a host in minor orders or merely tonsured as well as real ecclesiastics, received their first education in grammar and composition and arithmetic. As we draw near to the fifteenth century a knowledge of reading, writing, and ciphering was becoming more diffused, but the learned complete layman was almost confined to Italy, where a literary education of laymen, however restricted in numbers and scope, had survived the Dark Ages and became notable by the close of the thirteenth century.

The Universities

The home of the higher education of the time was the universities or *studia generalia* which had struggled into life in the twelfth century, and took final shape and multiplied after the year 1200. At first there were only four or five of these international institutions. Salerno in Southern Italy, the oldest, was the school of medicine, isolated and anomalous. Bologna, following the national Italian bent, was the greatest centre of the study of the Roman Civil and the Canon Law, other studies being pursued but subordinate. Paris was the capital of European theology and metaphysics, where clerks from all Europe thronged. Montpellier rivalled Salerno in medicine. Oxford was a minor Paris. By secession, by development of pre-existing schools, and by deliberate

foundation, there arose newer universities. Cambridge was
colonized from Oxford in 1209, Padua from Bologna in 1222.
Frederick II founded Naples in 1224, Alfonso X renewed
Salamanca in 1254, Gregory IX created Toulouse in 1230.
In the fourteenth century Eastern Europe began to have
universities of its own. The Emperor Charles IV instituted
the University of Prague, chiefly for Germans and Czechs,
in 1348, and was imitated by Casimir the Great at Cracow
for Poland in 1364. All these universities, along with others
in France, Italy, and Spain, possessed the privilege, by
prescription or grant, of the *ius ubique docendi*, of granting,
that is, degrees which gave the right to teach in any of
them. To them flocked the clerks of all countries : in them
dwelt the thinkers and teachers ; from them swarmed the
prelates, the bureaucrats, and administrators of Christendom. They led and formulated the public, informed opinion
of Europe. Fortified by charters, indispensable to Pope and
secular rulers, their members were mainly supported by
church revenues, for the most part the incomes of non-
resident benefices, at once a justifiable employment of endowments and a crying abuse. By the year 1300 these
powerful corporations were ranked beside the *Regnum*
and the *Sacerdotium* as the *Studium*, centred at Paris,
the third divinely ordered guide and ruler of Christian
men.

It was only by degrees that they attained a stable organi- Their
zation and privileges. Besides the immense need that State Develop-
and Church had of them, there was the difficulty of con- ment
trolling and protecting the promiscuous, disorderly throng
of students—from boys of fourteen upwards—who congre-
gated within them. Riots and faction fights among the
students themselves, riots with sometimes wrathful, sometimes greedy and oppressive townsmen, quarrels with ecclesiastical authorities, the fear of heresy, the zeal for sound
learning and doctrine, the wish for the finished product in
see or Roman Curia or administrative office, all contributed
to their development. In 1200 Philip Augustus of France
confirmed the exemption of Parisian scholars from the secular
courts ; in 1231 Pope Gregory IX made them finally independent of the Chancellor of the Bishop of Paris. A similar
evolution took place elsewhere. The result was that the

universities became self-governing corporations with practically full jurisdiction over the acts of their members, and privileged against the world outside.

Their Organization The organization of these populous universities varied from place to place and had not finished its development at the close of the fourteenth century, but, as was to be expected, there were certain common features, which were analogous to those of the ordinary craft-gild. The fully licensed teacher had to be tested and accepted by his fellow " masters " or " doctors " after a definite period of training. Beneath this doctorate were the " bachelors," analogous to the journeymen, who had obtained their " degree " by attending the regular instruction and performing exercises, and who were allowed to lecture on the less advanced subjects. Below there were the mass of students, like apprentices, who were qualifying themselves, often without success, for the bachelor's degree. In Paris, which was typical, it took six years to become a Master of Arts, and at least fourteen to become a Doctor of Theology. Then, the universities were divided into departments of studies, the Faculties of Arts or Philosophy, Medicine, Law, and Theology, which each had its separate course of training. Within this general resemblance the divergences were great. Two **Masters' and Students' Universities** leading types may be distinguished, the " Masters' Universities," like Paris, in the north, and the " Students' Universities," like Bologna, in the south. As its name implies, the Masters' university was nearer the normal gild and ruled by its fully qualified Masters or Doctors ; it was also usually characterized by the predominance of the more numerous Faculty of Arts, which provided a training not merely designed for a special profession and was considered a suitable preliminary for the other faculties as well. At **Paris** Paris the Faculty of Arts was divided into four " Nations " —France, Normandy, Picardy, and England—amid which the countries of Europe were roughly allotted, and each " nation " was under an elected Proctor. The Congregation of the Faculty voted by " Nations " and was presided over by a Rector, also elected for a short term, who by 1300 was the real ruler of the University. Though the superior Faculties had an equal voice with that of Arts, the facts that their members were fewer and largely masters of Arts as well made their Deans become eventually the Rector's subordinates. Some variety of this organization appeared in the other Masters' Universities.

In the second type, the students, including the bachelors. ruled the University. At Bologna, the source of the system, Bologna the Faculty of Law was predominant, in which the students, coming from all countries, were more mature, and the teaching doctors were handicapped by being citizens of Bologna and intensely anxious to maintain its profitable vogue. The Students of Law were divided into the Ultramontane University of foreigners and the Cismontane of Italians; each was subdivided into "Nations," each had a Rector; the Rectors together presided over the Congregation of both Universities. A University of Medicine and Arts existed beside those of Law; a Faculty of Theology was only established in 1352. By this organization the students protected themselves against their hosts and tradesmen and enforced a severe discipline on their teachers, whose lectures were minutely supervised; the boycotting of culprits was a weapon hard to parry. Yet mutual interests left the examination for a degree in the hands of the Colleges of Doctors of the Civil and Canon Law—destruction of its value was not contemplated. Those Colleges were confined to Bolognese citizens; other doctors might teach or practise Law elsewhere. This narrow policy, degenerating into the succession of hereditary teachers, resulted at last in the pre-eminence of Bologna being transferred to Padua.

The predominant course of study in the northern uni-The Faculty versities was that of Arts or Philosophy, in which the works of Arts. of Aristotle and his commentators held the all-important Aristotle place. This meant a devotion to Logic and Dialectic and Metaphysics, which proved a valuable mental training, for they provided a discipline and practice in valid reasoning and criticism, most beneficial in a time emerging from semi-barbarism. This dominance of Aristotle had not come about without a struggle. In the twelfth century there had been a dawning interest in the Latin classics as literature, but the age was not really ripe enough for a true appreciation of them. Aristotle's works, too, had to be known and their study to be permitted by the Church, for they were Greek

and essentially heathen. The Aristotelian logic had been
the foundation of the dialectic of the twelfth century;
towards its close his works on natural science began to
filter through by means of translations from the Arabic,
mainly *via* the Moors of Spain. The capture of Constantinople by the Latins in 1204 led to versions of the *Physics*
and *Metaphysics* direct from the Greek in clumsy but usable
translations. This meant more accuracy, but it did not
mean the restriction of Arabic influence, for besides the
translations the commentaries of Moslem philosophers, especi-
Averroes   ally of the last and greatest, the Spaniard Averroes, were
powerful with all and accepted by some as the only true
interpretation of Aristotle's thought. Doctrines of a pan-
theistic nature, the denial of the immortality of the soul,
the belief in the eternal existence of the world, were all
deduced from Aristotle and enshrined in Averroes' Commentary, and directly they became known in the universities
they found adherents and excited the alarm of the Church.
Paris was their centre, and was the theological capital of
Christendom, the special care of the Papacy. In 1210 the
reading of Aristotle's books on philosophy and their commentaries was forbidden by a synod at Paris; in 1215
Robert de Courçon, the papal legate, prohibited them in
more precise terms; prohibitions were repeated by the
Popes in 1231 and 1263. But these decrees were never
obeyed at Paris or elsewhere, and in 1366 papal policy had
so far changed as to make the study of Aristotle's philosophy
a necessity for the degree of Master of Arts. This revolution
merely confirmed the practice of well over a century. It
was partly due to the appearance of thoroughly reliable
translations from the Greek, among which those of the
Fleming, William of Moerbeke, Archbishop of Corinth, round
Scholastic   about the year 1260, were conspicuous, but mainly due to
Philosophy   the exposition and commentaries of the great orthodox
philosophers, led by the Dominicans, Albertus Magnus of
St. Thomas   Cologne (1207–80) and Thomas Aquinas the Neapolitan
Aquinas   (1224–74), who constructed a strictly orthodox system of
philosophy on Aristotelian lines. These thinkers followed
on a long succession of twelfth-century theologians who,
chiefly in the cathedral schools of North France, had developed the study of Christian metaphysics, while indefatig-

able translators had recovered from Arabic versions remnants of ancient learning in that earlier renaissance.[1]

The works of St. Thomas Aquinas, of which the *Summa contra Gentiles* and the *Summa Theologica* were the chief, crowned the edifice of scholastic philosophy, the principal study of the " schoolmen " of the universities. We cannot enter into the best known of their subjects of discussion, the bone of contention of " realism " and " nominalism," which may be loosely adumbrated rather than described as the question of the objective reality of " universals," the species or the kind, apart from the particular individual object,[2] or their method of dialectic by which this theme and others equally important to them were disputed and expounded. Their method was essentially deductive ; they endeavoured to establish their views by reasoning from fixed premises, and accepted authoritative statements in fixing their premises. Aquinas's synthesis of philosophic theology represents the triumph of a variety of " realism " ; it was also the best conciliation of authority and reason— of the interpretation of competing, sometimes infallible, sometimes venerable and revered pronouncements, of Scrip-ture, Councils, Church Fathers, and classic sages, of the deductions to be drawn from them, and of the results of pure, *a priori* reasoning on the model of Aristotle. He covered the whole range of Christian doctrine, the theory of knowledge and existence. His aim was to show that the results of pure reasoning supported and were conform-able with the Christian revelation. The true results of philo-sophy, built on and transcending Aristotle, the use of the human reason, could not contradict, nay, must in their more limited sphere agree with revealed verities. By reason man could apprehend and partially prove the nature and structure of the universe and Christianity itself. Reason could not, indeed, scale the heights of faith, but it led infallibly towards them.

These studies, besides the rival orthodox systems they

[1] See the preceding volume of this series.

[2] Thus is " mankind " an objective reality, or is each particular man only to be admitted as such ? The realists held the first opinion, the nominalists that " mankind " was merely a mental classification of indi-vidual men. The ultra-realists held the Platonic doctrine of " ideas," the ultra-nominalists that " universals " were mere words.

produced, gave birth naturally to heresy, to learned, philosophic heresy and disbelief distinct from the popular rough-
and-ready heresies of the Albigenses and Waldenses. Learned
heresy centred in Averroism, a belief in the infallibility of
Aristotle as expounded by Averroes. Thus Averroes' tenets
of pantheism, the eternity of the material world, and the

The Averroists denial of the immortality of the soul were for the Averroists
irrefutable metaphysical truths. The most notorious cham-
pion of this incompatibility of the results of reasoning with
the Christian revelation was Siger of Brabant, whose views
were condemned in 1270 and 1277, and who died in prison.
He never in words denied—in fact he affirmed—the truth
of the Christian revelation ; his sincerity is an open question ;
but his followers in the fourteenth century, who were not
condemned, declared openly for two contradictory verities,
the Christian revelation which they loudly accepted, and the
discoveries of reason after Aristotle which they declared
irrefutable. Barrenly intransigent as the Averroists were,
they at least upheld a coherent method of thought as against
the gymnastic dovetailing of a crowd of isolated texts and
pronouncements into a traditional theology with a logical
system of different origin.

Methods of Teaching The method of teaching and study was indeed favourable
to the deductive thought of the orthodox and Averroists
alike. The lecturer expounded and glossed the authoritative
books to his class ; the disputations, which were obligatory,
discussed philosophic questions on the basis of authoritative
pronouncements and accepted general positions, manipulated
and built upon with all possible subtlety of deductive reasoning and dialectic. If Aristotle furnished the main text-books
of the six years' course of Arts, the accredited compendium
of Christian doctrine, the *Sentences* of the twelfth-century
Peter Lombard, and books of Scripture were the staple of
the fourteen years' course of Theology. For most theologians
the Arts degree was a necessary preliminary, but after bitter
conflict the Friars established a privileged position. The
Dominicans were from the start a learned order, the Franciscans rapidly became an order with many learned members.
In the Faculty of Theology, which they entered without taking
the Arts degree on being sent to a university, they produced
the most brilliant doctors and took the lead.

With the achievement of the Dominican St. Thomas Duns Scotus
Aquinas, the constructive period of scholasticism ended.
With the Franciscan John Duns the Scot (*c.* 1265–1308)
from Maxton in Berwickshire, the dissolvent period began.
" The subtle doctor " undermined the massive harmonious
structure of Aquinas by denying the compulsive force of his
philosophical arguments as to, for instance, the immortality
of the soul. He stressed the sphere of simple revelation as
against philosophical proof. For him the infinity of the
Creator stood first ; goodness and truth were the effects of
God's unfettered will, not the conditions of his essence. The
incipient scepticism of these views was a sign of the times ;
it began the party of " Scotists," and heralded the rise of
a new " nominalism," though Duns himself had held to a
modification of " realism." Durand of Saint-Porçain maintained that the individual object alone is " real," and that
" universals " were only the general concepts and classification formed by the mind which observed individual objects
and their common qualities. The English Franciscan, Wil- Ockham
liam of Ockham (*c.* 1300–*c.* 1350), went farther. To him
the intuitive perception, the sensible impress, of an object
is the sole method of reaching facts. The unity, the infinity,
and the attributes of God are metaphysically probable
opinions only. We know them by faith alone. After
Ockham, the school of the Ockhamists or " moderni " attracted all the moving spirits. A fundamental scepticism in
the validity of metaphysical demonstrations of ultimate
truth possessed them, and their exercise became more and
more a play of the intellect.

Yet there was another tendency of slow growth to which Grosseteste
Ockham and his followers contributed. This tendency was and Bacon
born at Oxford in the thirteenth century. Its harbinger
was Robert Grosseteste, the learned Bishop of Lincoln (1175–
1253), who was not only a philosopher and teacher, but also
declared that mathematics, the properties of lines, angles,
and figures, were a necessary foundation for natural science.
He was followed by the prophetic figure of the Franciscan
Roger Bacon, who rebelled fiercely against the *a priori*
systems and philosophers of his day. He was not without
patrons, for he wrote his *Opus maius* at the bidding of Pope
Clement IV (1265–8), but he fell out with his order, and,

ill-liked as he was, was imprisoned in 1278 for some of his views on astrology.   Later he obtained his release and died at a great age at an unknown date.   Bacon's immense originality led him to insist on the novel idea that experience and experimentation were the true method of natural science,[1] and were capable of discovering the secrets of nature and of enabling mankind to attain a knowledge and control of natural means unsuspected by the past.   He advocated the acquisition of knowledge of all kinds, languages, geography, optics, alchemy, and astrology.   He revolted against the weight of authority which oppressed his age.   Aristotle had rendered philosophy as perfect as it could be in his time.   It could be given vast extension by the experimental method.   There was nothing unorthodox in this, nor did Bacon contest the value of deductive reasoning.   But the inductive method, which he declared to be the most valid instrument of progress, was strange and unwelcome, and indeed embedded in the fantasies of alchemy, and ignored by the regnant scholasticism of the thirteenth century.

Scientific Tendencies

Roger Bacon did not merely leave occasional prophecies of what men might be able to do and invent to astonish a later age which achieved them ; he left an abiding influence on some " moderni " of the fourteenth century.   For the Ockhamist Nicolas d'Autrecourt, experiment was the true source of knowledge, apart from faith ; men should not be obsessed by Aristotle and his commentators.   Jean Buridan, Albert of Saxony (ob. 1390), and Nicole Oresme (ob. 1382) proposed scientific theories on motion and gravity—Oresme believed in the daily revolution of the earth and opposed the prevailing astrology—which rested on observation and calculation and anticipated the better-founded explanations of later centuries.   In their own day, however, they were isolated thinkers whose disciples were few.

Civil and Canon Law

Besides Philosophy and Theology there was the third great subject of study, that of Law, divided into the Civil and the Canon Law, which formed separate, though kindred systems, the provinces as a rule of separate specialists, although doctors of both were not uncommon.   At Paris, indeed, by decree of Pope Honorius III in 1219, and of

[1] The Picard Pierre de Maricourt was his precursor.

King Philip the Fair in 1312, only the Canon Law could be taught, but this was an extreme case. The subject matter of the Civilians was the codification of ancient Roman Law, the *Digest* or *Pandects*, the *Codex*, and the *Institutes* of the Emperor Justinian (*ob.* 565); that of the Canonists was the *Decretum*, the universally accepted codification compiled by the monk Gratian *c.* 1141 from the older Church Law proceeding from Councils and Popes, and from the canons of subsequent Councils and the evergrowing mass of the Decretals of the Popes. In 1234 Pope Gregory IX issued a codification of the new material since Gratian up to his time in the five books of *Decretals* (the *Liber Extra*) compiled for him by the Catalan Raymond of Penyafort. To this were added in 1298 by Pope Boniface VIII the similar codification of the *Sext* (*Liber Sextus*), and in 1317 the *Clementines* by Pope John XXII. Finally, there were the *Extravagantes*, never codified but collected in the fourteenth century.

While the Canon Law was a living, increasing body of law under which men lived, enforced in the Courts Christian which covered Western Europe and by the supreme tribunal of the sovereign legislator, the Pope, the Civil Law remained Influence of an ideal jurisprudence, immensely influential on the varying Civil Law secular laws of Europe, but never actually coinciding with them, even in Italy and South France where it was theoretically considered to be the common law so far as custom and statute did not suspend or modify it. This did not diminish its vogue or restrict its effects, for it gave the logical, reasoned law suitable for a community advancing into civilization. From it could be derived the principles, the rules, and the individual prescriptions the age was seeking. Under its guidance, the old barbaric formalism vanished, and the customary law of an elementary agricultural community gave way to that of a developed society with its new needs and organization. The lawyers of Europe, whatever law they applied, were trained in it.

About the year 1200 was the hey-day of the Glossators, the teachers of the Civil Law by way of annotation (*glossæ*) and compendium (*summæ*). They settled and explained the text, they quoted parallels, reconciled contradictions, derived or emphasized underlying principles, and illustrated the text by concrete cases. Their work was finally summed

up in the *Glossa Ordinaria* of Accursius of Florence (1182–
c. 1260).   Besides their strictly legal influence, their activity
was invaluable, for they began the criticism of sources of
information, the induction of principles from a comparison
of instances, the reasoned application of principles and precedents to the manifold and incessantly new variety of life
in a changing society very different from that to which the
legislation of Justinian was adapted.   This mental training
became a fecund constituent of medieval civilization.   With
the exhaustion of their method they were succeeded by
another type of jurisprudent, the Commentators, of whom
Bartolus of Sassoferrato (1314–57) was the greatest.   From
a scientific point of view this new school was a retrogression,
for it was no longer the inductive investigation of the source
which counted most, but its application with a fine-spun
logic by deduction to actual conditions, where the Roman
law more and more was compulsory legislation owing to the
labours of the Glossators.   Now the deductive reasoning of
the Schoolmen, rendered infinitely pedantic and finickingly
subtle, ruled among the Civilians.   Yet the Commentators
did make Roman Law a living law once more, and transformed it from an example and a model into a suitable
framework of State and society.   It would take us too far
to give even an outline of the advances made from 1100 to
1400 ;   but reasonable proof and evidence, appellate jurisdiction, personal responsibility, free contract, the authority
of the State and its ruler, the application of consistent reason
and equity to the settlement of human transactions and
disputes, were among the tangible effects of this prolonged
development.

Influence of Canon Law   The effects of Canon Law, itself modelled largely on the
Civil, were similar and even more direct and practical, for
it was enforced by its courts from the start in its detail.
There appellate jurisdiction, the sovereign authority of the
Popes, the reasoned application of principles and analogies
to actual cases were visible facts of daily life.   So, too, it
was informed by a moral code, both higher and more individual than the elementary and often barbaric customary
ethics of the past.   That it was too legal, that the letter
of the law and adroit perversions of the spirit by means of
manipulation of the letter were embedded in its heart and

seemed to deny its own ideals, was too true and the source
of many ills. But the result was not all veneer. The standard of human morals and behaviour was raised. Life was
more guided by knowledge and reason, if pedantic and wily,
not by the instincts and consecrated habits, noble and ignoble
in their dim-sighted savagery, of the Dark Ages. This was
the work of the jurisprudents, mainly Italian, and a chief
contribution of Italy to the growth of medieval civilization.

The bifurcation of jurisdiction and authority, the fact Political
that every man was under two systems of law and coercive Thought
courts, the secular and the spiritual, was decisive for the
trend of medieval political thought. The omnicompetent,
self-sufficing, watertight State did not then exist. Christen- The
dom was considered as a unity under two sets of authorities, Gelasian
the spiritual which guided men's souls to salvation, and the Theory
secular, which safe-guarded their bodies and temporal interests, which kept the peace and warded off the infidel. These
were the " two swords " of the Gelasian theory. The one
class of authorities culminated in the Pope, the other in the
Emperor. Only the Pope's power was real and enforced,
that of the Emperor was a shadowy pre-eminence, and the
secular power was really shared among kings and local potentates. This dismembering and localization of its functions
were first its weakness and later its strength. But there
was also the undenied superiority of the " spiritual sword,"
for its end of salvation was all-important and everlasting.
How far did that superiority go, how far and in what sphere,
if at all, was the " temporal sword " independent, was the
theme of the political theorist of the day.

As we have seen,[1] the papalist theory upheld with little Papalist and
compromise the supremacy of the " spiritual sword " vested Imperialist
in the omnicompetent Pope, even if, rated at the lowest Views
expression, he intervened in ordinary temporal affairs, nar-
rowly limited, " ratione peccati." The Emperor was but
his vicegerent, perhaps his nominee, at any rate approved
by him. The " temporal sword " was ultimately the Pope's,
although its use was delegated to the secular officers. The
imperialist theory, on the other hand, held without much
argument by kings and civilians, maintained a stricter
Gelasian view, that the " temporal sword " was conferred

[1] Chap. I., p. 20.

directly by Christ on the Emperor for completely independent exercise; and in practice the other kings considered that the Emperor possessed only a representative pre-eminence over themselves.

Aristotle's Politics

Political thought was given greater definition by the progress of scholasticism and law in the thirteenth century, but a new and vital element was added by the translation and study of the *Politics* of Aristotle. This at last supplied a reasoned analysis and theory of political institutions, and Moerbeke's translation, with Aquinas's commentary, produced both new versions of older theories and completely new theories as well. Mere adoption of Aristotle's system was naturally impossible. It had to be blended with the dominant conception of Christendom and ecclesiastical power, and Aristotle's city-state of antiquity found but few analogies, and those distant, in the Italian communes. *A priori* theories combined with alien facts produced a great but somewhat heterogeneous advance of fettered ingenuity.

Aquinas and Ptolemy of Lucca

Aquinas himself expounded firmly the supremacy of Pope and Church; " the Empire," he said, " was changed from the temporal into the spiritual." But, under the Papacy, he had a clear view of the lay State, large or small, a localized political community, whose monarch should be limited, had better be elected, and could be deposed by his subjects. Ptolemy of Lucca, the continuator of Aquinas's *De Regimine Principum*, even borrowed from Aristotle the opinion that different forms of government might suit different peoples. He, too, upheld in terms that the Pope was the true Emperor as well, and this papalist theory received its most precise expression in the *De potestate ecclesiastica* (c. 1320) of Augustinus Triumphus : all secular rulers were delegates and subordinates of the omnicompetent Pope, from whom all Christian men derived their rights and possessions.

Dante

The old-fashioned imperial theory found its first reasoned exponent, and perhaps its last, in the poet Dante in his tract *Monarchia*, written probably in support of the Emperor Henry VII about 1312. The new Aristotelian, yet scholastic, spirit is shown by the intensely abstract argument by which the necessity of a universal Empire for the government of mankind is proved, and also by the recognition of the fitness of local autonomy of the component States of various kinds which existed—the Emperor is a kind of supreme arbiter. Thus with the truly medieval insistence on the inherent virtue of unity Dante is aware of the separate kings, barons, and communes of Europe. The realities of nations, feudalism, and republics show dimly through the imaginative cloud of his reasoning. The proof that the Roman Empire of the past is the universal Empire of his theory is, however fragile, an appeal to historic fact ; and the refutation of the Papacy's claim to be the unitary head of Christendom is met both by shrewd legalistic argument from Scripture texts and law and by the scholastic distinction of the two ends of man, temporal prosperity and eternal salvation, each with its independent guide, the Empire and the Papacy, the dual hierarchy which actually existed. The " epitaph " of the Empire, as an utterly unreal theory, the *Monarchia* is yet evidence of the movement of thought.

At the same time novel, even radical, thought was Pierre appearing. That of Pierre Dubois, a provincial French Dubois lawyer of Coutances, is perhaps more important as a symptom of decaying old and arising new ideas than as a reasoned contribution to theory. His aim was to secure the peace of Christendom and to recover the Holy Land by making the King of France supreme in Europe. The Pope was to cede his temporal rule and authority to the King of France, and to establish the Papacy too in France. By feudal law, by war, and by diplomacy, the King of France could then set up a universal dominion. What emerges is the strong nationalism of Dubois, his perception of the evils of the Pope's secular dominion, his realization that the Empire was merely a German State, his belief in the rights of secular sovereignty, all current facts seen in daylight. John of John of Paris Paris, the Dominican, was a thinker. He opposed papal absolutism over the Church and defended the independence of the " temporal sword " in the hands of kings ; he declared the inexpedience of temporal power and wealth being conferred on the clergy—they were mere grants harmfully bestowed by secular princes. Further, and it was a great step towards rationalism, he opposed in the course of his argument the allegoric interpretation of Scripture texts, on which so much far-reaching theory had been built. This was to strike at the root of older theory—Dante himself, one may note, was making a timid approach to it, the first whisper of a transformation.

Marsilio of Padua

The most brilliant political theorist of the Middle Ages, however, was the physician Marsilio of Padua, who with the help of the French Averroist John of Jandun, composed his *Defensor Pacis* in 1324 apropos of the contest between Pope John XXII and the Emperor Lewis the Bavarian. Marsilio had absorbed Aristotle's *Politics* far more thoroughly than his contemporaries—to him, being a Paduan, the ethos and conception of the city-state were more intelligible than to them—and his original mind drew the faltering arguments of such French thinkers and statesmen as John of Paris and Guillaume de Nogaret to radical and startlingly modern conclusions. He was a creative system-maker. The driving motives which led him on to views prophetic of the French Revolution and the nineteenth century were first, the hatred of ecclesiastical privilege and domination, secondly, a keen realization of the ills wrought to Italy by papal secular authority and secular ambition—here he anticipated Machiavelli—and thirdly, his rather casual adhesion to the Spiritual Franciscans, with their ideal of poverty, in their contest with John XXII. Lewis IV's situation gave him his opportunity. But his motives are absorbed into his zeal for his revolutionary conception of the State.

Marsilio's cardinal doctrine is the omnicompetence and self-sufficiency of the State, the natural organization of human society, endowed with a natural and therefore right and necessary evolution, structure, and functions. The supreme and absolute authority in the State is its *legislator*, the assembly of its citizens. Thus Marsilio is a democrat, though in his *legislator* mere numbers are not to outweigh the superior worth of its better members. The decrees of the *legislator* form positive and the only compulsory law; thus it is an Austinian sovereign. It elects the executive, the *pars principans*, whether vested in one man or a board, and prescribes its functions. Hereditary monarchy, when practised, is merely due to the decree of the *legislator*. The entire activities of the citizens, whether laymen or ecclesiastics, are subject to the *legislator's* prescriptions; it admits no concurrent jurisdiction. This scheme, utterly in conflict with the dual authority, ecclesiastic and secular, then in vogue, required a detailed refutation of the claims of Pope and Church, and here Marsilio was as bold as in his politics. The allegoric interpretation was scouted, the Gelasian attitude in any form condemned. Marsilio traces the growth of papal power by historical induction from well-known sources. St. Peter never received the " plenitude of power " from Christ ; he was never Bishop of Rome ; if he was, his personal position, whatever that was, was never handed down to the Popes. Papal power was the result of slow accretion and usurpation. The mass of Canon Law had no validity. Few and only early Councils were made really General by the participation of the laity, and even their canons, though binding on the conscience, were only enforceable by the *legislator*. Further, General Councils, with the same powers, should be held, elected by the various *legislatores*, to preserve orthodoxy in doctrine and the united action of Christendom. The whole coercive power of Pope and priesthood vanished ; they were merely spiritual advisers, the Pope being president and chief by a historical evolution, and functionaries of the State. They were bound to live in complete and apostolic poverty. There was no essential distinction between the orders of priests and bishops. Transgressions of the Gospel Law, sin and heresy, were, as such, only punishable by Christ in the future life. Excommunication was a function of the State ; so were laws against heresy, although it might be unwise to make them. In short, Marsilio is a thorough Erastian. He declines to discuss the alternatives of a world-State or a plurality of States, but his system assumes the latter, though the communities which form the State (*regnum vel civitas*) may be graded by dependence one on another. The Empire is merely assumed, when it is mentioned, as the greatest of States.

William of Ockham, Marsilio's contemporary and fellow- Ockham rebel, was unlike him primarily a schoolman, and his political utterances derive partly from his sceptical philosophy and partly from his convictions on Apostolic Poverty, which led naturally to disbelief in the temporal power of the Papacy. An accent of philosophic doubt pervades his writings. He doubts even the infallibility of a General Council, in which he suggests women ought to take part. Unity and the Empire may be temporary expedients. But he upholds the

independence of the State, and denies the papal plenitude
of power.   He was a powerful dissolvent to inherited theories.

Ægidius
Colonna.
Wyclif.

The last development in this period comes from England
in Wyclif's work, *De Civili Dominio* (*c.* 1375), which com-
bines the irruption of feudal ideas into political theory with
a new conception of the Church.   The friend and councillor
of Pope Boniface VIII, Ægidius Colonna, had introduced a
feudal complexion into his treatise, *De Ecclesiastica Potestate*,
written in support of extreme papal claims.   All men held
rights and property, like vassals, on trust on condition of
" righteousness " (*iustitia*), and that righteousness meant
loyal submission to Church and Papacy.   If men did not
fulfil the condition, they lost their rights.   About 1350
Fitz-Ralph, Archbishop of Armagh, transformed this argument by making " righteousness " moral righteousness, obedience to God's commandments.   This view was taken over
by Wyclif.   Only the good man possessed property or jurisdiction in the eyes of God ; the bad man was *ipso facto*
deprived.   Applied to the hierarchy of the Church, his
doctrine annulled the authority of its frequently sinful
members, including the Pope.   The idea of the visible
Church, in which and by loyal membership of which salvation was assured, was smitten by this exacting argument ;
individual holiness was made the criterion.   The spread,
however, of Wyclif's teaching and its indirect effects belong
to the following volume.   Here its future importance can
only be suggested.

Common
Ideas of the
Feudal Age

Law

Apart from ambitious thinkers, there was the less systematized thought of lawyers and politicians.   Three ideas
were dominant, though not universal, the supremacy of law
and custom, the contractual view of obligations, and the
derivation of legal authority from above.   Law was conceived
of, not as made by decree, but as handed down from old
time, depending on God's ordinance and the nature of men
and their communities.   It was conceived to be declared
and applied rather than added to and amended.   The force
of precedent was enormous, and change, which was continually in process, appears, one might say, in disguise.   Men felt
that kings and potentates were under the law, not above it
or its masters.   Here the Civilians were working a slow
alteration.   They held, as jurisprudents and as bureaucrats,

that the royal power was absolute, that it made the law and was above it. In the mid-fourteenth century their doctrine was winning ground in France, at least.

Feudalism was in essence a system of private contract Contract between suzerain and vassal, and as feudalism was the reigning method of government it maintained in being a contractual view of the community. Rulership was a matter of mutual obligation, the State a structure of mainly inherited contracts and consent. If the king was pre-eminent, he had his duties to his vassals, and they their rights, that their counsel and consent were necessary to him, that taxes beyond and outside the customary should be granted by them, that monarchy in fact was limited by a mass of agreements.

Yet the right to rule came from God. The king was Rulership the Lord's Anointed. Even if the monarch was elected by God's authority flowed from him downwards, and the most feudal Ordinance of jurisdictions was a delegation from above; it was not conferred by a sovereign people. This religious view was the faith of St. Louis; it gave an overwhelming sanction to kingship, and it is easy to see how it could combine with the Civilians' conception of the non-contractual State under its prince to produce later absolutism and to refute the rival theocracy of the Papacy. While more general schemes amused the philosophers, these wider-spread, almost instinctive notions mingled, in opposition or coincidence, to form and change the actual constitutional laws of the European countries.

The Latin literature of these centuries covered most Latin subjects besides those treated above : sermons and hymns, Literature legends of the saints, secular poems and love songs, diplomatic letters and official documents, chronicles and biographies. Overlaid with new words and new senses of old words, it was grammatical and had a certain style of its own. There were mechanical rhythms, the *cursus*, according to which sentences were constructed. It now seems more interesting and less faded when its wording is tinged with the vernaculars. But far more racy of the time, and living as literature, were the works in those vernacular tongues Vernacular themselves.[1]   Literature

The unquestioned leadership among the vernaculars in

[1] Cf. Chap. I, pp. 5, 27, 35.

Langue d'oïl and Langue d'oc the year 1200 belonged to the two languages of France, the Langue d'oïl and the Langue d'oc. In them by the progress of over a century the vulgar tongue had received a higher degree of polish and elasticity ; men of other lands were beginning to write in them ; they set fashions in other languages. Yet French verse was even then verging on a decline in inspiration which continued through the fourteenth century ; its old themes were becoming hackneyed ;

The Romantic Epic its new, whatever their merits, were missing greatness. The romantic epics which pullulated were losing themselves in tedious length and in the repetition of old effects, which were not now so faithful a transcript of actual manners as their predecessors. Of the main themes, the cycle of Charlemagne, born of feudal anarchy, was perhaps ageing most ; that of Arthur and the Round Table was perhaps less affected, for in its fanciful wonderland and chivalry, it was still attractive to the courtly society of knights and ladies ; that of Alexander and Rome, with its marvels of eastern legend and fantastic invention, was perhaps always less popular. It is noticeable, too, that the original milieu, the minstrel chanting to an audience at feast or gathering, was getting out of date for the upper classes. With greater literacy, narrative poems were now being written to be read, commonly no doubt aloud, and their vogue did not disappear. By a further transformation the epic material in the thirteenth century was being converted into narratives in prose, the easier, more direct medium, and in prose, ever longer and more conventional, they continued to the end of the Middle Ages. A mystic piety and religiosity had appeared among them by means of the development of the story of the Holy Grail, which appealed to the age of Innocent III and St. Louis, and modified the voluminous Arthurian cycle.

The Troubadours The epics were in the main in Langue d'oïl, the language of the *trouvères* ; in Langue d'oc the troubadours had developed their complicated, artificial lyric poetry on the theme of *courtois* love, the idealized devotion of the knight to his chosen lady, always married and held up as unattainable. Here, too, the original inspiration was dying out— the Albigensian wars killed it—the last of the series almost was Theobald of Navarre and Champagne, a somewhat futile figure in the politics of 1230.

Meanwhile, other genres of poetry were emerging, and it is noticeable that much of them responded to the taste of the rising bourgeois class and the clerks from the universities, moralizing, coarse in temper, and satiric. The animal romance of Reynard the Fox was a satire on contemporary society. The religious drama both edified and entertained the townsmen ; it also gave scope for realistic characterization. The instructive, didactic poem was the popularization of learning. A satiric, realistic lyric appeared in the thirteenth century, to be succeeded in the fourteenth by the artificial versification of the *lai*, the *ballade*, and the *rondeau*, in which most subjects, but chiefly conventional love, were turned out with machine-like dexterity. Here Guillaume de Machaut (*ob.* 1377) was the master of the commonplace. But the dominating work was the allegoric *Roman de la Rose*, in which the life of the lover was described in endless personifications of emotions and circumstances. This was begun by Guillaume de Lorris, *c.* 1237, and continued in endless couplets and digressions on life and society by the cynical Jean Clopinel of Meung *c.* 1278. The effect of this rather vapid learned allegorizing mixed with cynical realism and dispraise of women was to close the spontaneous period of verse and to give rules for its manufacture.

But if poetry really receded, prose advanced.[1] Historians appear in the vernacular, lively, coloured, and direct. Ernoul of Palestine told of the Third Crusade and its sequel, a naïve, childlike Herodotus. Geoffrey of Villehardouin and Robert of Clari recounted the conquest of Constantinople in 1204, the one a tendentious and propagandist defender of the leaders, the other an unsophisticated representative of the knights of the rank and file. The garrulous Joinville from Champagne wrote in his old age his reminiscences of St. Louis, the ingenuous and truthful portrait of an age and its Saint. In the fourteenth century the Walloon Jean le Bel of Liége described contemporary events minutely at first hand, and his successor the Picard Jean Froissart, in his lengthy chronicles, described his century from the point of view of courts and knights under the rule of formal chivalry.

Later French Poetry

French Prose

[1] It may be noted that books on customary law were written in French, German, and Spanish in the thirteenth century, a sign of the growing capacity of the vernacular and of the ability to read it.

Vivid, detailed, and anecdotic, his work is an immense
tapestry of men, women, and their doings, reckless of accuracy but vividly truthful in atmosphere and setting. He
reported to his public their life seen through their own eyes.
We have travelled from the annals and memoirs to impres-
sionistic history.

Spanish
Vernacular
Literature

The use of the vernacular, for prose as well as poetry,
partly native and spontaneous, partly influenced by France,
was seen in other countries. King James I of Aragon (*ob.*
1276) wrote in Catalan the chronicle of his reign. Muntaner
(*ob. c.* 1330) and Desclot, both Catalans, each wrote works
that were far from being mere chronicles. There was composed in Castilian the General Chronicle of Spain at the
command of Alfonso the Learned. It was an age of historical
ballad-making in Spain, full of action, drama, and emotion,
a purely Spanish product.

Italian

In Italy we see the imitation of the troubadours give
way to a native and greater literature. It was at the court
of the Emperor Frederick II that the transition began to
take place by the adoption of Italian as the literary vernacular language instead of Langue d'oc. With the fall of
the Hohenstaufen the centre of Italian civilization moved
northward to Tuscany, and it is in Tuscany, and more
especially in Florence, that the greatest poets and prose-
writers appropriately appeared, with the result that the
Tuscan dialect has become the standard literary Italian.
Guido Guinizelli (1240–76), however, the founder of the
dolce stil nuovo, who raised the idealization of woman to a
degree exceeding the troubadours, was a Bolognese. He
was succeeded by the Florentines, Guido Cavalcanti and

Dante

Dante Alighieri (1265–1321). The achievement of Dante,
the greatest poet of the Middle Ages, one of the greatest
of any age, can only be briefly indicated. He cast the
mould for Italian after him, he gave the deepest, truest
utterance to the Middle Ages and foreshadowed the Renaissance, and he produced in the *Divina Commedia* a work
of undying excellence—a spiritual inheritance for mankind.
The *Comedy* completed the triumph of the Tuscan idiom :
its style and phrase influenced all subsequent Italian authors.
It expressed and embalmed the Middle Ages, so soon to
change, in their typical ideas and attitude to life, their

philosophy, their thought, their science, their art, their passions and aims. It was the prelude to the Renaissance, not only by summing up the civilization already attained, but by showing the tinge of novelty, the sense of style, the appreciation of the classics, the characterization of his personages, the precise observation of external nature. We see in this learned layman, in his allegory of the future life, the germs of that transformation which was to make the actual world and men in this life the mainspring of thought. Finally, on its intrinsic merits, the magnificent, unequalled planning, the weight and profundity of thought, the depth and poignancy of emotion, the range of subject, the beauty and felicity of phrase, and the varying, stately music of its rhythm, it has never ceased to cast a spell on posterity.

With Petrarch (1304–74) and Boccaccio (1313–75), Flor- entines both, came the beginnings of humanism, the cult of the classics as the embodiment of a higher civilization, which might be recovered by their intensive study. Each showed the changing temper of the age. Petrarch, an exile all his life, was a clerk and pluralist of Avignon, a traveller, who later settled at Arquà in the Euganean Hills above Venice. He had a singular power of influencing the minds of cultivated men, partly because of the timeliness of his advent. In Italian literature his *Rime*, sonnets and odes, on the introspective theme of his love for the Provençale Laura, set the vogue for centuries. More modern than Dante, they became the manual of lovers and poets. In his Latin works, again, he is more modern, however sincerely orthodox he might be in his acceptance of the medieval tradition of the religious life. He was the open foe of the wire-drawn deductions of the schoolman and the legists. He sought his philosophy in the secular wisdom of the classics. The ancients were his heroes. In imitation of them, he sought to revive their style, their solid reasoning, their lucid view of life. He set on foot the search for long-neglected Latin authors, the intensive and sympathetic study of both long-known and new-found works, the idolatry indeed of the remains of classic Antiquity. In fact, the advance of medieval civilization in Italy, so classic in temperament, so near to Byzantium and its survivals, had made Italians more capable of being in touch with and of partially understanding the classical spirit.   North of the Alps that sympathy was yet lacking.

Boccaccio   Petrarch's contemporary Boccaccio, a home-bred Florentine, was in part, as a humanist, his obedient follower, but he also made an original contribution to his time. Italian prose in Dante's *Vita Nuova* was already a delicate instrument of expression. Boccaccio made it a varied, supple language, informed by classic taste and rationality: the use of Latin, indeed, had proved an implement to educate and develop the vernacular. Like Petrarch, he became a model for the future. The naïve simplicity and pedantic devices of his predecessors, in short, gave way to a modern style. Still more marked was his secular attitude to life, his objective realism, his intense appreciation of the actual world before him. His greatest work, the *Decameron* (*c.* 1350), a medley of stories, grave and gay, poetic and coarse, idealistic and sensual, portrayed the life of his day with a colour, a vivacity, and love of the individual fact, which heralded and in part created a new era.

Dante, Petrarch, and Boccaccio were the founders of Italian literature, which flowed from them. While in France we can trace traits and symptoms which still exist, there is a gulf between the old literature and the present. That gulf is bridged by these three Tuscans. It is significant that Petrarch and Boccaccio divined the yet unknown treasures Greek literature contained for their revival of Antiquity. Petrarch vainly tried to learn Greek; Boccaccio obtained the first miserable translation of Homer. It was a portent rather than an achievement.

Tuscan Chronicles   Italian vernacular literature of the fourteenth century includes other notable works—like the Chronicles of the Florentines, Villani and Compagni, the one with the comprehensive range of the European merchant, the other with the shrewd intensity of the local trader—but they do not possess this modernity. Turning to Germany, we are again in the full medieval current. German vernacular literature in the thirteenth century was largely inspired by that of France. The French cycles were rehandled and paraphrased, sometimes in masterly fashion as in Wolfram of Eschenbach's (*ob. c.* 1220) *Parzival*; the love poetry of both troubadour and *trouvère* found a rival in that of the *minnesinger*, who

German Vernacular Literature

clustered round Herman I, Landgrave of Thuringia. But
there was also a native Germanic cycle of marked national
characteristics. The old legends of the race, the tales of
Siegfried and Dietrich of Bern (Theodoric the Ostrogoth),
were continually retold under the Hohenstaufen and their
successors. The famous *Nibelungenlied*, composed *c.* 1190, The *Nibe-*
shows an ethos, more primitive than that of the chivalric *lungenlied*
age. Loyalty to kindred and personal war-leader wears an
aspect of fierce and noble barbarism : the duty of blood-
revenge, the devotion of the sworn-companion to his lord,
the sense of destiny to be bravely met are dominant. In
a more conservative land, folk-tales centuries old retained
their original standards of heroism. These qualities do not
desert the later lays, but they are mingled with a less earnest
love of mere marvels and endless adventures, the exaggeration
of accepted chivalry in the fourteenth century.

Yet the most realistic and the best story-telling of the The Ice-
Middle Ages arose in the prose sagas of Iceland, the traditions landic Sagas
of the Norse, held tenaciously in memory and told in the
long winter evenings ; for this the Icelanders developed an
almost perfect technique. Snorri Sturluson (*ob.* 1241) wrote
the *Heimskringla*, the finest series of royal biographies of
the time, beside which others seem faded. The anonymous
sagas of Icelandic heroes, written down in the thirteenth
century, have an even higher merit. Forceful narrative,
incisive characterization, an impressive simplicity, dramatic
action and speech, make the life of that corner of Europe
more alive and understandable than that revealed by the
chronicles, poems, and treatises of other lands. It was the
literature nearest to the people of any in Europe, and preserved and developed, perhaps on that account, a keen sense
of objective reality. The Icelanders walk out of the page
in their habit as they lived.

The dominant art of the thirteenth and fourteenth cen- Gothic
turies was that of architecture, and to it the other arts of Architecture
painting and sculpture were subordinate and ancillary. By
the year 1200 the great architectural creation of the Middle
Ages, the so-called Gothic style, had already been evolved.
The pre-eminent intellectual interest of the age was religious
and theological, and Gothic was in essence the art of church-
building so as to fulfil the needs of the Christian cult and

ideals.   Architecture was necessarily conditioned by the builders' knowledge of engineering, and Gothic was the result of
the slow discovery of the means of collecting the thrusts of
superimposed weight and converting the sidelong, outward
pressure into vertical pressure through spaced conductors to
the ground.   Romanesque, the earlier architecture, had relied
on the massiveness of its structure, its walls and towers ; its
windows could only be small ; its round arches and barrel
roofs required all the support of its thick and solid masonry.
The triumph of Gothic rested on the pointed arch and ribbed
roof, by which the downward thrusts were collected on
comparatively slender columns ; the invention of the flying
buttress topped with a pinnacle allowed the weight and outward thrust of the lofty clerestory to be canalized to the
ground.   The walls could thus become mere screens, with
vast window spaces of stained glass, hung on the tense skeleton
of pointed arch, column, and buttress.   Space, loftiness,
light and colour, and complexity of design could thus all be
combined for the uses of the cult in a many-celled, athletic,
soaring structure of marvellous beauty and variety.   Mystery
and awe, a reasoned, logical system, the reigning dogmas of
religion, the pageantry and ceremonial of rite and procession,
a devotion at once hierarchic, monastic, and popular found
therein their expression and their home.

Spread of
Gothic over
West Europe

The native land of Gothic, from which it radiated at
varying speeds over Europe, was the Île de France, and it
was there that the greatest among many masterpieces were
achieved.   The cathedrals of Amiens, Chartres, and Rheims,
the Sainte Chapelle at Paris of St. Louis were among them.
Into Spain Gothic spread at the end of the thirteenth century, into Germany a little earlier, in both replacing the
native varieties of Romanesque.   It came into Italy with
the Franciscan and Cistercian movements, but always retained its alien, borrowed character.   The Italians borrowed
the pointed arch and the wide spaces suitable for preaching,
but not the large windows, out of place in a sunlit climate,
or the flying buttress and thin walls.   If the solid wall was
not strong enough, they even tied the vaults with rods.   For
them Gothic was not an engineering secret, but a means of
picturesque variety like the coloured stones in which they
built it.

For the Gothic builders, sculpture and painting were means of decoration and doctrinal instruction rather than independent arts, and this affected their use apart from building ; men decorated a book of hours or a romance with miniatures and borders and an ivory box with carven figures. Thus the Gothic church was coloured with painted designs on the stone-work and with the rich hues of its stained glass. Its surface was varied with the mouldings and floriated capitals of its arches and pillars, the statuary of its portals, and the carving of its woodwork. This decorative aim, as civilization and skill advanced, combined with zeal for realism in detail ever more proficient. The sculptured figures of the portals grew steadily more life-like. In the thirteenth century they are expressive of doctrine and divinity, as the building they inhabit is clearly ruled by its ritual purpose. But in the fourteenth century the balance begins to tilt in favour of observant realism. Statuary less obviously subserves the building, while it becomes more human and anecdotal. The details and monuments of the buildings themselves eclipse somewhat for the artist its traditional plan and purpose. Ornament is developed and multiplied for its own sake, while still remaining a decoration rather than a work of art complete in itself.

Gothic Sculpture and Painting

Growing Realism

Certain national traits can be noticed in this decorative Gothic style as it spread. The French becomes elegant and vivacious, the Spanish solemn and sumptuously elaborate, the German forcefully realistic. But the subjects remain the same, the Gospel story, tales of the saints and from Holy Writ, the doctrinal scenes of Christianity, in the romances scenes of chivalry, and more and more often grotesque fragments of homely life peering out of naturalistic foliage. Its purpose, to decorate, instruct, amuse, and catch the eye, is always evident. A spiritual change, however, took place in Italy. There, the symbolic, rigid Romanesque imagery had been more patently surcharged with Byzantine hieratic severity than elsewhere ; the uncouthness of northern Romanesque had been absent. When change came during the thirteenth century, it was due to the impact of realism and the influence of late Roman monuments and sepulchral sculpture under the guidance of the native Italian instinct for beauty of form and for composition, creating a unified

Beginning of the Italian Renaissance

scene of imaginative life out of the separate realistic elements transferred to the artistic design. Mural painting in the unbroken wall spaces of Italy had always there held a peculiar importance, and it is in the frescoes of Giotto (1266–1336) that the new spirit attained conscious and epoch-making expression. He " knocked a hole in the wall," by creating an illusion of three dimensions on a flat surface. In the scenes of the legend of the Virgin and the life of Christ in the Arena Chapel of Padua, his figures not only live and move with dramatic emotion, they are palpably part of a single scene, intent on the event, and are integral parts of the landscape setting. The picture has become the realistic yet imaginative re-creation of a crowded moment of life, seen as a whole, and acting as a unity on the spectator. Line and colour, background and realistic personages are fused into one conception compounded by the artist from the actual world he saw.

Giotto, in short, had reached the Renaissance. His followers and rivals in the fourteenth century might be more conservative and less inspired ; the Sienese painters, Duccio, Martini, and the Lorenzetti, might surpass him in colour and grace, while failing in his greater qualities ; none the less, his achievement was unforgettable, and set Italian art on the new roads which led to a new ideal of art a century later.

SUGGESTIONS FOR READING ON CHAPTER X
I. UNIVERSITIES AND LEARNING

Cambridge Medieval History, vol. vi, chapter xvii ; vol. vii, chapter xxv : vol. viii, chapter xxiii.

Glotz, G., ed. : Histoire Générale, Le Moyen Âge. Vol. viii. La civilisation occidentale. Paris, 1933.

Rashdall, H. : The Universities of Europe in the Middle Ages. Ed. Powicke, F. M., and Emden, A. B. 3 vols. Oxford, 1936.

Thorndike, L. : University Records and Life in the Middle Ages. Columbia University Press, 1944.

Haskins, C. H. : Studies in the History of Mediæval Science. Cambridge, Mass., 1924.

Kimble, G. H. T. : Geography in the Middle Ages. 1938.

Sarton, G. : Introduction to the History of Science. Vols. ii and iii. London, 1931, 1947.

Galbraith, V. H. : The Literacy of the English Kings. Proc. Brit. Acad., 1936.

II. SCHOLASTICISM
A. SOURCES

St. Thomas Aquinas : Summa contra gentiles in Opera Omnia. Rome 1882 ff. ; Summa Theologica. Ibid.

Dante : *La Divina Commedia.* Many modern editions.
Peter Lombard : *Sententiae.* Several editions.

B. Modern Works

Cambridge Medieval History, vol. v, chapter xxiii ; vol. vi, chapter xix.
Glotz, G., ed. : *Histoire Générale,* as above.
Gilson, E. : *La philosophie au moyen âge.* 2 vols. Paris, 1922.
Wulf, M. de : *History of Medieval Philosophy.* Trans. Messenger, E. C.
3 vols. London, 1935, in progress.

III. LAW AND POLITICAL THOUGHT

A. Sources

St. Thomas Aquinas and Ptolemy of Lucca : *De Regimine Principum* in
Opera Omnia. Rome, 1882 ff.
Selected Political Writings of S. Thomas Aquinas. Transl. by J. G. Dawson.
Oxford, 1948.
Aegidius Romanus : *De ecclesiastica potestate.* Ed. Scholz, R. Weimar,
1929.
Pierre Dubois : *De recuperatione Terrae Sanctae.* Ed. Langlois, C. Collection des textes pour servir à l'étude et à l'enseignment d'histoire. Paris,
1891.
John of Paris : *Tractatus de Potestate Regia et Papali. In* Goldast, M.,
Monarchia S. Romani Imperii. Vol. ii. Frankfort, 1614.
Marsilio of Padua : *Defensor Pacis.* Ed. Previté-Orton, C. W. Cambridge, 1928.
Guillelmi de Ockham Opera Politica. Ed. J. G. Sikes. Manchester, 1940.
(Only one volume so far published.)
Dante : *Monarchia.* Ed. Moore, E. Trans. Wicksteed, P. H. Temple
Classics. London, 1904.
Trémaugon, E. : *Somnium Viridarii. In* Goldast, M., *Monarchia S.
Romani Imperii.* Vol. i. Hanover, 1612.

B. Modern Works

Cambridge Medieval History, vol. vi, chapter xviii ; vol. vii, chapter xvi,
vol. viii, chapter xx.
Gierke, O. : *Political Theories of the Middle Age.* Trans. Maitland, F. W.
Cambridge, 1900.
Poole, R. L. : *Illustrations of the History of Medieval Thought and Learning.*
2nd edn. London, 1920.
Carlyle, R. W. and A. J. : *History of Mediæval Political Theory in the
West.* 6 vols. Edinburgh, 1903–36.
McIlwain, C. H. : *The Growth of Political Thought in the West.* London,
1932.
d'Entrèves, A. P. : *Mediæval Contributions to Political Thought.* Oxford,
1939.
Lagarde, G. de : *La naissance de l'esprit laïque au déclin du moyen âge.*
3 vols. St. Paul-Trois-Châteaux, 1935 ff.
Woolf, C. N. S. : *Bartolus of Sassoferrato.* Cambridge, 1913.
Previté-Orton, C. W. : *Marsilius of Padua.* Proc. Brit. Acad., 1936.
Workman, H. B. : *John Wyclif.* 2 vols. Oxford, 1926.
Vinogradoff, Sir P. : *Roman Law in Medieval Europe.* Ed. Zulueta, F. de.
Oxford, 1929.
Armstrong, E. : *Italian Studies.* Ed. Ady, C. M. London, 1934.
Ullmann, W. : *The Medieval Idea of Law.* London, 1946.

Ullmann, W. : *Medieval Papalism : the political Theories of the medieval Canonists.* 1949.

IV. LITERATURE

A. Sources

Chronicles and other works show the Latin prose of the period. For verse see Raby, F. J. E., *History of Christian Latin Poetry*, Oxford, 1927 ; *History of Secular Latin Poetry in the Middle Ages*, 2 vols., Oxford, 1934 ; and Waddell, H., *Mediæval Latin Lyrics*, London, 1929.

For editions of the vernacular prose and verse, the bibliographies of modern histories of national literatures may be used. Translations of the Icelandic Sagas, the *Nibelungen Lied*, and some French romances are in Everyman's Series. Translations of the Catalan Chronicles are listed in the Suggestions on Chapter VIII, of Villani and Dino Compagni in Suggestions on Chapter XI. J. G. Lockhart's Spanish Ballads are available in reprints.

B. Modern Works

Cambridge Medieval History, vol. vi, chapter xxv.

Glotz, G., ed. : *Histoire Générale*, as above.

Lavisse, E., ed. : *Histoire de France.* Vols. iii and iv.

Bédier, J., and Hazard, P. : *Histoire de la littérature française illustrée.* Vol. i. Paris, 1923.

Paris, G. : *Mediaeval French Literature.* Temple Primers. London.

Chaytor, H. J. : *The Troubadours.* Cambridge, 1912.

Garnett, R. : *History of Italian Literature.* London, 1908.

Fitzmaurice-Kelly, J. : *A New History of Spanish Literature.* Oxford, 1926.

Gardner, E. G. : *Dante.* London, 1923.

Ker, W. P. : *Epic and Romance.* London, 1896.

Saintsbury, G. : *The Flourishing of Romance and the Rise of Allegory.* (Periods of European Literature.) Edinburgh.

Snell, F. J. : *The Fourteenth Century.* (Periods of European Literature.) Edinburgh, 1899.

V. ART

Cambridge Medieval History, vol. vi, chapter xxii ; vol. viii, chapter xxiv.

Evans, J. : *Art in Mediaeval France, 987–1498.* Oxford, 1948.

Glotz, G., ed. : *Histoire Générale*, as above.

Lethaby, W. R. : *Mediæval Art.* 2nd edn. London, 1912.

Fergusson, J. : *History of Architecture.* 3rd edn. London, 1893.

Jackson, T. G. : *Gothic Architecture in France, England, and Italy.* London, 1915.

Morey, R. : *Mediaeval Art.* London, 1948.

Ruskin, J. : *The Seven Lamps of Architecture.* 3rd edn. Orpington, 1880.

Viollet-le-Duc, E. : *Essai sur l'architecture militaire au moyen âge.* Paris, 1854.

CHAPTER XI

THE DEFEAT OF THE PAPACY BY FRANCE

IF we look at Western Christendom as a whole in the Predomin-
thirteenth century, it will be seen that such unity and ance of the Church and
central organization as it possessed—and they may the Papacy
be overrated—consisted of the Catholic Church and the in Western
monarchic Papacy. The Church only had an articulated Christendom
administration and a common law spread over all Europe.
The Church and its chief intervened for better or worse
under some form or other in almost all secular affairs high
and low. The philosophy and the learned literature of the
time emanated from clerks. The bureaucrats of the secular
monarchs were largely clerks. The education of the time
was centred in the universities, and these were the haunts
and training-schools of clerks. The movements of the
century which had the widest, most popular, and deepest
appeal were those of the mendicant orders of Friars. The
heretical movements which the Church fought and feared,
whatever their variety, were anti-clerical movements. The
Church was the most pervading, and seemed to be the most
powerful factor in society. Its driving-power and cohesion
centred in the Papacy. As the Papacy rose to its full height
under Innocent III, as it defeated the Empire and Sicily
under Innocent IV and his successors, its hold on the Church
and its activities grew tighter and more penetrating. Under
its ægis scholastic philosophy developed into the all-embracing
system of Aquinas. Monk and friar, prelate and inquisitor,
merchant and lawyer served its interests. Then towards
the close of the century we see it faltering under the con- Their decline
gestion, the multiplied labours, the tortuous political inheritance, and still more the ethos of its own success. The
Christian faith, with its fervours, hopes, and fears, has been
frozen into a governmental, political system directed by
lawyers and men of affairs. They do their worldly job to
an accompaniment of trite and sounding phrases, but the

shaping energy of their predecessors has left them. That victorious, expansive zeal has deserted them for the champions of other causes. A crushing defeat, however obstinately retrieved, revealed how much loss of belief in the Church's motive could mean loss of the Church's prestige and influence. The fourteenth century sees the Papacy and the Church struggling ever less convincingly for privileges, income, land, rights and gains here and there. Their victories only speeded the ebb of confidence, ready for the crowning disaster of the Schism. A sceptical spirit, as we have seen, loosened the fabric even of the thirteenth-century philosophy.

Philip III of France. The new Royal Ministers

In this decline the defeat of the Papacy by the French monarchy forms a landmark, revealing the weakness of old forces and the strength of new, and thereby itself a force to shape the future. The death of St. Louis supplied an almost immediate proof of the hold the kingship had acquired on France, for under his son, Philip III (1270–85), an honest, easily led nonentity, its progress was unimpeded. The government was carried on by confidential ministers, belonging to the newly formed class of legists and the like, who were coming to the fore in the royal bureaucracy. Whether physicians, like Pierre de la Broce, or lawyers or plain knights, they were laymen, and their standpoint was that of the Civil Law. They believed in the king's autocracy in the mode of Justinian. Their methods in cases which had a political bearing were those of the pedantic, wily, grasping legalism of the time, in which an adroit use and straining of the letter of the law often became unscrupulous chicanery ; and this odious side of their activity was ever more manifest and habitual. Where feudal independence or inconvenient privileges were to be curtailed, by hook or crook, by exalting the royal prerogative or by pettifogging quibbles, these lawyers, strong in the king's power and wealth and the reverence felt for him, seldom failed to attain their end. In spite of their faults and their greedy self-interest, it is clear that they benefited France, for the royal authority grew greater, and its past and present gains were continuously consolidated. Royal government was better than disorderly feudalism or selfish, short-sighted town oligarchies, and the people felt it. Besides, if local particularism and the aversion felt by the South for the North and by province for province continued unabated, a national patriotism existed too, whose only expression and bond was the king.

Philip III's reign was marked by successes and failures, neither much due to the king himself. In 1271, after the Tunisian crusade, died the king's uncle, Alphonse Count of Poitiers and Toulouse, and his great inheritance fell to the Crown. Thus the best of Languedoc came under direct royal sway. The English king had, indeed, claims on parts of it under the treaty of Paris of 1259,[1] but only obtained the Agenais by the treaty of Amiens in 1279. Meantime in 1273 Philip gave to the Papacy another part of Alphonse's lands, the little Comtat Venaissin in the Arelate on the River Rhone. Subsequent events made this cession in the Empire a political success, for it proved one of the factors which fixed the Papacy at the neighbouring city of Avignon under the shadow of the French throne. Another annexation of immense importance was achieved by the marriage in 1284 of the king's eldest son, Philip the Fair, to Joanna, Queen of Navarre and Countess of Champagne. Navarre, the land-locked, barren little Spanish kingdom mainly to the south of the Pyrenees, was of small importance save as a means of entry into Spain, but rich and fertile Champagne was in the heart of northern France, an essential province for the growth of the monarchy. The kings never let go this invaluable inheritance.

Philip's failures were connected with the personal policy of his uncle Charles of Anjou. Under that dominating influence he endeavoured, with the Pope's aid, to be elected to the vacant throne of the Empire, but this project, useful to Charles, most deleterious to the real interests of France, was baffled by the firm resistance of Pope Gregory X, who furthered the election of Rudolf of Habsburg.[2] More fatal was the crusade of Aragon undertaken to recover Sicily for Charles after the Vespers and to enlarge the Capetian dominions by dethroning Peter III and replacing him by Philip's younger son, Charles Count of Valois. Philip himself led to the crusade the largest army yet assembled by a King of France, but the obstinate Catalan defence, the summer heat, and the sea-victory of Admiral Loria half-destroyed it, and led to the king's death.[3]

Philip III's Annexations.

Toulouse

Champagne

The Crusade against Aragon

[1] See above, Chap. V, p. 116.   [2] See above, Chap. VII, p. 148.
[3] Cf. above, Chap. IV, p. 93.

Philip IV
the Fair

Philip IV the Fair (1285–1314) has been called an enigma, for he was silent and reserved, no worker, and his contemporaries thought that he was merely guided by his ministers. Yet he chose them consistently and their policy remained the same. It is hard to resist the inference, made without hesitation about many of whom we are told less or as little, that the formally devout, stalwart, hunting, uncommunicative king was master in his own house and chose congenial instruments. He may have resembled so far his descendant Henry VIII of England, when Cardinal Wolsey ruled for him and was deemed his viceroy. Philip never came out into the open, yet he was never absent from critical events. He inherited the aureole of the crown, and the staff of able, bold, unscrupulous, and flint-hearted bureaucrats, with whom kingship was the first article of faith. He chose from them truly terrible ministers, and supported them fearlessly. We may guess that he was aware that the loyalty of France had given him a giant's strength, and he used it like a giant. For him and for his creatures formal legality in religion and politics took the place of a moral conscience. It was an attitude of mind which with less consistent ruthlessness was characteristic of his time, the result of a long habit of appealing to the law : legal procedure was righteousness. This harmony with and excess of a reigning prepossession largely explains his success.

His Conflicts
with Boni-
face VIII

The cardinal fact of the reign of Philip the Fair was his conflict with Pope Boniface VIII and its victorious outcome, which was decisive for the course of European history. It was concerned with the closely allied and interwoven questions of clerical immunity and taxation, the papal claim for ultimate secular supremacy and moral supervision in politics, and the royal counter-claim for unfettered rule over the kingdom of France and complete independence in secular affairs. Obviously, these great questions raised the whole issue of sovereignty between State and Church, of papal prerogative, of the unified direction of Europe by the sacerdotal Papacy, and of the separatist rule of their peoples by the lay national kings. In the contest the papal theory was precisely formulated, and was repudiated.

The first step in the divergence was made in the treaties of Canfranc (1288) and Tarascon (1291) with Aragon, by which the Aragonese crusade was abandoned, and Charles Problem of
Clerical
Taxation of Valois compensated with the counties of Anjou and Maine surrendered by his father-in-law Charles the Lame of Naples. The crusade had been accompanied by the grant of tenths of clerical annual incomes in France, decreed by the Popes to finance the king in the war, if only partly applied to the professed object. The problem of finance was by now pressing in the European States. With their bureaucracies, their costly wars, and the increasing expense of more efficient government, the old revenue from demesne lands, customs, tolls, and feudal incidents was becoming insufficient. Direct taxation of income and property was frequently necessary. Lay subjects were liable for these new burdens, and gave with some grudging. The Church theory admitted the justice of the old feudal exactions, but not that of the new. The clergy, in short, objected to being at scot and lot with the laity for the common purpose of the realm. The Pope, in the curial theory, was sole disposer, even sole true possessor, of all Church endowments. New grants from them could only be made by his decree in the interests of religion. To reluctance on grounds of principle was added the fact that the Papacy needed taxation of the clergy in the form of " tenths " for its own political crusades, and a double taxation of clerical property by both Pope and king was a heavy burden even on the vast ecclesiastical lands.

Conflict came, therefore, when Philip the Fair after the conclusion of the Aragonese dispute was embroiled, as we shall see, with England in 1294. For the war he demanded grants from the French clergy in their synods. The protests of the malcontents found a new Pope at Rome, Boniface VIII.

The overbearing and despotic Pope had come to the Aims of
Boniface
VIII throne in a most difficult moment.[1] He had the Sicilian War on his hands ; the administration of the Church was out of gear ; and the Papacy was suffering from the political shifts and entanglements, the degradation of its aims and methods for half a century. Worldly as he was, he held the highest view of the power and functions of the Papacy. He would play the part of Innocent III on a later stage against more powerful adversaries. He looked on the Church as a great governing machine, and was unconscious,

[1] See above, Chap. IV, p. 94

perhaps, how much that very fact had weakened its hold on men's consciences. Determined to abate no papal right, eager to dominate the world as a splendid autocrat, he was also eager beyond measure to exalt his own family, the Gaetani, to be the greatest of the Roman nobility, and pursued his and their ambitions and vendettas without scruple. He was regardless of the hatred he aroused, which was bitterest in the Roman Curia itself, where his fierce temper and autocratic bullying had full play.

The earlier years of his Pontificate

His abilities and his faults were soon shown. He revoked all the acts of Celestine V and the still unexecuted " expectations " of benefices granted since 1292. He completed the peace with James II of Aragon, thereby advancing the war with Sicily.[1] He undertook the codification of the Decretals issued since Gregory IX, and in 1298 published the *Sext* (the Sixth book of Decretals), by which the Canon Law was brought up to date and clarified. In short, as far as administration went, he brought system and order. But a dark side was shown, too, in his nepotism and in the imprisonment of his unfortunate predecessor, Peter Morrone, who soon died in 1296. The doubts as to the validity of a papal abdication were still entertained among the Spiritual Franciscans and whispered among the many malcontents of the Curia.

Clericis laicos

In this uneasy state of things came the first dispute with France. Boniface had no mind to see the clerical subsidies used to promote secular wars ; he needed them, too, for his own war with Sicily. He was a legislator, and dealt with difficulties by far-reaching enactments. In February 1296 he issued the thorough-going decretal *Clericis laicos*, by which all subsidies by the clergy to the lay rulers were forbidden, unless granted by the Pope. The open challenge was taken up at once. Edward I of England followed a north Italian precedent by outlawing the English clergy till they consented to pay. Philip the Fair took the offensive against the Pope : he banished foreign merchants from France and stopped the export of bullion and letters of credit. By paralysing the Italian mercantile system he deprived the Papacy of the bulk of its resources. Boniface vainly reiterated in the bull *Ineffabilis* of September 1296 the papal claims to supervise

[1] See above, Chap. IV, p. 95.

the political conduct of the king " ratione peccati," on the ground of sin, for such acts had their moral side. The French responded by the new weapon of pamphlets : the king had the independent rule of his kingdom ; the clergy ought to take their share in the public burdens. Important for their effect on opinion, these pronouncements only supplemented Philip's material measures, and Boniface slowly retreated. The bull *Romana mater* of February 1297 The Pope's began his surrender ; in July 1297 the bull *Etsi de statu* surrender to completed it. The king could receive clerical subsidies Philip IV without papal consent in case of necessity, of which he, and not the Pope, was to be the judge. Special favours accompanied this : Louis IX was canonized ; even Pierre Flote, the king's chief minister, was gratified by personal favours ; Boniface consented to arbitrate between Philip and Edward as a private person only. In fact, the cause of the lay State had been won, and other kings gradually obtained in practice like powers to those of the King of France.

One reason for Boniface's surrender was his quarrel with Boniface's the Roman house of the Colonna. In the first year of his feud with pontificate he had fallen out with the two cardinals of the the Colonna family, Giacopo and Pietro, and the chief laymen, Stephen and Sciarra. The reasons were partly political—the cardinals inclined to peace with Sicily and conciliation to France ; partly family and personal—the Pope favoured some other Colonna in a disputed inheritance, and was rapidly forming by purchase a vast estate in the southern Campagna for his nephews, which threatened to eclipse all rivals ; and partly religious, for Cardinal Giacopo was a friend to the Spiritual Franciscans, who denied that Boniface was true Pope. Matters came to a head when in May 1297 Stephen seized a convoy of the Pope's treasure at the gates of Rome, the purchase money for fresh acquisitions. Within a week Boniface deposed the cardinals and confiscated their lands. The Colonna replied that Boniface was no Pope, but a simoniacal tyrant. The Pope's resource was to proclaim a crusade against the schismatic house, the final degradation of the Holy War when it was used, not against Saracens or infidels, but against his private enemies. Yet it was success-ful. The Colonna fortresses fell by 1298 ; Palestrina, the chief, was levelled with the ground ; the Colonna themselves made humiliating submission, and then fled to spread evil rumours of the Pope in France and Italy.

The Jubilee of 1300

Boniface advanced to more ecumenic schemes in the institution of the Jubilee of 1300. He decreed that all pilgrims to Rome, who visited the seven basilicas in that year in penitence, should receive, like crusaders, full pardon for their sins. The antiquity of the new custom was assumed : every hundred years there was a Jubilee. It suited the Pope's temper to consolidate partial, local indulgences in one great festival ; as the prospect of a crusade to win back Palestine receded, it offered a peaceful substitute which exploited and increased the glory of the Papacy and the Eternal City. Diplomacy and remarkable organizing talent were required. Peace was secured among the warring States of North Italy and the routes made safe. The provisioning, housing, and policing of the swarms of pilgrims in Rome were carried through. The city reaped a golden harvest, and the Papacy a handsome increment of income. Boniface was uplifted beyond measure. He was improving the organization of the turbulent Papal States, and scheming by negotiations with Albert of Germany to add Tuscany

The Crisis at Florence

to them. This and his relations with his bankers brought him into Florentine domestic politics. In the rapidly growing city there were at least four strata of inhabitants : (1) the nobles or magnates, partly feudal, partly banking merchants, always riotous with their incessant vendettas, excluded from the government and under laws of exception, but none the less dominating the actual magistrates ; (2) the wealthy *popolani* of the Greater Arts, who were merchants, bankers, and lawyers ; (3) the *popolani* of the Lesser retail Arts, prosperous, but having only a subordinate share in the government ; (4) the swarming employees of the Greater Arts and the petty handicraftsmen, who had no part in the government, but a large part in revolutions. Since the Ordinances of Justice of 1293 a marked fissure had become

Black and White Guelfs

evident in the governing groups. The Blacks represented the extreme Guelf nobles, entrenched in the *Parte Guelfa*, and a number of bankers and merchants of European commerce. They held to the valuable alliance with the Papacy. The Whites were moderate Guelfs from the same classes,

who believed in conciliation, save with their domestic foes,
and objected to be tied to the Pope's chariot-wheels. The
whole political division was dominated by family and commercial rivalries. Though a leading Black noble, the
" baron " Corso Donati, might aim at tyranny, as a whole
neither party thought of disturbing the existing constitution.
Both wooed the Lesser Arts and the unenfranchized handicraftsmen. Both aimed at crushing the rival faction. In
1300 the Whites, led by the Cerchi, the wealthiest bankers
in Europe, had gained the upper hand, and Corso Donati
had been exiled. They resisted Boniface's moves to direct
the city's policy, in which the papal bankers, the Spini,
who were Blacks, were involved, while at the same time
faction hatred broke out into open violence, and the leading
Blacks were sent into exile, along with Whites indeed who
were soon recalled. Boniface resolved to enforce submission.
Charles of Valois came to Italy with armed force in 1301
on his way to the Sicilian war. He was sent first as Peacemaker to Florence by the Pope, and was admitted on
November 1 into the city by the trembling Whites. This
was the signal for revolution. Corso Donati entered the city **Expulsion of**
and roused his faction and the mob. The Whites were **the Whites**
plundered and soon proscribed by the triumphant Blacks.
Their subsequent efforts to re-enter by force were failures.
Yet Florence under the Blacks maintained her independence
of the Papacy, and Donati met his death later in an attempt
to overthrow the constitution. A more famous victim of
these civil broils was the poet Dante, who went into lifelong banishment in 1302 with the Whites.

Charles of Valois, who had done the Pope's work in **The second**
Florence, failed, as we have seen,[1] in Sicily, but before that **dispute with**
failure the second and fatal breach between Boniface and **Philip IV**
Philip the Fair had begun. The immediate origin of it lay
in the case of Bernard Saisset, Bishop of Pamiers in Languedoc. The bishop was a hasty, intemperate southerner, who
hated the French of the north and was far from a devoted
subject of the king. He was also at odds with his neighbours,
and it seems that Philip and his councillors decided to teach
recalcitrant prelates a lesson by his condign punishment.
Saisset was haled suddenly to Senlis to an assembly sum-

[1] See above, Chap. IV, p. 95.

moned there in October 1301. He was charged with an extraordinary catalogue of crimes, based on most inadequate evidence, which were taken as proved. This broadcasting of exaggeration and calumny was to be the favourite method of propaganda for Philip's acts of tyranny. This time Pierre Flote was the king's spokesman, but the procedure shows the hand of another adviser, a lawyer of Languedoc, Guillaume de Nogaret, grimly anti-clerical and a fanatic for the monarchy, a product of the Albigensian persecution and the enforced Catholicism of his country. Then Boniface was astounded by the demand for Saisset's deposition and degra-dation, so that the king's hand might be freed in his punishment. Here was a fresh attack on clerical immunity, following continuous clerical taxation and Philip's alliance with Albert of Germany whom the Pope had not recognized. Boniface resolved to fight on the general question. In December 1301 by the bull *Salvator mundi* he suspended all the recent concessions to the King of France, and in the *Ausculta fili* bull *Ausculta fili* he delivered a bitter lecture to Philip on the faults of his government, more especially with regard to the Church ; the king, he declared, was subject to the Pope—not to think so was to be an infidel. Meantime he summoned the French prelates to a council at Rome in November 1302 for the reformation of the kingdom of France.

Philip once again took up the challenge. His ministers circulated a forged and offensive parody of *Ausculta fili* along with a similar forged reply of the king. Then, with the ground thus prepared, an assembly of nobles, clergy, and bourgeois, the ancestor of the later States General, took place at Paris in April 1302, in which Pierre Flote upheld, with general assent, the absolute independence of the king in temporal matters and denounced the extortions and greedy provisions of the Pope in France. The Pope in return pressed his superiority " ratione peccati " in a wrathful speech, and held his council, which some third of the French prelates, chiefly from the south, attended. On November 18 *Unam* he issued the celebrated bull *Unam Sanctam*, in which the *Sanctam* claims of his predecessors were given precise legal form. Both swords belonged to the Papacy, the spiritual for direct exercise, the temporal to be exercised by kings under the Pope's supervision. To be subject to the Pope was necessary for salvation. Characteristically in this controversy he answered effective acts by an alarming pronouncement on general doctrine. "My master's sword," Pierre Flote had said, "is of steel, the Pope's of verbiage." Yet events seemed to play into Boniface's hands. The French army had been routed at Courtrai and Pierre Flote slain. When Cardinal Jean Lemoine came to France to treat, the king was at first conciliatory.

It was not for long. Guillaume de Nogaret, more bold and far more unscrupulous than Flote, became the king's chief adviser. It seems that Lemoine, who like many at the Curia hated his master, played the traitor and reinforced the ugly rumours spread by the Colonna. A scheme of fierce aggression and wily propaganda was resolved upon. At an assembly of notables in March 1303 Nogaret denounced the Pope as a usurper, a tyrant, a criminal, an unbeliever, given to every vice, and captured thereby, largely by slander, French opinion. Meanwhile he was dispatched on a secret mission to Italy, leaving the work of propaganda to continue. His mission was startling: to capture the Pope and bring him for trial before a general council of the Church. *Mission of Guillaume de Nogaret*

Both sides prepared for a final struggle. Philip in further assemblies and by diligent propaganda defined the case against the Pope and ranked public opinion behind him. Boniface secured the alliance of Albert of Germany and accepted peace with Sicily. He was unaware of his real weakness. He was hated in the Curia and in the Campagna, where the Colonna and a crowd of dispossessed nobles, whose lands had been purchased for the Gaetani, sought their *vendetta* and were too near to the Papacy to be restrained by reverence. While Boniface was at his native place, Anagni, completing a bull of excommunication and suspension of Philip, Nogaret and his band of local adherents on September 7, 1303, entered the little city by the treachery of the Pope's captain of the guard. He spent some hours in forcing his way into the Pope's palace, which was fiercely defended by the Gaetani, but ingress was at last achieved through the cathedral. Boniface was found lying on his bed, clasping the cross and defiant. " Here is my neck, here is my head," he replied to his enemy Sciarra Colonna. But Nogaret could not complete the abduction of the Pope *The Outrage of Anagni* he had captured, and the townsmen turned against him. On the 9th they rose and forced him from the city. The Orsini came to escort the Pope to Rome through the anarchic Campagna, and there worn out by disease and mental agony he died on October 11. Legends of senile insanity at his end were at once spread. His life had been violent and tyrannic. He had the appetite of glory of the future Renaissance. His nepotism and greed of gain had been flagrant. But his fall was due to his attempt to maintain unchanged, with pedantic legalism, the authority of Innocent III at a time when the secular powers had grown immensely stronger, while the spiritual prestige of the Papacy had decayed owing to the misuse of its powers and that worldliness of which the " magnanimous sinner," Boniface himself, if we dismiss malignant slander, was a crying example.

Pope Benedict XI

The new Pope, Benedict XI, a pious Dominican, was conscious of his weakness. He at once forgave King Philip, but refused pardon to Nogaret and his accomplices. How far this attempt at compromise was feasible was concealed by the Pope's sudden death on July 7, 1304. There succeeded a prolonged vacancy, for the cardinals were obstinately divided between the pro-French and the Bonifacian factions. At last by a tortuous and discreditable intrigue the pro-French secured the election of Bertrand de Got, Archbishop of Bordeaux, a seeming Bonifacian who had really come to a secret, if vague, understanding with Philip the Fair. He

Pope Clement V.

The Babylonish Captivity

took the name of Clement V (1305–14), and at once startled even his supporters by ordering the Curia to join him beyond the Alps. The " Babylonish captivity " of the Papacy had begun.

The " captivity " was largely due to Clement's personal character. He was timid, irresolute, and constantly ill, perhaps with cancer. He turned the disaster of Anagni into utter defeat, for he succumbed time and again to Philip's pressure. He feared " to scandalize our dear son, the King of France." The warring state of Italy may have excused for a while the exile of the Papacy from Rome; Clement made it permanent in 1309 by settling in the little Provençal

The Papacy of Avignon

city of Avignon on the east bank of the Rhone close to the papal possession of the Comtat Venaissin. There surrounded by the cardinals, whom he made French by numerous creations, he was both protected and terrorized by his close neighbour and compatriot, Philip the Fair.

Philip IV and Nogaret held continuously over the head of the shrinking pontiff the threat of a posthumous process, as a preliminary to condemnation, against his predecessor Boniface VIII. This was not only necessary for Philip's exculpation and Nogaret's safety but also to complete the victory of the lay monarchy of France over papal pretensions. It was also a most formidable weapon of offence to make the Pope pliable in disputed questions, for the spectacle of the dead Pope's trial as a usurper and heretic, and the exposure of the accumulated scandals, true and untrue, of the Roman Court, would be a deadly blow to the prestige and good name of the Papacy. Clement almost immediately annulled *Clericis laicos* and *Unam sanctam* as far as France was concerned, a curious proviso, and restored the Colonna to their cardinalships and lands. This did not fulfil Philip's demands, and a new problem was soon involved with the old, the destruction of the Knights Templars.

The Process against Boniface VIII

The Order of the Temple had long been unpopular for its pride and money-making propensities—it had taken with success to advanced finance, and in France acted as the king's treasurer. Since the fall of Acre in 1291 it had lost its *raison d'être*, for the Knights did not, like the Hospitallers, secure a new field of action in the East. The conduct of individual knights laid it open to reproach and encouraged hostile rumour. Its wealth attracted the covetous eyes of the needy French government. Financial exhaustion, indeed, was probably one of Philip's chief motives in destroying the Order, for he kept their French lands during his insolvent reign ; another was possibly the wish to abolish the dangerous non-royal force of 2,000 knights cantoned in France. In any case, in 1305 he decided to destroy them, and the ruthless Nogaret was placed in charge to collect evidence. Two years of underground work produced a sufficient amount of evidence of malpractices for Philip to place before the Pope at Poitiers in April 1807. Clement promised an inquiry, but this was not enough. In September Nogaret was promoted to be keeper of the royal seal ; on October 13, by secret orders, all the Templars in France were thrown into prison, and their lands seized by the king's officers. This

The Knights Templars

Philip's Attack on the Order

coup d'état, which even the Pope feebly blamed, was followed
by a proclamation accusing the wretched knights of heresy,
idolatry, and the worst immorality, Nogaret's usual method
of propaganda ; and the prisoners were put to prolonged
torture to extort confessions of the imputed crimes.   Almost
all, including the Grand Master, gave way : " I would say
that I have killed God," said one in fear of the flames.

The confessions, indeed, were worthless, but they were according to the law.   With them before him, the Pope began
his inquisition, and asked for a general sequestration of the
Order's property throughout Christendom.   But once the
French Templars were brought before the Pope's deputies,
they retracted their confessions, and Clement took the affair
into his own hands.   This was dangerous, and the French
Government resorted once more to propaganda.   Clement's
own notorious nepotism and greed were denounced ; the
imputed crimes of the Templars insisted on.   An assembly
at Tours in May 1308 was imbued with the royal views.
Clement was squeezed into surrender by a second interview
with the king at Poitiers.   A new inquisition by prelates
on whom Philip could rely was ordered ; similar measures
were to be taken outside France ; and a General Council was
summoned to Vienne to decide the question for October 1310.
Still things did not go well for the king.   Numbers of French
Templars still retracted their first confessions.   In Spain
and Germany, outside Philip's influence, the Knights were
acquitted.   In England, in spite of torture, the result was
that nothing was proved.   In Cyprus, too, the Knights
were acquitted and only executed by an act of political
vengeance of their enemy, the king, Henry of Lusignan.
Then came another stroke of policy in France.   In May
1310 sixty-three Templars, who had retracted, were burnt
as relapsed into heresy, and this terrified the rest.   Meantime, in 1308, Philip and Nogaret used their most efficient
weapon : they pressed their accusations against Boniface
VIII.   Clement saw himself obliged to open a process, which
at last took shape in 1310.   Once the accumulation of
scandals, however dubious, began, his remaining courage
vanished.   By the final date of the Council of Vienne,
The Council   October 1311, he was ready for a humiliating transaction.
of Vienne.   The king himself came with troops to Vienne to overawe the

Council. Clement refused to hear the Templars' defence, and, fearing an adverse vote of the prelates, in April 1312 dissolved the Order on his own authority on grounds of expediency. Their goods were decreed to the Hospitallers, to whom, loaded with debts and charges after a number of years, they eventually came. Already, he had obtained the cessation of the process against Boniface. The price was high. In April 1311 he erased from the papal registers all bulls against Philip and his instruments. Philip was even praised for his laudable zeal against Boniface. Nogaret, Sciarra Colonna, and their accomplices at Anagni were absolved. At last, in May 1313, the edifice of reconciliation was crowned by Celestine V being declared a saint under his private name of Peter Morrone. This shame-faced bull was not published, and Dante could still place the dead hermit in perpetual limbo for his " gran rifiuto," the abdication which after all was wise.

There remained one last act of the Templars' tragedy. The Grand Master, Jacques de Molai, and some other dignitaries after long imprisonment were brought to final trial in 1314. When they asserted their and the Order's innocence, they were declared relapsed and burnt at the stake. Clement, Nogaret, and Philip soon followed their victims to the grave.

The means which Philip and his ministers used in their attack on Boniface VIII and the Templars were iniquitous. They would hardly have been successful had not both Papacy and Order sunk deeply in public opinion, and had not a new awe and loyalty surrounded the French monarchy. They signalized the triumph of the lay State over the ecclesiastical hierarchy and its chief, a triumph which was never really reversed. Under Clement at any rate the " Babylonish captivity " of the Papacy was a literal fact. It might seem a just retribution for the papal policy during many decades. But the methods employed engendered long-lived evils. The heaping up of incredible slander, torture, and inequity became characteristic of French legal procedure till the Revolution of 1789. They, like the similar disregard of elementary justice in the Inquisition, deformed European criminal law for centuries. They gave a sanction to degrading popular superstitions of witchcraft and demoniac intervention. They increased the heartless cruelty they displayed. But they were symptoms as well as causes. The ideals of knighthood and of religion, which, if truly exemplified by few, had taken so powerful a share in raising Western Europe out of furious barbarism, were becoming more formal and external as they were more widely accepted as a code by the many. An adherence to the letter of the law dispensed with the indwelling spirit. The institutions and ideas were still strong and had no worthy rival, but the sap was retreating to their roots. The winter of discontent was showing signs of its approach.

SUGGESTIONS FOR READING ON CHAPTER XI

A. Sources

(i) Documents

The Sext. *Liber Sextus Decretalium.* In *Corpus Juris Canonici.* Ed. Friedberg, E. Vol. ii. Leipzig, 1879–81.

Dupuy, P. : *Histoire du différend d'entre le Pape Boniface VIII et Philippes le Bel.* Paris, 1655.

Finke, H. : *Acta Aragonensia.* 3 vols. Berlin, 1908–22.

Lizerand, G. : *Le dossier de l'affaire des Templiers.* (Classiques de l'histoire de France au moyen âge.) Paris, 1923 [with French translation].

(ii) Chronicles, etc.

Villani, G. : *Historie Fiorentine.* Muratori, *Rerum Italicarum Scriptores.* Vol. xiii. English selections by R. E. Selfe and Philip Wicksteed. London, 1906.

Compagni, D. : *Chronicle.* English translation in Temple Classics. London, 1906.

Nangis, G. de : *Gesta Philippi III* and *Chronicon.* Bouquet, *Rerum Gallicarum et Francicarum Scriptores.* Vol. xx.

B. Modern Works

Cambridge Medieval History, vol. vii, relevant chapters.

Digard, G. : *Philippe le Bel et le Saint Siège, de 1285–1304.* Paris, 1937

Glotz, G. : *Histoire Générale, Histoire du Moyen Âge,* vol. vi : *L'Europe occidentale de 1270 à 1380,* pt. i. Paris, 1940.

Hughes, P. : *A History of the Church,* vol. iii. London, 1947.

Lavisse, E., ed. : *Histoire de France.* Vol. iii (as for Chapter V).

Langlois, C. V. : *Philippe le Hardi.* Paris, 1877.

Mollat, G. : *Les papes d'Avignon.* 6th edn. Paris, 1930.

Boase, T. S R. : *Boniface VIII.* London, 1933.

Finke, H. : *Aus den Tagen Bonifaz' VIII.* Münster, 1902.

Gregorovius, F. : *History of the City of Rome in the Middle Ages.* Eng trans. Hamilton, Mrs. Vol. v, pt. 2. London, 1906.

Gardner, E. G. : *Dante.* London, 1923.

Armstrong, E. : *Italian Studies.* Ed. Ady, C. M. London, 1934 ; and some works on Italy listed for Chapter III.

CHAPTER XII

THE DECLINE OF THE PAPACY AND THE CHURCH

THE decline of the Church in the fourteenth century The Popes
is especially associated with the long residence of of Avignon
the Popes at Avignon, the " Babylonish captivity,"
as the poet Petrarch termed it.   This decline, however, was
of old date.   It was only accentuated in this period.   Under
the Popes of Avignon over-centralization and over-taxation
of the Church, the over-development of the governmental
machine, the diversion of the papal revenues to secular,
territorial warfare, the decay and ossification of the local
administration of the dioceses, all of which had long been
in progress, grew to an immense degree.   The Popes of
Avignon did not create, but they increased these evils.   Their
attempts at reform were spasmodic, and commonly vitiated
by their own greed of money and excessive grasp on power,
not to mention the disasters of the times for which they
were not responsible.

Seven Popes occupied the Chair of St. Peter during this
period, men as a rule of capacity and good intentions.
Clement V was, as we have seen, weak and greedy of money, Clement V
which he showered on his relations ; led by a natural preference for his countrymen, he gave the French, and more
especially the South French, cardinals an enormous preponderance in the Sacred College, which his successors, just
as naturally, only increased.   It was this that rooted the
Papacy in its temporary residence at Avignon.   As far as
was possible in an ecumenic institution, it became French,
and the Curia was manned by Frenchmen.   On Clement's
death, fierce dissensions broke out between the Gascon
cardinals favoured by him, the Italian remnant, and the
other French members of the College.   After two years an
agreement was only reached under pressure from the King
of France, Philip the Tall.   The choice fell on the Cardinal-
bishop of Porto, Jacques d'Euse from Quercy in Languedoc,

John XXII who took the name of John XXII (1316–34). Although he was seventy-two at his accession, this Pope left an indelible mark on the Papacy. He was arbitrary and nepotistic, passionately fond of despotic power, but he was a clear-sighted lawyer and an organizer. He systematized the centralizing monarchy of his predecessors. He met opposition by fierce persecution. He left behind him a needless quarrel with the Empire and the fruitless wars of Italy. By a natural reaction against John's hard shrewdness the **Benedict XII** next Pope, Benedict XII (1334–42), was the Gascon Cardinal Jacques Fournier, an ex-inquisitor and monk. This rigid man and poor politician endeavoured without great success and with much unpopularity to reform the Curia, the clergy, and the monastic Orders. His reforms were honestly meant and dealt with acknowledged evils, but he lacked the statesmanlike skill to enforce them or to check the luxury of his own court. Such success as he had was endangered and the finances of the Papacy were seriously impaired by the con-**Clement VI** duct of his successor, Clement VI (1342–52). This was a Limousin, Cardinal Pierre Roger, Archbishop of Rouen, a noble cleric and chancellor of the King of France. He was the least conscientious of the pontiffs of Avignon ; his personal morality was dubious ; his love of splendour and luxury and his reckless gifts and provisions dissipated Benedict XII's savings and led the Church into permanent embarrassment, almost insolvency. " My predecessors did not know how to be Popes," he replied to a remonstrance. He was, however, a profuse patron of art and learning, a brave man who faced the Black Death at Avignon and put a check on the accompanying panic-struck fanaticism, and a statesman unlike the Pope who replaced him, another Limousin, **Innocent VI** Innocent VI (1352–62). Clumsy and vacillating by nature, Innocent VI met hard times and harsh judgements. It was in his reign that the Free Companies, bred in the Hundred Years' War, ravaged Provence and threatened the papal residence of Avignon itself. A first invasion in 1357 resulted in the re-fortification of Avignon. In 1360–1 the bands, out of employ owing to the treaty of Brétigny, besieged the city and only retreated in return for a heavy bribe. The next **Urban V** Pope, Urban V (1362–70), was saintly and learned, the admired of his contemporaries. He even had the courage

o return to Rome in 1367 during the short-lived peace
secured by Cardinal Albornoz. If his resolution broke down
under difficulties and he made his way back to Avignon in
the year of his death, he had set a precedent which was
irresistible. Rome was no longer much more dangerous
than Avignon. The worthy Gregory XI (1370–8), like all *Gregory XI*
these Popes a south Frenchman, found himself obliged, if
he wished to avoid revolt in the Papal States and perhaps
a schism, to transfer the Papacy to its seat at Rome once
more in 1377. He listened to the impassioned appeals of
St. Catherine of Siena. He was, indeed, ready to flee to
Avignon when he died, but his death at Rome caused first
the election of an Italian Pope, and then the revolt of the
French cardinals and their election of a rival Pope, who
returned to Avignon. The Great Schism began, and, with *The Great*
Western Europe divided between the competing Papacies *Schism*
of Rome and Avignon, the evils in the Church reached their
worst.

The papal court at Avignon had a bad name with con- *The Papal*
temporaries. English and Germans looked on it as abusing *Court*
its economic wealth and power in favour of France. The
Italians never forgave the desertion of Rome, which seemed
emphasized by the purchase of Avignon from the Countess
of Provence, Joanna I of Naples, in 1348. The poet Petrarch
described it as " the sink of vice, the sewer of the world."
Cardinals and curialists were said to be given up to luxury.
The crowd of courtiers and benefice-seekers brought immense discredit. The Popes were almost invariably profuse
in the promotion and endowment of their relatives. But
nepotism, greed, and vice were no strangers to the Curia
in Italy. As the centralization of the Church and the
numbers of functionaries grew at Avignon, they were naturally there displayed on a larger scale. The extravagant
splendour of Avignon was certainly marked. The fourteenth
century saw an increase in pomp and show and costly luxury
of life in all courts, and the Curia led the way. The cardinals entertained princely retinues ; the Pope kept more
than royal State ; magnificent festivals were the order of
the day ; building and the arts found generous patrons.
With intense bitterness men saw the endowments of the
Church despoiled and squandered.

Centralization was increased and money extorted in most
departments of papal activity. First, there was the system
of papal appointments and provisions, i.e. the collation to
benefices, either actually vacant or merely in prospect of a
vacancy, by the Pope in disregard of the ordinary electors
or patrons if ecclesiastics. This was of old date, and served
several purposes besides that of deciding disputes or remedy-
ing neglect. It endowed learning, it promoted adherents,
it conciliated kings and potentates by appointing their candidates, it brought in a large revenue by the special taxes
it imposed on benefices which were thus filled, and, as important as any, it supplied incomes for the Pope's bureaucracy headed by the cardinals, the worst pluralists in Christendom. In the actual conferment of minor provisions, there
was little system ; petitions for them were commonly granted,
but this conferred no absolute right to a benefice, only a
strong claim which might need adjudication ; no proper
record was kept of grants ; there might be several papal
expectants waiting, one after another, for the same benefice,
and, on a vacancy, there might be rivals appointed by the
ordinary collators. It was the parent of continual litigation
between the claimants. But a system of the papal rights
was developed by the decretals of general " reservations."
Innocent IV had won an unenviable notoriety by his reckless
use of provisions to further his political ends. These were
so to say, haphazard. Clement IV in 1265 decreed that all
benefices which were vacated by the death of the holders
while at the Curia should be " provided " by the Pope.
The categories of benefices under this general reservation
were extended by Boniface VIII and Clement V, and John
XXII codified the system in 1316 by the bull *Ex debito*
under which all benefices held by curialists and a host of
others were subject to general reservation. He did, indeed,
attempt, though more in show than fact, by the bull *Execra-
bilis* (1317), to lessen the evils of non-residence and pluralism
by forbidding the accumulation in one person of benefices
with " cure of souls " ; but by the time of Gregory X
practically all benefices of which the right of collation belonged to ecclesiastics were reserved permanently or temporarily by the Pope. The practice of " providing " to
bishoprics had reached considerable proportions, varying

according to the country concerned, in the thirteenth century. The continual disputed elections owing to the absence of a majority rule—for only the better (*sanior*) party was supposed to carry its candidate—gave perpetual excuse for a papal appointment, in which political or curial motives were predominant. In the course of the fourteenth century the Popes claimed to provide to all sees. It was largely a phantom claim, for they provided commonly the royal candidate, subject to occasional promotions of curialist officials. In Germany, where the practice was more abusive, and bishops and abbots were princes of the Empire, the papal commands were defied by force ; their bearers ran some personal risk, and the Popes ended in saving their face by renewed provisions in favour of the hostile candidates. In England, the Statutes of Provisors and Præmunire gave the king and the ordinary collators, too, a weapon with which to resist. None the less, on the Continent the Popes won as far as formal law was concerned, and in any case reaped rich advantage to their finances. Centralization in short triumphed in its most inefficient and vexatious form.

One result of the irresponsible way in which provisions were made was to produce incessant litigation in the papal judicial courts between rival claimants of benefices. But this was only part of the immense judicial business arising out of the Canon Law which came before the Curia. The fact that the appellate jurisdiction of the Pope could be invoked at any stage in a Canon Law case immensely increased the numbers of such appeals, for it was not worth while to incur the delay and expense of appealing through the lower Courts Christian to obtain only reversible decisions. In these cases the Pope commonly appointed a local commission to investigate and decide ; in more important actions, the cases were tried and decided at Avignon. Papal justice was expensive and dilatory and in all cases a rich harvest of fees accrued. For the benefit of finality justice and its profits were centralized with universal consent and discontent in the Papacy. *Judicial Centralization*

Thus the gain to be acquired from provisions and litigation was one chief source of the income of the Curia. Besides the large fees and fines, the Popes claimed other casual receipts of importance. The goods of intestates were a *Taxation of the Clergy*

thirteenth-century source of revenue. John XXII secured
the *spolia*, i.e. private property of dead bishops and abbots
Urban V declared himself the heir of all ecclesiastics in
France and England.   At the same time the Popes demanded
the incomes of all vacant benefices.   Clement V, too, introduced the taking of annates or first fruits, which John XXII
the "father of annates," characteristically systematized
This meant the first year's net income of all benefices granted
by the Holy See.   By a more unscrupulous greed Urban V
annexed the procurations, i.e. the sums payable to bishops
for their entertainment during their visitations of their
dioceses.   Naturally, the visitations ceased while the tax
now papal, remained, and the supervision of local clergy
faded away.   Lastly, there was the open taxation of the
clergy by means of "tenths" of their incomes, or the more
attractively named "charitable subsidies."   For the raising
of all this revenue collectors were established in the different
countries, who received the sums due and transmitted them
directly or through bankers to the Curia.   Payment was
enforced rigorously by the ecclesiastical penalties for sin
which thus became the ordinary means of extortion.   On
one day in 1328 a patriarch, five archbishops, thirty bishops
and forty-six abbots were excommunicated for unpaid debts
to the Papacy [1].   Poets, chroniclers, and theologians all declaimed against the insatiable greed of the Curia.

Papal
Expenses

Crusades

Large part of the papal revenues, especially after the days
of the extravagant Clement VI, went to the splendour and
upkeep of the papal court.   But their wars accounted for
the Popes' heaviest expenses.   Of the wars the Crusade was
the most justifiable.   Alone among Christian princes the
Popes made the defence of Christendom from the infidel a
permanent aim of their policy.   The aggression of the Turks
in Asia Minor and defence of the Eastern Empire demanded
large sums, and the Popes subsidized and occasionally
organized naval and military expeditions.   The capture of
the island of Rhodes in the Ægean by the Knights Hospitallers
in 1310 gave an excellent base of operations ; in view of

[1] Bertrand de St. Geniès, Patriarch of Aquileia, paid to the Curia 20,000
florins of debts owing by his predecessors, and died himself in 1350, owing
still 2,550 florins after paying large amounts for his own liabilities to the
Curia. Aquileia was a wealthy princedom.

Turkish piracy the Venetians were useful allies ; and besides
minor operations Clement VI organized a considerable and
fruitless crusade to the Archipelago under Humbert II of
Dauphiné (1344–51).[1] But this expenditure was insignificant
beside that for the Italian wars. As absentees the Popes Italian Wars
of Avignon seemed more desirous of conquest and domination
in Italy than had been their Roman predecessors. They
feared to lose Rome ; they feared the Empire, the tyrants,
and the republics. They insisted on their sovereignty of the
Papal States. Dominion over Italy was the main object
of their foreign policy, for expulsion from Italy seemed
dangerous to the Papacy itself.

The Italian wars,[2] both successful and unsuccessful, but
never attaining their main purpose, began with the settlement at Avignon. Clement V fought and defeated Venice
in the War of Ferrara from 1308 to 1313 ; yet the native
house of Este soon recovered its practical independence.
John XXII attempted to overthrow the Ghibelline tyrants
of Lombardy, the Visconti and Della Scala, and to make his
own dominion in Romagna real. This crusade—for all wars
of the Church were now crusades—lasted from 1320 to 1834,
and in spite of some transitory successes of the legate in
charge, Cardinal Bertrand du Pouget, ended in complete
failure. It had been chequered by the last contest with
the Empire under Lewis the Bavarian. The progress of the
Visconti and the insubordination of the Papal States, where
papal rule was nearly a nullity, incited Innocent VI in 1853
to undertake a war of reconquest under the warlike cardinal,
Gil Albornoz. The war and diplomacy of ten years failed Albornoz
to overthrow the Visconti, but did subdue the Papal States
to submission and order. On the cardinal's death, however,
papal government deteriorated ; the French officials were
detested ; the Pope fell out with the republic of Florence ;
and a general revolt of the Papal States followed in 1875.
The atrocities of the Pope's mercenaries aroused hatred, but
they were eventually victorious. In March 1378 Florence
was accepting peace when Gregory XI died. In these long
and costly wars the Popes had gained little that was substantial. Their sovereignty in the Papal States was acknowledged, it is true, yet the component fractions, communes,

[1] See below, Chap. XIX, p. 409.   [2] See below, Chap. XVI.

tyrants, and nobles, after Albornoz' death acted in practical autonomy. The interference of the Empire was checkmated, and the struggle between the two titular heads of Christendom slipped out of sight when Charles IV abandoned all pretence of directing Italy. On the long theoretical dispute between the two swords the circumstances of its disappearance make an illuminating commentary.

The Papacy and Germany

To Germany, as will be seen later, the earlier Popes of Avignon may be described as uniformly hostile. They seemed to repay themselves for their loss of prestige by exalting their claims and intensifying their interference there. Clement V used the opportunity of the interregnum after the death of Henry VII to formulate papal suzerainty of the Empire in the most precise legal terms. John XXII, anxious to keep the imperial throne vacant, provoked the long contest with Lewis the Bavarian which only ceased under the accommodating Charles IV. Throughout, the Papacy appears as the fomenter of civil war and the suspension of government.

The Papacy and France

France suffered more than any country from papal exactions. It had, however, the satisfaction of being the eldest daughter of the Church. The Papacy became a French institution. Yet the " captivity " of the Popes may be exaggerated. Anti-German as they were, they attempted to mediate in the interests of peace and accommodation in the Hundred Years' War. But their bias was naturally French and loans to the French kings from papal resources betrayed their partiality to the sceptical English, and deprived them, to the detriment of their far successors, of spiritual influence. In a sense, not in doctrine but in unpopularity, the Avignon Papacy sowed the seeds of the Reformation in Germany and England.

Evils in the Church

Dioceses and Secular Clergy

The decline of the Papacy at Avignon was a symptom and an exacerbating cause of the evils in the Western Church. Non-residence, pluralism, political and unfit appointments, the perversion of spiritual powers and penalties to financial extortion, the substitution of vexatious administrative legalism for religious fervour, were all producing a cumulative effect. The bishops were statesmen, soldiers, and administrators. Their subordinate officials transacted diocesan business with minute attention to the letter of the law and

its abundant profits. Inspiring supervision had ended in
laxity and extortion. A great part of the revenues of the Appropria-
parishes had been alienated by the practice of appropriation, tion and
i.e. the gift of the cure of souls in them to a monastery, dence
which thereupon appointed a vicar with the lesser fraction
of the endowment as his salary. This was, indeed, better
than the appointment of an absentee rector who paid his
substitute chaplain as little as he could. Both practices
together resulted in the parishes being in charge of poorly
paid deputies. They meant that the ability and learning
as well as the revenues, if not always the virtue, of the
Church were diverted from the parishes to the better rewarded
and more ambitious careers of both ecclesiastical and secular
life. The concubinage, meanwhile, of the clergy was barely Concubinage
concealed, and extremely frequent. In France the terrible
calamities of the Hundred Years' War were no doubt chiefly
responsible for the actual desertion of parishes and the ruin
of their churches, but the exactions of the Curia unquestionably added to the distress. So did the mortality among the
parish clergy due to the Black Death and its sequels, and
this was a cause of impoverishment and inefficiency which
acted all over Europe. Here, too, the policy of the Curia,
in spite of remissions, did little to help on the needed
recuperation.

To the decadence of the secular clergy must be added the Monasteries
decadence of the monasteries. It had always been difficult
to maintain the strictness of the first enthusiasts among
their successors, but while monasticism still appeared to be
the only true Christian life and monks still led religious
opinion, reform after reform occurred in old foundations and
new orders or congregations, each with its stiffening or imitation of the Rule of St. Benedict, sprang up. That pre-
eminence and inspiration were ceasing at the beginning of
the thirteenth century. Uncloistered or secular life in the
new and better conditions of the time did not seem so ill,
the lead of public opinion passed from the secluded monks,
and the Christian ideal seemed better exemplified in the
social orders of mendicant friars. At the same time a widespread falling off was observable among the monks themselves. Besides sporadic failings and the necessary percent-
age of unfit monks, there were flagrant cases of degenerate

monasteries. More important was the general diminution
of fervour. The rule was slackly observed and interpreted
by lenient local customs in favour of indolent comfort ;
discipline decayed ; pomp and luxury increased ; the passion
for building, the bad management of vast estates, and an
expensive standard of life combined to place a large proportion of monastic houses in financial distress. Much of
this was attributed by men of the age, in their belief in
government, to the lack of supervision. The ordinary
Benedictine house was autonomous, subject only to episcopal
visitation, not welcomed or effective ; and some very great
houses were only subject to the Papacy. Innocent III's
remedy was to federate the Benedictine monasteries by means
of triennial provincial chapters for correction and standard-
ization. The measure no doubt hindered decay. None the
less decline continued. In the fourteenth century the old
abuses and slackness had increased ; flesh-eating, indolence,
and mismanagement were rife ; and it is noticeable that
learning—always the vocation of few—had deserted the
monasteries, as is shown, for instance, by the cessation of
the series of great monastic chronicles. As a result, new
monasteries were no longer being founded by the pious
laity. Only the very strict and undecayed Charterhouses
retained their hold on their esteem. Even additions to the
endowments of existing houses were rare, save in return
for " corrodies," i.e. the maintenance of pensioners. This
was really the purchase of annuities, often with bad financial
and moral results to the monasteries. Worst of all, perhaps,
was the growing habit on the part of the Popes of granting,
or allowing the grant of abbacies *in commendam*. By this
practice, the main revenues of a monastery were enjoyed
by an absentee cardinal or prelate, as time went on by
laymen too, and the monks were left to indiscipline and
irreligious poverty. Swarms of apostate monks, the *gyrovagi,*
contaminated society and brought discredit on the rest. In
1336 Pope Benedict XII endeavoured to check and regulate
these abuses by the bull *Summi magistri*. He decreed and
systematized the provincial assemblies ; he enforced strict
claustration, so much disregarded, and exclusion of the
laity ; he made provisions for good finance ; he reintroduced
a modified austerity. Learning was revived by the regula-

Reforms of
Benedict
XII

tions for sending selected monks to the universities and for the instruction of novices. This was legislation ; its effective observance, especially after Benedict's death, was doubtful. The Hundred Years' War in France, wars, politics, and the general lack of enthusiasm elsewhere produced decadence with little reduction of pace. The Black Death hit the monasteries hard. They never made up again the numbers of their inmates, nor did the comparative fewness of the monks mean greater selectness of their members. By the outbreak of the Great Schism the Rule of St. Benedict, so far as literal observance went, seemed passing into oblivion. This was not only the case of the autonomous Benedictines. It was equally marked among the federated Cistercians ; after the Black Death the decayed institution of lay-brothers was abandoned, and the farming of the Order was done by lease-holders or hired labourers ; the monks became mere landlords. Wholesale reform was necessary and demanded, but the individual conviction and effort which could give it seemed lacking, though the Brethren of the Common Life began such a movement in Friesland *c.* 1380.

More serious for the Church's influence and still more **The Friars** indicative of the decline of the ascetic ideal were the formalism and disrepute of the Friars. We have seen [1] how the Franciscans by the year 1250 had become divided into the " Conventual " majority and the " Spiritual " minority. The **Conventual** first were prepared to accept routine and the enjoyment of **and Spiritual** property ; they saw no difficulty in the subterfuge by which, **Franciscans** in gloves, they did not touch with the naked hand the coin they were given. The second adhered passionately to absolute poverty and partly owing to persecution withdrew in hermitages from the workaday world. In the bull *Exiit qui seminat* (1279) Nicholas III attempted a compromise. The Franciscans' possessions were declared the property of the Papacy ; they had merely the use of them, and the use of them should be ascetic. This did not satisfy the Spirituals, who gained a transitory success when Celestine V constituted them a separate Order. But Boniface VIII immediately cancelled this best act of the hermit Pope, nor was peace brought by Clement V, whose bull *Exivi de Paradiso* (1312) forbade landed endowment. John XXII, like the

[1] See above, Chap. II, pp. 59–61.

Persecution of the Spirituals

despot he was, proceeded to extremes against the recalcitrant Spirituals. A sharp persecution (1318), reinforced by the Inquisition and the stake, began their extermination, and was continued by Benedict XII. The apocalyptic views inherited from Joachim of Flora, and perverted by commentators into an " Everlasting Gospel " with the coming reign of the Holy Spirit, had for eighty years been rife among the Spirituals. Now under persecution their extremer members formed little heretical ascetic communities, mainly in Italy, generally known as Fraticelli, and in the divided and warring land, especially in Naples, where Robert the Wise showed them some sympathy, they succeeded in surviving. But the practical and legal Pope went farther. In 1322 he revoked the temporizing and quibbling *Exiit qui seminat* and vested their property in the Franciscans by law. This

Condemnation of the Doctrine of Poverty

was sincere. Then in 1323 he issued the dogmatic bull *Cum inter nonnullos*, by which the Franciscan doctrine that Christ and the Apostles lived in absolute poverty was declared heretical. Strangely enough, the Order which had been content to enjoy possessions hated their legal ownership and loathed abandoning the opinion of St. Francis. Some even revolted under the minister general, Michael of Cesena, who with William of Ockham and others took refuge with John's enemy, Lewis the Bavarian. They and their confederates fulminated against the heretical Pope ; Ockham introduced a new scepticism of papal claims ; their ally, Marsilio of Padua, produced his revolutionary work. Yet the Pope subdued the majority of the Order, and Benedict XII consummated the victory. The attitudes both of the Franciscan malcontents and of the Papacy were a sign of the legalistic temper of their day, which construed poverty in a purely legal fashion. Poverty in law was what the Franciscans wanted, and what the Pope denied them. Yet John XXII's action has a further significance : it marks the abandonment of the long-regnant, idealistic dream of the sanctity of utter poverty by the official Church. Always evaded, it was now flouted, though asceticism retained its old reverence.

Rivalry with Parish Clergy

Some of the weakness of the Franciscans may be attributed to their and other Friars' competition with the secular clergy over the often profitable rights of preaching, of hearing confessions, and of burying their devotees. Here Boniface

VIII was on congenial ground when he evolved a workable
system of compromise, but the bitterness of the struggle
long remained.　John XXII suppressed with his accustomed
vigour the doctrine advanced by some opponents of the
Friars that not even the Pope could deprive parish priests
of the right to confess their parishioners.

In this controversy the Dominicans were equally involved. The
They too had declined from their primitive self-abnegation. Dominicans
Most convents were holding property in the fourteenth
century, yet they were poor and discipline was weak.　Individuals were allowed to obtain private incomes.　" Poverty,"
it has been said, " remained in common, wealth became
personal."　After the Black Death, the practice of " limitors "
arose.　A friar, called a limitor, farmed the profits of a
district, and lived on the surplus left after his rent to his
convent had been paid.　It does not seem that the efforts
for reform promoted by Innocent VI had any success.
Gregory XI did more by instituting a cardinal protector
of the Order and revoking all dispensations from the Rule.

The Black Death seems to have affected both regular and The Black
secular clergy mainly for the worse.　Naturally a larger Death
proportion of the conscientious Friars and clergy perished
in ministering to their flocks than of the selfish and negligent.
But if the pestilence increased existing decay, it also stimulated a revival of religious feeling.　Reform from below,
from the subaltern ranks of the clergy, is discernible just as
the Great Schism began.　It was more effectual than reform
from above by the Pope's decretals.

The Popes at Avignon were at continual war with heresy Heresy
and in parts of Europe with considerable success.　Catharism
had already received mortal blows in Southern France and
Italy in the thirteenth century.　It survived, though persecuted, in Bohemia and south-east Germany, confused inextricably with other heretical beliefs.　In its original stronghold among the Bogomils of Bosnia it maintained itself
unmixed until the Turkish conquest, when its adherents went
over to Islam.　Waldensianism was strong in the western
Alps and Dauphiné, though it was much diminished by
energetic persecution under Pope Gregory XI.　It had off-
shoots in the peasant communities of Bohemia which provided
a favourable environment for the spread of the extreme

Hussite movement of the Taborites in the fifteenth century.
The characteristic heresies, however, of the fourteenth century
were newer.   There were the extreme Spiritual Franciscans
with their apocalyptic interpretations of Joachite prophecies.
There were the Fraticelli who mingled fanatical Franciscanism
with pantheism, not to mention wild and credulous sects
believing in an incarnation of the Holy Ghost as were the
Lombard followers of Fra Dolcino.   There were the illumin-
ists of Germany and the Netherlands, who frequently combined pantheism with antinomianism.   Under leaders like
Ortlieb of Strasbourg and Marguerite de la Porète of Brabant
they were widely diffused among the religious lay associations

Mysticism   called Beghards and Béguins.   The pious mysticism of the
influential German Dominican Eckehart was strongly tinged
with pantheism.   Mysticism, often perfectly orthodox, was
indeed the favourite refuge of fervently religious minds in
an age when official religion ceased to satisfy.   All these
movements, save orthodox mysticism, had one quality in
common.   They were anti-clerical, opposed to the wealthy,
legal, hierarchic Church ; and the Church saw in them
deadly enemies to itself and the Faith.   Persecution was
most severe under John XXII, who destroyed heresy in
South France.   It did not cease under his successors.   The
vigilance and the terrors of the Inquisition were seldom in
abeyance.   But to prevent the continual resurgence of

John XXII   heretical views proved impossible.   By an odd fate John
XXII himself nearly proved a heretic.   He thoughtlessly
promulgated disheartening views on the state of the blessed
between their death and the Last Judgement.   The theologians rose against him in favour of the immediate joys of
Heaven ; the schismatic Franciscans declaimed ; and the
Pope, usually so self-willed, surrendered at discretion.   The
old view that Heaven at once succeeded the pains of Purga-
tory, which is enshrined in Dante, was a necessary solace
to much-tried humanity.

The better   In describing the decline of an institution, stress must
side   necessarily be laid on the causes and features of that decline.
The healthier side attracted less notice then and is less
prominent now.   That under all disadvantages piety and
good works and zeal remained widespread is clear.   The
heretics themselves were often examples of it.   Worthy

prelates, devoted clergy, and fervent evangelists found a
ready response in the people. It was a time of educational
foundations in lieu of monastic, such as the College of Navarre
at Paris in 1314 by the queen of Philip the Fair. The
Popes were zealous patrons of learning and the universities.
Benedict XII founded the university of Grenoble. Urban V
promoted others as a generous and sympathetic patron.
New channels were being dug for the intellectual and moral
life of Europe.

It was, however, in the Eastern missions that the zeal of Churchmen was seen with least alloy. St. Francis had revived the ideal of converting the infidels by persuasion. In 1253 one of the most worldly of the Popes, Innocent IV, created the society of *Peregrinantes propter Christum* (Travellers for Christ) from select Franciscan and Dominican friars. The heathendom of the Mongols gave a better opportunity of conversion than the rival monotheism of Islām. Adventurous missionaries, such as John of Pian-Carpino (1245) and William of Rubruquis (1252), ventured across Central Asia. Others worked more daringly among the Moslems. The saint of the movement was the Catalan Raymond Lull (1235–1315), whose zeal at last brought him martyrdom at Bougie in Barbary. Lull saw that conversion could only be carried on by missionaries who knew the oriental languages. He himself could speak and write Arabic, and he taught the language to others. Clement V was convinced, and the Council of Vienne decreed six schools of Oriental Languages. Under John XXII, who actively encouraged them, missionary friars were at work in Persia, Turkestan, and China. There was a Christian Archbishop of Peking. If these missions decayed in the second half of the fourteenth century owing to political revolutions in the Far East and the spread of Islām in Central Asia, they do not testify the less to the devotion and courage still alive among the Friars in an age of decadence.

Missions to the East

Raymond Lull

SUGGESTIONS FOR READING ON CHAPTER XII

A. Sources

Baluze, S.: *Vitæ Paparum Avenionensium.* Ed. Mollat, G. 4 vols. Paris, 1914–27.
Villani, G., and M. E., and H.: *Historie Fiorentine.* As for Chapter XI.
Nangis, G.: *Chronicon.* As for Chapter XI.

Les grandes chroniques de France (St. Denis). Ed. Delachenal, R. (Chroniques des règnes de Jean II et Charles V. Paris, 1910).

Murimuth, Adam de : Continuatio chronicorum. Rolls Series. London, 1889.

B. MODERN WORKS

Cambridge Medieval History, vols. v, vi, vii, relevant chapters.

Lavisse, E., ed. : Histoire de France. Vols. iii and iv, relevant chapters.

Mollat, G. : Les papes d'Avignon. 6th edn. Paris, 1930.

Barraclough, G. : Papal Provisions. Oxford, 1935.

Coulton, G. G. : Five Centuries of Religion. Vols. i–iii. Cambridge, 1923 ff.

Mollat, G. : La fiscalité pontificale en France en XIVe siècle. Paris, 1905.

Lea, H. C. : History of the Inquisition of the Middle Ages. 3 vols. New York, 1887.

Lea, H. C. : History of Sacerdotal Celibacy in the Christian Church. 3rd edn. 2 vols. London, 1907.

Underhill, E. : Mysticism. 12th edn. London, 1930.

Bréhier, L. : L'église et l'orient au Moyen Âge. 5th edn. Paris, 1928.

CHAPTER XIII

THE APOGEE OF THE FRENCH MONARCHY

THE spirit of centralization and autocracy which dis- The King's
tinguished the Papacy pre-eminently in the thirteenth Bureaucracy
and fourteenth centuries was also to be seen in the
French monarchy. Not only did the bureaucratic ministers
who surrounded the King of France restrict feudal independence and enlarge royal intervention ; they also persistently developed the central administration into organized,
specialized departments, the homes of a sedulous routine.
The lay element among these ministers steadily grew in the
thirteenth century. The bourgeois clerks and the " chevaliers
du roi," who were either bourgeois in origin or taken from
the petty nobles, had received a legal, not an ecclesiastical
education. They were permeated with a legal and secular
spirit ; their Gospel was the Civil Law, however expert they
might be in feudal and customary jurisprudence. To exalt
the royal power, which had made them, and which they
looked on, with some justice, as the true means of good
government, was their continuous policy.

The parent organ from which departments were born was The Curia
the Curia Regis, the fluctuating assembly of vassals, great Regis
and small, household officers, and confidential servants, in
which and with the help of which the king transacted his
business. After a long and slow evolution the Curia by the
end of the reign of Philip the Fair had been subdivided in
administrative practice. For justice there was the Parlement The Parle-
of Paris, now a professional supreme court of law for the ment of
realm. This again was subdivided into different " chambers " Paris
which dealt with the different stages of legal business, one
being set apart for criminal cases. To the Parlement came
the more important legal actions of the royal domain, the
cases involving the special royal protection of churches and
private persons outside the domain (whose number was large
and increasing), the numerous *cas royaux*, which, like treason,

were reserved to the Crown's justice everywhere, cases arising out of the delay of justice in the feudal courts, and the growing mass of simple appeals from the justice of the vassals and of the royal *baillis* and seneschals, who held the local courts of the domain.   The sittings of the Parlement with the extension of its business grew constantly longer till after 1328 it was in permanent session.   Under this régime feudal justice was slowly withering before the better justice of the king, and the independence of all but the greatest vassals was gradually destroyed.   In fact, the administration of justice was the strongest means the kings possessed for making themselves supreme in France.   In this they resembled the Popes in the Church.

The *Chambres des Comptes et aux deniers*

The royal finances, the receipts and expenses, were in charge of the *Chambre des Comptes*, which had evolved partly under the influence of the Norman Exchequer.   It was given its final organization by Philip the Tall, but it was not the unique financial organ.   The receipts and expenses attributed to the royal household were managed by the *Chambre aux deniers*.   The royal treasure until 1295 was stored in the house of the Knights Templars at Paris ; after that date it was moved, save for a brief interval from 1303 to 1307 when it was again at the Temple, to the Louvre under royal treasurers.

The Hôtel du Roi

More migratory than these departments at Paris was the Hôtel du Roi which accompanied the king wherever he happened to be, whether in his residence at the capital or in the provinces.   Besides the more domestic officers, there were two of the first importance, the Chamberlain, till 1275 the head of the Hôtel's finances, but continuously one of the king's most intimate counsellors, and the Keeper of the Seals, who was the chief of the secretarial staff, the Chancery. Although the Chancellorship was left vacant since 1227 on account of its too feudal associations, its functions were performed by the Keeper, who thus had the charge of all administrative orders, legislation, and diplomatic correspondence.   Pierre Flote and Guillaume de Nogaret were successively Keepers of the Seals.   Pierre de la Broce, who guided Philip the Bold until his fall and execution in 1278, and Enguerrand de Marigni, who passed for all-powerful in Philip the Fair's last years, were Chamberlains.

These men and their like were members of another insti- tution, the King's Council, which advised him on all questions of policy and government. It varied in numbers and personnel from time to time. Philip the Tall gave it formal shape, with monthly meetings, but even then the informal meetings of those Councillors who were told off to attend the king must have been equally important.

In contrast with this elaborate distinction of functions in the central bureaucracy stood the unity of the local adminis- tration. The royal domain, now the greater part of France, was divided into *baillages* in the north and *sénéchaussés* in the south. There were some thirty in 1314. The *bailli* or the seneschal represented the king in all matters, judicial, administrative, and police. Even the great vassals who adjoined his government were under his supervision. He himself was supervised by the central departments and by *enquêteurs* sent down by the king, who sometimes created more abuses than they cured. Grievances of the subjects were rife under these resistless officials. Even more than the *baillis*, their pettier subordinates, *prévôts*, *baïles*, and the innumerable serjeants, were blamed for extortion and tyranny. None the less the prosperity of medieval France reached its highest point under the sons of Philip the Fair.

The power of Philip the Fair made him unquestionably the greatest king in Christendom. Princes of his house ruled in Naples and Hungary, and he hoped to enthrone another as Emperor. In 1308 he strove for the election of his brother Charles of Valois, in 1313 for that of his son Philip the Tall. These efforts failed. More wise and more successful were Philip's personal encroachments on imperial territory, which began the long advance of France eastwards over French-speaking lands. The infinity of complicated and scattered fiefs gave him opportunities all along the frontier. Disputes between the archbishop and citizens of Lyons gave him the city, the key to the Rhone (1307). This was a frank annexation. The episcopal town of Toul in Lorraine accepted his protectorate (1300). The Bishop of Viviers, west of the Rhone, became his vassal (1305). So did the Count of Bar for his lands west of the Meuse (1301) and the Count of Hainault for Ostrevant on the Scheldt. Philip's influence extended farther than these annexations. It resulted in his son Philip the Tall marrying the heiress of Franche Comté, though this proved only a temporary gain to the Crown.

Encroach-
ments on
Guienne

Valuable as were these acquisitions, they weighed little with Philip compared with his designs on the two greatest fiefs of the Crown, Guienne and Flanders. The position of Guienne, in the nature of the case and under the conditions established by the Treaty of Paris in 1259, was bound sooner or later to produce a conflict between France and England. The King of France could not easily put up with the fact that a great and wealthy fief of his kingdom should be in the possession of a powerful foreign monarch, who set a bad example to other great vassals and was a possible rallying-point of feudal independence and disaffection. His ministers and Parlement naturally endeavoured by all possible means to reduce the duchy of Guienne to the same status as other French fiefs by a perpetual legal aggression. Appeals were constantly entertained; insubordinate vassals of Guienne were encouraged by the intervention and support of the supreme suzerain at Paris; royal officials took every opportunity of interference on the frontier; the full execution of the retrocessions of 1259 in the Limousin, Quercy, and Périgueux, and Saintonge was evaded. At the same time, a disposition was manifested to take advantage of disputes, under the fully developed feudal suzerainty of the day, in order to put an end to the English dominion by confiscating the duchy to the Crown under form of law. On the other hand, the King of England, now Edward I (1271–1307), though hampered by his own belief in thirteenth-century feudal jurisprudence, just as naturally maintained as much as he could the ancient, all but autonomous rule of his predecessors in Guienne and was inclined to govern it as an English province. Guienne, with its ports and vineyards, was too valuable a territory to lose. The situation was aggravated, too, by the conflicts of the English and Gascon seamen with those of France, for the seafaring of the day, although mercantile in essence, was inextricably mixed with piracy. Quarrels over fishing and dues led to fighting and fierce retaliation

Edward I
and Guienne

Edward I, an organizer and reformer in all things, took his territory in Guienne and Gascony very seriously. He made two long stays in the duchy, 1273–4 and 1286–9, and,

by encouraging old towns, founding a number of *villes neuves*
there called *bastides*), improving administration, and enforcing order on the turbulent Gascon nobles, increased its
prosperity and made it incidentally more valuable to himself.
At the time there was no dynastic hostility between the two
kings.   In 1279 Edward's queen, Eleanor of Castile, received
the county of Ponthieu on the Channel which came to her
by inheritance, and Edward himself obtained the Agenais.
In 1286 southern Saintonge was at length surrendered to
him by Philip the Fair.

It may have been Edward's success in Guienne coupled
with his own release from the dispute with Aragon which
made Philip take up a definitely aggressive policy.   In 1293
something like a sea-battle occurred on the Breton coast
between the Gascon seamen and the Norman.   Edward was
summoned as their duke to appear before the Parlement
of Paris to answer for the Gascons' wrongdoing.   He sent
his brother Edmund, Earl of Lancaster, the stepfather of
Philip's queen, to arrange a settlement.   Edmund agreed
to hand over the six chief fortresses of Guienne, in feudal
fashion, during the inquisition into the facts.   Meanwhile
fresh frays occurred, and the Parlement of Paris promptly
in 1294 declared the duchy forfeited for breach of vassalage.
Philip probably found the opportunity given by possession
of the fortresses too tempting to be resisted, but it meant
war between the two kingdoms.   Gascony was conquered
for the most part from 1294 to 1296 ; the French shipmen
were active in the Channel and contemplated an invasion
of England.   Edward was preoccupied meantime in Wales
and Scotland ; in 1295 Philip began a long-lived national
friendship by accepting the alliance of King John Balliol,
the King of Scots, who was just then defying his exacting
overlord, the King of England.   Henceforth in an Anglo-
French war England was always threatened at home by
the Scots.

In 1296, however, Edward's hands were freed by the
temporary conquest of Scotland, and Philip's aggressiveness
raised up another enemy in Guy of Dampierre, the Count
of Flanders.   Owing to the fact that the Flemings were the
chief buyers of English wool, there was a natural tendency
to friendship between England and Flanders, which in 1294

[marginal notes:] War with Philip the Fair

Philip's Attack on Flanders

had led to a proposed marriage between Guy's daughter and Edward's eldest son. This alarmed Philip, who had been pursuing the policy of legal intervention in the fief of Flanders as he had in the fief of Guienne. He imprisoned Guy until the match was given up, and later took control of the chief towns of Flanders. Edward, on his side, was laboriously buying allies, including King Adolf of Germany, among the rulers on the eastern frontier of France. It was a repetition of King John's policy in 1214. The only sure recruit to this league was the wronged Count Guy, who revolted from France in February 1297. But Philip continued his victories. As will be seen, he had powerful partisans among the Flemish townsmen. His general, Robert Count of Artois, won the battle of Furnes over Guy ; when Edward came to Flanders, he could do nothing, the other allies did not appear, and England was in ferment over Edward's taxation, while Wallace drove the English out of Scotland. The truce which the King of England was obliged to make was followed in 1298 by the arbitration of Boniface VIII, which made no mention of Flanders. This provisional peace was confirmed in 1299 by the marriage of Edward himself to Philip's sister and the betrothal of the Prince of Wales to Philip's daughter Isabella. The question of Guienne was still to be settled. Fortunately for Edward, Philip's defeat in Flanders, his quarrel with the Pope, and the hankering of the Gascons for their duke rendered the French court conciliatory at last. In May 1303 the Treaty of Paris restored Guienne to Edward as it was ten years before. The real problem which provoked hostilities was thereby adjourned to another generation.

Peace with Edward I

Philip's Conquest of Flanders

The causes of Philip's ill-success in Flanders were both nationalistic and social. Flanders was not a mere French fief : the larger part of its inhabitants spoke the Low German Flemish tongue ; they felt the French to be foreigners and therefore disliked them. In the social conflict [1] Philip both gained and suffered owing to his class allies. Count Guy (1278–1304), unlike his predecessors, fell out with the town oligarchies of patricians, who so much diminished his power and he favoured the discontented small masters and employees. The patricians turned (1287) to the suzerain, the

[1] See above, Chap. IX, pp. 181–82.

King of France, who seized the opportunity of intervening
in the country. The patricians became known as *leliaerts*
(men of the fleurs-de-lys) while their adversaries called themselves *clauwaerts* (men of the claws of the lion of Flanders,
the count's blazon). With the alliance of the *leliaerts*
Philip's progress was easy. In 1300 he invaded Flanders,
annexed it to the Crown, and took Guy prisoner. He had
united to the royal domain the wealthiest part of the French
kingdom. But the foundations of his power in Flanders
were weaker than he thought. The gildsmen and cloth-
workers detested his partisans, the patricians. The new
taxation of the king was heavy; Jacques de Châtillon, his
governor, and the French mercenary garrison were loathed
as alien tyrants. Under the eloquent demagogue, the weaver
Peter de Coninc (" the king "), discontent ripened into
revolution. On May 17, 1302, the weavers of Bruges rose
and massacred the French and their friends in " the Matins The Matins
of Bruges " (May 18) to the number of 3,000. The other of Bruges
towns joined the revolt with the same violence.

Philip took up the challenge and sent a splendid feudal Battle of
host under the Count of Artois. So did the sons of Count Courtrai
Guy, John and Guy of Namur, who hastened to take the
lead of the insurgents. At Courtrai, on July 11, the customary wild feudal charges of the French were routed by
the pikes and trenches of the Flemish weavers and peasants.
So great was the carnage of knights that Courtrai was named
the " battle of the spurs " from the golden spurs of the
dead. The Count of Artois and Pierre Flote were among
them. It was an epoch-making event, for it was a victory
of bourgeois over knights, of infantry over feudal cavalry,
and it eventually led to the preserving of Flanders from
absorption in France.

Philip strained the resources of his kingdom to avenge Continua-
Courtrai with little result save the uncertain victory of tion of the
Mons-en-Pévèle (1304). Yet he weakened the resolution of War with
the enemy house. Count Robert of Béthune (1304-22), Flanders
Guy's eldest son and successor, agreed to the humiliating
peace of Athis-sur-Orge (June 1305), by which, in return
for his countship, the walls of the Flemish towns were to
be destroyed, an enormous indemnity paid, and the Walloon,
i.e. the French-speaking, district of Flanders—Lille, Douai,

and Orchies—were delivered to the king as security. This hard treaty could not, however, be executed owing to the resistance of the Flemings. Conferences and legal proceedings before the Parlement of Paris succeeded one another without much result. At last in 1314 open war broke out again, but by this time Philip had wearied his own subjects by his exactions for his fruitless campaigns. In the effervescence of discontent he died on November 30, 1314.

Philip the Fair's success in brigading the public opinion of France in his support in the great crises of his reign was furthered by the development he gave to the assemblies of the vassals of the Crown. Such assemblies were characteristic of the thirteenth century, and it is a striking evidence both of the disunity of the French provinces and of the self-sufficing prestige of the king that their evolution into a system of Estates, i.e. a general assembly representing the main classes of vassals—clergy, nobles, and bourgeois—took place so late in France under Philip. His predecessors had from time to time held great meetings of their Curia for consultation on important affairs. St. Louis had summoned on occasion assemblies of bourgeois representatives on matters which concerned them. But the first recorded meeting of the three orders in the State was in 1290, when they sent each a letter to the Pope, and this is mentioned by no chronicler. In 1302, however, the gravest crisis of the reign, the dispute with Boniface VIII, was at its height. Philip needed a staunch kingdom behind him, and the means adopted was a general convocation of the Estates of France. In February there met at Paris in person or by proxies the clergy, the nobles, and the representatives of the towns. They came to discharge a part of their duty as vassals to aid and counsel their suzerain, and not only vassals-in-chief but also sub-vassals were included in this loyal service from the whole of France. This assembly is consequently ranked as the first States-General of the kingdom, corresponding to the English Parliament and the Cortes in Spain. If the term is anachronous because it was not yet invented, and because little originality and no finality existed in the method of meeting and consulting, the assembly of 1302 is the undoubted ancestor of the later States-General and exercised a decisive influence on the development of its descendants.

Death of
Philip the
Fair

The States-
General

Next year the need for intensive propaganda against Boniface produced a fresh mixture of experiment and reversion to partial precedents. An assembly of the Three Estates took place at Paris, but in Languedoc a similar meeting was held separately, and in addition commissioners traversed the kingdom to gain adhesions from persons and corporations, an old device in taxation. In 1308 came the affair of the Templars, and now the precedent of 1302 was followed. A full " States-General " of the entire realm was summoned at Tours in May 1308, which was duly convinced in favour of the king. The system of treating with assemblies of the various districts, however, sufficed, or perhaps was more efficient, in raising taxation till August 1314, when the exigencies of the endless Flemish war induced Philip for the first time to demand subsidies from a full " States-General " at Paris. The aid was promised, but the difficulties in obtaining the performance of the promises showed that enforced unanimity under the king's eye had its limits as a method of propaganda.

The common characteristic of this tardy evolution of the States-General under Philip the Fair is that they met as an unwelcome duty, arbitrarily imposed by the king's will for the momentary needs of his policy. Their consent to the decisions put before them was not necessary. They only came to hear and obey. They came into being late, after and not before the doctrine of the fullness of royal power had been defined by the legists. They eminently lacked the unifying forces in like assemblies of older date in other countries. Not only were the Three Estates from the start rigidly separate and unsympathetic to one another, but the provinces of France seemed incapable of a common initiative. Of themselves they and their deputies always acted apart. They were only in unison in obeying the king's command. *Defects of the States-General*

The vast expense of Philip's wars was a source of continuous embarrassment to the royal government. Even in time of peace, the old sources of revenue, income from the demesne-lands of the Crown, dues and tolls, and the ancient feudal incidents,[1] did not suffice for the normal royal needs, which bureaucratic and improved government brought about. *Royal Revenue*

[1] See above, Chap. I, pp. 25-26.

To devise new sources of income was an imperative necessity which weighed upon Philip's ministers and deformed his **Clerical Taxation** policy. The taxation of the wealthy clergy was one justifiable resource, which led to the conflict with Boniface VIII. As we have seen, the Crown normally received the feudal incidents due for ecclesiastical fiefs; it exercised, too, the *régale*, the occupation of episcopal lands and the taking of their income during the vacancy of a see. Twice the Pope granted to Philip annates, a year's income of all benefices vacated and re-filled. But, as a result of the quarrel with Boniface, the power to receive " clerical tenths " of ecclesiastical revenues by consent of the French clergy became a permanent right of the Crown. These subsidies, already almost annual on one ground or another, were levied constantly at varying rates by Philip the Fair. The same **Lay Taxation** principle was applied to the laity. The general subsidies, commonly assented to by local assemblies, were levied from 1294 onwards either on income or property or both together; they might be a hundredth, a fiftieth, or a twenty-fifth, on income even a tenth. No one was exempt. In 1302 half of the silver plate of the kingdom was ordered to be brought to the Mint. Commutation of military service both from nobles and non-nobles was another frequent source of income. All were liable to serve; only a selection was needed or practicable. The practice of commutation was combined with the subsidies. Much money, of course, was lost on the way to the Treasury. Bargains had to be driven with communities averse to new taxation; great vassals were conciliated by a share in its profits. But the principle of universal, direct taxation by the Crown was established.

Indirect taxation was increased early in the reign, in 1292, by the introduction of the vexatious *maltôte*, an *ad valorem* tax on sales, which hampered the commercial class. The ordinary customs on export and import were of old date. **Debasement of the Coinage** None of these devices, however, filled Philip's empty purse. Great loans from the Italian bankers, small loans, usually compulsory, from functionaries and moneyed men, were used from the start. A worse expedient was tampering with and debasing the coinage, which won for Philip the name of the " false coiner." The silver coinage was that worst affected, and owing to the accounting methods of the time in France the inflation, as it would to-day be termed, could be accomplished in two ways, actual debasement of the metallic currency or an arbitrary elevation of its current purchasing power. Accounts were reckoned in a book-keeping money, never coined, of *livres*, *sous*, and *deniers tournois*. The actual coins in use were the gold *écu* of St. Louis, the gold angel of Philip, and the silver *gros tournois*. There was no fixed rate of equivalence between the coins in use and the money of account. This fact inspired the financial juggling of Philip's ministers in spite of the protests of the wiser Italian bankers. The first method was to increase by decree the rating of the coins in use in relation to the money of account. Thus the value of the *gros tournois* and the gold angel was arbitrarily raised in *livres*, *sous*, and *deniers*, in which debts and dues were reckoned. It damaged creditors and favoured debtors, especially the Crown, which had large debts and payments to make, and could thus use fewer coins for the purpose. But current prices refused to co-operate ; they rose in the money of account even when they remained stable in the coined money in use if that retained its intrinsic value. This, however, was not the case, for Philip also resorted to the second method, debasement, i.e. the use of less silver and more alloy, in the current coins. This practice began in 1295 ; it reached ruinous proportions in 1303 in the midst of the troubles with Flanders and the Pope. It met for the moment the needs of the Treasury by direct inflation, but it was most harmful to creditors and moneyed men, and eventually to purchasers, and consumers. For besides the intense uncertainty introduced by the decreasing intrinsic value of the coins and their exalted artificial rating in the money of account, current prices again refused to comply with royal finance. All articles grew dearer as the intrinsic value of coins fell. This was not the worst, for too sudden reformation caused its confusions also. In 1306 the " good " *gros tournois* of St. Louis' day was reissued, the debased coins were devalued to their intrinsic worth, and both were rated at lower and more correct figures respectively in the money of account. Now it was the creditors and the tax-gatherers who profited, and in any case transactions were made more complicated. The value of money became bewildering when debasement began again worse

than before, and another abrupt and transitory return to
good coins in 1313 did not help matters. Trade was suffering severely, silver was emigrating and becoming scarce in
France, and the Treasury itself in spite of passing, immediate gains was suffering. A publicist in the king's
service, the theorizing Pierre Dubois, estimated his personal
losses since 1295 at 500 *livres tournois*.

Spoliation of
Templars,
Italians,
and Jews Meantime taxes, loans, and debasement of the coinage
were supplemented by tyrannical spoliation of victims who
were unpopular. The most notorious instance was the persecution of the Templars with its terrible accompaniments.[1]
Philip also turned on the Jews and the Italians. The Jews
of France were a wealthy and learned community, but, as
was the case elsewhere, they were isolated by their faith
and exposed to the fanatical hatred of their Christian neighbours. The occupation of usury which most of them followed
was opprobrious and productive of constant friction with
their debtors. The royal house, too, cherished a traditional
enmity against them. Philip Augustus had once, in 1182,
expelled them from the royal domain. St. Louis, always a
man of his time, had burnt hundreds of copies of the Talmud ;
an unconverted Jew was outside the pale of his sympathies.
Philip the Fair, after sporadic hostilities, considered them
fair prey. In 1306 they were suddenly arrested throughout
France, their property was confiscated, and themselves
expelled. The debts due to them were ferreted out and,
usurious as they were, were rigorously collected for the
benefit of the Treasury. No one pitied them or remarked
the inconsistency—indeed by heavy special taxation rulers
had long shared in their profits—but in comparison with
Christian lenders the Jews were later regretted as " good-
natured " usurers.

The Italians, or " Lombards " as the French called them,
had woven themselves, more than the Jews, into the economic
life of the country. They were the bankers and creditors
of the king and the great nobles. Mouche (Musciatto
Franzesi) and his brother Biche (Biccio), the Florentines,
were ministers of the king, and played a part in the outrage
of Anagni. The bulk of the import and export trade of
France was in the hands of these Italian merchants. Their

[1] See above, Chap. XI, pp. 237-39.

factors and agents and smaller independent adventurers overran the country, lending, trading, and filling minor financial employments. They were naturally disliked as usurers and exploiters, and were suspect to king and people, for the manipulation of the money-changes which were in their hands and which they alone understood. The results of the king's financial errors were attributed to them : " they upset the circulation of our coinage." The interest on debts at the high rate prevailing, 43 per cent., due very largely to the risk involved, was looked on as outrageous extortion. Every now and then the king suddenly attacked them. In 1277 and 1291 they were all arrested. In 1296 they were banished in order to put pressure on Boniface VIII. But they paid heavily for the permission to trade, and the attacks were mainly an excuse for extraordinary plunder by the king. This, too, was the chief reason of Philip's last attack. In 1311 he banished all the Lombards from France, seized their property, and proceeded to impound and collect the debts due to them. It shows both the financial strength of the Italians that they recovered from these enormous losses and the indispensable nature of their commercial activity that they were soon readmitted by Louis X. The worst sufferer was France. What with these disturbances, the Flemish war, and the disorganization of the currency, the fairs of Champagne ceased to be the nodal point of North European trade. The main route of commerce began to move eastward.

By the end of his reign Philip the Fair himself, though not the monarchy, was grown unpopular. His hand had been too heavy on all classes of his subjects. The obedient Church of France was discontented. The feudal nobles found their franchises incessantly invaded, their justice taken from them, their tournaments and private wars prevented. Continuous exacting taxation alienated the bourgeois. The monetary experiments exasperated all. The last provocation was the renewed war with Flanders and its subsidy. It is significant that resistance, though widespread, was local and provincial. The provinces of France, Normandy, Burgundy, Champagne, Languedoc, Picardy, and Auvergne, acted separately. Leagues in each were formed (1314), in which the secondary nobles took the leading part, the towns and the Church being somewhat in the background.

As a result, the grievances put forward were mostly feudal, and compiled in defence of local custom against the centralizing intervention of royal officials. Philip hastily abolished the subsidy just before he died.

Louis X

Philip the Fair's reign was so crowded with important events and so decisive for the monarchy and its policy that his immediate successors merely seemed to carry on its unfinished work. His eldest son, Louis X (1314–16), sacrificed the chief minister, Enguerrand de Marigni, to the court enemies he had offended, but de Marigni's execution was of little importance beside the question of the Leagues. Here the solution adopted was that of granting provincial charters to appease particularist sentiment and feudal instincts. The monarchy, in short, retreated on points of detail, but not as to its own supreme, overriding authority. Particularism and feudalism were given a longer life; no check on royal absolutism was introduced. The bourgeois, for whom feudal turbulence and feudal rights had no attraction, soon rallied to the Crown, and in the next reign the Leagues decayed and died. Only the problem of the succession kept one or two alive a little longer than the rest.

The Succession Problem

The question of the succession was new. Hitherto, each Capetian king had left a son to succeed him; the problem of inheritance by or through females had never been mooted. But when Louis X died unexpectedly in June 1316 he left a young daughter and a yet unborn child. A regency in any case was necessary, and on this the first important step was taken. The regent for St. Louis had been the queen-mother, but now Philip the Tall, Count of Poitiers, the next

Philip V the Tall

brother of Louis X, assumed the office. When a posthumous son, John I, was born to Louis in November, he lived only a few days, and Philip the Tall had himself crowned at Rheims in January 1317. His accession was not unresisted. Eudes, Duke of Burgundy, and the Leagues of Burgundy and Champagne supported the claims of Louis' daughter Joanna (Jeanne), a claim justified by the law as to some fiefs though not as to others. However, Philip V carried the day. Joanna's claims were bought off; an assembly of prelates, magnates, Parisian bourgeois, and doctors of the University at Paris laid down the principle that no woman could inherit the crown of France, and this decision was

accepted by the kingdom. In a few years it was unquestioned law.

Philip V (1316–22) was by taste an organizing, legislative His work
king. Perhaps because of the original doubtfulness of his as Ruler
title, and because of the lively discontent with the arbitrary
measures of Philip the Fair, he encouraged the convocation
of Assemblies which continued, still in experimental forms,
the tradition of " States-General." Commonly, however,
the representatives of the Estates did not meet in the same
town ; the separation into North and South, at least, became
clearer. The assemblies, too, might complain and advise ;
they did not legislate. That task was the king's, and he
was constantly performing it. He organized in detail the
Hôtel du Roi, the Council, the Parlement, the Chambre des
Comptes, the administration of finance and forests, and he
attempted vainly to introduce a uniform and reformed
coinage. Yet by his reforms he had only earned dislike
when he died, leaving three daughters.

Franche Comté in the Empire, which Philip the Tall
acquired through his wife, went to his eldest daughter,
Jeanne, the wife of Eudes Duke of Burgundy, but now there
was no doubt that his younger brother Charles the Fair, Charles IV
Count of La Marche, was heir to France. Like his prede- the Fair
cessor, who had at least secured a firm hold on Lille, Douai,
and Orchies, he was involved in alternate peaces and preparations for war with Flanders, with the variation that the
new Count Louis II, in trouble with his insurgent subjects,
was inclined to the French side. In Guienne Charles the
Fair made more progress in the traditional policy. Frequent
appeals to the Parlement of Paris and royal intervention
created a state of friction, which was brought to war when
Charles obtained the *pariage* or condominion of Saint-Sardos
in Agenais from its *seigneur* and proceeded to build a fortress
there. The English seneschal of Gascony had recourse to
force. Charles, after the usual legal steps, declared Guienne
and Ponthieu confiscated to the Crown, and in 1324 invaded
the duchy. The English king was then the incompetent
Edward II, whose own kingdom was on the brink of civil
war. Little besides Bordeaux and Bayonne soon remained
to him in Gascony. Meantime, his wife Isabella, Charles's
sister, patched up a peace of Paris in March 1327. By this

Ponthieu and most of Guienne was restored to the Prince of Wales, soon to become by the English revolution Edward III. Charles kept Agenais; the absorption of the duchy by the Crown had begun anew.

Extinction of the Direct Line
Charles IV was the last of the direct Capetians. When he died in February 1328 he left only daughters behind him, although the queen was expecting another child. The question of the regency and the succession was raised again.

SUGGESTIONS FOR READING ON CHAPTER XIII

A. Sources

Funck-Brentano, F. : Documents pour servir à l'histoire des relations de la France avec l'Angleterre et l'Allemagne sous Philippe le Bel. *Revue Historique*, xxxix. 1889.

Langlois, C. V. : *Textes relatifs à l'histoire du Parlement.* Collection des textes pour servir à l'étude et à l'enseignement de l'histoire. Paris, 1888.

Laurière, E. J. de : *Ordonnances des Rois de France de la troisième race.* Vol. i. Paris, 1723.

Nangis, G. de : As in suggestions for Chapter XII.

Picot, G. : *Documents relatifs aux États Généraux et assemblées réunis sous Philippe le Bel.* Collection des documents inédits sur l'histoire de France. Paris, 1901.

Villani, G. : As in suggestions for Chapter XII.

B. Modern Works

Cambridge Medieval History, vol. vii, relevant chapters.

Glotz, G. : As given for Chapter XI.

Lavisse, E., ed : *Histoire de France.* Vol. iii.

Lehugeur, P. : *Histoire de Philippe le Long.* Paris, 1897.

Landry, A. : *Essai économique sur les mutations des monnaies dans l'ancienne France.* Bibliothèque de l'École des Hautes Études. Paris, 1910.

Dieudonné, A. : *Les monnaies françaises.* Paris, 1923.

Langlois, C. V. : *La chancellerie royale depuis l'avènement de St. Louis jusqu'à celui de Philippe de Valois.* Paris, 1895.

Pirenne, H. : *Histoire de Belgique.* Vols. i. Brussels, 1929.

Funck-Brentano, F. : *Philippe le Bel en Flandre.* Paris, 1897.

Lodge, E. C. : *Gascony under English Rule.* London, 1926.

CHAPTER XIV

THE DECLINE OF FRANCE IN THE HUNDRED YEARS' WAR

ONE thing was certain in the problem of the succession to Charles the Fair. No woman could inherit the crown of France. But who was the nearest male heir ? Was it the nearest male kinsman of the late king, whether related to him either through females or through males ; or was it his nearest kinsman in the male line only, i.e. by agnatic descent ? If the latter was the case, then the provisional regent, and if the queen gave birth to a posthumous daughter, the king, was Philip, Count of Valois, the son of the Charles of Valois, the younger brother of Philip the Fair, who had been an important figure in recent European history. If, on the other hand, relationship through females counted, the regent and possible king was Edward III of England, nephew of Charles IV through his sister Isabella ; Edward was nephew, Philip of Valois only cousin of Charles IV. The question was at once put to an assembly of magnates at Paris. The distaste for a foreign king was obvious ; the inconveniences of a method of succession through females, which might result in a nearer heir through females to Charles IV, a grandson, being born years after, were perhaps foreseen ; the natural legal argument that a woman could not transmit a right she could not possess was urged. In consequence Philip of Valois was declared regent, and when the widow of Charles IV gave birth to a daughter, he was crowned king. The " Salic law,"[1] so called from an ancient provision of the law of the Salian Franks by which a woman could not inherit land, was thus established as the rule for the succession to the French crown.

There were some concessions to be made. Joanna, the

The Salic Law

---

[1] The term is of later date.

daughter of Louis X and wife of the Count of Évreux, could not be denied the kingdom of Navarre, which her uncles had, somewhat irregularly, retained. Her claim to the county of Champagne, her grandmother's inheritance, was bought off by the grant of less dangerous fiefs, Mortain in Normandy and Angoulême. Pressure had to be put on Edward III, who was still in the power of his mother and her lover Mortimer. He did homage to Philip in 1329, but only in 1331 admitted that the homage was " liege " with the strictest duties of vassalage.

The last Capetians, in spite of the ephemeral outburst of the Leagues, had accomplished the triumph of the monarchy over feudal independence, but they had not modified feudal instincts and ideals. These last captured the monarchy itself on the accession of a great appanaged *seigneur* in the person of Philip VI. As Count of Valois, Anjou, and Maine, he had never acquired the true legally monarchic instincts of princes born in the purple. He was a great noble crowned. And, as it happened, feudal ideals in the
fourteenth century had become formalized into a code of behaviour for the knightly classes which, while it embodied some of the essential advances made in restraint of conduct and a higher standard of duty since the eleventh century, was nevertheless largely a matter of form and convention. The knight of chivalry was to be adventurous, reckless, combative, generous and frank to his equals, meticulous on the point of honour, liberal to prodigality. He was to live a life of display, festivities, hunting, and feats of arms. Forethought, statesmanship, unromantic good government, and humdrum administration were beneath him. Chivalrousness itself was limited to the fit recipient, another knight or a noble dame. These ideals Philip VI brought to the throne. His abilities were limited, his manners not popular, his political interests lay in vast and showy schemes for a crusade, he left administration to underlings without possessing any power of direction, but on the other hand he was only too at home in the chivalric *milieu* and its inconsequent mode of carrying on the business of a great State. Like other mediocrities in difficult situations he was blamed for inherited deficiencies in the State which he could not prevent, and for the lack of foresight into the new conditions of

warfare which he shared with the society which surrounded him.

The new reign opened with a victory in Flanders which confirmed the chivalrous prejudices of the king and the nobles. Since the battle of Courtrai Flanders had been in constant turmoil. There was a steady tendency to evolve in the towns a balanced government by " members " representing the diverse interests of the classes of the inhabitants. The merchant-employers and landlords formed one member, the employees of the cloth-trade another, the craft gilds of small masters others ; the number of members varied from town to town. The same phenomenon appeared elsewhere in the Low Countries. In Dinant, the employees in the metal industry, which was organized on a capitalistic basis for exportation, took the place of the cloth-workers ; in Liége and Utrecht, where the export trade was of small account, it was the gilds of small masters who seized in violent warfare power from the hereditary oligarchy of patrician landlords and in spite of set-backs achieved by the mid-fourteenth century a constitutional predominance. But in Flanders, as elsewhere, the patricians did not submit to their defeat, and not only the small masters of the retail trades but also the different sections of the cloth-workers, weavers and fullers, were bitter rivals for power. The Count, Louis of Nevers (1322–46), the son-in-law of Philip the Tall, and his nobles linked their fortunes with the *leliaerts*, for the trade-gilds and clothworkers were no less insubordinate than the *leliaerts* had once been. Against the renewed dominance of the count and his allies, a new revolution broke out in 1323 in Bruges and Ypres, and among the peasants, whom the nobles were endeavouring to reduce to serfdom. It was peculiarly ferocious, a war of the poor against the rich. Count Louis was himself at one time made prisoner, and he appealed to his suzerain the King of France. Philip zealously embraced the feudal cause and invaded Flanders. On August 23, 1328, the Flemish peasants and workmen under Peter Zannekin rashly left their entrenched camp on Mount Cassel and attacked the king's army. The mounted French knights could then charge to victory and slaughter. Flanders lay at the feet of count and king.

The Flemish Towns

Battle of Mount Cassel

None the less the Flemings were indomitable, and a new and temporary ally was given them in Edward III of England. The friction over Guienne, its boundaries, and the royal intervention in the duchy had gone on increasing. It seemed clearly leading to the loss of the duchy. Edward had had his hands tied by his Scottish wars ; he only gave up the project of conquering Scotland after 1336. Besides the help given by Philip to the Scots, the persuasions of the French exile, Robert of Artois, who had vainly claimed the county of Artois and had been banished by Philip for forgery in the consequent legal proceedings, urged Edward on to war.

In September 1336 he revived his claim to the French crown in a Parliament, and, after long parleys, at last assumed the title of " King of France," and sent in November 1337 his formal defiance to Philip of Valois. The new style ended his vexatious vassalage to the French monarchy, with the precarious hold on the valuable duchy of Guienne which it involved, for the duchy was thus absorbed into his kingship of France. It was natural, too, for a king so ambitious of conquest and martial fame to insist at the first opportunity on his hereditary claims to a great realm. Edward was no less an adventurous knight of chivalry than his rival, but he had far more practical ability. If politically he lived from hand to mouth and recklessly mortgaged the future in his pursuit of warlike fame, if he shared the complete lack of strategical conceptions in war which was character-istic of the time, he yet could handle his army in battle in the way he had been taught, and as a ruler could take opportunities, and comply with the suggestions of events. He could drive the governmental machine, and his overseas expeditions showed that he could organize a victory if not win a campaign. But his real and practical aim, as appeared in negotiations for a settlement before the Pope, was to secure the independence of Guienne from the irritating suzerainty of the Crown of France. In return, he would abandon his claim to the kingdom. Meantime, his scheme

of war was the old one—to erect a great confederacy on the north-east frontier of France and make an invasion from that quarter. He gained the alliance of the Count of Hainault, the Duke of Brabant, the Margrave of Juliers, and others, and above all that of the Emperor Lewis IV

f Bavaria, all of them bought by large English subsidies.
Count Louis of Flanders was unalterably loyal to Philip,
but the Flemish townsmen were gained by a skilful stroke
f policy. In August 1336 Edward forbade the export of
English wool to Flanders. It meant a complete stoppage
f the cloth-trade, the ruin and starvation of the towns
which lived on it. A revolution in Ghent placed a rich *Jakob van*
patrician, Jakob van Artevelde, at the head of affairs in *Artevelde of Ghent*
1337. He obtained the raising of the wool embargo from
Edward, and practically became dictator of all Flanders,
while the count fled to France. Philip had already, in May
1337, begun the Hundred Years' War by declaring Guienne
confiscated to the Crown.

The Hundred Years' War, as its name implies, lasted with *Periods of*
intervals of peace and truce well beyond the limits of this *the Hundred*
volume. It only ended, and then by no treaty, with the *Years' War*
final expulsion of the English from Guienne in 1453. In
this volume, it falls into three main periods, the first till
the Peace of Brétigny in 1360, the second of precarious
peace till the renewal of war in 1369, and the third until
the death of Charles V of France in 1380. The first was the
period of French defeats, the second of recuperation, and
the third of reconquest.

At the outbreak of war in 1337 it might well seem that *Relative*
Edward III was recklessly bold in undertaking a life-and- *strength*
death struggle with the French monarchy. The odds, how- *of the*
ever, so far as victory and not the conquest of France was *Combatants*
concerned, were by no means so much against him as they
appeared. It was true that France as a whole was loyal
to Philip VI and hostile to the foreigner. Its population
and wealth were vastly greater than those of England. Its
cavalry were the most renowned in Christendom, valiant,
loyal, and flushed with recent victory. But there were
weaknesses, too. Of the four remaining great fiefs of France,
only Burgundy could be depended on : Guienne was sub-
stantially loyal to its English duke, whose government was
good and flattered its particularist instincts ; Flanders was
an English ally ; and particularist Brittany, with its Celtic-
speaking districts, was likely to hold aloof at least. More
serious was the state of the finances and the army. Philip's
revenues from the demesne, dues, customs, and tolls barely

Philip's
Armies

sufficed for his expenses in peace. Even with papal aid
which he got, he needed for war extraordinary and un
popular subsidies, consented to unwillingly by the assemblie
and hard and long to collect. Then the army was, howeve
levied, of a completely old-fashioned feudal kind. It mainl
consisted of the heavily armoured knights and men-at-arms
who fought in wild, disorderly charges. They might com
for the prescribed term of feudal service, too short for a
campaign ; they might be hired out of the proceeds o
commutation for the service of the *arrière ban* and of sub
sidies ; but they were of the same character in any case
commanded by their feudal lords, without discipline or an
conception of tactics, and hampered by their heavy weapon
unless matched by a similar force and on ground suitabl
for a tournament. The infantry, mainly foreign mercenaries
armed with the cross-bow, from Italy or Germany, wer
despised and levied hastily at need. This was the army t
which Philip, who waited for the storm to break befor
making preparations, trusted for his defence.

Edward III's
Armies

Edward on the other hand had obtained large supplie
from Parliament for a popular war, and possessed the mean
of raising a field army of incomparable efficiency, trained i
new methods of fighting and new tactics in the Scottis
wars. Feudal service had been replaced by the privat
troops, called " retinues," of the king and great lords. Thes
were paid for by the king and were to some extent disciplined
They consisted of the armoured knights and men-at-arms
of " hobelars," a kind of mounted infantry, largely archers
and of foot archers. Besides the " retinues," large forces o
foot archers were called out from the counties by commission
of array. In addition to the fact that great numbers o
these levies had seen service in the Scottish wars, the practic
of archery with the long-bow was insisted on among th
peasantry, and thus a reservoir of potentially efficient infantr

Their
Tactics.

was established. For this kind of army new tactics had bee
developed. The knights dismounted in a defensible positio
and acted as pikemen with their lances in the centre ; th

The Archers

archers, also on foot, formed forward curving wings ; som
knights were told off as a small body of cavalry. If th
enemy could be induced to attack, they were riddled b
arrows from the flanks before they closed, and then repelle

by the pike-like lances of the centre. Horses could hardly be induced to charge on the line of steel points. The essential feature of these tactics lay in the superiority of the long-bow as a missile weapon. Edward I had borrowed it from the Welsh. Over five feet long and drawn to the ear, it shot at least three arrows to one of the cumbrous cross-bow, and had a greater range and penetrating power than the short-bow drawn only to the chest. In the hands of trained archers who could be protected from charges it brought victory.

Some years passed, however, before Edward was able to show his military superiority. He relied too much on un-stable coalitions to overcome the larger forces of the King of France. In 1338 he crossed to Flanders and at Coblenz on the Rhine was declared by the Emperor Lewis Vicar of the Empire against France, but only in September 1339 could he assemble his dearly bought allies and invade Picardy. He never got far ; for the season was late, no town sur-rendered, and Philip declined to make the attack which was necessary for his tactics. Next year Edward secured the active alliance of the Flemish towns under Artevelde, to allay whose feudal scruples he quartered the arms of France with those of England and acted as reigning king of the uncon-quered realm. Philip now tried to prevent a new invasion by attacking the English army as it came again by sea. He collected the ships of north France with their fighting seamen, who had already raided the English coast, and added to them royal ships of war and galleys from Genoa. This fleet on June 24, 1340, met the English at Sluys on the Flemish coast, where Edward wished to disembark. The result was a complete English victory, the first in the war, which gave Edward the command of the sea. But again he could not bring his enemy to battle ; he could not capture the single town of Tournai, his money gave out, the Scots, now the invariable allies of France, were making war on him, and he was glad to make the truce of Esplechin.

A new base of operations, after this failure, was given Edward by the disputed succession to the duchy of Brittany. When Duke John III died in 1341, this was claimed by his niece Jeanne, daughter of his deceased brother Guy, and by his youngest brother John, Count of Montfort. Jeanne was married to Charles of Blois, nephew of Philip VI ; she

Edward's Failures in Picardy

Battle of Sluys

The Suc-cession to Brittany

and her husband were accepted by French-speaking Brittany, John of Montfort by the Breton speakers of the west. Curiously enough, King Philip declared for the female claimant, and invested her husband. By the same paradox, Montfort appealed to Edward, who thereupon supported the male line. A long civil war began in Brittany, in which English and French joined and neither expelled the other.

Meanwhile the great coalition was breaking up. The Emperor made his peace with France in 1341 and revoked the vicariate conferred on Edward. The other allies followed suit. The Flemish towns, with their incurably narrow local outlook, had fallen out among themselves. The great towns endeavoured to destroy the rival industries of the smaller. Bruges and Ypres hated the leadership of Ghent. The count's party re-formed, as men found that export of cloth was no less necessary to them than import of wool. Lastly, the weavers of Ghent wished to dominate the other crafts and interests in their town. They defeated the fullers with much slaughter in May 1345. The blame of these troubles fell on the dictator Artevelde, who was accused of wasting public money on his personal ends. Edward's refusal at Sluys in July to resume the war in Flanders was fatal to him. In a few days he was massacred by the insurgent weavers of Ghent. Class and sectional war followed in the Flemish towns, the rest of the gilds combining against the weavers. The death of Count Louis at Crécy was an advantage to his house, for the new count, Louis of Maele, was bred in Flanders and popular. Still, it was not till January 1349 that he captured Ghent, the stronghold of the weavers. Thenceforward, Louis of Maele with much adroitness held to a middle way between France and England. Neither wished to drive him to active alliance with the other side.

The great war meantime had revived in Guienne itself. Earlier Philip had made some progress in the slow reduction of the duchy. In 1345 the Earl of Derby, for Edward III, began the counter-offensive. The English rule was more liked than the French, and his army showed its quality; he recovered a stretch of territory. When John, Duke of Normandy, Philip's heir, attempted to win it back in 1346, his failure was followed by a fresh departure. Derby made

Fall of Jakob van Artevelde

War in Guienne

a " chevauchée," a merciless raiding and ravaging expedition Derby's
in French territory through Poitou. This terrible method "chevau-
of warfare, which abandoned sieges and solid acquisitions, chée"
was now to afflict France.

Edward had prepared are inforcing army for Guienne on Edward III's
the news of the Duke of Normandy's invasion. Contrary "chevau-
winds and the advice of a Norman exile, Godefroi d'Harcourt, chée" in
led him on July 17, 1346, to land in the Côtentin with some Normandy
20,000 men. His command of the sea since the victory of
Sluys gave him the choice of the point of attack. From
La Hougue he conducted a devastating march, putting the
wealthy land of Normandy to fire and sword. The rich
port of Caen was captured and ruthlessly sacked. Thence
he passed to cross the Seine at Poissi ; he dared not attack
Paris, but aimed at conducting his " chevauchée " across the
Somme to a safe end in Flanders. Philip, who had shown
indecision throughout, was now in pursuit with a much
larger force. Yet Edward slipped across the Somme by a
ford near Abbeville in spite of the resistance of local levies.
He could not now be pinned down and starved out, but
could choose a defensive position if the French would attack
him in it, and retreat again northwards if they would not.
Such a position he found at Crécy. On August 26 Philip Battle of
came up and took the bait. The English cavalry were dis- Crécy
mounted on rising ground. Between and outside their three
battalions, the archers jutted forward in angular formation
protected by stakes and trenches. There was a reserve of
mounted men. The English had their backs to the afternoon
sun. The first attack was made by Genoese cross-bowmen,
who made a poor show with their bowstrings damp from
heavy rain, and their aim impeded by the sun now coming
out, and their slow volleys were easily dominated by the
long-bows. As they turned in flight, the French knights
charged furiously over them. Fifteen vain frontal charges
were made, which, as men and horses fell under the English
arrows, hardly got through to the English lines. The battle
ended in total rout, with some 3,000 French dead, among
them 1,200 of knightly rank. John, the blind King of
Bohemia, Philip's friend, and Louis of Flanders were among
the slain.

After this crushing victory Edward could march north

and undertake the siege of the port of Calais. How important he deemed the capture of the town is shown by the fact that he was willing, in an age when sieges could rarely be long continued, to spend nearly a year before it in his fortified camp, while Philip vainly attempted a rescue and David King of Scots invaded England from the north. But David was defeated and captured at Neville's Cross on October 17, 1346, and Calais was at last starved into surrender in August 1347. It was made an English town, for long the staple of the English export trade. It secured the Straits of Dover and gave a permanent entry into France for two centuries. None the less, the length of the siege revealed the weakness of Edward's position. No French fortified town, outside Guienne, willingly submitted to him. The superiority of the defensive in siege-warfare at the time made a siege to be successful impossibly long. An army could not usually be kept together for it, nor funds be found to pay the troops. This meant that France was unconquerable. In fact, after Calais the exhausted combatants made a general truce, which lasted till 1351. Before it ended, Philip VI died in August 1350, and was succeeded by his son John II, surnamed " le Bon," the genial.

Although King Philip was not the man to meet emergencies, or counter a new method of warfare, or even conduct a skilful foreign policy, his reign was not without successes or reforms which were on the lines initiated by his predecessors. The penury of King James III of Majorca, most of whose lands had been conquered by his suzerain and cousin Peter IV of Aragon, gave his other suzerain, the King of France, the opportunity of buying in 1349 his fief of Montpellier for the royal domain. This important university and trading city was in itself a valuable acquisition, and moreover one more foreign ruler was eliminated from the South of France. More valuable still was the acquisition of Dauphiné in the imperial kingdom of Burgundy or Arles. The reigning Dauphin, Humbert II, was an inefficient prince of the dominant chivalrous type, who wavered between schemes of earthly glory as a crusader and thoughts of a religious life. He had lost his only son, and was loaded with debt. In 1343–4 he raised funds for a crusade by selling the succession of Dauphiné to the eldest son of the reigning King of France or the king himself, if no son was yet born to him. In 1349 after the failure of his crusade he became a Dominican, and completed the transfer, again for a handsome sum, by surrendering his State to Charles, Philip's grandson and eventual heir. In this way, Dauphiné was united by a permanent personal tie with the Crown of France, though governed by a separate title as a fief of the Empire. A tongue of French territory extended now from the River Rhone to the pass of Mont Genèvre. France touched at last on her natural frontier of the Alps.

In internal government Philip VI and his ministers con- *Internal Government and Taxation* tinued in considerable detail the work of the Capetians in organizing and improving, at least in outward form, the bureaucracy and administration. The jurisdiction of the Church courts was restricted. But the necessity of raising money for the wars caused the most significant changes and great distress. The famous *gabelle*, or salt monopoly, was introduced in 1341, and was to become a permanent source of royal revenue. The "tenths" of the clergy, too, were with papal consent raised every year. Large loans were borrowed, more especially from the francophil Popes at Avignon to the diminution of their influence elsewhere. More than all subsidies and aids for the war were collected from the French people.

These subsidies furthered the growth of the assemblies *Provincial Estates* and gave them legal privileges. The local Estates of the provinces made grants in return for the redress of grievances and the acknowledgement of their control of extraordinary taxation. More marked was the solid form given to the *The States-General* States-General, which could speak for the whole kingdom. They met, and this weakened their power, in two assemblies, the States-General of Languedoïl and those of Languedoc. But the king could only obtain grants in return for redress of grievances, and had to listen to sharp criticism on his policy, in which the truces, his most beneficial measures, were signalized by his angry subjects.

In these years the distress of the once prosperous kingdom *Distress of France* was increasing. The English ravage had done immense harm to wealthy districts. Heavy taxation did its part, while debasement and revaluing of the coinage on the model of Philip the Fair impeded every business transaction, to the ruin of trade and the eventual damage of the Crown. Even secret debasement was introduced in 1349 as a method of inflation.	Vexatious and arbitrary government interference to prevent speculation in the coinage added to the troubles of debtors, creditors, and business-men.	Only the most wary could come through without loss.	Then in 1348 the

The Black Death

first onset of the Black Death depopulated France.	No remedy could be found till it wore itself out.	France suffered, indeed, in this with all its neighbours, but it was a debilitated kingdom which faced the English war under John II.

John II the Good

The new king was another valiant knight of chivalry, less capable than his father.	Slow-witted and obstinate, he was spendthrift and greedy and given to outbursts of rage. The ministers he relied upon did not improve his government : they were, as was traditional, new men, and were intent on personal gain and devoid of scruple.	While they increased discontent with the abuses of the government, King John himself was losing the people's confidence by his arbitrary behaviour.	He suddenly executed without trial Count Raoul of Eu, the constable of France, and promoted Charles of Spain, of the disinherited line of de la Cerda,[1] to wealth and power.	This favouritism embroiled him with the most sinister personage of the time, Charles the Bad,

Charles II the Bad of Navarre

King of Navarre.	Charles the Bad was exceedingly dangerous.	Besides his kingdom of Navarre he possessed the county of Évreux and great fiefs in Normandy and north France, including Meulan and Mantes near Paris.	Still more serious were his pretensions to the throne.	He was the grandson, born in 1332, of King Louis X, and if the nearest male relative through females was the true heir, he might seem to have a better claim than Edward III [2]; he declared his mother Joanna's renunciation made before his birth to be invalid.	With this ambition, his abilities—he was a cunning intriguer, an orator, and of popular manners —and his treacherous, grasping, and unscrupulous character made him the evil genius of France for years.	He began as the son-in-law of King John, but became his irrecon-

[1] See above, Chap. VIII, p. 155.

[2] That is, if the doctrine of "representation" (later universal) was accepted.	He was the grand-nephew through a brother, Edward the nephew through a sister of Charles IV.	He "represented" his grandfather Louis, though more distant in degree than Edward who only represented Isabella.

cilable foe when he murdered his private enemy, the constable Charles of Spain in 1354. Thereupon he began to treat with the English, a partition of France between Edward as king and himself with enormous fiefs being the aim and joint campaigns the means to it. Twice the alarmed John bought him off by great concessions at Mantes and Valognes (1354, 1355), but these were hollow peaces. Charles the Bad was inciting the Dauphin Charles against his father, and stimulating the resistance of Normandy to the taxes for the English war. On April 5, 1356, John perpetrated another arbitrary act. He arrested and imprisoned the King of Navarre at a feast given by the Dauphin at Rouen, and executed his chief adherents. It meant disloyalty in Normandy and elsewhere where Charles the Bad had friends.

Meantime, the royal government was in high disfavour. The renewal of the English war and the emptiness of the Treasury, accompanied by the worst debasement of the coinage yet known, forced the king to submit to severe The War limitations of the monarchy by the States-General of 1355,[1] but at any rate he was enabled to raise very large and inefficient armies. The war was going badly after its definite renewal in 1354. The English were winning in Brittany ; a short ravage by Edward III in Artois was outdone by a terrible " chevauchée " of his son, Edward " the Black Prince " of Wales, in autumn 1355 through Languedoc, which ruined over 500 towns and villages. Next year, the Duke of Lancaster (the Earl of Derby of earlier campaigns) ravaged Normandy with the aid of the Navarre partisans, while the Black Prince with some 7,000 men conducted another " chevauchée " to the Loire so as to effect a junction with the northern force. John, who had not intercepted Lancaster, now came south with a large army, from which the prince retreated. At Maupertuis, close to Poitiers, John Battle of was tempted to attack the enemy in a strong position. Poitiers Once more the French mounted knights were mown down by the English arrows, and John's attempt to make a more resolute charge by dismounting his main force only made it more helpless and immobile, while receiving a flank counterattack of horse and foot as well. The defeat was crushing, Captivity of and John himself was taken captive to England. John II

_____
[1] See below, p. 286.

Regency of
the Dauphin The young Dauphin, who acted as regent during his father's captivity, was faced with a terrible crisis. Not only had the official English campaigns caused great misery : France was now the prey of the Free Companies continually quartered on the country. These were levied by mercenary captains on the model of the English " retinues." English, Welsh, Breton, Gascon, French, in origin, whichever king they claimed to serve they lived on the plunder of the peasant and reduced the larger part of France to ruin. The French nobles as a fighting force and the bureaucracy as a government were discredited. The King of Navarre had a powerful following. It was in these circumstances that the

The States-
General Tiers État, the bourgeois, of the States-General attempted to assume control and reform the kingdom. In this movement the States-General of Languedoïl, meeting at Paris, took the lead ; those of Languedoc, meeting at Toulouse, while making analogous conditions to their grants, were less thorough-going and far-reaching in their policy. The Languedoïl assembly of December 1355 seriously limited the

Limitation
of the
Monarchy monarchy. They granted a subsidy and taxes to maintain 30,000 troops, but they were to be gathered in by men they elected and spent under the States' own supervision, exercised at subsequent meetings. For this purpose the kingdom was divided into financial districts called *élections* with officials called *élus*, a system which outlasted the Middle Ages, although the election of the officials by the States from which the names were derived very soon disappeared. Further, in future the king was bound to consult the States-General before levying an aid or summoning the *arrière ban*, which was really the levy of a composition-tax. The right of the subjects of resistance to official oppression was recognized. The troops raised were to be organized by the States' delegates.

Étienne
Marcel The spokesman of the Tiers État in 1355 was a wealthy cloth-merchant, Étienne Marcel. His trade connected him with Flanders and its self-governing towns, and he schemed to introduce a kind of parliamentary government. Though no orator, he could organize and lead his fellows. As provost of the merchants of Paris he was used to judge and administer. Beside him stood a capable speaker, Robert le Coq, Bishop of Laon, a partisan of Charles the Bad. When the States-

General met again in October 1356 after the Battle of
Poitiers, under Marcel's leadership they demanded the punishment of evil counsellors, and the election of a Council of
State by themselves to govern the kingdom. Although the
Dauphin gained time by a visit to the Emperor Charles IV
at Metz and by agreeing to the less onerous demands of the
States-General of Languedoc, yet when the States-General
of Languedoïl renewed their meetings, he was obliged to
make great concessions in March 1357. The administration
should be reformed from top to bottom, the coinage placed
under control of the States, and certain representatives
of them added to his Council. A subsidy was granted in
return.

But these successes of the States-General were fragile. Contest with
The Dauphin was hostile and gained support in the provinces. the Dauphin
King John from Bordeaux announced a truce with the
English and annulled the subsidy. The States-General
themselves in their frequent sessions soon consisted only
of the Tiers État, for nobles and clergy abstained from
attendance, and even the Tiers État now represented only
a fraction of the towns, a quite small group led by Paris,
for the others were not so radical. However, they obtained
a new, if doubtful, ally in the King of Navarre, who escaped
from prison and entered Paris, where he displayed his orator-
ical gifts and forced the Dauphin to reconciliation. Meantime all the north of France, in spite of King John's truce,
suffered under the pillage of the bands of English and
Navarrese partisans, who reached the neighbourhood of
Paris. In February 1358, in view of the reaction of feeling
towards the Dauphin and the rumours of a peace with
England and King John's return, the States-General forbade
the assembly of provincial Estates, and Marcel, who dreaded
his own overthrow, incited his partisans to murder the
marshals of Champagne and Normandy, two of his opponents,
in the Dauphin's presence. The Dauphin was compelled to
take the title of " regent " instead of " lieutenant " in order
to invalidate his father's acts. He could not be prevented,
however, from quitting Paris in March and holding loyal
assemblies in Picardy and Champagne. It was now a case
of civil war, when a new outbreak occurred.

The peasants of the open country were suffering intolerably

The
Jacquerie

under the brigand-like Companies of English and Navarrese partisans. Their wrath was directed against the nobles who could not defend France, and were often themselves in the Companies. At last, on May 28, 1358, they rose in insurrection in the Beauvaisis under the leadership of Guillaume Karle. The Jacquerie, as it was called from Jacque, the by-name of a peasant,[1] spread in a few days over Picardy and the Île de France. Some small towns, such as Senlis, joined the movement. Everywhere the châteaux of the nobles were pillaged and destroyed. The Dauphiness and 300 great ladies were almost captured at Meaux, but were rescued by two Gascons, the Count of Foix and the Captal de Buch, returning with their retinue from crusade in Prussia. This was partly a defeat of Marcel, for, at first disapproving, he had later allied with the Jacquerie and planned the attack on Meaux. But the King of Navarre could not desert his own order. He led the nobles of his faction against Guillaume Karle, and on June 10 defeated the ill-armed Jacques. Within a month the insurrection had been put down with atrocities of vengeance worse than the peasants' own outrages. Some 20,000 were said to have perished. The lot of the peasant in France had turned definitely to the worse.

Charles the Bad, however, was still pursuing his schemes. Marcel, now desperate, made him Captain of Paris, for the Dauphin had become strong enough to besiege the city. In July the rebel provost even introduced some English soldiers of the bands near into Paris, while Charles the Bad negotiated with Edward III's representatives. But the Parisians were nearly unanimous against the English, and an ever stronger party supported the Dauphin. Marcel was forced to dismiss the English soldiers, and then on July 31 was himself struck down by his opponents as he went the round of the walls, perhaps to admit the King of Navarre. His chief friends were executed, and on August 2 the Dauphin entered Paris. He was wisely lenient to subjects now devoted. The monarchy was restored.

Murder of
Marcel

Reasons for
his failure

The failure of the constitutional movement, itself due to the misfortunes of the war, was the consequence of its own weakness. However discontented, France looked to the king

[1] The *jacque* was the short tunic of peasants.

for relief. The nobles and clergy early deserted the cause. The Tiers État were divided; Marcel had but scattered supporters outside Paris. The King of Navarre lost his popularity as his treason and ambition became evident. Languedoc had held aloof; even Languedoïl was a parcel of provinces, only united in allegiance to the king. Nor had Marcel and his friends, new to national politics, the statesmanship to devise a moderate compromise which would retain general acceptance. Indeed, such a compromise was hardly possible where traditional monarchy, class divisions, and provincial separatism were so strong.

The Dauphin was master of a ruined, anarchic realm. State of He had neither money nor an army. The Free Companies France of English, French, and other races were overrunning and devastating three-quarters of France, even taking or ransoming towns. Yet the resistance hardened; town and village defended themselves; Companies and bands on the French side fought well if ravaging in their turn. When King John agreed to a treaty which ceded in full sovereignty the old Angevin lands from Normandy to the Pyrenees, the States-General of May 1359 rejected it and continued the war. For the moment Charles the Bad of Navarre, deserted by Edward III, became loyal for a heavy bribe. Edward III, Fruitless whose own kingdom was feeling the strain, now made his Campaign of supreme effort. With a magnificent army he left Calais in Edward III October 1359 and marched to Rheims, where he hoped to be admitted and crowned. But he was met by a new plan of campaign. Everywhere the inhabitants and French troops took refuge in the fortified places, which Edward could not delay to besiege. Shut out of Rheims, the English proceeded vainly to Paris and then to Chartres, losing horses, baggage, and men in a stormy winter. The defensive battle in which they were certain victors was never offered them. The Scots were renewing their alliance with France; Winchelsea across the Channel was sacked in a French raid. Edward III could only give up his larger hopes and insist on his minimum demand, which at last the French were willing to concede. At Brétigny, near Chartres, on May 8, 1360, a treaty was Peace of signed. In return for abandoning his claim to the crown, Brétigny Edward was ceded in full sovereignty Guienne with additions — Poitou, Saintonge, Agenais, Périgord, Limousin, Quercy,

Angoulême, Rouergue, and Calais. King John was to be ransomed for 3,000,000 gold crowns, of which 600,000 were to be paid at Calais when he was set free. This preliminary treaty was finally confirmed on October 24, 1360, at Calais. Only 400,000 crowns could be paid ; hostages were given for the remainder of the ransom. More difficult and important were the mutual evacuation and surrender of the lands ceded by the French or held outside them by the English. Till that was accomplished, the final renunciations of the crown of France by Edward and of the suzerainty of Guienne by John were withheld, a diplomatic fact of the greatest moment.

On his return to France King John endeavoured to keep his word. The cessions, slowly enforced against the will of the inhabitants, were completed by 1364. Money was hard to procure, and the king was spendthrift as before. Before his death he had only paid 800,000 crowns in all. Meantime the wretched kingdom was a prey to the Free Companies. They were now independent under their leaders, like the ex-tailor, Sir John Hawkwood, and amid ravage and atrocities put the districts through which they wandered to ransom. If they were cleared from Normandy by the Breton royalist soldier, Bertrand du Guesclin, they defeated a royal army at Brignais near Lyons in April 1362, and aimlessly devastated Languedoc. They had nearly captured the Pope in Avignon.[1] At the same period the recurrence of the Black Death came to complete the general misery.

The ravages of the Free Companies

The Succession to Burgundy

Although incapable, John seemed always fated to decide the course of history. In November 1361 a difficult question of succession was raised by the death of the last male of the Capetian line of Burgundy, Philip of Rouvres. He was not only Duke of Burgundy, one of the ancient great fiefs, he was Count of Artois with other lands in France, and Count of Franche Comté in the Empire. Of his inheritance, Franche Comté and Artois with Rethel in Champagne went to his great-aunt, Margaret, daughter of King Philip the Tall, widow of Louis Count of Flanders and mother of Louis of Maele, then Count of Flanders. John could, however, claim to be the nearest heir to the duchy of Burgundy, and he asserted his right, only to grant the duchy immediately to

[1] See above, Chap. XII. p. 242.

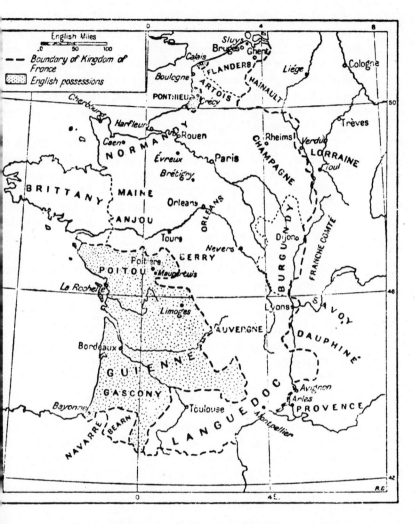

Map legend:

English Miles

Boundary of Kingdom of France

English possessions

FRANCE AFTER THE TREATY OF BRÉTIGNY IN A.D. 1360

Philip the
Bold be-
comes Duke
of Burgundy
his youngest son, Philip the Bold, who had fought by his side at Maupertuis. He endeavoured, too, to gain for Philip Franche Comté by investiture from the Emperor. It was not an unwise stroke of policy to substitute an appanaged prince for a great vassal of the older type, but, as it happened, King John thus founded the Valois line of Burgundy which was to strive to erect a " middle kingdom " and to bring the greatest dangers upon France.

Death of
John II
John's end was characteristic. His son Louis, Duke of Anjou, one of the hostages for the unpaid ransom, broke his parole and escaped. The chivalrous king insisted on returning to captivity at London, where he died on April 8,
Charles V
the Wise
1364. His death was most fortunate for his kingdom, for his son, Charles V the Wise, was quite a different sort of man. Instead of the reckless knight of chivalry he appears as a valetudinarian student, living a life of regular magnificence in his palaces in the Île de France. He had a love of law and order. Learned for a prince himself, he was a friend of learned clerks, who translated for him Aristotle and Livy into French and composed for him treatises on government. He believed in taking counsel of his subjects—in assemblies of notables, who even elected his chancellors. For all that, he held firmly to his prerogative—he was the heir of St. Louis. If he gave his subjects sound money and good government, he taxed them heavily for his splendour and his policy. He showed both an enlightenment and a meanness preluding another age to that of chivalry. He tolerated the Jews and curbed the Inquisition. His policy, which was so successful, was informed with an adroit cunning and a legal chicanery not far removed from faithlessness and fraud. But, after St. Louis, this merciful, hardworking prince was the best of his line.

Bertrand du
Guesclin.
Defeat of
Charles the
Bad
His first task was to quell his namesake, Charles the Bad, again in revolt, this time claiming the duchy of Burgundy. By good fortune Charles V now had a military leader in Bertrand du Guesclin, a hard-fighting Breton veteran who understood war as a business. In May 1364 du Guesclin defeated the Navarrese at Cocherel under the Captal de Buch. He captured the King of Navarre's dangerous towns of Mantes and Meulan on the Seine which threatened Paris. If Charles the Bad was too strong, especially in Normandy,

o be conquered, he was reduced in March 1365 to a peace
which gave him Montpellier in place of Meulan.

Almost at the same time peace came in Brittany, which Peace in
he war between the rival dukes had made for years the Brittany
happy hunting-ground of Edward III's captains. At last,
in September 1364 the younger John of Montfort defeated
Charles of Blois, who was killed on the field, at Aurai. Du
Guesclin himself was captured. In the following April Duke
John was recognized by the King of France.

The most serious problem before Charles the Wise was Gradual
that of the Free Companies who infested his kingdom. reduction
The first scheme was to enlist them as crusaders to aid the of the Free
King of Hungary against the Turks. But their abominable Companies
behaviour in Alsace roused the Germans against them.
Charles IV, who had favoured the plan, turned them back
from the Rhine in July 1365, and a new outlet had to be
found. An opportunity was given by civil war in Castile.[1]
Peter II the Cruel was hostile to France, and at feud with
his bastard brother, Henry of Trastamara, who pretended
to the crown. At the end of 1365 Bertrand du Guesclin
induced most of the Free Companies to follow him to Spain
to support the French ally, Don Henry. They were victorious
and Henry was crowned king, but this meant their prompt
return to France. Fortunately, King Peter obtained the
alliance of the Black Prince, then ruling Guienne, and again
the Companies marched to Spain, on the English side, to
win the battle of Nájera (Navarete) in April 1367, when du Battle of
Guesclin, fighting for Henry, was once more made prisoner. Nájera
This was the last of the Black Prince's victories and it was
fatal for him. Peter the Cruel kept none of his promises ;
the prince fell ill and never recovered his health. When he
withdrew to Guienne, Trastamara renewed the war. The
last act was a new expedition (1368-9) of Du Guesclin and
the defeat and death of Peter. For France, the benefit of
the Spanish war was the extinction of the Free Companies.
Battles, hardships, debauch, and disease half-exterminated
them. The remnant were easily and sternly dealt with by
Charles's government.

The chief aim of Charles V's policy was to reconquer the Charles V's
territories lost to England by the treaty of Brétigny. It New Army

[1] See below, Chap. XVII, p. 375.

was largely for this end that he reformed his army. Beside
providing for the fortification of towns and castles and the
training of his subjects in the cross-bow, he paid for com
panies of soldiers, mainly nobles, similar to the English
" retinues," who formed a kind of regular army. A new
arm was the artillery, introduced thirty years earlier, but
now improved sufficiently to be of value in the siege
warfare which it was later to revolutionize. Further, a
royal navy was instituted under the Admiral, Jean de
Vienne.

The Flanders   Charles's diplomacy was exercised in isolating England by
Succession   a system of alliances. Louis of Macle of Flanders planned
(1364) to marry his daughter and heiress, Margaret, to the
Earl of Cambridge, Edward III's youngest son. With the
Pope's aid Charles broke off the match, and (1369) married
Margaret to his own brother, the Duke of Burgundy. The
price was the retrocession of Lille and Douai to Flanders,
but not only was the alliance and succession of Flanders and
Nevers secured, but that of Louis' still living mother, Mar
garet, Artois and Rethel in France and Franche Comté in
the Empire. In this way, for a great temporary advantage
Charles built up the future power of the Dukes of Burgundy,
which was to dominate French history in the fifteenth century
and give union to the Netherlands. The alliance of King
Henry of Castile, with his valuable navy, was the natural
outcome of Charles's help in the war of succession ; it was
enlarged later by the adhesion of Portugal and cemented
in 1371 by the pretensions of Edward's son, John of Gaunt,
Duke of Lancaster, to the Castilian throne, when he married
Constance, the daughter of Peter the Cruel.

Renewal of   Meanwhile the treaty of Brétigny was breaking down.
the Hundred The ceded districts were most unwillingly subjects of the
Years' War
King of England, and their discontent came to a head when
the Black Prince, deeply in debt after his Spanish campaign,
laid a heavy hearth-tax, imitated from France, on Guienne.
In 1368 the malcontent Gascon nobles appealed to Charles
as suzerain, and, taking advantage of the fact that the
final renunciations of French suzerainty and Edward's claim
to the French throne had never been exchanged, Charles
entertained the appeal and summoned the Black Prince
before the Parlement of Paris in 1369. The prince took up

the challenge, and war was declared in May, Edward III renewing his title of King of France.

French propaganda and pro-French feeling had an immediate effect. Périgord, Rouergue, Quercy, part of Gascony, and the county of Ponthieu in the north at once transferred their allegiance to Charles. A piecemeal, methodical conquest began. The Black Prince, dying of dropsy, did indeed in 1370 recapture revolted Limoges, and perpetrate a terrible massacre of the inhabitants, but he had to be carried in a litter for the campaign and soon after withdrew to England. The only effective method of war of the English remained the ravaging " chevauchée," and now Charles and du Guesclin, his Constable, had devised the countering strategy. Du Guesclin refused to attack the enemy in their chosen positions. He followed and harassed them with effective, sudden onslaughts. No town or fortress opened its gates, and the invaders, short of food, could only march through the country to their own remaining strongholds. The great campaigns of Sir Robert Knolles in 1370 and of the Duke of Lancaster in 1373 only resulted in loss of men and horses. The English, too, lost the command of the sea. On June 23, 1372, the Earl of Pembroke was defeated and captured by the Spanish fleet under its Genoese admiral, Boccanegra, off La Rochelle. This victory enabled Du Guesclin to conquer Poitou and Saintonge. Meantime, the French ships plundered English ports along the Channel. When a two years' truce was arranged in 1375 Edward III only retained the coastland from Bordeaux to Bayonne and the town of Calais. Maladministration at home, the exhaustion due to the impossible task of conquest, and the fact that Edward III himself was sinking into dotage, crippled England. The Black Prince died in 1376, and the king in June 1377, leaving his kingdom and the renewed war to his grandson, Richard II, under an incompetent council.

Charles V was using his victory to get rid of the disloyal great vassals. Duke John IV of Brittany had sided, not unnaturally, with Edward III. The Bretons' sympathies, however, were French, and in 1373 almost all the duchy was conquered by Bertrand du Guesclin. Charles seized (1378) the opportunity to confiscate it to the royal domain. But he had overlooked the racial particularism of the in-

(marginal notes:) Conquests from the English

Battle of La Rochelle

Deaths of the Black Prince and Edward III

Breton War

habitants. They were Bretons before they were Frenchmen.
Even du Guesclin was averse to the annexation. John IV
was recalled, and later made his peace with his suzerain.
More successful were the proceedings against the habitual

Overthrow of Charles the Bad

traitor, Charles the Bad of Navarre. He had secretly again
allied himself to Edward III. When the truce was ended
in 1377 he even schemed to poison the King of France.
Discovery of the plot in 1378 led immediately to the conquest of his vast Norman fiefs by du Guesclin in spite of a
relief expedition of the Duke of Lancaster. Henry of Castile
overran the kingdom of Navarre. Charles the Bad died
ruined in 1387 ; it was not till later that his son Charles III
recovered his French domains.

As his health failed Charles V endeavoured to close the
English war by a generous peace, but the question of
suzerainty proved insoluble. Though du Guesclin died in
1380, the last English " chevauchée " of the reign from
Calais proved as abortive as the former. The war was left

The Great Schism

dragging on. So, too, was the Great Schism in the Church.
After much consultation the king decided to revolt from
Urban VI and take the side of Clement VII. Strong reasons
were adduced for his action, but it is hard to resist the conclusion that a French Pope at Avignon was too valuable a

Death of Charles V

political asset to be given up. While Charles was busily
engaged in obtaining adherents abroad to his Pope, he died
on September 16, 1380.

Internal Government

His death was a public misfortune, for he had rescued
France and governed well. Good order and the careful
minute reform of the administration were the keynotes of
his reign. After his first troubles the coinage was kept
sound. He sternly repressed the abuses of clerical immunity
and feudal privilege, even if private war could not be wholly
done away with. The nobles in one way or another were in
the king's pay, and their castles were at his disposal. The
privileged towns were submissive and well treated. The
States-General were regularly summoned for the grant of
taxation, although the king steadily endeavoured to make
their grants permanent and removed from their control.
Finance was necessarily of first consequence for a splendid
king with a great war on his hands. Besides the careful
management of the demesne lands, Charles levied the *gabelle*

or salt-monopoly, which after 1360 was permanent, the tax on sales and wines, and the new hearth-tax or *fouage*, first raised for King John's ransom, the most oppressive of all for the poorer folk. He withdrew the collection of taxes from the States-General : the *élus* became his officials, super-vised by the *généraux* at Paris—the great fiefs were not exempt, although the *seigneurs* were conciliated by receiving a share of the proceeds. While the *fouages* were raised directly, however, the indirect taxes on sales and wines were farmed out, thus giving rise to severe abuses of long con-tinuance.

Charles's fault, indeed, was the financial oppression of his reign inflicted partly by his own extravagance, partly by the greed and corruption of officials, on the ravaged, ex-hausted, and depopulated country. France was deep in misery, and the king, much as he did for revival, did not spare his subjects. Bitter discontent was seething in the people when he died, if suppressed by the gratitude and affection that were felt for him. On his death-bed he abolished the hated *fouage*. This was to leave the problem of economy to the regency for his young son Charles VI. To sum up, France was reviving in 1380, it was again the first State in Europe, but the fall in prosperity since the succession of the House of Valois had been immense. The debasement of morale by the long, ferocious war, the reckless indiscipline of chivalry, the decay of public spirit, the strife between the ideas of a centralizing monarchy and of a population full of unredressed grievances, and perplexed by desires for provincial independence and for a share in govern-ment, were of evil omen for the reign just begun.

Exhaustion of France

SUGGESTIONS FOR READING ON CHAPTER XIV

A. SOURCES

(i) *Documents*

Cosneau, E. : *Les grands traités de la Guerre de Cent Ans.* (Collection des textes pour servir à l'étude et à l'enseignement de l'histoire.) Paris, 1889.
  Ordonnances des rois de France de la troisième race. Vols. i–vi. Paris, 1723 ff.
  Rymer, T. : *Foedera.* 20 vols. London, 1704–35.

(*ii*) *Chronicles*

Froissart, J. : *Chroniques.* Trans. Berners, Lord. 6 vols. London, 1901–3.
Grandes Chroniques de France. Ed. Paris, P. Vols. v–vi. Paris, 1836–8.
Murimuth, Adam : *Continuatio chronicorum.* Ed. Thompson, E. M. Rolls Series. London, 1889.
Villani : as in suggestions for Chapter XI.
Baluze : as in suggestions for Chapter XI.

B. MODERN WORKS

Boutruche, R. : As given for Chapter IX.
Glotz, G. : *Histoire générale, Histoire du Moyen Âge,* vol. vi. *L'Europe occidentale de* 1270 *à* 1380, pt. ii. Paris, 1941.
Cambridge Medieval History, vols. vii and viii, relevant chapters.
Lavisse, E., ed. : *Histoire de France.* Vol. iv, pt. i.
Delachenal, R. : *Histoire de Charles V.* Paris, 1909–31.
Denifle, H. : *La désolation des églises, monastères, et hôpitaux en France pendant la Guerre de Cent Ans.* Vol. i. Paris, 1899.
Landry, A. : as in suggestions for Chapter XIII.
Luce, S. : *La France pendant la Guerre de Cent Ans.* 2 vols. Paris. 1892–3.
Oman, C. : *History of the Art of War in the Middle Ages.* 2 vols. London. 1924.
Perroy, E. : *La Guerre de Cent Ans.* Paris, 1946.
Pirenne, H. : *Histoire de Belgique.* Vol. ii. Brussels, 1922.

CHAPTER XV

THE DYNASTIC RIVALRIES IN GERMANY: SWITZERLAND

THE death of the Emperor Henry VII in August 1313 produced first an interregnum and then a civil war in Germany. There were immediately two candidates for the vacant throne, Henry's son, the minor King John of Bohemia, and the Habsburg Frederick the Handsome, the senior Duke of Austria. Each of these had a party among the princes. John could count on the Archbishops of Mainz and Trèves, Frederick on the Archbishop of Cologne and the Elector Palatine, Rudolf of Upper Bavaria. It is noticeable that the preference for a lesser count, so marked previously, had now disappeared. The Electors had found by experience that such an election merely meant the emergence of a new rival house among the greater princes of the Empire. They now hesitated between candidates already powerful. Frederick's chances were, however, damaged by ill-success in a war on his hands. Elector Rudolf quarrelled with his younger brother Lewis, Duke of Upper Bavaria, over the regency for their young cousins, the Dukes of Lower Bavaria, and this ended in involving Duke Frederick and his Habsburg brothers. Lewis repelled an Austrian invasion of Bavaria by a brilliant victory in November 1313 at Gammelsdorf near the River Isar, which brought him into the first rank of princes. Thereupon the Luxemburg party, seeing that King John, opposed by the Papacy, had no chance, turned to the victor. But a valid election was hard to obtain owing to the doubts as to which rival princes were the Electors. Further, the Habsburg party remained obdurate, and there was no majority rule to decide an election even if it was agreed who should elect. When the election took place on October 19–20, 1314, five Electors, the Archbishops of Mainz and Trèves, King John of Bohemia, the Duke of Saxe-Lauenburg, and the Margrave of Brandenburg,

Rival candidates for the Throne

Double Election of Lewis IV and Frederick III

elected Lewis IV, while the Archbishop of Cologne, the
Elector Palatine, the Duke of Saxe-Wittenberg, and Henry
of Carinthia, who still claimed Bohemia, voted for Frederick
(III).   Lewis IV secured the regalia and coronation at Aix-
la-Chapelle, Frederick was crowned at Bonn by the correct
archbishop, the Elector of Cologne, both important assets
in contemporary opinion.   There was nothing to decide the
issue but war.

The rivals were evenly matched.   Both belonged to the
reigning chivalrous type of ruler.   Both were personally
popular.   Neither was a strong character.   In ability Lewis
the Bavarian was much the more gifted, but he was changeable to a degree, a maladroit opportunist, who had only one
thing at heart, the increase of the dynastic possessions of
his house of Wittelsbach.   He cannot be blamed for not
attempting to restore the monarchy, for that was impossible
when no one wished it, but he did nothing for Germany,
or to remedy its confusion.

Civil War   Low Germany to the north was indifferent to the struggle.
In south Germany the war was waged indecisively, partly
owing to the reluctance of the rivals to risk a pitched
battle, partly owing to the lukewarmness of their partisans.
Fortifications could usually hold out in the short sieges of
fourteenth-century armies.   So external events caused the
chief alternations of fortune.   The crushing defeat of Frederick's abler brother Leopold in 1315 by the Swiss at
Morgarten [1] crippled the Austrians for a while.   The disaffection of the Bohemian nobles in 1317 for King John,
Lewis's best ally, turned the balance against the Bavarians.
At last, in 1322, the Habsburgs made a great effort.
Frederick, with Hungarian allies, invaded Bavaria from the
east ; Leopold from Swabia and the west.   But Lewis IV
did not allow them to unite..   With John of Bohemia, whom
he had reconciled with his nobles, and other princes he fought
Battle of   Frederick on September 28 at Mühldorf on the River Inn.
Mühldorf   The stubborn resistance of his footmen and dismounted
knights and the opportune flanking charge of the Hohenzollern Burgrave of Nuremberg won the day.   Frederick,
his brother Henry, and 1,400 prisoners fell into the hands
of the victor.   No such battle had been fought in Germany

[1] See below, p. 319.

for many years, and Lewis seemed secure on the throne. He used his victory to enfeoff his eldest son, Lewis, with the March and Electorate of Brandenburg, which had lapsed to the Crown by the extinction of the Ascanian margraves in 1320. This was in accordance with precedent, but it disappointed John of Bohemia, who only got Upper Lusatia of the Ascanian inheritance.

A new enemy now arose in Lewis's path. The Papacy being vacant in 1314, neither of the rival Kings of the Romans had requested papal approval. But when John XXII became Pope in 1316, he declared himself for the time neutral between their conflicting claims. The fact was that Pope John dreaded a new Emperor and his intervention in Italy, and so did his ally, King Robert of Naples. The safest course was to keep the Empire vacant. For this policy, the papal claims, now distended to their utmost, provided a means and an incentive to the masterful Pope. On the death of Henry VII, Pope Clement V had issued a bull declaring in set terms that the Empire was a fief of the Holy See, that the Pope's approbation was necessary for a valid election, and that during the vacancy of the throne the Pope directly ruled the Empire. Acting on these lines, John XXII considered the throne vacant until he decided for one claimant or the other. He appointed King Robert his Imperial Vicar in Italy, and declared both Lewis's and Frederick's appointment of vicars as invalid. The victory of Mühldorf was a blow to him, and his fears were soon justified, for Lewis sent a Vicar to Italy to help his Ghibelline enemies of Verona and Milan. The Pope's counter-step to this action was marked by all the extremist energy of his arbitrary character. In a *monitorium* of October 8, 1323, he declared Lewis culpable of having acted as King of the Romans before his election was confirmed by the Pope and of aiding heretics in the person of Visconti of Milan. Within three months Lewis was to lay down his usurped title and his subjects were to renounce him under pain of excommunication and forfeiture.

Lewis asked for an extension of time for his defence, which was granted for the narrow term of two months. But he was disposed for resistance, and after the manner of Philip the Fair, though with less resources and conviction,

Attitude and claims of Pope John XXII

Breach with Lewis IV

prepared a counter-attack. At Frankfort in January 1324 he declared the independence of the Empire and the sufficiency of his election and coronation to make him King of the Romans without papal approval. Then the Pope proceeded to extremities. At the end of the two months, on March 23, 1324, he excommunicated the king, with further threats on continued resistance. Lewis replied on May 22

Appeal of Sachsenhausen

by the Appeal of Sachsenhausen. In this, besides his Frankfort claims, he espoused the cause of the revolted Franciscans under Michael of Cesena.[1] John XXII was a heretic and therefore no Pope, since he denied the absolute poverty of Christ and the Apostles. The king appealed to a General Council of the Church. John XXII's answer on July 11 was to pronounce Lewis's election null, and to deprive him of his hereditary possessions, if he did not submit.

The *Defensor Pacis*

Almost at the same time as these sweeping documents there appeared the most remarkable product of the dispute, the *Defensor Pacis* of Marsilio of Padua and John of Jandun, with its doctrine of the supremacy of the lay State and of the invalidity of the papal theocracy.[2] The authors soon fled from Paris to join the revolted Franciscan leaders at Lewis's court. Their treatise decorated a struggle which was but an inefficient imitation of former controversies. Neither Pope John nor Lewis could rouse formidable opposition to one another. Germany took little notice of John's decrees; the Church still considered John Pope.

Reconciliation of Lewis IV and Frederick III

Leopold of Austria, indeed, schemed to bring in Charles IV of France as Emperor, but the captive Frederick came to terms with Lewis IV in 1325. He was to be joint-king, a title which he bore till his death in 1330, although he did not function as such. An offer of Lewis to abdicate in his favour in 1326 if the Pope would accept him as king was shattered on John XXII's refusal, but completed the reconciliation with the Habsburgs and thus ended the civil war in Germany. A Polish invasion of Brandenburg, instigated by the Pope, did not affect the security of Lewis's position.

Lewis IV's Italian Expedition

It was now that Lewis IV endeavoured to strike at his adversary by an Italian expedition on the model of his predecessors. In alliance with the Ghibelline despots of the north he entered Italy in March 1327 and received the Iron

[1] See above, Chap. XII, p. 252. [2] See above, Chap. X, pp. 210-11.

Crown at Milan. In January 1328 he reached Rome, welcomed by the Colonna and the Ghibellines. His adviser seems to have been the political theorist Marsilio, whom he made his vicar in Rome, and whose revolutionary views were now almost whimsically applied. An assembly of the Roman people gave Lewis the signory of their city; the imperial crown was placed on his head by their four lay delegates. Another assembly deposed Pope John as heretic and traitor, while a Franciscan, Pietro of Corvara, was elected Pope as Nicholas V. John XXII, meanwhile, had proclaimed a crusade against his enemy. But all these proceedings were devoid of serious result. The crusade fell flat; Lewis barely attempted to attack the Guelfs. His Italian supporters fell away. He beat a slow retreat, reaching Germany in January 1330, and the anti-Pope, whom he abandoned, submitted to John. The vain expedition might have shown the combatants, as it did their successors, that the question of the Empire was a dead issue in Italy.

His Lay Coronation at Rome

His Anti-Pope

The contest between Papacy and Empire now became inextricably mixed with the territorial ambitions of the three great houses of Wittelsbach, Luxemburg, and Habsburg. King John of Bohemia, already aggrieved by not obtaining Brandenburg, now set his eyes on a new inheritance, also desired by his rivals. Henry, Duke of Carinthia and Count of Tyrol, the ex-king of Bohemia, had no male heir, but a daughter, Margaret Maultasch (" of the ugly mouth "). The two remaining Habsburg brothers, Albert II and Otto, were his nephews by his sister. In 1330 King John of Bohemia gained the hand of Margaret for his younger son John Henry and with this marriage hoped to gain the succession of Tyrol for his house. But while King John was occupied in an attempt to gain a kingdom in north Italy,[1] the Emperor made a secret partition treaty with the Habsburgs; they were to have Carinthia, himself Tyrol. He naturally feared to find the Luxemburgs hemming him in on the south, yet he endeavoured to keep the peace with King John, who on his return from Italy in 1332 was at war with Austria and Poland. John was to exchange Tyrol and Carinthia for Brandenburg.

The Succession to Tyrol and Carinthia

With these negotiations attempts to make peace with the

[1] See below, Chap. XVI, p. 339.

Pope were involved.   Lewis was ready to abandon his theological allies and their policy, in which he had merely taken
an opportunist interest, and to accept absolution if he might
retain the Empire.   But John XXII insisted on the nullity
of an election unconfirmed by the Papacy, and he still aimed
at Lewis's deposition and a new election.   In this resolution
he was backed by King Philip VI of France, who coveted
the imperial kingdom of Burgundy or Arles.   In 1333 John
of Bohemia came forward with a new plan.   Lewis IV was
to abdicate in favour of his cousin and John's son-in-law
Henry the Elder, one of the Dukes of Lower Bavaria ; France
was to gain the kingdom of Arles in pledge for a large sum.
This met the Pope's views but not those of King Robert
of Naples, who dreaded being the vassal of Philip VI for
his county of Provence.   Lewis IV, who had at first seemed,
as a diplomatic move, to agree, took courage and denounced
the scheme, on the encouragement of the few Italian cardinals.   The aged John XXII, who was emerging with
difficulty from his controversy on the state of departed
souls,[1] then took occasion on his death-bed in December 1334
to unveil the true objective of his policy by decreeing the
separation of Italy from Germany and the Empire, a *brutum
fulmen* disregarded by all.

The death of Duke Henry of Carinthia in April 1335
made the Emperor still more eager for reconciliation with
the Papacy.   He enfeoffed the Habsburgs with Carinthia
and south Tyrol, his own sons with north Tyrol.   King
John, wounded at the moment in a Paris tournament,
could do nothing, but while the Habsburgs took and kept
Carinthia and Carniola, the Tyrolese held firmly to Margaret
Maultasch.   To gain the Curia, Lewis became more and more
yielding ;   at last, in the autumn of 1336, he offered to
abandon his title of Emperor until crowned in the ancient
form, to do penance by crusade, to renounce the Appeal of
Sachsenhausen and his Franciscan allies, whom he professed
not to have understood, and to accept the papal approbation
of his kingship.   Benedict XII, the new Pope, was himself
perhaps inclined to conciliation, but Philip VI and Robert
of Naples were utterly opposed to it ;   they ruled the Pope,
who had also John XXII's doctrine to uphold.   His un-

[1] See above, Chap. XII. p. 254.

bending attitude, as he himself foresaw, threw Lewis into an English alliance and a stiffer resistance.

In July 1337 the Emperor took Edward III's pay [1]; The John of Bohemia was the ally of France. The German Declaration princes as a whole were indignant at the Pope's exorbitant of Rense claims and ready to assert the independence of the Empire. When an embassy from them to the Pope failed anew, feeling was strong enough to produce a meeting of all the Electors except the King of Bohemia on July 16 at Rense near Coblenz on the Rhine. There they declared that the chosen of the Electors, whether unanimously or by a majority, was rightful King of the Romans, without the need of any papal confirmation; the King of the Romans was ruler of the Empire; only the honour of his formal coronation as Emperor at Rome belonged to the Pope. In August, at the great Diet of Frankfort, where princes, counts, barons, and imperial towns were all represented, this declaration was made a law of the Empire. The aggression of the Popes had at last hardened the custom of the Empire into constitutional law.

Lewis IV's fortunes seemed now at their height. He created Edward III Imperial Vicar for the war with France. The last recalcitrant among his Wittelsbach kinsmen, Henry of Lower Bavaria, submitted. Even John of Bohemia yielded to the current among the princes and did homage. But Lewis was incapable of a consistent policy. He still hankered after papal recognition, territorial gains, and an Italian expedition in the old style. France had been the obstacle to reconciliation with the Pope. When Philip VI after Sluys begged the Emperor's mediation, Lewis made an alliance with him in 1341, revoked Edward's vicariate, and made vain proposals to Benedict XII. While the Electors thus found themselves deserted by their chief, Lewis raised new enmities over the Tyrolese succession. Countess Margaret Maultasch lived on bad terms with her The divorce husband John Henry of Luxemburg. In 1342 the marriage and re- was annulled by a complaisant bishop, and Lewis not only marriage of confirmed this but also as Emperor, by a usurpation of papal Margaret prerogative, gave a dispensation for the re-marriage of Maultasch Margaret with his eldest son, Lewis, Elector of Brandenburg,

[1] See above, Chap. XIV, pp. 276-7, 279.

since the marriage was within the forbidden degrees of
kinship. He even enfeoffed the bridal pair with Carinthia.
Thus the Luxemburgs and Habsburgs were again rendered
hostile and the Pope flouted.   Clement VI, who had succeeded
the less resolute Benedict XII, at once renewed the process
started by John XXII, and repeated its condemnations in
1343.   It was clear that Electors and princes were inclined
to abandon the Emperor.   Yet Lewis once more conciliated

The Habsburgs acquire Carinthia

the Habsburgs by re-enfeoffing them with Carinthia, and
renewed the most abject offers to the Papacy : everything,
including abdication and the surrender of his theological
allies, of whom the chief, except William of Ockham, were
dead, but not the acknowledgement that papal confirmation
was necessary for a legitimate King of the Romans.   These
offers were refused once more.

Meanwhile the Electors, led by the Luxemburger Baldwin
of Trèves and the new Archbishop of Mainz, appointed by
papal provision, were thinking of deposing an Emperor who
could not either maintain the policy of Rense or make peace.
A new storm over succession to territory embittered the

The Succession to Holland and Hainault

disaffection.   In September 1343 William of Avesnes, Count
of Hainault, Holland, Zealand, and Friesland, died without
male heirs.   Hainault went by law to his eldest daughter,
the Emperor's wife : the other counties were vacant, and
Lewis granted them to her at once.   This not only offended
the other relatives but alarmed the Netherland house of
Luxemburg. If King John, blind and exiled, was not
dangerous, his heir Charles, the regent of Bohemia, was
ready for civil war as the Pope's ally.   In April 1346 Clement
VI called on the Electors to proceed to a new election ; in
the same month Charles came to a secret agreement with
the Papacy.   He promised personally to await papal confirmation before he was crowned or acted as King of the
Romans, not to enter the Papal States without papal permission, to enter Rome only for the day of his imperial
coronation, to revoke all Lewis's acts.   This was enough.

Election of Charles IV

On July 11, at Rense, five Electors, the three archbishops,
the King of Bohemia, and Duke Rudolf of Saxe-Wittenberg,
elected Charles IV as king.   The two Wittelsbach Electors,
the Count Palatine and the Margrave of Brandenburg, were
not present.

Charles's reign began badly. The Imperial Free Cities and many princes would not recognize the " Parsons' king." He shared in the defeat of Crécy, and after coronation at Bonn—for Aix-la-Chapelle was for Lewis—he slipped in disguise back to his kingdom of Bohemia. An attempt to conquer Tyrol failed. But his way was cleared by Lewis's Death of death on October 11, 1347, from apoplexy while hunting. Lewis IV Lewis IV had really retained the throne till his death ; he had greatly increased the territorial power of the Wittels-bachs, his guiding desire. But his inconstancy, his in-ability to keep faith with his allies, his interference in Italy, had lamed his resistance to the overweening papal preten-sions. None the less, this dreary, indecisive struggle taught the new men of both parties : it was the last, if unimpressive, End of contest between Papacy and Empire. Charles IV was contest of willing to leave Italy alone, except for the occasional assis- Empire and tance given to the Pope ; he himself accepted papal con- Papacy firmation : thus papal fears were allayed and papal claims given a shadow of fulfilment. The Papacy on its side was satisfied by the real abandonment of Italy and no longer made the constitutional denial of papal suzerainty and its implications, which the German Diets and laws maintained, a *casus belli*. The theoretical contest died out ingloriously when its material cause was removed.

Charles IV's unchivalrous, businesslike character was Charles IV's suited to the new time. Like his namesake, Charles the Character Wise of France, he was a cultured, administrative prince, who shone in diplomacy and in organization, too, when he had anything to organize, as in his hereditary kingdom of Bohemia. He was a linguist, master of five languages, French, German, Czech, Italian, and Latin. Of chivalric recklessness or romantic devotion to the dream of the Empire he was incapable. His successor Maximilian called him " the father of Bohemia and the stepfather of the Empire," but the Empire had long been orphan, and little more was possible. Charles would never quit the substance for the shadow. Still he did see and endeavour to remedy the crying evil of the German constitution—the uncertain, disputed elections to the Empire. His practical good sense showed him that the impossible attempt to rule North Italy, where he had sojourned a year or two as his adventurous

father's representative, was not worth the steady hostility
of the Papacy. He had the legal and diplomatic acumen to
preserve formal rights, such as those over the kingdom of
Burgundy, which brought some little immediate profit and
might be of future value, if only to bargain with. This
sober, disillusioned, sickly figure worked to build the near
future, not to resuscitate the distant past.

The reduc-
tion of the
Wittelsbachs
On Lewis IV's death King Charles was able to lead a
successful expedition from Bohemia to the Rhine, when most
of Germany submitted to him. The Wittelsbachs held out,
but they were too numerous and divided, while none of them
possessed much capacity. The Empress-dowager with her
younger sons had the Netherland counties ; the Elector
Lewis of Brandenburg and his elder brothers had most of
Bavaria, now that the Dukes of Lower Bavaria were extinct ; the Elector Rudolf II and his kinsmen of the elder
branch of the house held the Palatinate of the Rhine round
Heidelberg and the north corner of Bavaria, called now the
Upper Palatinate. It was not till January 1348 that the
two Electors, together with the Duke of Saxe-Lauenburg
and the ex-Archbishop of Mainz, who had been deposed and
replaced by Clement VI but not expelled from his principality, agreed to elect Edward III of England. The latter
had, however, been gained over by Charles IV by means of
recognizing the claims of the Empress's sisters, one of whom
was Edward's queen, Philippa, to the Netherland inheritance,
and he sensibly refused the Wittelsbachs' offer of the imperial
burden. Frederick of Meissen, their next candidate, also
would not stand. Charles now found a new weapon. An
impostor appeared, claiming to be Waldemar, the long-dead
Margrave of Brandenburg, the last Ascanian. He found a
large following in the March, and the Ascanian branches of
Saxony and Anhalt accepted him. So did Charles, while
the belated election of an anti-Cæsar, Count Günther of
Schwarzburg in Thuringia, by the Wittelsbach party in
January 1349 proved a flash in the pan. He soon abdicated
and died. Meanwhile, the embarrassed Wittelsbachs were
making peace. Charles married the daughter, Anna, of the
Elector Palatine, with part of the Upper Palatinate for prospective dower. At the peace of Eltville, the Bavarian
dukes submitted on easy terms. Charles gave up the false

Waldemar, who was left to his enemies to conquer, and surrendered all claims to Tyrol. He could then proceed in July 1349 to a new coronation at Aix-la-Chapelle.

Ill-luck and their own divisions continued the decline of the Wittelsbachs. In 1351 Lewis the Elder exchanged the March of Brandenburg with two of his brothers, Lewis the Roman and Otto, against the sole possession of Upper Bavaria. On his death in 1361 this and Tyrol fell to his son Meinhard. Directly the latter died unmarried in 1363, Tyrol was taken, with the consent of Margaret Maultasch, by the Habsburgs led by Rudolf, now the senior Duke of Austria. Upper Bavaria was seized by Stephen of Lower Bavaria, the eldest Wittelsbach duke, who thereby mortally offended his two brothers of Brandenburg. To injure him, they made a treaty with the Emperor, that, if they died sonless, Brandenburg should go to Charles's heir Wenceslas and his other sons. In 1364 Charles used the contest of Duke Stephen of Bavaria with the Habsburgs over Tyrol to obtain another succession treaty. If either Habsburgs or Luxemburgs became extinct, their lands should be inherited by the surviving house. Strangely enough, this treaty came into force by the extinction of the Luxemburgs. Duke Stephen failed in his war with Austria and renounced Tyrol in 1369. Meantime, Otto, now sole Elector of Brandenburg, had in 1365 given the government of his lands to the Emperor for six years, but this arrangement was overthrown by the local nobles. Otto, whom Charles was pressing to abdicate, at length turned to his kinsmen. A league was formed of the Elector Palatine, the Bavarian dukes, other princes, and Hungary against the Emperor in 1371. But Charles was lucky and skilful. The Elector of Mainz, an opponent, died ; Lewis of Hungary was diverted by the acquisition of Poland and made truce in 1373 after a half-hearted campaign in Moravia, and later contracted an alliance with his former foe. The Wittelsbachs by themselves could make no headway. After an invasion of Brandenburg, Otto resigned himself to the treaty of Fürstenwalde in August 1373. The government of and succession to Brandenburg were ceded to Charles, who had already bought Lower Lusatia from a temporary mortgagee. Otto retained his title and electoral rights till his death childless on pilgrimage in 1379. The

Decline of the Wittelsbachs

net result of this tangle of treaties, alliances, marriages, and wars was that, though they retained the much-divided Palatinate and Bavaria, and a branch ruled part of the Netherlands in isolation, the Wittelsbachs lost their position as one of the greatest houses of the Empire. The aims of Lewis IV had in fact been stultified largely by the unlucky consequences of the absence of primogeniture.

The Black Death
It was during the first years of Charles's reign, in 1348–51, that the Black Death swept over most of Germany, only certain districts such as East Franconia and Bohemia escaping owing, it may be imagined, to the absence of black rats which spread the disease. It caused the same heavy mortality as elsewhere, and recurred in 1367 and at later periods with the universal result of checking the growth of the population. Its first onslaught produced in unorganized Germany more undisciplined effects even than in other parts of Europe, In south Germany the fanatic movement of the Flagellants arose and spread over the country until it was

Massacres of the Jews
rigorously suppressed. Connected with it were the terrible outbreaks against the Jews which destroyed their prosperity in Germany. Precedents had already been given in 1298 and 1336–8 by popular massacres of the Jews in all south Germany. Now in 1348–9 some 350 Jewish settlements were attacked by the mob on the charge of causing the plague by poisoning the water, and over 200 communities were wiped out. Though there was a remnant left, especially in Austria, the centre of European Judaism was thenceforth in the east in Poland.[1]

Charles IV crowned at Rome
For the completion of his imperial status Charles required a Roman coronation, and he did not care under what humiliating conditions he obtained it. In 1354 Germany was quiet enough for him to make a hurried journey to Rome, where he was crowned in April 1355, and to return as hastily. He raised some money by the sale of titles and privileges, all that remained to him of the imperial prerogatives in Italy, but no Pope could take offence at the obedient monarch's behaviour. Yet this contemptible exhibition of the " pedlar " of titles, as the Italians thought him, sealed the Peace between Papacy and Empire. A second journey, more of an expedition, in 1368–9, was even under-

[1] Cf. above, Chap. IX, p. 184, and below, Chap. XVIII, p. 395.

taken at Pope Urban V's request to support his return to
Rome from Avignon and to secure some sort of peace in
Italy, but though Charles again came back to Germany with
a full purse he failed deservedly to help either Papacy or
Empire. He had only confirmed the separation of Germany
and Italy.

Although Charles IV was mainly concerned with the
government of his kingdom of Bohemia,[1] as was natural
considering the lack of means and instruments to govern
Germany, he made distinct endeavours to give some kind
of peace and order in the German kingdom. This was done
mainly by the encouragement of the *Landfrieden,* the local *The Land-*
associations for the maintenance of peace in given districts. *frieden*
The oldest of them was the Westphalian in the north. The
Franconian, Bavarian, and Rhenish *Landfrieden* were founded
under Lewis the Bavarian ; under Charles others arose. The
rulers, nobles, and towns, who formed them, guaranteed for
definite periods the safety of travellers and mutual defence.
Transgressors were placed under a kind of outlawry, and, if
powerful, were coerced by the united force of the association.
If the *Landfrieden* could not put down private war, they
mitigated its effects, and gave some security in a land under
countless rulers.

The worst evils in Germany, however, because they were *The Golden*
the parents of all the others, were the uncertainty surround- *Bull*
ing elections to the crown, which was the cause of so many
civil wars, and the fact that even a universally recognized
Emperor was in his own person the only link binding the
country together, for the Diet of princes and imperial towns
which he summoned was amorphous and unorganized, in
spite of its undoubted powers in taxation and solemn legislation—the towns indeed were only subordinate members of
the assembly in which they yet had a right to appear by
their representatives. The greatest triumph of Charles's
German policy was to provide a certain constitutional election, and to call in the Electors as an organized College to
the Emperor's assistance as a bond of union. The obvious
need of a defined system of election and the advantages
offered to the Electors themselves helped him to carry
through his scheme. A Diet at Nuremberg in November

[1] See below, Chap. XVIII, pp. 397-99.

1355 approved the main provisions of the Golden Bull which
he issued on January 10, 1356. They were supplemented
and confirmed in a Diet at Metz at Christmas 1356. The
Golden Bull, so called from the golden seal occasionally
affixed to imperial charters, settled first of all which seven
princes were the Electors of the Empire. The Archbishops
of Mainz, Cologne, and Trèves, the Elector Palatine of the
Rhine, the King of Bohemia, the Margrave of Brandenburg,
and the Duke of Saxe-Wittenberg. The Dukes of Bavaria,
who by family treaty since 1329 had enjoyed a vote in
alternation with the Elector Palatine, also a Wittelsbach,
were thus excluded. So, too, the Duke of Saxe-Lauenburg
lost the electoral vote to his cousin of Saxe-Wittenberg, now
the only Elector of Saxony. This, however, in view of the
practice of co-inheritance, was not enough. The electoral
dignity was attached to definite lands of the lay Electors,
which were to descend by primogeniture. Thus, there could
be no doubt who the Electors were of the Holy Roman
Empire. Further, the majority principle, affirmed at Rense,
was established : if a majority of Electors, meeting at Frankfort, agreed on a candidate, he was the legitimate King of
the Romans to be crowned at Aix-la-Chapelle. No notice
was taken of the Pope's claim to confirm or nominate the
king or to rule the Empire during a vacancy. On the contrary, the Elector Palatine was *ex officio* regent in the south,
the Elector of Saxony in the north. The seven Electors
were strengthened and propitiated by special rights. The
King of Bohemia's absolute autonomy was confirmed, but
the other Electors were given practically sovereign rights in
their lands : they could coin money and judge without
appeal ; it was high treason to rebel or plot against them.
They were to meet as an imperial council at least once a
year. In fact, they were added as a possibly efficient central institution to the Empire. Thus, as far as law could
do it, a disputed election was prevented, and papal claims
thrust tacitly aside. The Pope protested, but he had no
incentive to make him push the matter farther : the Empire
had become German.

Disintegra-
tion of
Germany

The defects of the Golden Bull were obvious on the
surface. It did not make—no law could have made—the
Emperor as Emperor any wealthier or any more powerful ;

it gave him neither demesne, nor army, nor revenue, nor bureaucracy, the four great desiderata of the German monarchy. Germany remained a collection of nearly independent princes and towns, engrossed in private policies and wars. The only members of the Empire who gained by it were the Electors. The towns were discouraged, for it vainly forbade them to form any leagues save the *Landfrieden*. The princes were annoyed at the Electors' status. In fact, Rudolf, the senior Duke of Austria, took it so much to heart that he had forged imperial charters, two of them purporting to be issued by Julius Cæsar and Nero, which practically severed Austria from the Empire. Charles not unnaturally was suspicious, and called on the humanist Petrarch for an opinion, which was unfavourable to the duke, a faint intrusion of the Renaissance into Germany. Rudolf took up arms on the rejection of his charters, and was only pacified when he obtained Tyrol in 1364. He died the next year and the division of the Habsburg lands between his brothers weakened the rival dynasties to the Emperor.

That division emphasized one merit of the Golden Bull, the primogeniture introduced into the lay Electorates. Although it only applied to a particular territory in each case, it was to prove slowly infectious by example. Before its clear advantages, the inveterate German custom of subdivision among co-heirs was at long last to give way. But this was long after Charles IV's time, and he could not have foreseen it. What he did aim at was the avoidance of double elections to the Empire, which came to pass, aided by his Bull, in the century following his death.

Charles's practical and disillusioned diplomacy was well illustrated in his dealings with the kingdom of Burgundy or the Arelate. There the imperial authority, always trifling, tended to annihilation not only before the autonomy of the great vassals but before the aggressions of the King of France. No attempt was made by the Emperor to alter existing facts, but he was careful to emphasize and use his formal suzerainty and thereby to keep it intact and in some degree profitable. In 1365 he even went through the long-disused ceremony of coronation at Arles, the last Emperor so to do. More important were his frequent acts of sovereignty in the shape of expensive charters to the princes and nobles, the real

Charles IV and the Arelate

rulers of the land.   In 1356 at Metz he obtained the homage
of Charles of France for Dauphiné and of the Duke of Burgundy for Franche Comté.   In the same year he made the
Dauphin imperial vicar for Dauphiné, and the Count of
Savoy for his lands;   in 1378 he even made the Dauphin
imperial vicar for all the Arelate, save the Savoyard territory.   If these grants, except in Dauphiné, were only temporary, they gained recognition of the Emperor's legal
supremacy, while submitting at a price to the inevitable
French advance.   The suzerainty, thus unheroically maintained, was to be of some value in preserving Franche Comté
for later Emperors.   It but little affected the gradual solidification of the Arelate into its four chief divisions, Savoy,
which since the late thirteenth century included Vaud to
the north of Lake Geneva, Franche Comté, Provence under
its Neapolitan dynasty, and Dauphiné, which was already
French.

The Free Companies   It was a sign of the disintegration of Germany and the
isolation of its northern parts that Charles IV left the Hansa
League and the neighbouring princes to fight and win their
war with Waldemar III of Denmark by themselves.[1]   He
did, however, take action when the Rhine was threatened
in 1365 by the Free Companies on their way to Hungary
from France,[2] a " crusade " which he himself had furthered.
But the army which he collected to repel them from Alsace
committed the same atrocities as the *routiers* had.   It gave
no encouragement to Germans to rely upon the Emperor.

The Luxemburg Lands   Charles's real interests, however, in which perhaps he
also saw the best chance for the restoration of an effective
German monarchy, lay in the increase of the territorial possessions of the house of Luxemburg.   In pursuing this aim
of aggrandizing his family, which was that of every recent
Emperor, he followed a much more consistent and coherent
scheme than Lewis the Bavarian.   That scheme concerned
the east.   His ancestral land of Luxemburg he gave as a
duchy in 1354 to his youngest brother Wenceslas, who had
married the heiress, Joanna, of the duchy of Brabant.   But
Duke Wenceslas left no children when he died in 1383, and
no new Luxemburg branch was founded in the Netherlands.
On the other hand Charles IV was building up a half-Slav,

See above, Chap. IX, pp. 186–87.   [2] See above, Chap. XIV, p. 293.

ialf-German power round the kingdom of Bohemia. To
Bohemia with the overlordship of Moravia and Silesia, he
added Lower Lusatia in 1368, Brandenburg in 1373, and
part of the Upper Palatinate in 1353. In this way a solid
block of Luxemburg lands was created, which might possibly
be increased by the inheritance of Austria owing to the succession treaty of 1364 and even by Hungary if a match
between a Luxemburg and the heiress of the kingdom could
be arranged. The block could be the centre of Luxemburg
control of the Empire. Charles did not, however, venture
to disregard entirely the rights of junior members of his
house. In his last will he left to his eldest son Wenceslas
Bohemia and its overlordships with western Lusatia ; to his
second son Sigismund the electorate of Brandenburg ; to his
third son John, a new duchy of Görlitz, i.e. eastern Lusatia,
and the Neumark province of Brandenburg. His dead
brother, John Henry, the ex-Count of Tyrol, had already
received the Bohemian fief of Moravia, and left it to his
own sons. In each branch Charles established primogeniture
with eventual rights of succession to the others. But it
was to be more the chance of the failure of heirs than his
planning which continued the unity of his possessions.

The crown of Charles's schemes for his family was the The
election of the heir to Bohemia, Wenceslas, to be King of Election of
the Romans during his father's lifetime, the first election of Wenceslas
the kind since the days of Frederick II. In view of the
increasing power of the Luxemburgs and the jealousy felt
for it, this was a difficult project. But the Electors and
other important princes could be bought, no new thing in
imperial elections. Charles paid in cash and in grants of
privileges, and by pledging imperial free towns, nominally
a part of his demesne, to the covetous princes. He had then
to conciliate, by characteristic double-dealing, imperial law
and his own undertakings to the Papacy on the subject of
papal confirmation and suzerainty. He suddenly informed
Pope Gregory XI, then at war with Florence, that Wenceslas would be elected in two months' time and forthwith
crowned. The Pope protested that his approval should be
received before the coronation. Charles, supported by the
Electors, would only defer each ceremony for the illusory
period of ten days, which did not allow time for the Pope's

reply. On June 10, 1376, Wenceslas was elected at Frank fort, and on July 6 crowned at Aix-la-Chapelle. Not til then did Charles send an antedated petition for confirmation and Wenceslas accept his father's engagements of 1346 Gregory received the new move perforce with favour, bu recognition was only given by the rival Popes of the Schism Henceforth their claim was tacitly abandoned.

War with the Swabian League Charles's shabby diplomatic success, however, left hin at war. He had never been a good friend to the Imperia Free Towns, and had even legislated against their league in the Golden Bull. He had taxed them for his wars an bribes. To pledge them to princes was to endanger thei freedom. In 1376 a Swabian league of towns was forme to resist. Charles put them to the ban of the Empire, bu he failed to capture Ulm, and his princely allies, led by th Count of Wurtemberg, were routed by the townsmen at th battle of Reutlingen next year. Charles then made a peac at Rotenburg, by which the towns were secured agains being pledged and their leagues were permitted. He arrange in 1378 a favourable treaty between the League and Wur temberg. Thus, against his will he had contributed to th

Death of Charles IV development of the Free Towns. Soon after, on Novem ber 29, 1378, he died after years of painful disease, leavin the Empire and Bohemia to King Wenceslas. It is con ceivable that he might have benefited Germany more tha he did, but to abandon the pursuit of the impossible and t accept, with some pompous disguise, existing facts, was rea service, and the Golden Bull, whatever its faults, prove durable by what it abandoned no less than by what i created.

A feature of Charles IV's reign, on which he hardl exercised any influence, was the increasing tendency—w can call it no more—of some of the border territories o Germany to form separate conglomerations with a charac teristic life of their own, large enough and distinct enoug to give birth in the future to new states and nations. Th Bohemian kingdom which he ruled had always been a Sla annex, not an integral part, of the Empire, but he strength

The forma- tion of the Netherlands ened its autonomy and enlarged its boundaries. The Lo Countries or Netherlands at the mouths of the Rhine an its great tributary, the Meuse or Maas, continued to drif apart from the main current of German politics and to form a group of provinces linked together by conditions of life and mutual proximity. As some of them spoke a dialect of north French—Walloon—and one of them, Flanders, was mostly a French fief while others were immediately on the French borders, they tended to form a characteristic civili-zation which showed both German and French affinities. The principalities of this region, Flanders under its count, Hainault, Holland, and Zealand under a branch of the Wittelsbachs, Luxemburg and Brabant under Charles's brother, and the prince-bishoprics of Liége and Utrecht, were engrossed by politics and problems dictated by their pro-vincial circumstances, and involved largely in manufacture and commerce. In them all the system of " Estates "— **Their** nobles, clergy, and towns—had taken root, and the power **Estates** of the princes was thereby severely limited. In 1356 Duke Wenceslas was obliged to accept the charter known as the *Joyeuse Entrée* of Brabant ; in 1373, after long struggles the Prince-Bishop of Liége submitted to the Peace of the Twenty-two, which placed the administration under the supervision of a board of the three Estates. It is to be noted that of the Estates the towns with their wealth were the most powerful. Meantime within the towns the class- **Their Towns** strife was in progress through the fourteenth century. In Brabant, with the duke's support the oligarchic patricians held their ground till the end of the period. In the city of Liége the *métiers* of small masters and their followers waged nearly a century of war against the landlord patricians from 1312. In spite of reactions each peace usually marked a step in advance for them till in 1384 the government of the city passed to the thirty-two gilds. In Utrecht, like Liége not a town of one great industry, the same results were achieved. More commonly a division of power between patricians, small masters, and cloth employees (or at Dinant the smiths) was arrived at. Throughout these controversies the Emperor and his suzerainty played no part.

Another district which dropped into practical isolation **The Habs-** was the south-eastern duchies of the house of Habsburg. **burg Lands** Until the death of Duke Rudolf IV in 1365 the Habsburg magnates held together under their senior duke, and ended by ruling a solid block of territory, Austria, Styria, Carinthia,

Carniola, Istria, and Tyrol, from the Danube to the Adriatic
Rudolf shrewdly created a university for his dominions at
his capital of Vienna.   After his death, however, subdivision
could not be resisted and soon lamed the Habsburg power
His two brothers Albert III and Leopold II founded the
lines of Austria and of Styria respectively.

The forma-
tion of
Switzerland

But meanwhile the power of the Habsburgs in their
homeland of Swabia had shrunk before a new insurrectionary
league, the Swiss Confederation, which ended by cutting off
from Germany its southernmost province.   Up to 1218 the
mountainous districts between the Rhine, the Jura Moun
tains, and the Alps had been under the sway of the Dukes
of Zähringen, who were entitled Rectors of Burgundy.   When
that house became extinct, there was no longer an inter
mediary between the fiefs and districts and the Emperor
In the German-speaking, Swabian district to the east of the
River Aar, the greatest feudatories were the Counts of Habs
burg, whose domains stretched from the Rhine and Lake
Constance to Interlaken.   But in the Romance-speaking land
to the west the Burgundian Counts of Savoy established a
dominion.   A junior member of the house, Peter II, whose
appanage was Chablais to the south of the Lake of Geneva
succeeded in forming the barony of Vaud to the north of it
as far as Morat, by means of diplomacy, war, and the money
derived from the generosity of his nephew Henry III of
England.   Among minor powers were three imperial free
towns, Zurich, Bern, and Solothurn, whose prosperity was
mainly due to the transit trade from the Alpine passes.
There were, however, three small rural districts in the centre
round the Lake of Lucerne to which the new St. Gothard
route over the Alps gave importance.   These were the future
Forest Cantons of Uri, Schwyz, and Unterwalden.   As count
or as imperial or monastic " advocate," the Habsburgs had
here the chief rule over a population of free or serf peasants ;
but in Uri and Schwyz there existed also an association of
the inhabitants called the *Markgenossenschaft* for the management of the common pastures.   For the Hohenstaufen the
control of the St. Gothard route, opened by the construction
of the famous Devil's Bridge in the ravine of the River
Reuss, was of great value for the connexion of Germany and
Italy, and in 1231 Uri was given a charter as imperial domain ;

its Markgenossenschaft became a *Landsgemeinde.* When
Rudolf II of Habsburg turned against Frederick II Schwyz
received a similar privilege. But Rudolf III of Habsburg,
the King of the Romans, renewed the domination of his
house : Schwyz was subjected, the imperial advocacy of
Urseren south of Uri was given to his sons.

It was this reduction to the state of a Habsburg pro- The Swiss
vince which proved the origin of the Swiss Confederation. Confedera-
Scarcely was the irresistible Rudolf dead than the three tion
malcontent districts formed in August 1291 a sworn permanent alliance (*Eidgenossenschaft*) for mutual peace, mutual
defence, and the exclusion of alien officials. They joined
with Albert of Austria's jealous neighbours against him, and,
although he had the best of the fighting, Uri and Schwyz
obtained from his rival King Adolf of Nassau confirmation
of their direct dependence on the Empire. Albert's victory
in the civil war, however, and his accession to the German
throne in 1298 gave him the upper hand until his murder
ten years later. In this period of Austrian rule later legend
placed the baseless and familiar story of William Tell. With
Albert's death came the final revolt ; in 1309 King Henry VII
renewed the old grants to Uri and Schwyz and gave Unterwalden the same privileges. Still the independence of the
three cantons was insecure. When Henry VII died (1313),
they prepared to defend themselves and naturally held by
King Lewis the Bavarian against his rival and their enemy,
Frederick the Fair of Austria. The Habsburg dukes retaliated by a commercial blockade, and in 1315 Leopold I, the
most energetic of them, invaded the three cantons in force
from the north and the west. He himself from the north,
confident of victory, entered Schwyz by the defile of Morgarten. But here on November 15 his crowded, helpless Battle of
men-at-arms, unable to charge or turn, were routed with Morgarten
great slaughter by the nimble Swiss mountaineers rushing
on them from the higher ground. His none-too-devoted
footmen also took to flight. This victory of peasants and
footmen over mounted knights ranks with Courtrai as a
political and social event. It was a blow to feudal rule and
feudal warfare. It preserved the new Confederation, which
obtained a sort of recognition from the Habsburgs by a
series of truces from 1318 onwards.

The Swiss, as they were soon named from their best-known canton of Schwyz, were not long in obtaining adherents from other unwilling subjects of the Habsburgs or neighbours who dreaded them. Of these the chief were the wealthy free towns of Bern and Zurich, and the only less prosperous Habsburg subject, the town of Lucerne, which was the northern outlet of the route through the three Forest Cantons. Lucerne first concluded a perpetual alliance with them in 1332, and although compelled to return to the Austrian obedience, this alliance was not abandoned by it. Zurich underwent a social revolution in 1336, under the leadership of its burgomaster Rudolf Brun, which associated the craft-gilds in the government beside the patricians,[1] and, in hostility with the Habsburgs whose rights were imperilled, allied in turn with the Swiss in 1352. The allies seized on the contiguous districts of Glarus and Zug. Duke Albert II of Austria in a strenuous campaign was only able to recover the two last and his purely feudal rights by the peace which followed. Bern, meantime, was engaged in strife with her feudal neighbours. Over them she won the great battle of Laupen in 1339, and, while remaining friendly with the Habsburgs, strengthened her position by a perpetual alliance in 1353 with the Forest Cantons. The siege of Zurich by the Emperor Charles IV in person, in support of the Habsburgs, did result in a partial submission of the town in the peace of Ratisbon in 1355, but his quarrel with Duke Rudolf IV changed his policy. He favoured the Swiss who reconquered Zug, and in 1368 the Habsburgs acknowledged the loss by the " truce of Torberg."

By these wars and slow acquisitions the Swiss Confederation was being solidified round the kernel of the Forest Cantons by means of a network of alliances. The so-called
Priests' Charter (*Pfaffenbrief*) of 1370 gave some degree of internal unity by its common provisions. In 1375 a new danger for the whole country increased the Swiss prestige. The French noble, Enguerrand de Coucy, endeavoured to support his claims on part of the Habsburg inheritance by an invasion at the head of mercenaries of the Free Companies, the so-called Guglers. From their rapine the lands round the River Aar were delivered more by the efforts of

---

[1] Cf. above, Chap. IX, p. 179.

Bern and the peasants than by their ruler Duke Leopold III
of Austria. Leopold III, however, who held the Swabian
lands of the Habsburgs, was busy increasing his power, and
fell out both with the Swiss and with the Swabian league
of towns north of the Rhine. Peace was soon made with
the latter ; the duke then endeavoured to repel the Swiss.
But in 1386 at Sempach, north of Lucerne, his dismounted **Battle of**
knights proved no match for the mountaineers, and he him- **Sempach**
self was slain. This victory was followed in 1388 by that
of Näfels, where Albert III of Austria was repulsed from
Glarus. A truce of Zurich in 1389 confirmed the Swiss
conquests and was made a peace in 1394.

The Swiss Confederation now consisted of eight Cantons, **The New**
for Zug and Glarus were become full members, and an ally, **Cantons**
the town of Solothurn. The Covenant of Sempach (1393)
gave a military law for the whole. Otherwise, the confederates seemed diverse enough. The peasants of the forest
cantons, the craftsmen of Zurich, and the patricians of Bern
were under different institutions. But they formed a solid
block of land among the mountains ; they spoke the same
dialect ; they were bound together by interest and tradition.
Without a thought of separating from Germany or the
Empire, they had acquired in resistance to the Habsburgs
a character of their own and a joint autonomy which marked
them off from the straggling, shifting leagues to the north.
Yet it needed over a century of independence and expansion
before they were to feel themselves a separate people.

When Charles IV died in 1378, Germany had become a **Germany**
collection of States, which were still being increased in num- **in 1378**
ber by the practice of subdivision. A characteristic of these
territories was the scattered formation and ragged outline
of even the smaller of them owing to the varying chances
of inheritance, grant, or partition. There was much overlapping of feudal rights too, which was only gradually giving
way to the exclusive jurisdiction of one ruler. Four types
of government predominated, the ecclesiastical and the lay
principalities, the towns imperial or dependent on a prince,
and the Knights of the Empire sprung from the ancient
royal domain. Of these the ecclesiastics, the prince bishops **Ecclesiasti-**
and abbots, were numerous and powerful. In the west and **cal Princes**
centre of Germany their principalities clustered thickly.

They had become a preserve of the greater and lesser nobles who filled the cathedral chapters and dominated the abbeys. Although the Popes of Avignon succeeded among many bitter struggles in enforcing their right of provision as against canonical election, the profit they obtained was mainly financial, for their appointments were made from local nobles or imperial protégés ; in fact, influence on these appointments was still a valuable resource of the Emperor. The

Lay Princes lay princes were of very varying degrees of wealth and power. Even with the subdivision of their lands, the Electors of Brandenburg, the Dukes of Brunswick-Lüneburg, the Margraves of Meissen, the Counts of Holstein in the north, and the Dukes of Bavaria, the Elector Palatine, the Hohenzollern Burgraves of Nuremberg, and the Counts of Wurtemberg were important potentates ; lesser rulers, like those of Baden in the south, Hessen and Nassau in the centre, Juliers and Cleves on the Rhine, Mark, Mecklenburg, Pomerania, and Ascanian Saxony in the north, were far from

Free Towns negligible. Among the self-governing towns few ruled much land outside their walls. The imperial towns possessed a greater legal security for their independence : those held of a prince of the Empire might enjoy greater prosperity, but were always exposed, and were all later subjected, to the

Knights of authority of their overlord. The Knights of the Empire,
the Empire who existed chiefly in Franconia and Swabia, ruled their generally tiny lands like any prince, but they were one of the evils of the time just as were the poorer nobles within princely territory. The practical cessation of the Empire and its activities left this class without resources or employment. They eked out their living and gratified their fighting tastes by plundering merchants and peaceful neighbours. The robber baron or knight was a decadent and sordid successor of the chivalry of the Hohenstaufen age. The *Landfrieden* and the leagues of towns were mainly directed towards curbing their depredations. So too was much of the energy of the greater princes.

Princes and   The princes, however, and the self-governing towns,
Towns whether imperial or not, were at odds. The more active the prince the more eager was he to enforce his authority, when it legally existed, on so valuable a part of his territory as a flourishing town, or to acquire from the Emperor

rights over a free town contiguous to his lands. The towns
on their side feared for their autonomy, and were anxious to
extend their sway over the neighbouring country-side both
for a securer food-supply and for the acquisition of useful,
non-trading burghers in the shape of small proprietors outside their walls, the *Pfahlbürger*. After the time of Lewis
the Bavarian, when both parties co-operated in *Landfrieden*,
these causes of dissidence led to leagues of the free towns
alone for their common defence. Charles IV, himself an
aggressive prince, in the Golden Bull vainly forbade them
and more effectively the admission of *Pfahlbürger*. In 1376
two great town-leagues were formed, a Swabian of imperial
towns and an upper Rhenish from Mainz to Strasbourg.
These leagues, as we have seen, were not without success
against the princes; if defeated in the field, the burghers
were unconquerable within their walls; but the scattered
towns were far too isolated and therefore divergent in their
local interests to hold together permanently like the Swiss.
The same narrowness was visible in their relations with the
Empire. Their contributions were the richest source of
imperial finance, but, besides their justifiable fear of being
pledged to the princes as a security for loans or reward for
support, they were most unwilling to give supplies for imperial
schemes. Like the princes, they looked merely to their local
or mercantile interests, not in any way to Germany as a whole.

While the political life of the German kingdom was so
weak as to be nearly moribund, it was showing considerable Growth of
vigour in the several districts. Not to mention the Hansa Estates
League and the other towns, this was manifested in the
activity of the stronger princes and in the growth of a system
of Estates in their territories. Princes like the Ascanian
Margraves of Brandenburg, the Elector Palatine, and others,
bishops, dukes, and counts, were busy converting their
heterogeneous feudal rights into a genuine sovereign
authority over a defined stretch of territory, to become in
fact territorial monarchs (*Landesherren*). They were taming
their own vassals and setting up a government of nominated
officials. While themselves bound to the Emperor only as
his feudal vassals, they were making their own nobles their
subjects. But, as was the case with other contemporary
rulers, the expense of their government was exceeding their

ancient revenues, and for extraordinary taxation they needed the consent of their subjects, which they obtained by means of assemblies of Estates. The clergy, nobles, and town representatives met, as in France, in the first place to vote subsidies to the prince. From this function they advanced till no princely law could be issued or weighty matter resolved without their concurrence. Thus the fractions of Germany were developing not only a government but a constitutional life of their own.

Peasants As we have seen,[1] the class which often suffered in this tangled process of the dissolution of Germany and the rise of the small German States was the peasantry. Although there were exceptions, the peasant was more heavily taxed for the support of the prince and his officials, suffered under the reactionary feudal jurisdiction and exactions of impoverished nobles, and was a victim of the petty wars and disorder. Growing peasant discontent was an ominous symptom in Germany at the close of the fourteenth century.

SUGGESTIONS FOR READING ON CHAPTER XV

A. Sources

(i) Documentary

Constitutiones et Acta publica imperatorum et regum. Vols. v, vi, viii, *Monumenta Germaniae Historica.* Legum Sectio, IV. 1909 ff.

Winkelmann, E. : *Acta Imperii inedita saeculi XIII et XIV.* 2 vols. Innsbruck, 1880–5.

Krammer, M. : *Quellen zur Geschichte der deutschen Königswahl und des Kurfürstenkollegs.* Vol. ii. Leipzig, 1912.

(ii) Narrative

Johannes Victoriensis : as in suggestions for Chapter VII.

Matthias von Neuenburg ; as in suggestions for Chapter VII.

Limburger Chronik (in Old German) : Ed. Wyss, A. *Monumenta Germaniae Historica.* Deutsche Chroniken. Vol. iv. Hanover, 1883.

B. Modern Works

Cambridge Medieval History, vol. vii, relevant chapters.

Pirenne, H. : *Histoire de Belgique.* Vol. ii. Brussels, 1922.

Kaser, K. : *Das späte Mittelalter.* Gotha, 1921.

Fournier, P. : *Le royaume d'Arles et de Vienne.* Paris, 1892.

Oechsli, W. : *Schweizergeschichte.* 4th edn. Zurich, 1912.

Jarrett, Dom Bede : *The Emperor Charles IV.* London, 1935.

Hauck, A. : *Kirchengeschichte Deutschlands.* Vol. v.

Clarke, M. V. : *The Medieval City State.* London, 1926.

Lindner, T. : *Deutsche Geschichte*, as in suggestions for Chapter VII.

---

[1] See above, Chap. IX, pp. 192–93.

CHAPTER XVI

ITALY, 1290–1380

IN the last years of the thirteenth century the conditions The Two
of the two halves of Italy, the kingdom of Naples in the Halves of
south and the many city states of the north, provided a Italy.
violent contrast between the two in almost every way.
Naples had entered the road of decadence, economically and Naples
politically, though the mere size of the kingdom rendered it
still the most powerful Italian State.   In government it was
an autocratic, bureaucratic, but feudal monarchy under the
Angevin Charles II ; it was immune from the rapid, revolutionary changes of the north.   But though the monarchy
endeavoured to follow the paternal centralization of the
Emperor Frederick II, its spirit was changed and its success
was gone.   Feudal privilege and feudal jurisdiction were now
rampant.   The barons, whether French or Italian in origin,
were out of hand ; ecclesiastical privileges were overgrown ;
the royal officials were corrupt ; noble, prelate, and official
almost equally oppressed the peasants and townsmen beneath
them.   A fossilized feudalism, incapable of reform or progress, fettered every activity.   In economics decadence was
even clearer.   The country was becoming poverty-stricken.
Much of the land was never very fertile.   Frederick II had
already overtaxed it, and the ruinous wars and schemes of
the Angevins completed its exhaustion.   Agriculture and
trade withered under extortionate royal and baronial exactions and monopolies.   Manufacture and the growth of a
prosperous *bourgeoisie* were made practically impossible,
while the indebted kings were bound to favour the exploitation of their subjects by their Florentine and North Italian
creditors.   South Italy, in short, was entering on the period
of retrogression, poverty, and maladministration which was
not to end for centuries.

Far otherwise was the condition of the centre and north North Italy.
of Italy.   Here politically there was infinite division : the

The Papal States   city state, even if it was ruled as at Rome by a feudal nobility or merely clogged in its working by its subject nobles as so often in Lombardy, was supreme.   If the Papal States seemed to constitute a wide monarchy in the centre, stretching from sea to sea and from the Garigliano to the Po, the Pope's suzerainty over them was vacillating and intermittent.   No land was more splintered among really autonomous powers, the nobles and towns of the Patrimony of St. Peter round Rome itself, the hill-cities of Umbria and the March of

Tuscany and Lombardy   Ancona, and the communes of the plain of Romagna.   Tuscany was divided between four great cities, Florence, Siena, Pisa, and Lucca, some smaller towns, and the remnants of the feudal lords.   Lombardy was partitioned in like manner, while the republics of Venice and Genoa held its outlets to

Political Instability   the two seas.   Extreme political instability was the characteristic of all these territories, and the sources of it were manifold.   The country nobles, though fighting a losing battle, were recalcitrant subjects hard to tame, and their endless feuds, the very breath of their life, were the cause of ceaseless turmoil.   Large numbers of them were town-nobles and citizens as well, and in this capacity not only rent their city with their faction-fights and disorder but struggled for political predominance.   Against them was ranged, as we have seen,[1] the *popolo*, composed of merchants and tradesmen, who were determined to oust them from power and reduce them to order.   Nor was this the only dissidence of classes.   The petty shopkeeper, in Florence the Minor Arts, resented the lion's share of power engrossed by the wealthy trader, and below the gildsmen in the larger cities came a numerous throng of wage-earners, who had no part in the constitution.   In this unbalanced state of the internal forces of the communes, with faction and class warfare almost endemic and rooted in the civic habits, the rivalry of city with city, each passionately desirous of its own autonomy and scarcely less eager for dominion over its neighbours, was expressed in the great feud of Guelfs and Ghibellines, which crystallized the internal factions and gave a foreign policy and system of alliances.   Revolutions at home were abetted from abroad.   Swarms of exiles of the defeated party were scattered among rival cities or held out

[1] See above, Chap. IV, pp. 99–100, and Chap. XI, pp. 232–33.

in the countryside. The victors oppressed the vanquished who were allowed to remain.

In general, in the struggle of nobles and *popolo*, which was but one element, however important, in these civil broils, the *popolo* were the winning side. Yet the commune was showing signs of decay. Where true republican government by magistrates and councils survived, as in Tuscany, the misrule of dominant and insecure factions, and executives incapable of giving justice and order, was widespread. The vogue of tyranny, however, was growing in Lombardy ; in Milan, Verona, and Ferrara it had become permanent ; in other towns the commune had an intermittent life ; Padua and Bologna retained a more vigorous, if stormy, freedom. Tyranny, in fact, with all the disadvantages of arbitrary despotism, gave internal peace and justice to the ordinary citizen and fostered, as a rule, his economic interests.

Economically, indeed, the cities of central and northern Italy were reaching the height of their prosperity, whether free communes or despotisms. It is remarkable how gilds and gildsmen, in spite of wars and disturbance, carried on their business with unremitting activity. Fertilized by the Eastern carrying trade and the revenues of the Papacy, the greater cities developed their manufactures, such as the cloth of Florence, for export, and their banking, in which they were almost unique in the West. Florentine banking firms, like the Cerchi and the Spini, handled the papal revenues, financed the wars of popes and kings, and mingled as principals or agents in most money transactions of Western Europe. They were the first amassers of capital and inventors of credit, and they reaped the advantage. The Florentines, it was said, were a " fifth element," for they were found everywhere. In the wake of this activity and in a smaller sphere the lesser towns followed. " Early capitalism " displayed and let loose individual enterprise. *Economic Prosperity*

Yet the political ills of Italy were only too apparent in the year of Jubilee. The faithless egoism of tyrants and faction-chiefs, the wars for trade and aggrandizement, the persecution of defeated opponents, and the intense instability of all governments increased the general unrest of which they were the outcome. In 1302 even the " wise " Matteo Visconti of Milan fell before a coalition of rival neighbour *Milan and Florence* tyrants and Milanese malcontents in a Guelfic reaction, Guido della Torre of the rival Guelf house set up a severer despotism at Milan with a guard of 2,000 uniformed troops, and Matteo waited in exile " till the sins of the Torriani should be greater than his own." In Florence, in 1308, the last attempt of the " baron " Corso Donati to seize the government, supported by the unenfranchized poor, failed and he himself was killed in his flight. His death sealed the victory of the rich *bourgeoisie*, the bankers, merchants, and manufacturers of the Greater Arts, who henceforth controlled the complicated Florentine constitution. The day of the half-feudal fighting nobles had ended in Florence at least, and it is noticeable that their fall coincided with the permanent use of professional mercenaries. The Peace of Caltabellotta had left unemployed large numbers of Catalan soldiers who lived by war. A numerous band were shipped off eastward to Constantinople, and made history in the Balkans as the Great Catalan Company. Others by means of Robert, King of Naples, sold their swords in Italy. It was Diego de la Rat and his 300 troopers who saved Florence and its oligarchs from Corso Donati. The bourgeois gildsmen had never been so efficient as the nobles in war. Now, while the nobles were outclassed by professional soldiers, they more and more abandoned their inexpert militia service, which was alien to their habits and disastrous, or at least harmful, to their business, and relied on mercenaries.

Catalan Soldiers

Venice.
The War
of Ferrara

Troubles on a larger scale were produced by the ambition of Venice to control the mouths of the Po and with them the whole eastern outlets of Lombardy. The occasion was given in 1308 by the death of Azzo VIII of Este, the tyrant of Ferrara, then on the chief branch of the Po. Not venturing to leave Ferrara to his bastard son Fresco, Azzo hit on the expedient of bequeathing the town to the latter's legitimate son Folco under his father's guardianship ; but this arrangement was opposed by Azzo's younger brothers and by Pope Clement as well. Fresco on his side received the support of Venice. Clement was already haunted by that fear of losing the Papal States which so continuously stirred the Popes of Avignon ; Venice frankly desired to increase her great trading privileges to the extent of monopoly and dominion. Fresco, however, was weak at home and unable to prevent the army the Pope collected from his jealous neighbours from entering Ferrara; he ceded the town-fortress Castel Tedaldo and his rights to Venice in October 1308. Clement was willing to grant the city for a tribute, but Venice demanded absolute dominion and drove out the papal forces. Clement, now roused, saw his strength in this particular quarrel. His legate, Cardinal de Pélagrue, easily raised a large crusading army, for no Lombard town wished to see Venice in Ferrara, and the Papacy could strike at the Venetians throughout Christendom: their goods were declared confiscate, themselves were to be enslaved. It was a bull fiercer than any of Boniface VIII. In August 1309 the Venetians suffered a terrible naval defeat on the Po by Francolino and were driven from Ferrara. Yet in spite of their losses they did not submit to the Pope till 1311, and it was only in 1313 that peace was finally signed with a partial loss of their ancient privileges.

Discontent at this foolish war and aspirations after a faction tyranny of the Lombard sort seem to have been the main causes of a conspiracy which shaped all the later history of Venice. Three nobles, Bajamonte Tiepolo, called "the great knight" by the people, a Querini, and a Badoer, plotted to overthrow Doge Gradenigo and his oligarchic clique in the name of popular liberty. All three had estates on the mainland and were thus affected by Lombard traditions. Their popular following was small. On June 15, 1310, they attempted to take armed control of Venice. But Gradenigo was ready for them and they made a poor show in the fighting. Banishment was the chief punishment inflicted, which enabled Bajamonte to be a minor danger for many years. To safeguard the State from revolution, a special committee of safety was set up, the famous Council of Ten, which, at first temporary, was prolonged until it was made permanent in 1335. With the Doge and his councillors, its numbers were really seventeen. Its function was to preserve the State and its morale. Its secrecy and the unlimited power which it was given made it on occasion master of the republic. Secret and vital matters were its province, and its secrecy and occasional severity surrounded it with dread, which together with much later corruptions have created a legend of its iniquity. But its procedure was

Tiepolo's Conspiracy

The Council of Ten

usually equitable, it kept the members of the wide patrician
oligarchy disciplined to the law, and as its members were
elected in the Great Council and changed every year, it was
representative of the ruling class.   Acting by the side of the
ordinary officials and the large debating council of the Senate,
it kept Venice for long the best administered State in Europe.

The helpless weariness of strife and revolution, meanwhile, were producing an unreasoning hope in some miracu-
lous saviour, of which we have the echo in Dante's famous
" veltro (greyhound)." [1]   Fra Ubertino da Casale, the Spiritual Franciscan, following the Joachite tradition, wrote of
the new age of the Church that was to come with the fall
of the corrupt and worldly hierarchy.   The very fact of the
Papacy's humiliation under Boniface VIII and its exile in
France seemed to herald the end of an era.   Strangely
enough, an answer seemed to come to these hopes and
despairs.   In 1308 there was elected King of the Romans
Henry VII of Luxemburg, a man almost obsessed with the
shadowy ideal of the Holy Roman Empire and its mission
in Italy.   To Henry his office appeared as the career of a
knightly emperor in a romance of chivalry.   He was the
supreme arbiter, the bringer of justice and peace, the protector of the weak and oppressed.   In his rightful domain of
Italy, which was suffering from the abeyance of the Empire,
it was his God-given task to cure her anarchy and confusion
by the restoration of the Empire.   Himself neither Guelf
nor Ghibelline, he would reconcile the pernicious factions
which had lost the reason for their existence, remove oppression, and replace incessant wars by a just sway which, like
St. Louis', would respect others' rights and enforce its own.
He came at the call of many exiles who demanded justice
and relief.   Dante, most probably during his expedition,
expressed in his *Monarchia* the legend of the Empire's origin
and Henry's own idealistic conception of the Emperor's
functions.   The rivalry of Papacy and Empire seemed dead,
for the Pope himself was the patron of his enterprise.
Clement V, indeed, genuinely afraid to go to his see of Rome
in the prevailing anarchy, was very willing that a pious

The Emperor Henry VII

---

[1] *Inferno I*.   " Veltro " is possibly an anagram of " ultore," the avenger
of Henry VII and the wrongs of the defeated.   " Exoriebit aliquis nostris
ex ossibus ultor."

Emperor, who no longer had any real footing in the peninsula, should allay the storm for him and clear off some of the evil legacy of the past. Guelf Florence had flouted his legate Napoleon Orsini in Tuscany in pursuit of her ambitions and feuds, and, tepid though he was, he issued cordial bulls of approval.

The realities of the Italian situation were unknown to the romantic Henry, and were not fully unveiled to Clement. The exiles thought seldom of the ideal of the Empire or of reconciliation ; they looked to the Emperor to tip the balance in their favour and to enable them to gain the upper hand over their adversaries. Ghibelline rulers, like the Della Scala, hoped to legitimize their dubious authority by imperial diplomas and thus to consolidate it. The Guelfs, whether tyrants or free communes, saw with anxiety the unavoidable approach of a German army, to which their own divisions and precarious hold on power and its unwelcome support by the Pope made it difficult to offer resistance, and which, by Henry's programme, meant the dangerous rehabilitation of their enemies. Robert of Naples, who was even in less case to resist the papal mandate, feared for his kingdom of Naples and his influence farther north. Though he played with the hope of making profit out of the expedition by the projected marriage of his son, the Duke of Calabria, with Henry's daughter and the cession of the kingdom of Arles as her dowry, his real interests were shown by his alliance with the Tuscan League, and his garrisoning Romagna, of which the Pope made him Vicar in 1310 after the expulsion of the Venetians from Ferrara. This last appointment might have warned Henry of Clement's doubts, but it was only the Florentines who openly urged him not to enter Italy. When he came, it was the Florentines who strained every nerve to organize resistance.

Henry VII entered Italy in October 1310 by the Mont Cenis Pass, accompanied by some 5,000 men mostly hailing from the lands along the Rhine. His war-chest consisted of a wagon full of specie, on which sat trusty knights for its security. This was in keeping with the romantic, old-fashioned character of his enterprise, and stands in glaring, instructive contrast with the advanced credit-system of his Florentine foes, who could dispose of far greater sums. At

Feeling in Italy

Arrival of Henry VII in Italy

first his progress was triumphant. His kinsman, Amadeus V Count of Savoy, and the Lombard Ghibellines joined his standard ; the Guelfs could do no less amid the prevailing enthusiasm for the peace-bringing Augustus. City after city sent in its submission, and on December 23 he appeared before Milan at the head of 12,000 men, largely Ghibelline exiles, such as Matteo Visconti. Guido della Torre had thought of opposition, but his fellow tyrants would not back him up and he ended by sullenly submitting. Henry could on January 6, 1311, receive the Iron Crown of the kingdom of Italy, or rather an imitation of it, for the real crown, handed down from the days before Charlemagne, had been pawned by Guido and was not to be found. He now developed his idealistic policy. All exiles, of whatever party, were to be restored to their rights and property. Milan itself made him its *signore*, and imperial vicars were dispatched to rule the Lombard communes. For a moment he appeared to be accomplishing his mission among universal rejoicing. But realities almost immediately broke through the surface of an imaginary triumph. His Germans and the subsidies he demanded were intensely disliked. On January 12 Visconti tricked the deposed Guido into a joint revolt and then held aloof while the Torriani were defeated and driven from Milan. King Henry despite himself found that he was a Ghibelline. At the news of the Milanese fighting, the Guelf communes, headed by Cremona and Brescia, burst into revolt, and Henry, seeing in them faithless peace-breakers, committed fatal errors. When Cremona, overawed by his speedy approach, humbly again submitted, the harshness of the punishment he inflicted and the razing of her walls stirred Brescia to desperate resistance. It needed a four months' siege from May to September to starve the city to surrender. Thus the glamour of Henry's coming largely disappeared, while Florence and her league hardened in their enmity and King Robert slowly abandoned his attitude of passivity. When Henry reached Genoa, although he was loyally received there and was given the government, he heard that Robert had sent troopers under his brother John, Count of Gravina, to Rome to aid the Guelf Orsini.

Henry's reply was to accept the overtures of Frederick II of Sicily, Robert's mortal enemy. He became, indeed, more

formidable as chief of the Ghibellines. Greeted with enthusiasm by the Pisans in March 1312, he marched along the
Tuscan coast to Rome which he reached in May. Here the
situation had changed to his disadvantage. In 1310, with
the Pope's patronage, his envoy, Louis of Savoy, the Baron
of Vaud, had been appointed Senator to rule the city; but
since the Count of Gravina's entry in December 1311 the
Vatican and the central district were held against him by
the Guelfs. Henry occupied the Ghibelline and Colonna
quarters, but days of street fighting failed to force a way to
St. Peter's across the Tiber. In the end, he received the
imperial coronation on June 29 in the Lateran basilica at Henry VII's
the hands of reluctant cardinals, who protested that the Coronation at Rome
Pope's commission only authorized them to crown him in
the traditional St. Peter's. But he was isolated in Rome,
and was soon forced at the alarmed Pope's command to
make an armistice with Robert. Then he marched north to
undertake a vain siege of Florence. The city gates were not
even closed, for the Emperor's army was far too small to
capture a less powerful town. Henry was now anxious for
a decisive war on King Robert and the Guelfs. He adopted
the extreme Ghibelline view of the subjection of Naples to
the Empire, declared Robert dethroned as a rebel, and
seconded zealously by the Pisans and the Ghibellines, prepared at Pisa a campaign to conquer Naples in 1313. Clement
V, become naturally ardent on the other side, threatened
excommunication, and a new struggle of Papacy and Empire
was imminent. The immediate odds were not against Henry,
since Robert was devoid of courage, Frederick of Sicily was
an imperial ally, and reinforcements were expected under
his son John of Bohemia. But at the very beginning of his
second progress south on August 24, 1313, Henry fell a
victim to fever at Buonconvento near Siena. His death, so Death of
opportune as to be set down to poison, dissolved his army Henry VII
and the Ghibelline league. Cause and leader vanished
together, when he was interred at Pisa. It was strange that
the ideal of the Empire should have appeared most clearly
in this belated and anachronous enterprise, which was the
death-struggle of a dying order of things against the growing
new. The war signalizes the victory of bourgeois capitalistic
Florence over chivalry in the service of an obsolete theory.

Robert of
Naples

At the death of Henry VII King Robert seemed to be on the way to an Italian kingdom. He was chief of the Guelf faction. Pope Clement, claiming to rule in the vacancy of the Empire, gave him the title of Imperial Vicar of Italy. In Lombardy, he enlarged the County of Piedmont, which had been reconstituted by Charles II in 1305, by the acquisition (1312) of Asti, hitherto a free commune, and of Alessandria (1310); Pavia, Parma, and Reggio recognized him as their *signore*. He was papal Rector of Romagna, and Vicar of Ferrara, keeping out the house of Este, whose chief, Francesco, was murdered in 1312. In Tuscany, he was Signore of Florence, Siena, and Lucca since 1313 and head of the Tuscan Guelfic League. The Pope appointed him Senator of Rome. But Robert " the Wise " was not equal to his task. Though cunning and diligent, he was a mean man with too much on his hands, and he was obsessed with

War with
Sicily

the reconquest of Sicily. His forces and his anticipated revenues—for he lived on credit—were always being spilt on this always fruitless enterprise, when they were urgently needed in the north. A first unsuccessful invasion of 1314 ended in a truce. A second in 1316 was completely futile, followed by another truce. Frederick II on his side threw over the peace of Caltabellotta by associating his son Peter II in 1321 with himself. A great Neapolitan expedition in 1325 could not take Palermo; another in 1335 failed miserably, as did a fifth against Peter II in 1338; the capture of Milazzo in 1342 had no sequel. All that had been done was to cripple Robert's policy elsewhere, and to incur the damage of counter-attacks.

Uguccione
della
Faggiuola

A slow decline of Robert's power soon became visible in Central Italy. The Pisans in their straits made Uguccione della Faggiuola, a stout soldier, their Captain-General, and with a force of 1,000 of Henry VII's Netherland troopers, left behind in Italy, he was formidable. In 1314 he seized on the great Guelf city of Lucca. In reply to his attacks, backed by the Ghibellines of Lombardy, even Robert was forced to send troops in aid to Florence under his brother Philip, Prince of Taranto, the titular Latin Emperor of Constantinople; but the whole array of the Guelfs was on August 29, 1315, disastrously routed by Uguccione at Montecatini. The defeat would have been more fatal had not

Uguccione angered by his greed both of the Pisans and his chief Lucchese supporter, Castruccio Castracani. In April 1316, as he rode out to keep Lucca down, the Pisans rose and closed the gates behind him. Castruccio, who made Castruccio himself tyrant of Lucca, let him go, to die a few years later Castracani in the service of the Della Scala. It was Castruccio's attacks, and the persistent internal dissensions between Greater and Lesser Arts and the always feared magnates, who retained influence while excluded from office, which maintained Robert, though disliked, as Signore of Florence until 1322, and produced both the fettering of the mistrusted Priors by a new council of *Buonuomini* and the remarkable innovation in 1324 of determining the succession of all magistrates for some five years by lot. The measure showed both the incurable jealousy and mistrust of the Florentines and their not unjustified confidence in their own average ability. But a victory of Castruccio at Altopascio in September 1325 brought back the nearly useless Angevin suzerainty. Charles, Duke of Calabria, the heir to Naples, proved extortionate to a degree, and his death in 1328 was the occasion of a reform in the constitution. The lot was retained for the appoint- The Lot at ment of magistrates : the list of office-holders was elected Florence for some five years ahead, their names were written on wax balls and put into a bag (*imborsati*), and thence drawn as required. The city councils were simplified. There were to be two : the Council of the Popolo (300 members) of *popolani* only, and the Council of the Commune (250 members) of both *popolani* and magnates. Laws had to pass both councils. Short terms of office gave large numbers of the citizens some share in the government. This was a semi-democratic element, but the chief power in Florence remained to the wealthy merchant class.

Robert's dominion in Romagna withered speedily. His Robert loses officials gained an evil name, the licence and cruelty of his Romagna Catalan soldiery were intolerable, and the towns which he ruled slipped from him to native tyrants. In 1317 the out- raged Ferrarese rose in favour of Rinaldo d'Este and his brothers. Threats did not bend them, and two years after Robert's vicariate came to an end. But in Genoa, far more Gains Genoa important for him, the king scored almost the only success of his reign. Here after the death of Henry VII the rival

Ghibelline houses of Doria and Spinola continued their wonted broils with the result that the Guelf Fieschi and Grimaldi obtained the upper hand in 1317 and the Ghibellines left the city to bring on it a siege by the united forces of their party in Lombardy, led by Marco Visconti. King Robert could not allow the great sea-power, which dominated the Tyrrhenian Sea and his communications with his northern lands, to fall under the control of the Lombard tyrants. In 1318 he came to the rescue with a fleet and army. He was acclaimed Signore along with Pope John XXII, and in February next year his troops defeated the Visconti at Sestri Ponente. The war went on, but Robert's new acquisition remained his for many years.

The Visconti and Della Scala

Of greater moment for Italy was the rise of two wider Ghibelline States in Lombardy. Matteo Visconti of Milan and Cangrande della Scala of Verona were both fortified by the title, given by Henry VII, of Imperial Vicar of their cities. Matteo was a crafty statesman, who by good government won the loyalty of the Milanese and persistently extended his dominion. Piacenza was governed by his less able son Galeazzo ; in 1315, after a victory over the Angevin seneschal of Piedmont on the River Scrivia, he won over Pavia, and Alessandria fell to him, followed by Vercelli. The regional State, replacing the isolated city, was well on its way. Cangrande, the friend and host of the poet Dante, was a genial warrior in alliance with Matteo. His immediate foe was the free commune of Padua. In 1311 he began the war by the conquest of her subject, Vicenza, and closed it by a crushing victory outside Padua itself in 1318, which had the further result of the disappearance of Paduan liberty, for the defeated city gave itself a tyrant in the Guelf Giacomo da Carrara, who founded an intermittent dynasty.

Policy of Pope John XXII

These Ghibelline successes had been favoured by the long vacancy of the Papacy on the death of Clement V in 1314. When in 1316 the strong-willed John XXII was elected to the papal chair, the many years of the persevering and fatal wars of the Popes of Avignon to recover and increase papal supremacy in Italy began. More than anything else, this papal policy impeded the natural growth of larger States, and brought continuous war, foreign mercenaries, and foreign intervention. One ruling motive was the fear of imperial, that is, German, intervention in Italy. The memory of Henry VII and the revolutions he had caused and planned was still fresh. To conjure this danger, Pope John did not adopt the radical and impracticable proposition of Robert, that he should abolish the Empire, but pursued the course of Clement V : he reiterated that the Empire was a papal fief, that no one could be King of the Romans without his sanction, and that the rule of the Empire during a vacancy belonged to him. Thus he deferred to recognize either claimant of the imperial throne, Lewis the Bavarian and Frederick the Habsburg, and declared the imperial vicariates of Henry VII to be now invalid. He resented fiercely any attempt of either rival to interfere in Italy. Another motive was hostility to the ambitious Ghibelline tyrants of Milan, Verona, and Lucca. They could not fail to use German alliances and troopers on occasion ; they were the unremitting and dangerous foes of the Pope's Guelfic supporters like King Robert and the soi-disant papalists of Lombardy ; their expansion showed no signs of respecting papal rights. To combat them John XXII may have toyed with the idea of creating a native king of Lombardy—he made King Robert Imperial Vicar—but his permanent policy was to break up the new States by a league of threatened rulers under the guidance of the Papacy.

John XXII began by ordering the Ghibelline tyrants to abandon their imperial vicariates. When Matteo Visconti alone obeyed, but had himself elected Signore of Milan instead, while continuing his warfare with the Guelfs in Genoa and elsewhere, the Pope accused him of heresy and excommunicated him. The threatened Ghibellines held a congress at Soncino in 1318 and elected Cangrande their captain-general. Next year, in December, Luchino Visconti, one of Matteo's sons, defeated and killed King Robert's seneschal of Piedmont, Ugo del Balzo, at Monte Castello. This defeat, although Robert in the same year was made Signore of Guelf Brescia, determined the Pope on new measures. He sent in 1320 a legate, his nephew Cardinal Bertrand du Pouget, into Lombardy to organize a crusade against the Ghibellines, and engaged French troops under Philip of Valois, the future King of France, for the campaign. Philip, however, proved a broken reed. He was outnumbered near Ver-

His War with the Lombard Ghibellines

celli, treated with the Visconti, and hurried back to France,
while Vercelli and even Cremona surrendered to the Visconti.
Cardinal du Pouget was more trustworthy. In spite of the
rapid failure of a despairing project to obtain help from
Frederick of Austria, he condemned Matteo for heresy and
preached the crusade. In 1322, Matteo, whose hold on Milan
was weakened, abdicated in favour of his son Galeazzo, and
shortly afterwards died. The Visconti dominion crumbled.
In 1323 du Pouget besieged Milan itself. But now a new
factor emerged. Lewis IV, victor of Mühldorf,[1] sent envoys
to rally the Ghibellines; even Castruccio hastened to aid
from Tuscany while the German troopers in the Pope's service deserted to the other side. The siege was raised, and
the victory of Vaprio (February 1324) led to a Visconti
recovery. But the indomitable cardinal succeeded in forming a solid Guelf block south of the Po, Parma, Modena,
Reggio, and Bologna, where he made his residence.

Lewis IV
in Italy

Lewis IV's intervention began the new strife of Papacy
and Empire which lasted all his reign. He himself came to
Italy in 1327, partly to assert himself as Emperor, partly to
injure the Pope, partly perhaps because the trade with Lombardy had natural attractions for a Bavarian. He took the
Iron Crown at Milan, and then showed the curious inconstancy which marred his whole career. He suddenly seized
his host, Galeazzo Visconti, who was in enmity with and
accused of treachery by members of his own house. The
Visconti State was broken up, large sums were exacted, and
Lewis pursued his long march to Rome, creating Castruccio
his Vicar of Tuscany as well as Duke of Lucca, a novel
dignity for a tyrant, on the way. Pisa, temporarily Guelf,
was captured and given to the new duke, while a popular
revolution in Rome, angered at the Pope's absenteeism,
drove out King Robert's vicar. The expedition, however,
petered out miserably. Lewis, indeed, carried through his
unprecedented coronation and set up his anti-Pope, but he
was soon forced to retreat before Robert and the Roman
Guelfs. His return-march was inglorious. For a heavy
payment he had just re-installed Azzo Visconti, son of
Galeazzo, who had died, in Milan, and Azzo, not unnaturally,
at once turned against him. So did the Este tyrants of

[1] See above, Chap. XV, p. 300.

Ferrara, hitherto compulsory Ghibellines. Both houses carried through a reconciliation with the Pope. Yet Lewis assisted Ghibelline revolutions in the cities south of the Po before, subsidized by Visconti to get rid of him, he left Italy in December 1329. His most valuable adherent, Castruccio of Lucca, had already died in 1328. The glamour of the Empire, left by Henry VII, had faded in this inconsequent expedition.

Azzo Visconti had yet to reconstruct the Milanese State, but Mastino II della Scala was left by Lewis the most powerful tyrant in the north. To Verona and Vicenza, Cangrande had added in 1329 Treviso and Padua. With his help, a new tyrant, who founded a dynasty, Luigi Gonzaga, had replaced the Bonaccolsi in Mantua. In 1330 Mastino della Scala was besieging Brescia to bring the commune under his sway. Robert of Naples, the Signore, could do nothing. So the desperate Brescians brought a new invader into Italy by electing the romantic knight, King John of Bohemia, as King John their lord. King John had the personal prestige and per- of Bohemia sonal charm inherited from his father, the Emperor Henry VII, and his arrival with troops to the rescue produced a sudden enthusiasm for him. City after city—Bergamo, Cremona, Pavia, Vercelli, Parma, Reggio, Modena, and even Lucca—all declared for him in the confused faction strife left behind by Lewis IV. Cardinal du Pouget came to terms with him with a view of forming a North Italian kingdom, and the Pope agreed. But this was to alarm all the native powers. Guelf and Ghibelline, Visconti, Della Scala, D'Este, King Robert, Florence, and many others, in 1332 formed the league of Ferrara to expel the intruder. The forces of King John and the legate were routed twice in 1333 at Ferrara and Argenta. King John, disillusioned and fickle, left Italy, while the unfortunate Cardinal du Pouget, caught in 1334 by a revolt of Bologna, which he had made his headquarters and which was weary of ecclesiastical rule and its South French myrmidons, was thankful to escape to Avignon. The long efforts of John XXII had come to nothing.

The first thirty years of the fourteenth century had seen Tyranny in the extinction of most free communes of the north, due to Lombardy their own inability to suppress faction and secure a just and stable government, but the generation of tyrants of that

period, if they evidently served a public need, were among
the worst of their kind.   The greater men, the Visconti,
Della Scala, and D'Este, were the best.   Faithless treachery,
cruelty, furious revenge and murder, and capricious crime
characterized the common breed.   They were not even loyal
to their faction or their family.   A complete demoralization
set in among them in which personal ambition or appetite
ruled supreme, produced by the breakdown of institutions
and the long habit of remorseless faction feuds.   Seizing
power by violence, backed by insatiable, hireling mercenaries, such tyrants as the Vistarini of Lodi or the Bonaccolsi
of Mantua could never acquire the hold of a legitimate
dynasty or legal authority, and this stain of illegality rested
even on the greater houses, which really rescued the country
from anarchy and misgovernment.   The intervention of Pope
and Emperor, the feeble but continuous scheming of Robert
of Naples, intensified and prolonged the confusion, but did
not create it.   There was a general scramble for power, a
rivalry of districts, cities, systems of government, classes,
factions, and men, which was complicated by religious abuses,
by economic change, and by foreign mercenaries.

Decline of
Robert's
Power

The departure of John of Bohemia and the legate left
North Italy to its local tyrants.   Scarcely a free commune
now remained.   But the idea of a kingdom under an Italian
king was in the air.   Robert of Naples was no longer a candidate.   Fatally impoverished in his exhausted and turbulent
kingdom, still vainly wasting his scanty resources in the
Sicilian war, the most inefficient of allies, he lost ground
after the death of his only son and heir, the Duke of Calabria.
In 1335 Genoa threw off his already enfeebled dominion, and
was ruled by the Ghibelline nobles.   For the moment it

Mastino II
della Scala

seemed as if Mastino II della Scala, although far inferior in
statesmanship to his uncle Cangrande, would succeed in
patching together a real North Italian State.   Besides his
principal cities round Verona, he acquired in 1335, mainly
by purchase, Parma, Reggio, and Lucca.   But he had too
many local vice-tyrants, his ambitions were dreaded by
rival powers, the Florentines desired the outlet of Lucca, and
he unwisely entered on a trade-war with Venice.   He levied
greatly higher duties on Venetian merchandise passing north
and west through his lands and on the cattle and corn sent

from those lands to Venice. To crown all, he blocked the Po by a fortress. Venice was led back once more to mainland conquest, which she had abandoned after the disastrous Ferrarese war. She could not lose both her trade-routes westward and the food-supply essential for her sterile islands. In June 1336 an alliance against Mastino was formed by his neighbours, Venice, Florence, Azzo Visconti, the D'Este who had just reconquered Modena, and the Gonzaga of Mantua. Next year Mastino was attacked on all sides. Azzo Visconti besieged Brescia, the Venetians Padua, Charles of Luxemburg, King John's son, was tempted to seize Belluno. The decisive blow was the defection of Marsilio da Carrara, once tyrant and now assistant tyrant of Padua. He betrayed the trust of the Della Scala while he was their envoy at Venice. By agreement on August 3, 1337, he opened the gates of Padua to the enemy, who captured therein Alberto della Scala, Mastino's brother. Brescia fell to Azzo of Milan in October. Mastino resigned himself to these losses. By a peace of 1339 Marsilio da Carrara was restored to the tyranny of Padua as a Venetian client, and Treviso was ceded outright to Venice herself, which thus obtained a sure source for her food supply, an independent outlet to the north, and the freedom from transit dues on the lower Po. Two years later Mastino's garrison was expelled treacherously from Parma by Azzo da Correggio, while he sold Lucca to Florence. In this way the Della Scala fell out of the competition for the conquest of North Italy, although they remained the local tyrants of Verona and Vicenza.

The Visconti dynasty, on the other hand, starting with a greater city and more central position, produced also a remarkable series of able rulers, who in succession or in rivalry made steady progress. Azzo Visconti gave Milan internal quiet ; he encouraged her industries and rebuilt the circle of the walls ; unresisted within, he was busy in war and annexations. We have seen his conquest of Brescia, second only to Milan as a manufacturing city. Bergamo he obtained in 1332, Vercelli in 1334, Cremona, Como, and Lodi —the last from the brutal miller's son, Tremacoldo—in 1335, Piacenza in 1336. Pavia, ruled with his support by the local house of Beccaria, admitted his garrison in 1332 ; Novara was ruled by his uncle Giovanni, its bishop. Although this

Azzo and Luchino Visconti

territory was still far from compact, it was all contiguous.
Azzo was succeeded by his uncle, the warlike Luchino (1339–
49), who annexed Parma finally after an interlude of the rule
of the D'Este (1346).   But he also advanced westward :
Asti, already revolted from King Robert to the Marquess of
Montferrat, admitted him in 1840 ; on King Robert's death
and the misfortunes of the Hungarian attack on Naples, the
neighbours of the County of Piedmont gathered to the spoil,
the Visconti, the Marquess of Montferrat, and the Prince of
Achaia, the cadet of the house of Savoy who held the appanage of Savoyard Piedmont.   Luchino gained the profit :
practically all the Angevin possessions in West Lombardy,
including Alessandria, were his by 1347.

Tyrants in   Unlike Lombardy, Romagna was still the land of petty
Romagna   tyrants.   The warlike house of Malatesta held Rimini and
its neighbourhood, the Polenta Ravenna, where they had
been the last hosts of Dante, the Ordelaffi Forlì, the Man-
fredi Faenza.   The turbulent province, which produced the
best fighting men in Italy, was seldom at peace within and
without its cities.   More novel and symbolic of the times
was the surrender of the great commune of Bologna to
tyranny.   Long weakened by class and faction disorders,
Bologna never recovered from the rule of Cardinal du Pouget.
On his departure a year's anarchy ended in Taddeo Pepoli
establishing a tyranny, which was legalized by the title of
Papal Vicar (1337).

The Doge-   Even in Genoa the same causes were causing a trend
ship at   towards monarchy at least.   The ruling Ghibellines waged
Genoa   unsuccessful war with Aragon in help of the attempts of the
Sardinians to throw off the yoke of their Spanish master.
Meanwhile they were narrow and oppressive at home.   The
popular magistrate, the Abate of the Popolo, was nominated
now by them instead of being elected by the members of the
gilds ; the seamen on the ships were ill-treated without
redress by their noble captains.   At last in 1339 an insurrection broke out which created a doge as the single chief
of the State in the person of Simone Boccanegra, a descendant of the Boccanegra who had headed the *popolo* a century
earlier.   After five years (1344) Boccanegra wearied of the
strife with the still powerful nobles and abdicated, but the
dogeship was retained.

The same contrast between a clogged and miserable Florence instability in politics and a persistent efficiency in private business was shown in Florence in the years following the death of the Duke of Calabria. The new constitution had done little to cure the evils of the body politic. The magnates were still turbulent, powerful, and unfairly excluded ; the Minor Arts were denied influence ; the proletariat of the *popolo minuto* were still oppressed economically and without any share in the State save in its burdens ; more than all, the *popolani grassi* of the Greater Arts, which ruled the city, were divided by bitter family and business rivalries and were more than suspected of corrupt use of power to the commune's detriment. The government showed at its worst in a war with Pisa. Florence had long aimed at a wide territory in Tuscany and access to the sea. Pistoia, Volterra, and Arezzo (1337) were already hers. In 1341 Mastino della Scala sold her his outlying possession of Lucca, now useless to him. The Florentines occupied the town, but this roused the Pisans, then under the house of Gherardesca, to desperate efforts. They besieged Lucca, and, since the Florentine army was ill led and supplied, took it in August 1342. Discontent at Florence now came to a head. A wave of feeling rose for a single, efficient, uncorrupt chief. One of the captains employed in the army, Walter of Brienne, titular Duke of Athens, was familiar to the people for many The Duke of Athens years. He had never been particularly successful, either in his attempt to regain his Greek duchy or in his service at Naples and elsewhere, but he was a skilful intriguer of popular manners who created the impression that he was the man of the moment. In May 1342 he was appointed protector of the republic and his powers were rapidly extended over the whole government. He had the magnates and the *popolo minuto* behind him ; he made an inglorious peace, but still a peace, with Pisa. On September 8, 1342, he was made Signore for life by a tumultuous *parlamento*.[1] But the difficulty was to satisfy his own ambitions and those of his supporters at the same time. The magnates found themselves out of power, the *popolo minuto* were neglected as before, while the duke governed with greed and cruelty by

[1] The soi-disant general assembly which was at the base of the Florentine constitution.

means of abandoned instruments. Within the year all classes were temporarily united against his tyranny. Plots were formed which on July 26, 1343, led to furious insurrection. Besieged in the Palazzo della Signoria, the duke abdicated on August 1. He left the city enfeebled and the subject towns in revolt. Partly his incompetence, partly the number and power of the Florentine bourgeois had saved the city.

The crushing of the Magnates

At first, after the Duke of Athens' disappearance, a well-meaning attempt was made to abolish the Ordinances of Justice and to admit the magnates into the offices of the republic, but it did not last. The magnates displayed once more their inveterate, insolent disorder, while the *popolani grassi* desired to monopolize the government in the interests of their class. It is true that the dividing line between them was artificial and inconsistent, for the greatest magnates, like the Bardi, were bankers, and family rivalries had much to do with the legal definition. Yet on the whole it corresponded with the distinction between semi-feudal habits and those of bourgeois merchants. Both sides endeavoured to gain over the Lesser Arts of small shopkeepers and the mob of the *popolo minuto*, and in the competition the *popolani grassi* won. The end came tumultuously. Anticipating, it was said, an insurrection of the magnates, two leading houses of the *popolo grasso*, the Medici and the Rondinelli, led the shopkeepers and mob, on September 24, against their noble enemies. The organized riot spread ; it is noticeable that all the magnates in the main city surrendered promptly, and only those south of the Arno who could defend the bridges fought. Even there, when a bridge was forced, the Frescobaldi and Rossi were received into surrender. Only the Bardi held out and their palaces were burnt and sacked. There was little loss of life, but much of property. Once the work was done, marauding was quelled. The *popolo grasso*

Class Conflicts

then met their obligations by recasting the constitution. A considerable number of bourgeois or needy magnates were made *popolani* ; the Ordinances of Justice were restored with some alleviation ; the Priors were fixed at eight, of whom three were to be from the five " middle " Arts, three from the nine Lesser Arts, and only two from the six Greater Arts. The Gonfalonier was to come from each group in rotation. Thus for a while the " small master " class swayed the com-

mune to the disgust of the bankers and merchants, who felt
themselves injured in purse and power. Anti-clerical laws,
diminishing the province of the ecclesiastical courts and
papal intervention, did not, however justified, help their
business at Avignon ; the great house of Bardi failed in 1346,
owing to the too vast and speculative character of their loans
and " frozen credits," as the Peruzzi had done before them,
dragging with them to bankruptcy lesser firms. A reaction
was begun by playing on popular prejudice. First, the
weight of the Lesser Arts was lessened by forbidding any
one but a true-born Florentine to hold any office, for many
prosperous shopkeepers were recent immigrants from little
towns. Then, adherence to the Ghibellines, or suspicion of
favouring them, was on information punished by the same
incapacity. This enabled the Parte Guelfa, still the stronghold of the capitalists, to blot out from political life actual
or potential adversaries. Under a new disguise, rent by new
feuds, the Florentine oligarchy was reasserting its dominion.

It was in this time that the Black Death came to Florence **The Black**
as elsewhere in Italy. It reached Messina from Kaffa by **Death**
Genoese ships in January 1348 and spread over Sicily.
Thence it attacked Genoa, Pisa, Florence, and the towns of
Lombardy along the Po. Venice and the Adriatic coast
suffered equally. Curiously enough, Milan and some north
Lombard towns escaped this first visitation. Where it came
the plague lasted some five months, and may have carried
off a third or more of the population. The towns and the
poorer classes suffered naturally the most, for in densely
populated parts the infection was easiest. It is from Florence,
from the pen of Boccaccio in the prologue to the *Decameron*,
that there comes the most vivid description of the pestilence,
its rapid and fatal onslaught, the helplessness of patient and
physician, the dissolution of natural ties in the universal
panic, the dread of infection, the flight of some, the recklessness of others, the brutal courage of the collectors and buriers
of the dead. As elsewhere, the population did not easily
recover from its devastations, for it recurred for many years.
Its economic effects added to the unrest of the *popolo minuto*,
for it caused a temporary rise of wages, which later could
not be retained, and thus increased the tendency to a new
class revolt.

During these years a fresh scourge lacerated Italy, the free companies of professional mercenary soldiers who supplied the most formidable fighting forces in an age of perpetual warfare. They were for the time mostly foreigners attracted by the high pay and life of licence they could enjoy in their profession. In their rise they were fostered by the decay of the feudal and half-feudal nobility which had been the deciding factor in battles, and by the increasing absorption of the citizen footmen in their trade and peaceful occupations. The Emperor Frederick II and his partisans made large use of German soldiers, who were not personally engaged in the city factions or rivalry, and they remained an important source of the power of the Lombard tyrants. With Charles of Anjou's invasion came a certain number of French adventurers, but it was the employment of Catalans in the early fourteenth century that turned the scales in favour of foreign troops. Then came in succession the invasions of Henry VII, Lewis IV, and John of Bohemia. Each left behind many hundreds of soldiers, who took service with the warring tyrants and cities, and showed a faithless readiness to change their employer whenever they had a chance of better terms. Yet till 1339 this soldiery, unless hired, was disorganized. It was then that the peace between Mastino della Scala and Venice left a host of Germans without employment. A junior Visconti, Lodrisio, bold and ambitious, at enmity with his cousins against whom he had already conspired, seized the opportunity. He reminded the leaderless mercenaries that already the Catalans in the Balkans had formed themselves into the Grand Company. In imitation he organized them into the Company of St. George and led them to the conquest of Milan. But Azzo and the Milanese were the stronger; they routed the Germans at Parabiago, and captured Lodrisio. The example, however, was fruitful. When Pisa discharged her German horse in 1842, they became the Grand Company under " Duke " Werner of Uerslingen, who styled himself " the enemy of God, of mercy and pity," a style that he and his men thoroughly deserved. For a year they ravaged and blackmailed Tuscany, Romagna, and Lombardy till a combination of tyrants intimidated and bribed them into dispersing. When Lewis of Hungary invaded Naples, the mercenaries

gathered again, serving in the wars, and after them cam- Their
paigning, i.e. looting, living at free quarters, and blackmail- Ravages
ing, on their own account. Werner, with a new company,
ravaged both south Italy and the Campagna. Fra Moriale
(Montréal), a Provençal Hospitaller, was even more formidable. He organized his robber troopers as a little wandering
State, despoiling Central Italy and blackmailing the helpless
governments, in spite of an occasional defeat, until he was
captured and beheaded at Rome by Cola di Rienzo in 1354.
His lieutenant and successor, Count Lando (Conrad of
Landau), continued his career, and all Italy south of the Po
suffered under the marches of the Grand Company, whether
hired or not. At last in 1358 Florence summoned courage
to resist the pest and refused passage through her territory.
As Lando retreated towards Romagna, he was attacked by
the infuriated peasantry in the difficult mountain pass of
Scalella and suffered heavy losses. Next year, on renewing
the invasion, he was out-generalled by the Florentine com-
mander, the fighting Romagnol tyrant Pandolfo Malatesta.
Other successful resistance followed, and the looting brigandage of the Companies began to wane. But the institution
remained. War in Italy was carried on by Free Companies
of foreign adventurers, hired out by their leaders, who were
termed *condottieri* (men who received a contract of hire,
condotta), to the warring States. The Peace of Brétigny
(1861) brought fresh swarms of this soldiery into Italy ;
there were the two mainly English companies, the White
Company and the Company of St. George, the latter under
a famous general, the ex-tailor, Sir John Hawkwood, who
was known to the Italians as Giovanni Acuto. Less marauding than they had been, they seemed a necessary evil.
Italian nobles, mountaineers, and adventurous peasants took The Italian
to the trade, until Alberigo da Barbiano, a Romagnol, in 1378 Company
recruited an all-Italian Company of St. George. He was a
general of originality and organizing skill. By improving
accoutrements, bridles, and drill, he gave his heavy horsemen
a new power of manœuvre and solid formation. So successful was he that he drove the foreigners out of the military
market and created a school of scientific generals, who waged
the wars of the fifteenth century.

The recrudescence of the Free Companies of Adventure

has been due to the tragic demoralization of the kingdom
of Naples.   King Robert died on January 19, 1343, a ruler
who missed his real, if small, opportunities partly in consequence of the hereditary entanglements of his foreign policy
as the Pope's vassal and chief of the Guelfs in Italy, partly
because of his obstinate pursuit of the vain conquest of
Sicily.   During his long reign oppressive taxation destroyed
all chance of the recovery of economic prosperity and of the
formation of a healthy middle class.   A degenerate and out-
of-date feudalism produced mutinous anarchy without military strength, oppression without a purpose.   The ill-used
peasantry, crushed with exactions, misgoverned by bureau-
crat and baron, fell back into savage self-help.   For all these
ills the industrious and learned king had no remedy ; he did
not even try to find one.   The position of his heiress, Queen

Joanna I, eldest daughter of his only son, the Duke of
Calabria, was difficult from the start.   There had always
been a succession problem, for Robert was only the third
son of Charles II and his nephew, Charles Robert, King of
Hungary, who represented the eldest son, had claims which
were not set at rest by the Pope's decision in favour of
Robert.   In order to remove this danger, Robert married
Joanna to her cousin Andrew, the second son of Charles
Robert : thus the rival claims would be reconciled.   But
Joanna was gay and voluptuous, and Andrew rough and
reserved, while both wished to exercise the government.
Further, the junior branches of the royal family, the lines
of Taranto and Durazzo, were already at feud, and each had
designs on the kingdom.   In the discord of the queen and
king-consort Robert of Taranto became the lover of Joanna,
and Charles of Durazzo married her younger sister Mary,
aiming at the crown.   Plots were woven amid the corrupt
Neapolitan court, while King Lewis the Great of Hungary,
Andrew's elder brother, insisted with the Pope on Andrew's
coronation and full participation in the government.   But
when a papal legate came to Naples to perform the corona-

tion, Andrew was treacherously murdered on September 18,
1345, at Aversa, where he was staying with his wife.   Who
was behind the plot and the actual criminals remains dubious.
The titular Latin Empress, Catherine of Valois, the mother
of Robert of Taranto, appears almost certainly guilty—she

was aiming at the throne for her son—Queen Joanna was obviously callous and was deeply suspected, but without real proof; so also, but with much less reason, was Charles of Durazzo. King Lewis of Hungary had no doubts : he accused Joanna of adultery and murder, demanded her deposition, and claimed the throne. Meanwhile at Naples the minor criminals were hideously executed, Catherine pressed for the marriage of Robert and Joanna, and the rival princes armed. Pope Clement VI declared for a fair trial, and temporized, but he most feared the union of Naples and Hungary. Catherine's death next year allowed the fickle Joanna to cashier suddenly Robert of Taranto and soon to marry his younger brother Louis, whom rumour at once accused of Andrew's murder. Lewis of Hungary, however, King Lewis of Hungary's Invasion prepared his invasion, which gathered together fresh mercenaries, and in January 1348 reached Naples without resistance. Joanna and Louis of Taranto fled to Provence, and thence to Avignon, where the queen was acquitted by Clement VI.

Lewis of Hungary's uncontested reign in Naples was short. He had Charles of Durazzo killed in revenge for his supposed share in Andrew's murder ; he sent the Angevin princes to confinement in Hungary ; and he governed by foreign agents, while his German and Hungarian troopers lived on the country. In June the Neapolitan barons revolted, and Joanna and Louis of Taranto could return. Naples under Joanna I Lewis himself was back in Hungary, but his *condottieri* and mercenaries, Werner, Conrad Wolfart, Fra Moriale, and their like, spread in a terrible, marauding, faithless warfare over the wretched land. A second short campaign in 1350 by Lewis in person drove Joanna to refuge in Gaeta without any permanent conquest, and at last the Hungarian king gave up the struggle on terms. Joanna was duly tried again by the Pope and duly acquitted, an indemnity was paid, and peace was signed in January 1352. There was no internal peace, however, in Naples. The Free Companies continued their blackmail and depredations ; the princes of the blood, released from Hungary, fought, intrigued, and rebelled for power ; the nobles were more anarchic than before. Louis of Taranto, inspired by the capable Florentine adventurer, Niccolò Acciaiuoli, not only made head against these troubles but also most unfortunately, tempted by the island's factions and the youth of the two kings Louis and Frederick III, invaded Sicily. He had more success than his ancestors, but domestic wars called him back. On his death in 1362, Queen Joanna took as her third husband the dispossessed King of Majorca, James (IV), who was poor and not allowed any power. He was little in Naples, and on his death Joanna married again in 1376 : this time it was Otto, one of the Dukes of Brunswick, an approved soldier. The queen remained childless, however, and the nearest heir was her niece Margaret of Durazzo, who had married her cousin Charles, Duke of Durazzo. The pair were the natural heirs to the kingdom, and with the aid of Lewis of Hungary, in whose service Charles was, were recognized as such. Meantime, the anarchy of the kingdom and its misery under the

Peace with Sicily

Free Companies continued. The only relief was that the war with Sicily was at last given up, when in 1872 under papal mediation, it was agreed that the island should remain, as Trinacria, under the Aragonese dynasty, but as a tributary vassal kingdom under Naples. The terms were not kept, but the peace was. So ended the wasted effort of ninety years. It was the doubtful conduct of Joanna in the Schism which produced the next revolution. The Roman Pope Urban VI raised against her Charles of Durazzo, while Joanna gained allies by adopting the French Duke Louis of

Death of Joanna I

Anjou. In 1381 Charles III came with Hungarian troops, murdered Joanna, whom he had captured, and took the crown. He found the kingdom in a turmoil which his adventurous, troubled reign did not remove. The ancient division of Italy had been made more striking by the reign of the Angevins. Naples and Sicily were on a lower plane than the North.

Rome

From these dreary dynastic broils we turn to events which, however fleeting, were concerned with ideas, however chimerical. The city of Rome had suffered severely by the desertion of their see by the French Popes. There was no longer the papal court to bring wealth and great affairs. Its population dwindled and it was a prey to the incessant feuds of the nobles. Colonna, Orsini, and Gaetani, along with minor houses, carried on their furious strife, watched by the impotent papal vicars. Yet Rome was a place of pilgrimage and a bourgeois class subsisted still, with growing wrath at the nobles' anarchy and brigandage. In Rome the indignation and claims of the gildsmen were peculiarly coloured by the famous past of the city. They could not forget that their predecessors had been lords and conquerors of the world. The theories of the Empire and the Papacy were a perpetual reminder, and contemporary facts seemed a mere transitory perversion of their innate superiority. Fostered by poets and thinkers, by events like the Roman proceedings of Henry VII and Lewis IV, and by their own appetite for pompous phrases, these prepossessions made every attempt of the Roman *bourgeoisie* for better government take the form of a deluded parody of the classic past. The delusion was startlingly conspicuous in the fourteenth century, when dawning humanism, voiced with enthusiasm by the poet Petrarch, fed on memories of Livy and Virgil, exalted ancient Rome and Italy, and strove zealously to renew the glories of classic civilization. The coronation of Petrarch at Rome with the poet's laurel in 1341 was both a manifesto of the new tendency and an incitement to take idealized legends as solid, practicable facts. Only in such an atmosphere could the career and dreams of Cola di Rienzo (Nicholas, son of Laurence) have been possible. Cola was the son of a tavern-keeper and a laundress on the Tiber bank. He thus came from the lower *bourgeoisie*, but he had the nature of a scholar ; he educated himself, and became a notary. Like a true humanist, he was well read in the Latin classics, while the Roman monuments which enchanted his imagination led him on to read the inscriptions of the ancient republic and empire. This handsome enthusiast, who a century later would have hunted for manuscripts, was also a born orator and demagogue. He set himself to rouse his fellow-citizens to imitate their ancestors by explaining to them the memorials in their midst, while he evolved in his own mind a grandiose programme of revival and reform, which was indeed inspired by genius, but not by that of a realist. In his neurotic temperament the habitual self-delusion of the Romans and the theorist's belief in the power of words and systems urged him under the stress of conflict to the border-line of sanity. He became the prey to his own visions and ideals.

Cola di Rienzo

This learned demagogue first gained a foothold in politics when in 1343 a temporary bourgeois revolution in Rome resulted in his being sent as envoy to placate Pope Clement VI. The revolution failed, but the eloquent and learned Cola gained the Pope's personal favour. Some years of propaganda, speeches aided by allegorical pictures, enabled him to carry through his own revolution in May 1347. It was directed against the brigand, anarchic nobles, not in outward seeming against the Pope, who soon approved, and whose vicar was made co-Signore of Rome along with Cola di Rienzo himself. But Cola's plans went far beyond the restoration of justice and order and the subjection of the nobles, which he did in fact enforce during his administra-

His Programme tion. He schemed a real revival of the ancient republic, a federation of Italy in which all Italians should be Roman citizens, a reign of peace and justice and freedom, over which he should preside. For this end he summoned a congress of Italian states, and assumed an authority to which his good government and success and the charm of his dream gave a momentary vogue. But he was already unbalanced. He believed himself inspired by the Holy Ghost. The propagandist hoped to conquer by means of titles and pompous symbolic ceremonies in a realist world of fighting interests. He called himself " Tribune of Liberty, Peace, and Justice, Liberator of the Sacred Republic " ; he went through a solemn coronation ; he issued decrees annulling all grants in derogation of the Roman People's world supremacy. For the time he carried all before him ; flattering embassies came in ; he defeated a revolt of the great noble houses. But he lost the Pope's favour, as his plans and his disregard of the papal vicar became manifest. His own nerve failed him under the tense strain of his dangers, and his rule deteriorated. The Romans were expecting the Pope to proclaim another Jubilee, this time after fifty years, to relieve the poverty of the city ; now they were menaced with interdict instead.

His Fall When a new noble revolt in December was encouraged by the papal legate at Montefiascone, no one rallied to defend the quaking tribune.

His Life in Exile Cola escaped while Rome returned to anarchy. He eventually took refuge in the mountains of the Abruzzi among the heretic Fraticelli. There his speculations took a Ghibel-

line, Joachite turn.   He went in 1350 to Prague, hoping to
persuade the unadventurous Charles IV of Luxemburg to
enter Italy as its deliverer, reform the clergy and confiscate
their wealth, and place the new-made world under a trinity
of Pope, Emperor, and Cola as Duke of Rome.   He declared
that his own real father was Henry VII.   This did not appeal
to Charles, who kept him in prison as a heretic, but the
ex-tribune's personal charm and genius kept him unharmed.
At last, he was sent to Avignon, where he was imprisoned
and tried but not condemned.   Rather, he was admired and
pitied, while his ready imagination produced a new Guelf
scheme for the deliverance of Italy : all tyrants should be
expelled under the ægis of the Pope.   When Pope Innocent
VI in 1353 dispatched Cardinal Albornoz to Italy, he sent
him Cola di Rienzo as a useful instrument for governing
Rome.   In 1354 he was given his chance.   With money
borrowed from Fra Moriale's brothers he raised a troop of
mercenaries, and, appointed Senator by Albornoz, marched
on the city, which accepted him in August.   Everyone His Second
expected the admirable government of his earlier days, but Rule in
they were disillusioned.   Cola was arbitrary and neurasthenic. Rome and
Death
He became unpopular by his taxation and his executions.
He treacherously put to death the *condottiere*, Fra Moriale,
the brother of his benefactors, for the sake of his wealth.
Fra Moriale was a terrible freebooter who deserved his end,
but it was base in Cola.   In October the Romans rose ; they
shouted down the Senator whose voice might have charmed
them again, and he was miserably slain as he fled in disguise
from the Capitol.   It was his unhappy fate to be the visionary
genius in politics—he forecast the union of Italy—and the
Romans were too barbarous to be free ; yet his own defects,
vanity, perfidy, and a streak of madness, were glaring.   He
was no statesman, but a portentous embodiment of the
aspirations of his age.

The lead in North Italy was passing definitely to Milan
when Mastino II della Scala died in 1351 and left Verona to
his three corrupt and efficient sons.   The Visconti on the
other hand continued to furnish men of craft and strength. Giovanni
Luchino was followed by his surviving brother Giovanni, Visconti
Archbishop of Milan (1349–54), who could wield, as he once
boasted to the papal envoys, both crozier and sword, and was

an adept in the wiles and bribes of contemporary diplomacy. He restored the unity of the Visconti family by recalling from exile his nephews, the sons of his brother Stefano, and continued the expansion of the Milanese dominion.   It was becoming clear that cities preferred to lose their independence to a tyrant, to whom all his subjects were equal, than to a republic, which kept its conquests in mere subjection and reserved the rule to its own citizens alone.   The opportunity was given to the archbishop by the attempt of Astorge de Durfort, papal rector of Romagna, to drive the Pepoli from Bologna in pursuance of a half-hearted design of Pope Clement VI to quell the Romagnol tyrants.   The Pepoli, too weak to hold out, sold in 1350 their city to the Visconti. An interdict declared by the indignant Pope had no effect, his troops were bribed to desert, his cardinals were similarly corrupted, and Clement ended in 1352 by making the archbishop his tributary vicar of Bologna for twelve years. Florence, indeed, made war, but a stalemate ended in a general peace next year.

War of Venice and Genoa

Meantime Giovanni Visconti obtained with scarcely an effort a more important signory.   In 1350 the bitter rivalry for the Black Sea trade of " the two eyes of Italy," Venice and Genoa, broke into war in the Levant, and Peter IV of Aragon, who found Genoa always supporting the resistance to him in Sardinia, joined Venice.   In the east each side won victories, but in August 1353 the Genoese fleet in the west was utterly defeated by the Venetians and Catalans at La Loiera off the coast of Sardinia.   Genoa thereupon elected the Visconti her *signore* and the war became general.   Now the Genoese had their revenge in November 1354 in an equally complete victory over the Venetians at Sapienza off the Morea.   In the following year a reasonable peace was made under the auspices of the Visconti.   Each party agreed to respect the trade of the other in the Black Sea ; Genoese warships were not to enter the Adriatic nor Venetians the Gulf of Genoa.   The peace was too fair to please the two republics, which only accepted and observed it owing to exhaustion and pressing preoccupations.   Genoa took advantage in 1356 of the Visconti brothers' misfortunes to revolt and restore Doge Boccanegra.   This meant the final victory of the *popolo*.   Henceforward the government and doge-

Genoa under the *popolani*

ship were disputed for by rival families of rich *popolani* merchants. Power passed from the semi-feudal houses. When Boccanegra was poisoned in 1363, Gabriele Adorno was promptly made doge, to be replaced by his enemy, Domenico Campofregoso, in 1370. Though rent by habitual faction, the republic kept its Riviera, and in a victorious war with Cyprus in 1373, due to the usual competition with Venice, obtained heavy sums and the control of the port of Famagosta.

That Venice took no action over Cyprus was due to her Venice. own misfortunes. Discontent among the workmen of the Doge Falier Arsenal, due partly to the arrogance of young patricians, had been fanned by the disaster of Sapienza, and gave a cue to the ambition of the doge, Marino Falier, himself tied down by his fellow oligarchs and furious at a personal insult. But the plot was discovered in time by the Council of Ten, the patricians held together, and in April 1355 the doge was condemned and beheaded. The dramatic event sealed the constitutional powerlessness of the dogeship, however influential with his colleagues an individual doge might be. Far more dangerous to the whole State was the conflict with Hungary. King Lewis the Great was determined to annex Loss of Dalmatia, which with its islands and its forests was essential Dalmatia to Venice's ship-building and control of the Adriatic, and was also the natural littoral of his kingdom of Croatia. Since her annexation of Treviso and overlordship of unwilling Padua, Venice was far more vulnerable to a land attack. In 1356 Lewis besieged Treviso and invaded Dalmatia. He won all along the line ; in 1358 Venice was forced to cede Dalmatia. After this blow it is no wonder that the Venetian dominion began to totter. The native Cretans' dislike of foreign rule was reinforced by the indignation of the Venetian colonists, who were excluded from office, even in Crete, by the narrow policy of the oligarchy. They revolted together in 1363-4, but their own association with mere disorder and Venice's prompt energy caused a quick reconquest. Venice in fact was recovering. Faction always quickly withered there, whereas it drained Genoa like an ulcer. When Francesco Carrara of Padua, in alliance with Lewis of Hungary, made war again, Venice in 1373 defeated the Hungarian army at Fossa Nuova, and compelled Carrara to submit. In a few years she was able to begin the final and decisive struggle with Genoa, the famous war of Chioggia.

The War of Chioggia

The war began over the possession of the island of Tenedos, which the Venetians had forced the Emperor John Palaeologus to cede to them, and it became a life and death struggle. A victory of the Venetian admiral Pisani in the Tyrrhenian Sea was followed in 1379 by his annihilating defeat off Pola. The Genoese admiral Pietro Doria thereupon occupied the town of Chioggia at one entrance to the Venetian lagoon, and aided by Francesco Carrara of Padua, who held the mainland coast, he prepared to starve out the enemy city by a blockade. It was then that the patriotism and unity of the Venetians were best shown. With an improvised fleet under Pisani, first imprisoned, then restored to command, they succeeded in blockading the Genoese at Chioggia in their turn. Their fleet from the Levant came home just in time to ward off the Genoese relief squadron. At last in June 1380 the Genoese were compelled to surrender, and as Genoa was exhausted and torn by faction peace could be made in 1381. Venice had temporarily lost her mainland dominion—she gave Treviso to the Duke of Austria rather than to Carrara—but her real strength was unimpaired : her constitution had borne every test. Henceforth Genoa was in decline. The fratricidal struggle had fatally dimmed one of the two eyes of Italy and had lamed the defence of Christendom in the East.

The Visconti divided

The position of the three Visconti brothers, Matteo II, Galeazzo II, and Bernabò, immediately weakened on their succession to their divided inheritance. They had little to dread from the first Italian expedition of Charles IV, whose coronation at Milan they permitted in January 1355, and from whom they bought, like others, the useful Imperial Vicariate. When he hurried back to Germany, " having filled his empty purse," they shut their gates upon him. But the dissolute Matteo II was poisoned by his brothers as a family danger, and each survivor lost ground, Galeazzo in the west, Bernabò in the east. A league under the Marquess of Montferrat seized Asti and the neighbourhood in 1356 ; Genoa became independent ; and Pavia revolted under the Beccaria. Giovanni d'Oleggio Visconti, natural son of the archbishop, and deputy ruler of Bologna, threw off the yoke of his cousins ; Mantua and Ferrara joined the league against them. The league hired the Grand Company under Lando for the campaign ; but this was soundly beaten by Lodrisio Visconti, now loyal and reconciled, at Casorate. In 1358 came peace, which allowed the Visconti next year to capture Pavia, become for a while a free commune inspired by the Austin friar Bussolari. Thus the Visconti State held its own despite its losses.

Much more dangerous was the marvellous revival of the Papal State by Cardinal Gil Albornoz. This fighting Spanish prelate, already distinguished in the wars with the Moors of Granada, was a statesman of the first magnitude. In August 1353 he was sent to Italy as legate by Pope Innocent VI, who was alarmed at the wild anarchy round Rome and at the wide dominion in Romagna and the March of Ancona erected by the Malatesta. Well supplied with money and troops, the legate in 1354 made short work of Giovanni di Vico, the Prefect of Rome (save that of Emperor the most ancient title in Christendom), who was turning the Tuscan Patrimony into a principality. In an astonishingly brief time the whole Patrimony and Umbria were reduced to a kind of order ; free communes and feudal lords lived under papal control. In spite of some chequered fortune, next year the Malatesta collapsed, and received a remnant of their dominion as Papal Vicars. The years 1356 and 1357 saw the capture of Cesena from the Ordelaffi, but, while the legate attacked Forlì, which the Ordelaffi still held, he was thwarted by the intrigues of Bernabò Visconti, who was anxious with papal help to wrench Bologna from Giovanni d'Oleggio, and feared that it might go to the legate instead. As a result of Bernabò's efforts at Avignon, a new papal agent, Androin de la Roche, Abbot of Cluny, hampered and then replaced Albornoz for a year. On his complete failure Albornoz returned in December 1358, and Ordelaffi surrendered at last. Active war now began with Bernabò. Giovanni d'Oleggio, hard pressed by his cousin, in 1360 gave Bologna to the legate in return for compensation in the March of Ancona. Fresh Hungarian mercenaries were summoned and dismissed for bad behaviour, a league of hostile neighbours was formed, a crusade preached, Bernabò defeated in 1363, when Pope Urban V avoided extremities.

He again sent de la Roche, and in 1364 compensated Bernabò for Bologna by an enormous indemnity.   There was something to be said in favour of not breaking up the Visconti State, but the peace left Albornoz's work in danger.   The great soldier and statesman had also been a legislator.   In 1357 he issued the *Constitutiones Aegidianae*, which remained the basis of public law in the Papal States till the days of Napoleon.

The achievement of Albornoz and the dangers of Avignon, which no longer contrasted favourably with the Papal States, no less than his own religious feelings, led Pope Urban V to resolve to return to Rome.   With the Emperor Charles IV he arranged a joint appearance in Italy, where they would abolish the pernicious Free Companies, and the power of the Visconti, whose ambitious schemes were threatening Tuscany and preventing the peace of Italy.   In June 1367 Urban landed in the Papal States.   Soon after the league was arrayed against the Visconti.   But Albornoz died in August, and Charles came in 1368 only to mediate a peace and raise money by diplomas before he left again for Germany.   The Papal States were soon in commotion, as the papal government deteriorated.   Homesick amid war and rebellion, Pope Urban left for Avignon in 1370, where he died in the same year.   The war with the Visconti had already recommenced, and owing to Bernabò's aggression in Tuscany Florence took part.   With alternate success—the Visconti obtaining Reggio —it continued till 1375.   A truce then produced a new combination.   Florence had long been malcontent with the expansion of the Papal State and her social equilibrium had been endangered by the refusal of the legate at Bologna to permit the export of corn in famine years.   Now the same legate allowed Sir John Hawkwood, who had distinguished himself on both sides, to lead his unemployed company to the ravage of his Tuscan ally.   The Florentines in wrath allied with Bernabò, and stimulated by vivid appeals the angry, oppressed towns of the Papal States to revolt.   Pope Gregory XI replied by interdict, confiscation, and a European boycott of Florence, which responded by heavy taxes on the clergy and enthusiastic support of the special board for the war, called in scorn of papal sentences the " Eight Saints."

The revolt of the States of the Church and the fear of Pope
Gregory XI
in Italy a schism of the Italians if he remained at Avignon made the question of the Pope's return to Rome more pressing. Gregory XI's natural hesitation was diminished by the inter- vention of a saint, whose personality had secured her an extraordinary prestige, St. Catherine of Siena. Her ardent appeal for his return to his see seconded the argument from facts. In January 1377 the transfer of the Curia took place. Meantime the Pope had waged war with ferocious mercen- aries, who brought him success. A company of Bretons, with whom was the legate Robert of Geneva, in revenge for their losses in a riot perpetrated a terrible massacre at Cesena while the future Pope of Avignon hounded them on. As a result Bologna and the March of Ancona submitted. Flor- ence, too, though she struggled on gallantly with Hawkwood as her *condottiere*, was exhausted by her enormous mercantile losses. A congress was held at Sarzana in March 1378 which produced after Gregory XI's death a peace on easy terms.

The crisis of the war of the Eight Saints was followed in Discontents
in Florence Florence by revolutions for which the causes had long been accumulating, for the city was honeycombed by the rivalries and discontents of factions and classes. Power mainly lay with the wealthy Greater Arts, the Lesser Arts of " small masters " having a small share of it, and longing for more. Then there were the excluded classes of the Magnates and the *popolo minuto* or workmen. But within the Greater Arts there was a powerful group of great bankers and manufac- turers, partly Magnates or allied to them, who strove for an oligarchic control of the State. Their policy aimed first at reducing the influence of the Lesser Arts, and keeping their fellows of the Greater in subjection, and then at holding down the proletariat, who suffered under the low wages given by their employers and landlords. Their chief weapon lay in the institution of the Parte Guelfa, with its immense wealth, in which those Magnates who were commercial held a leading place. By the process of " admonition (*ammoni- zione*)," without proceeding to prosecution, the Parte Guelfa succeeded in excluding its rivals from politics under pretext of the now meaningless crime of Ghibellinism. In spite of reactions, led by the less oligarchic citizens, the Parte Guelfa by 1372 seemed to be achieving their purpose. But behind the Arts stood the ill-treated workmen, who found that the rise in wages after the Black Death was accompanied by higher prices. Their natural remedy was to obtain the jealously guarded privilege of forming Arts of their own with a share in the government instead of remaining mere subjects of the Arte della Lana. Already in 1345 a wool-carder, Ciuto Brandini, had led a movement for such associations and had been executed as a rebel. The only concession was the admission of the dyers to a share in the Arte della Lana. One of the chief preoccupations of the government was to keep the price of food low and thus allay the discontent of the poorer classes, but bad harvests, wars, and the difficulties of importation often rendered this impossible. In 1368 the workmen rioted for food, and the dyers went on strike for higher wages in vain. At the close of the War of the Eight Saints, the various discontents were allying together. The Lesser Arts sympathized with the *popolo minuto*, and large sections of the Greater Arts were hostile to the Parte Guelfa, while the rifts, due to family rivalries, among the oligarchs paralysed them—the wealthy Salvestro dei Medici, the first notable man of his family, even supported the movement behind the scenes. In July, 1378, the *popolani minuti* broke out into organized revolution, in which the Ciompi, i.e. the less skilled employees of the cloth-trade, took the lead. The government gave way : Michele di Lando, the ringleader, a wool-carder, was made Gonfalonier of Justice with a new board of democratic Priors. Three new gilds were formed from the workmen, the Dyers, the Jerkin-makers, and the Ciompi. But wages did not rise or prices fall, and the workmen of the Ciompi, assembling in Santa Maria Novella, elected a board of Eight to enforce further change. On August 27 they assaulted the Priors' Palazzo. But Michele di Lando, whether he realized that mere revolution was fruitless or had changed his views on insurrections when in office, headed the forces of order with prompt decision, and routed the insurgents. Meantime employment ceased and the proletariat had no means of reviving it. All other parties were united against them. The Art of the Ciompi was at once abolished, while the other two new gilds were allowed to subsist. In the new government the Lesser Arts had most sway. It lasted only three years, for it could

The Revolt of the Ciompi

not meet the difficulties caused by the poverty of the State,
the decline of the cloth-manufacture, the hostility of the
Greater Arts and the Magnates, the resentment of the Ciompi,
and the intrigues of ambitious demagogues.   Amid plots and
executions the Lesser Arts lost cohesion.   At last, in January
1382 the Greater Arts took action, and in a reform of the
constitution they were given the preponderance, while the
arts of Dyers and Jerkinmakers were dissolved.   Michele di
Lando and Salvestro dei Medici were among the banished.
In fact Florence, with her commerce and foreign policy, Restoration
could not be successfully ruled by a class of small shop- of Oligarchy
keepers, and very soon a narrow oligarchy of half-magnate
bankers formed a real government ; it was the culmination
of a tendency visible for a century.

The opening of the Great Schism saw Italy in conditions Italy in 1380
which held good until the French invasion of Charles VIII.
In the south Naples and Sicily were disorderly, decaying feudal kingdoms.   The Papal States were breaking up
again into little tyrannies.   Florence was reconstituting her
dominion in Tuscany.   Genoa had become second-rate ;
Venice had embarked on the conquest of the mainland.   In
Piedmont the Count of Savoy and his house were forming
a solid pre-eminence.   In the centre the Visconti were unifying Lombardy.   Although Galeazzo II, who died in 1378,
and Bernabò were singularly cruel and odious tyrants, and
extortionate as well, they kept order, provided justice where
they were not themselves concerned, encouraged economic
prosperity, and formed an administration.   The era of the
autonomous commune was over because it had proved un-
workable, but the era of the despots now established gave
little promise of stability or peace.

SUGGESTIONS FOR READING ON CHAPTER XVI

A. SOURCES

(i) Documents

Acta Aragonensia.   Ed. Finke, H.   3 vols.   Berlin, 1908 ff.

Acta Henrici VII.   Ed. Bonaini, F.   2 vols.   Florence. 1877.

Baluze : *Vitae Paparum Avenionensium.*   Ed. Mollat, G.   4 vols.   Paris,
1914 ff.

Briefwechsel des Cola di Rienzo.   Ed. Burdach, K., and Piur, P.   5 vols.
Berlin, 1912–29.

Constitutiones et Acta publica imperatorum et regum.   Vols. iii–vi, viii, as
in suggestions for Chapter XV.

(ii) Narrative

Mussatus, Albertinus : *Historia Augusta* and *De Gestis Italicorum.* Ed.
Muratori, *Rerum Italicarum Scriptores.* Vol. **x.**
   Nicolaus episcopus Botrontinensis. *Relatio.* In Baluze, *Vitae paparum
Avenionensium,* ed. Mollat. Vol. iii.
   Compagni, Dino : as in suggestions for Chapter IV.
   Villani, G. and M. : as in suggestions for Chapter IV.
   Dandolo, A. : *Chronicon Venetum.* Ed. Muratori, *op. cit.,* xii.
   Flamma, Galvaneus : *Manipulus Florum.* Ed. Muratori, *op. cit.,* xi.

B. MODERN WORKS

Cambridge Medieval History, vol. vii, relevant chapters.
Mollat, G. : *Les papes d'Avignon.* 6th edn. Paris, 1930.
Brown, H. : *Venice.* 2nd edn. London, 1905.
Davidsohn, R. : *Geschichte von Florenz.* Vols. iii, iv. Berlin, 1912 ff.
Gregorovius, F. : *History of Rome in the Middle Ages.*
Caggese, R. : *Storia di Firenze.* Florence, 1913 ff.
Muir, D. : *History of Milan under the Visconti.* London, 1924.
Foligno, C. : *Story of Padua.* London, 1910.
Clarke, M. V. : *The Medieval City State.* London, 1926.
Sismondi, J. C. L. de : *The Italian Republics.* Ed. Boulting, W. London.
Caggese, R. : *Roberto d'Angiò.* 2 vols. Florence, 1922–31.
Piur, P. : *Cola di Rienzo.* Vienna, 1931.
Rodolico, N. : *La democrazia fiorentina nel suo tramonto.* Bologna, 1904.
Ricotti, E. : *Storia delle compagnie di ventura in Italia.* Turin, 1893.

CHAPTER XVII

THE IBERIAN PENINSULA IN THE FOURTEENTH CENTURY

THE restriction of the Moorish dominions in the Iberian peninsula to the little kingdom of Granada in the south ended the period of the Reconquest, and changed the political conditions of the Christian States. Henceforward for many years, the warlike nobility and the Church turned their wealth and fighting instincts towards anarchic independence and resistance to the monarchy. The kings on the other hand pursued an aggressive policy of centralization and royal authority, influenced by the absolutist tendencies of the reviving Roman Law. The history of the peninsula is consequently filled by the conflicts between the rival forces, complicated by incessant dynastic disputes within the kingdoms, which were frequently involved with wars between several countries. Nor was it only the intense insubordination of the Spaniards which kept civil war alight : each province had a separate local life of its own, more marked in some, less in others, and this particularism was at once an obstacle in the way of the monarchy and a reason for the ultimate failure of attempts to put the monarchy in permanent leading-strings. Common action over a wide extent of territory for any length of time proved impossible. The sense of national unity was deficient.

To this stalemate, the Aragonese federation was a partial exception. The States which composed it did themselves form the distinct regions within which unity and continuity could be attained ; particularism here favoured co-operation under the restrictions it imposed. Further, Catalonia faced the Mediterranean, which gave a natural outlet for national energies and a foreign policy to the kings very different to the sporadic and casual relations which the other Iberian kingdoms entertained with Europe north of the Pyrenees. The conquest of Sicily by Peter III was but a continuation

Monarchy and Particularism

The Aragonese Federation

and a part of the expansion of maritime Catalonia over the
Mediterranean which began with the commercial enterprises
of Barcelona and the expulsion of the Moors from the Balearic
Islands and ended in the Spanish empire of Charles V.   This
was definitely a Catalan policy, for the three States of the
federation differed markedly from one another, although as
against Castile they showed a common capacity for organization and aptitude to make and maintain the rule of law.
Catalonia, with its Languedoc speech and traditions, was at
once the most advanced and the most conservative.   There
the feudal rule of the nobles over their serfs was most retro-
grade and oppressive ; there the trading towns were most
prosperous and autonomous.   The Catalan Cortes, with their
three houses, shared in legislation and voted subsidies ; they
supervised their kings, but were also least inclined to fetter
them too strictly ; the dynasty was itself Catalan and so
were its ambitions.   Aragon proper, however, was an inland
Spanish kingdom, united to Catalonia by little more than
the person of the sovereign and the occasional meeting of a
joint Cortes.   In its compact territory nobles and towns
could act together ; they were determined to limit the powers
of their kings, whose policy they disliked ; independent
isolation was their ideal.   Valencia, the joint conquest of
Aragon and Catalonia, was divided between the instincts of
both, but for long the Aragonese tendencies had the greater
sway, for if the towns were Catalan, the feudal nobles who
ruled over Moorish peasants were Aragonese.

Its last   The Aragonese expansion in Spain came to a close in
Annexations 1304 with the annexation of a small part of Murcia.   James
the Conqueror in 1266 had conquered the Moorish kingdom
of Murcia for his son-in-law Alfonso the Learned of Castile,
and with great loyalty had handed it over.   But war broke
out later when Castile sided with France against Peter the
Great, and ended at last in the further cession of this corner
of Murcia to the Valencian kingdom.   King James II (1291–
1327) the Just, indeed, made a fresh attack on Granada, in
concert with Castile, but his failure to take Almería in 1310
ended his ambitions in that quarter.   James's chief interests
were Mediterranean, though it is strange how little resulted
from all his great activity.   In 1298 he restored at the Pope's
Majorca   command the kingdom of Majorca and Roussillon, conquered

by Alfonso III, to his uncle and namesake James II, although he was able to insist on strict vassalage. When James of Majorca's son and successor Sancho died in 1324, his nephew James III succeeded him in spite of the King of Aragon's attempt at annexation. James the Just also aimed at a political superiority over the Barbary States which he never got. He began under the Pope's grant the conquest of the kingdom of Sardinia, but he had to meet not only the oppo- Sardinia sition of the islanders under the Judges who ruled their four principalities, but also that of the Pisans and Genoese, both of whom had possessions and partisans there. It was not till 1323 that James sent his heir Alfonso with an army and fleet which captured Iglesias, and not till 1326 that a Catalan sea-victory drove out the Pisans, and made the kingdom of Sardinia a restive dependency.

In his internal government James II's achievement was Internal more solid. The foreign wars of his father Peter the Great Government had been most unpopular in Aragon proper, and in 1283 the of James II king had been forced to grant the *Privilegio General* to the The "Union" of nobles and towns. The Cortes were to meet *Privilegio* every year; no military service was to be due outside the *General* kingdom; new taxation was only to be by grant of the Cortes; and no Aragonese could be punished without due legal process. Alfonso III had been in still greater straits at the beginning of his reign. The *Privilegio de la Unión*, The which he was compelled to grant to the Union in 1287, pre- *Privilegio* scribed that no proceedings could be taken by the king *de la Unión* against its members save before the Justicia and by permission of the annual Cortes, that the Cortes should elect members of the royal council, that the king should give security for his performance of his concessions, and finally that the Union could depose him if he broke his word. James II, however, while he did not keep these pledges, gained steadily in favour by his strict observance of the ordinary law; the more adventurous nobles found careers abroad. When it came to a final breach with the Union in 1301, he had the support of the Justicia and the Cortes against the grasping barons, and was able to break up the dreaded association. Even the Cortes in 1307 were made biennial, and that provision too was not kept. The Justicias, maintained in their great authority, were allies of a king who gave his subjects justice and peace. In Catalonia and Valencia meanwhile the Cortes were made triennial, in law at least. Bold warrior and crafty diplomat as James the Just was, his chief talent was for organization, in which he was a true king of his time, a contemporary of Edward I and Philip the Tall. Under him there appear real finance departments ; and both central and local administration and the courts of justice were developed as in other monarchies. Like his contemporaries, too, were the wide range and somewhat ineffectual character of his foreign policy, which extended all over the Mediterranean and even reached Germany.

Alfonso IV

His son Alfonso IV (1327–36) the Kindly, met with little good fortune. He lost the greater part of Sardinia to the Genoese in a revolt of the islanders, and his reign was clouded by the attempt of his second wife, Leonor of Castile, to oust her stepsons from the succession and secure it for her own sons. She obtained prodigal grants from the ailing king, but the opposition that they roused, especially in Valencia, was so great that they had to be recalled. On Alfonso's death the queen and her sons fled to Castile, leaving the throne to the rightful heir, a masterful personality, Peter IV, whose reign marked an epoch.

Peter IV

Peter the Ceremonious (1336–87) inherited to the full the ability, the hard, strong character of his line, of which he was the most unamiable representative. Cruel and faithless, devoid of scruples, he was, in his internal policy at least, wise and even moderate. There were two weaknesses in the Aragonese federation, the autonomy of the kingdom of Majorca under the junior line of the royal house, and the dangerous insubordination of the nobles of Aragon and Valencia. The Kings of Majorca had hitherto maintained themselves by oscillating between France, where they held the town of Montpellier, and Aragon. King James III, a valiant knight but incompetent ruler, fell out with both his suzerains. In 1341 he lost Montpellier to Philip of Valois.

Acquisition of Majorca

Meantime, his incessant friction with Peter IV, which was personal as well as political, had resulted in the King of Aragon's determination to dispossess him. On a trumped-up excuse Peter declared his fiefs forfeit and proceeded to their conquest. In 1343 Majorca was seized and Roussillon

SPAIN c. A.D. 1300

invaded : all James III's lands were conquered by 1344. By selling his rights in Montpellier to the King of France, he was able to make a desperate invasion of Majorca in 1349, but he was defeated and slain, though his son James (IV) remained a troublesome claimant till his death.   There was no doubt of the benefit to the Catalan sea-power and commerce accruing from the annexation of the Balearic Isles. Palma, the capital, was the half-way port for the western Mediterranean.   Peter IV endeavoured to add to them a really subject Sardinia, but though, in alliance with Venice, he defeated the Genoese, revolt always simmered in the island which he was never able to subdue.   The same Mediter-

Sicily ranean ambitions made him claim the throne of Sicily as male heir on the death of his kinsman Frederick III in 1377 ; here, while taking the title of king, he was obliged to be content with the acceptance of his son Martin as regent for the little queen, Maria, who was betrothed to his grandson Martin I of Sicily.   Peter did succeed, however, in obtain-

Athens ing the Catalan duchy of Athens and in appointing a governor. It was a sign of the times that the literary king, himself a chronicler, rejoiced in the possession of the Acropolis, " the most precious jewel that exists in the world."   The Renaissance had begun.

Although they gave political support to Catalan commerce, these gains were shadowy enough.   The dynastic wars with Castile, which will be told among the events of that kingdom, brought no profit.   Peter IV's real achievement,

War with like that of James the Just, was the reassertion of mon-
the archical authority in Aragon and Valencia.   Trouble began
" Union " in 1346 owing to a project of the king.   He had then no son by his first queen Maria of Navarre, he was at enmity with his brother James of Urgell, and he proposed to abrogate the existing law of Aragon, which did not admit a female sovereign, by making his daughter Constance heir to the crown.   This caused violent discontent : the king's brothers protested, the " Union " of Aragon was revived by nobles and towns alike in Aragon, and a like " Union " arose in Valencia in alliance with it.   At the Cortes of Saragossa (1347) Peter was forced to confirm the *Privilegio General* of Alfonso III and dismiss his Catalan councillors.   When he was safe in Catalonia, always on good terms with the dynasty,

the death of James caused an outburst of revolt. The royal troops were defeated in Valencia, and Peter himself surrounded in Murviedro. He now confirmed the Union of Valencia (1348) and gave a similar *Privilegio* to that of Aragon. For two months he was detained and humiliated. Then the outbreak of the Black Death gained him permission to retire to Catalonia. By this time, however, a royalist reaction had set in : Peter had, too, gained the alliance of Castile, usually his enemy. On July 21, 1348, he won the decisive battle of Epila over the Aragonese Union, capturing his other brother Ferdinand in the victory. The rebellion Victory of in Aragon collapsed after this defeat, executions were the Peter IV order of the day, and the furious king lacerated Alfonso's Privilege with his dagger when he annulled it. He was known henceforward as " Peter of the Poniard." Valencia's reduction followed. The capital city was besieged and compelled to unconditional surrender. The Valencian Union and *Privilegio* were abolished like those of Aragon, while punishments of horrible cruelty were inflicted on the chief rebels. The movement had been partly feudal, partly in defence of an oligarchical free government, and partly due to jealousy of Catalonia and distrust of the arbitrary and treacherous Catalan king. Yet Peter represented unity, order, and efficiency. If he crushed the great nobles, he maintained the older liberties ; the Justicia functioned as before, the Cortes retained their powers. In each State a commission of the last Cortes, the Diputación General, existed till the next Cortes met, with the duty of watching over the observance of the laws, the administration, and the finances ; that of Catalonia, the Generalitat, performed also some of the functions of the Aragonese Justicia. In fact, even under Peter of the Poniard the standard of individual freedom and of popular participation in the government was higher than elsewhere in Europe. " Our peoples are our good vassals and companions," said Alfonso the Kindly to his Castilian queen.

The cunning and cruel king did not find a better end Death of than he deserved. When he married his fourth wife, Sibilla Peter IV de Fortia, he turned against his elder son, John Duke of Gerona, born to him by his third wife, Leonora of Sicily. Deprived of his rightful office of lieutenant-general of the king, the duke appealed to the law and revolted. In the midst of the struggle Peter the Ceremonious died, deserted by all, at Barcelona. But he left to John I a flourishing realm with free institutions. Barcelona, the Catalan capital, was a maritime republic, and the Book of the *Consolat de Mar*, originating there, was generally adopted as a mercantile code by the shippers and traders of the Mediterranean.

Castile

In marked contrast to the law-loving and politically minded members of the Aragonese federation stands the wide and dislocated kingdom of Castile. Here the provinces, Old and New Castile, Leon, Galicia, Asturias, Biscay, and Andalusia, were far too unlike to act together, yet not self-contained enough to possess internal unity. Separated for the most part by natural barriers, by divergences of climate, soil, and configuration, they were yet fatally interconnected by their gradual conquest from the northern mountains. The ancient division between Leon and Castile ceased to have constitutional importance : the first united Cortes were held in 1250, and the separate Cortes ceased to be assembled in the fourteenth century. Besides the natural impatience of control and sectional particularism of the Spaniards, the chief causes of the anarchy of Castile were the over-mighty baronage and the over-mighty Church, both of which were fostered by the long wars of the Reconquest, with their prodigal grants of land, independent frontier fighting, and piecemeal resettlement. The great nobles were the *ricos hombres*, who possessed enormous estates and privileges. While the Lara were over-powerful in one province, Biscay, with its separate race and language, most of them, like the Haro, owned lands spread from north to south ; in the thirteenth century the establishment of primogeniture concentrated and maintained their power : they were thus less dangerous for unity but the more potent for general disorder. Below the *ricos hombres* were the fighting lesser nobles, the *hidalgos*, who followed in their train or fought for their own hand, the very material for anarchy. The right of private war and of disavowal of their allegiance gave their turbulence a kind of legality. The power of the nobles was further enhanced by the great military Orders, Santiago, Calatrava, and Alcántara, to which they furnished knights, who were not bound to celibacy; the Grand Masters of the Orders controlled widespread estates and a host of warriors. The Church, too, possessed enormous endowments throughout Castile. The great bishops and abbots had all the privileges and turbulence of secular nobles in addition to their ecclesiastical exemptions and revenues.

The towns and free peasants were less of a bulwark to the monarchy than might have been expected. Many of them were subject to great noble or prelate. The royal towns were more intent on their peculiar local privileges and customs, their *fueros*, than the general interests of the kingdom. It was characteristic that their main contribution to order was the formation of provincial leagues, the *hermandades* (brotherhoods), which did much to quell brigandage and to organize self-defence, but which replaced rather than helped the action of the king.

Thus no concerted, persistent action was taken either to support or to limit the royal authority. The Cortes were summoned by the king, who in law had free choice in determining their composition—there was no right to be summoned which was possessed by any individual magnate or city. Additional taxation beyond the customary revenue required their grant, or rather that of the town representatives, for nobles and clergy were exempt. Their power was great when assembled. Their complaints might occasion remedial laws. But they were neither efficiently organized nor united by common interest. *The Powers of the Cortes*

A further element of disunion was the existence of large numbers of alien races in the kingdom. The Moorish population of peasants and townsmen in Andalusia was still considerable. The Jews also were numerous and wealthy. Both Moors and Jews were segregated from the Christians in communities of their own. Treated with tolerance in the thirteenth century, they became subject to ever-increasing hostility and persecution early in the fourteenth. In any case they increased the radical incohesion of the Spanish peoples. *Moors and Jews*

One expression of the essential disunity of Castile was the diversity of the law. The traditional general law of the kingdom was the mainly Germanic *Fuero Juzgo*, which was revised and brought up to date in the *Fuero Real* of the *Castilian Law* learned Alfonso X in 1254. But side by side with the *Fuero Real* subsisted the numerous competing *fueros* of region, class, or town, which had the greater validity if they disagreed with it. When Alfonso X issued his codification of *Las Siete Partidas* in 1264, he introduced a valuable and ever more influential instrument of legal education, which steadily Romanized the conceptions of the lawyers, but which was not the valid law of the land. It was a leaven not an enforceable code. The actual laws of Castile were collections of local usages, clung to all the more because they were local and particularist.

The Monarchy

The Castilian monarchy, therefore, was weak save in prestige. Its legislative and administrative authority had few legal limits, but to enforce obedience the means at its disposal were insufficient. The instinct of personal independence and local self-will was too strong. It could not appeal to any national solidarity or political organization ; it was faced by over-mighty subjects and regional insubordination. To its difficulties may be added the mediocre statesmanship of its kings and political misadventures, minorities and civil wars, which crippled it.

Sancho IV

The difficulties of Sancho IV (1284–95), though largely of his own making in pursuit of his ambitions, were partly due to others. His alliance with France against Alfonso III of Aragon in 1287 caused the latter to free and support the Infantes de la Cerda, whom he had hitherto held in captivity when they took refuge with him. Alfonso, the younger de la Cerda, was proclaimed anti-king. Thus frontier war with Aragon was added to internal wars with the great houses of Haro and Lara and with Sancho's rebellious brother Don John. But there was also the Moorish danger. The storm-centre was always the coast at the Straits of Gibraltar, where crossings could be made between Africa and Europe. The Sultan of Morocco of the dynasty of the Banu Marīn had possessed himself of the coast town of Tarifa in Alfonso X's time. In 1292 Sancho captured Tarifa in alliance with Mohammed II of Granada and James II of Aragon. In 1304, however, when his son Ferdinand IV made a final peace with Aragon and the dispossessed Infantes de la Cerda, the two Christian kings made a great effort to subdue Granada, then under Mohammed III. But Granada was too strong

among its mountains and was now aided by Morocco. Both
James and Ferdinand failed in their attack.

Ferdinand IV, who began his reign as a minor amid Ferdinand
warring factions, died in 1312 leaving his son Alfonso XI IV and
an infant one year old. For twenty years Castile was a Alfonso XI
prey to the great nobles and rival princes, while Granada
won victories in the south. Such order as was kept was
due to the armed self-help of the Hermandad of Castilian
towns. When Alfonso XI came of age at fourteen, however, he showed a capacity to rule unseen in his immediate
predecessors. He painfully curbed the greedy princes and
turbulent nobility, resuming the possession of lost royal
estates. The Moorish wars with Granada and Morocco,
sometimes smouldering, sometimes in flame, continued to be
the chief preoccupation in foreign policy. Yet the ground
gained or lost was but small, though the danger from the
Banu Marīn of Morocco increased : Gibraltar fell to them in
1333. At last Ali of Morocco and Yūsuf of Granada made
a great joint effort. In 1340 they laid siege to Tarifa. On
October 30 Alfonso fought the battle of the River Salado to
relieve the town and won a decisive victory, which freed
Spain from African invasion. The Castilians were now aided
by Aragon and by volunteers from all Christendom who
were attracted by the fame of Alfonso. In 1344 he captured Algeciras, and he was besieging Gibraltar in 1350 when
he fell a victim to the Black Death. Although Gibraltar
remained untaken, the Moorish war had become a domestic
concern of Spain.

Alfonso's reign was important for Spanish institutions as Alfonso XI's
well as for war. The monarchy began to limit the autonomy Innovations
of the towns by the appointment of a royal officer in each,
the *corregidor*. Its resources, too, were increased by the
grant of a new tax, which became permanent, in 1342 during
the siege of Algeciras. This was the *alcabala*, a tax on all
sales, which was profitable to the Crown, but a perpetual
drag on the economic prosperity of the country. The
greatest advance, however, was in the law. The *Siete Partidas* had been steadily gaining ground among the lawyers,
and Alfonso was able in 1348 to issue the *Ordenamiento de
Alcalá*. By this enactment the *Partidas* were at length
made valid law, when they did not conflict with the *Fuero*

Real, the *fueros* of the towns, or the privileges of the nobles.
The limitations are significant of the dominance of regional
and class forces which moulded Spanish life.   But, even so,
the *Ordenamiento de Alcalá* made for unity and made for
progress.

The advance might have been greater had it not been
for the dynastic accidents which beset Castile.   Alfonso XI
had long neglected his second wife, Maria of Portugal, in
favour of Leonora de Guzman, by whom he had seven sons.
These were given wide lands : the eldest, Henry, was Count
of Trastamara and the second, Frederick, was Grand Master
of Santiago.   On Alfonso XI's death his only legitimate son,
Peter the Cruel, born of his first queen, succeeded.   He was
only seventeen and under the influence of his stepmother
and the Portuguese noble, Albuquerque.   Leonora de Guzman was promptly imprisoned and in a short time murdered
by the queen dowager.   Meantime, the anarchy and oppressions of the Castilian nobles and prelates revived, and Peter,
in his reprisals for turbulence and rebellion, was already
showing the ferocious cruelty and frantic violence, only too
characteristic of his time and country ; yet in him they were
marked enough to earn him his surname.   Unbalanced,
treacherous, and furious, he possessed none of the political
talent or moderation of his fierce contemporary, Peter the
Ceremonious.   He preferred murders to executions.   Garci-
laso de la Vega, governor of Castile, revolted at Burgos :
he was struck down in the royal palace.   Peter's bastard
brothers were soon in insurrection, and Henry of Trastamara fled to Aragon.   To strengthen the king, Albuquerque
arranged in 1353 his marriage with Blanche of Bourbon, a
grand-daughter of St. Louis ; but just at the time Peter
was engaged in a passionate *liaison* with Maria de Padilla :
he went through the ceremony of marriage with Blanche,
and then deserted her for Maria and imprisoned her.   This
soon led to Albuquerque being in revolt along with the queen
dowager, Henry of Trastamara, and his brother Frederick.
They treacherously captured King Peter at Toro, but he
escaped, defeated them, and wreaked a bloody vengeance.
Shortly afterwards in 1355 he fell out with Peter the Ceremonious of Aragon, and thus began an intermittent war
that lasted to 1361.   In the tangled revolts, repressions, and

Peter the
Cruel

appeasements of these years, it seems that Peter the Cruel
stood for good government against the turbulent nobles, but
his weapon was assassination : one victim was his bastard
brother Frederick, another Abū Saīd, the exiled King of
Granada, whom he himself murdered when he came as a
suppliant. Even legal executions were conducted with the
inhuman cruelty of the old law. When Queen Blanche died
in prison, he declared he had been married earlier to Maria
de Padilla, and had her son Alfonso recognized as his heir.

At last, in 1363, after the young Alfonso's death, Trasta- Revolt of
mara exchanged the rôle of mere rebel for that of pretender Henry of
to the throne, in alliance with Peter the Ceremonious, then Trastamara
once more in unsuccessful war with Castile. A new element
was imported into these endless, indecisive broils by the allies
hiring the Free Companies who were devastating France [1] to
enter Castile under the famous Bertrand du Guesclin. With
their aid Trastamara invaded Castile and was crowned as
Henry I in April 1366. But Peter the Cruel escaped to
Gascony and obtained the aid of the Black Prince. The
latter, with his veterans, proved too formidable for du
Guesclin and his troopers and for the Spanish light horse,
the jenneteers, at the battle of Nájera in 1367. Du Guesclin
was taken prisoner, fortunately for him by the Black Prince,
and Trastamara fled to Aragon. But Peter the Cruel did
not change his evil nature with his re-enthronement. He
began an orgy of executions of his disloyal subjects ; he,
too, largely no doubt from inability, but quite in keeping
with his character, performed none of his promises of money
or lands to the Black Prince. It was not long before Edward,
disgusted with his savage ally, and himself infected with a
mortal disease, led his starving, unpaid army back over the
Pyrenees. This left Peter open to new attack. Henry once
more entered Castile, supported by du Guesclin, who had
been ransomed, while Peter was forced to rely on the aid
of Mohammed V of Granada against Castile in revolt. On
March 14, 1369, du Guesclin routed the Moors on the plain
of Montiel. Peter escaped. From the castle of Montiel,
where he was besieged, he attempted to suborn du Guesclin,
but by the latter he was enticed out to his tent. There he Death of
was surrounded and Trastamara appeared. The two brothers Peter

[1] See above, Chap. XIV, pp. 290, 293.

grappled, and rolled on the ground, Peter uppermost, but a bystander intervened and enabled Henry to gain the advantage and stab his brother to death. In this furious scene not only Peter the Cruel but the monarchy of Castile received defeat, for Peter in his brutal way had been carrying on the contest of the Crown with the anarchic nobles, which in some form or another engaged most lands of Europe in the fourteenth and fifteenth centuries.

Henry II Henry II (1369–79), a bastard and usurper, occupied a shaking throne. He did not keep his engagements to Peter IV of Aragon and thus began a new war which only ended in 1375 when his heir John married Peter's daughter Leonora, a marriage which eventually brought her son Ferdinand to the throne of Aragon. But further, Ferdinand the King of Portugal claimed the crown of Castile, for his grandmother was a daughter of Sancho IV. So there was a war on that side, too, though Ferdinand made no progress. The Kings of Navarre and Granada joined in the fray. A new pretender appeared when the two daughters of Peter the Cruel by Maria de Padilla married two of the sons of Edward III of England, and John of Gaunt, the husband of the elder, Constance, took the title of King of Castile. But in this war Henry II had the best : his fleet defeated the English off La Rochelle. The danger was not removed, however, till after Henry's death when Gaunt's heiress married the heir of Castile.

To maintain himself, Henry II was obliged to court the nobles by prodigal grants of land and revenue, which impoverished the Crown, and gained him the title of *El de las Mercedes*, the generous. He flattered the Castilian passion for titles and honours by introducing from France the ranks of marquess and duke. Frequent sessions of the Cortes further restricted the independence of the monarchy, while they made the dynasty more secure. But at the end of the The Jews reign, the wealthiest trading class, the Jews, were already in decline : they had become hated by their Christian neighbours as alien enemies of the faith, and many of their alhamas or ghettos, within which they were obliged to live, had been sacked by du Guesclin's free companies in the civil war. The great industry of the land, however, sheep-raising for the much-prized merino wool, was never more prosperous.

The Mesta, or association of sheep-owners small and great, The Mesta
organized in 1273 by Alfonso X, was in its business a little
republic.   To its members belonged the many thousands of
sheep which migrated between summer and winter pastures
in north and south Spain and formed a characteristic feature
of Castilian life.

During this period the history of Navarre was either Navarre
parochial or subordinate to its greater neighbours.   The
basis of its society was Spanish and Basque, overlaid by
French influences due to the dynasty which ruled it, the house
of Évreux.   After the separation from France in 1328, the
kingdom was ruled by Joanna II (*ob.* 1843) and then by
Charles II the Bad (1849–87), who were frequent absentees.
The central administration was organized on the model of
France, but the Cortes were definitely Spanish, as was the
law, a collection of local *fueros*, although Philip the Fair had
produced a *Fuero General* which did not gain acceptance.
Navarre was a barren and poor country.   The Church, less
well endowed, was weaker than that of Castile, but the
numerous nobles were as stiff-necked as the Castilians and
the serfs of the countryside were at least free from arbitrary
exactions, while in the Pyrenees free peasant communes
subsisted.

Like Navarre Portugal possessed a regional unity which Portugal
was denied to Castile, but unlike Navarre and the greater
part of Spain it was a fertile land with the softer, more
equable climate of the Atlantic coast.   It received the first
downfall of the Atlantic rain-clouds which made luxuriant
the alluvial soil brought by the great rivers which crossed
the peninsula.   The mouths of these rivers, too, provided at
Lisbon and Oporto magnificent ports for the fertile hinter-
land and for the coastwise shipping which moved to and fro
from the Mediterranean to Flanders and England.   King
Dinis the Husbandman (1279–1325) seems to have realized Dinis the
that, with the extension of Portugal to the south coast by Husband-
the annexation of Algarve and with the final establishment man
of the more powerful kingdom of Castile in the land between
Portugal and Granada, it was better to develop his rich
inheritance than to attempt vainly fresh conquests.   Only
in 1295 did he extort a small retrocession of land east of the
River Guadiana during Ferdinand IV's minority, to which

was added the town of Olivenza in 1297 as the dowry of
the Spanish infanta who married his heir. Thus Portugal
attained her full limits. Dinis earned his surname. He
drained swamps and encouraged the cultivation and settlement of waste land ; he planted the pine-forest of Leiria to
hold back the coast dunes and provide future timber ; he
fostered mining and fishing ; he called in Genoese sailors to
build better ships—his admiral was Emanuele Pezagna, a
Genoese noble. Under him Portuguese sailors made the
voyage to the English Channel. The king, in fact, whose
ambitions lay in peace, is an exceptional figure among the
great rulers of the Middle Ages. He made possible the prosperity and enterprise of his country in the fifteenth century.
Its intellectual life also derives from him. He was a poet
and under him the Portuguese dialect, akin to Galician, took
shape as a national, literary language. He founded the
national university of Coimbra, which among other benefits
provided him with trained lawyers for the administration.
After the concordat of 1289 he succeeded in maintaining
peace with the Church, while insisting on the prohibition of
any more land being added to its vast estates. When the
Order of the Knights Templars was abolished, he continued
the Portuguese knights in their possessions under the new
name of the Order of Christ (1319), the only equitable solution of the problem which was effected. Beside Edward I
of England, Philip the Fair, and James of Aragon, he takes
the least famous, but the most beneficent place.

Dinis, however, himself caused dissension in his later
years by his affection for his bastard son, Afonso Sanches,
which brought on him the enmity of his legitimate son
Afonso IV (1325–57). The new king was more aggressive
than his father. He engaged in an unsuccessful war with
Castile to champion his ill-used sister, the Queen Maria, wife
of Alfonso XI (1336–9). When this was over he played a
leading part in the battle of the River Salado in 1340 as
Castile's ally, when the last formidable invasion from Morocco
was repelled. He fell out with his own son Peter, whose
devotion to his mistress, Ignez de Castro, alarmed him into
ordering her murder. Peace was only restored by the banishment of the actual assassins. Yet Afonso was a worthy
successor to Dinis. He codified the traditional laws of

Afonso IV

Portugal. He even risked a serious conflict with the Church by taking into his own hands the city of Oporto, whose bishop was an absentee at Avignon. The ten years' reign of his son Peter I (1357–67) was reckoned as the halcyon Peter I time of the earlier Portuguese kingdom. He kept the peace with his neighbours. His justice was stern and cruel : he tortured to death two of the assassins of Ignez de Castro. Equal justice for all and the strict maintenance of order were needs more often felt than satisfied in medieval States : Portugal was given them by Peter. In the Cortes of Elvas (1361) he terminated the conflict of jurisdiction between Church and State to the monarchy's advantage. The pre-lates complained of royal infractions of their franchises, and were answered by their confirmation so long as they were not contrary to the royal prerogative. But the rights of the towns were preserved, the administration was reformed, and a royal treasure was put by from the abundant revenue. To this prosperity Peter's son Ferdinand I the Handsome Ferdinand I (1367–83) brought decline. He was by nature spendthrift and inconstant, and to the misfortune of his kingdom had through his grandmother Queen Beatrice good claims to the throne of Castile on the death of Peter the Cruel. But his invasion of Castile was beaten back and retaliated. In 1371 peace was restored with the condition that Ferdinand should marry Henry of Trastamara's daughter Leonora. The fickle king immediately broke his word by marrying his mistress, Leonora Telles, who was already married. This provoked a Castilian invasion in 1372, which captured Lisbon, while Ferdinand's ally, John of Gaunt, the English pretender to Castile, never came to his aid. A humiliating peace in 1373 was the result. Ferdinand refortified Lisbon, and Henry of Trastamara's death in 1380 renewed the English alliance and the war. But the Earl of Cambridge (the later Duke of York), who brought an English army, effected little, and the Castilian fleet was victorious at sea and besieged Lisbon once more. Ferdinand changed sides again thereat. Shortly before his death his only child Beatrice was married accord-ing to a new treaty of peace to John I of Castile. She was to reign over Portugal under the regency of her mother, the hated Leonora Telles, who was suspected of adultery, and had incited one of the king's half-brothers, John, son of

Ignez de Castro, to murder his wife, her own sister. Amid
these horrors and with the profoundly unpopular subjection
to Castile in prospect, the reign closed. Yet Ferdinand's
government had its brighter side. Laws encouraged agriculture and shipbuilding. Lisbon was a wealthy port, and
Portugal, which imported most manufactures, produced wine
to exchange for them.

The
Monarchy
and the
Cortes

The government was of the Castilian type with far more
stress laid on the royal power and far less independence of
the great nobles and towns. Ferdinand could claim to be
absolute. Appellate justice had been acknowledged to be
the king's inalienable right since Dinis. The king made the
laws by his own authority, even if in answer to petitions of
the Cortes. The latter again resembled those of Castile in
their ill-defined composition and privileges and the lack of
cohesion between their three houses, although this was partially remedied by the joint committees called the *Diffinitors*.
They did, however, control the grant of taxation apart from
the ancient revenues of the Crown. In 1372 they refused a
general excise to Ferdinand I. But they had little of the
Spanish instinct of self-help. The Portuguese normally
looked to the king for remedial justice. It was when their
separate independence was threatened that their Iberian
particularism developed into a fervent national patriotism.

Granada

In essential prosperity the little Moorish kingdom of
Granada under the Nasrid dynasty excelled the rest of the
peninsula. Although in the recurrent wars with the Christians it lost a fringe of territory to Castile, the kernel of the
State remained intact, and the kings adroitly manœuvred
between their alternate enemy and suzerain to the north, the
Banu-Marīn of Morocco, and the kings of Aragon. Doubtless they were favoured by the disorders of Castile, but they
governed well. Their territory was populated by exiles from
Andalusia, whose industry made the plain of the Xenil a
garden. They fortified their capital and built their beautiful
palace of the Alhambra. Mohammed II (1273–1302) was
perhaps the most skilful in playing off Morocco against
Castile and in aiding Sancho against his father Alfonso X.
Mohammed III (1302–9) and his immediate successor survived the attack of Castile and Aragon with Moroccan help.
But after Yūsuf Abū-l-Hajjāj (1333–54) shared in the defeat

of the River Salado in 1340, effective aid from Morocco ceased. It was fitting that this literary and humane ruler, who protected non-combatants in his wars and established village schools, should make the last additions to the fabric of the Alhambra. Of his successors, Mohammed V (1354–9, 1362–91) was the faithful vassal of Peter the Cruel and the rebel of Henry of Trastamara. Granada's safety lay in the weakness of Castile and the wars of the Christian States among themselves.

SUGGESTIONS FOR READING ON CHAPTER XVII

Froissart's *Chronicle* contains notices of some Spanish events. The suggestions for Chapter VIII apply to this chapter also. To them may be added the *Cambridge Medieval History*, vol. vii, relevant chapters ; Storer, E., *Peter the Cruel*, Baltimore, 1910 ; and Daumet, G., *Étude sur l'alliance de la France et de la Castille au XIV⁰ et au XV⁰ siècles*, Paris, 1898; Glotz, G.. *Histoire générale, Histoire du Moyen Âge*, vol. vi.

CHAPTER XVIII

NORTH AND EAST EUROPE IN THE FOURTEENTH CENTURY

Scandinavia. General Tendencies

THE main fact of Scandinavian history in the fourteenth century is the predominance of the feudal tendency. As this power and insubordination of the landed nobility who possessed the chief fighting forces were later in Scandinavia than elsewhere in Europe, they showed somewhat different characteristics from the feudalism strictly so called as it had appeared earlier in the west. For one thing, except in Denmark, the vassal lords did not acquire the delegated public jurisdiction over their fiefs : they were powerful landlords of serf peasants. Again, except in the Danish duchy of South Jutland or Schleswig, fiefs never became legally hereditary ; heredity was confined to the ancestral estates only. Further, the practice of co-operation in national affairs was far too advanced at home and abroad for the great noble to rule isolated in his estates. In the struggle with the kings the nobles limited them by charters and assemblies and endeavoured to set up an oligarchic control by their own class. The kings on the other hand profited by the advance of civilization and the economic development of Europe to borrow money for their schemes and to pledge revenues in a tangle of alliances. An economic federation, the trading German Hanse towns, appears as a political power of the first magnitude.

Denmark

Denmark remained the most developed and populous of the Scandinavian kingdoms. King Eric VI Menved (1286–1319) spent his life in a vain attempt to defend the power of the monarchy against the nobles. In his reign the long contest with the Church over its immunities was won by the Archbishop of Lund, Jens Grand (1289–1302). The king was allowed to collect the *leidang* from the Church lands, but the Church retained its immunities and its dominion over its serfs. As the prelates were nobles by birth and their immunities akin to feudal disintegration, this was a quasi-feudal victory. But the nobles scored direct victories as well. Eric VI had succeeded as a child under the regency of his mother after the murder of his father Eric V, who had already been defeated by the Church and the nobles. When the nobles who had contrived the murder were driven into exile by the queen-mother, they allied with their sympathizing fellow nobles of Norway and began a war. A truce in 1295 restored them to their estates. King Eric, however, actively fought his losing battle, both at war and at peace with his neighbours of Norway and Sweden. But he was too ambitious : he prosecuted schemes of dominion over the south coast of the Baltic, over Mecklenburg and Pomerania, and exhausted his resources. He was compelled to admit the feudal autonomy of his kinsman, the Duke of Schleswig, and to pawn large domains, including the island of Fünen to the German Counts of Holstein, who assumed an ominous importance in Danish politics. Among his feudal foes was his brother Christopher—the disloyalty of the appanaged princes of the royal house was a chief cause of the weakness of the monarchy—and when he died childless, the rebel was elected king on the terms his noble allies dictated. Christopher II swore, the first Danish king to do so, to an election capitulation (1320). By this the king was made subordinate to the annual Parliament of nobles and prelates. He could not levy taxes, make laws, or declare war or peace without their consent. An appeal lay from his tribunal to the Parliament. The nobles could fine their peasants. Only three royal castles in Jutland were to be left standing, and the king was not to appoint Germans, whom he favoured, to his council. When Christopher tried to levy a tax, civil war broke out, which ended in his being driven out. Gerhard, a Count of Holstein, led the malcontents and was elected regent, while a Danish prince, his young nephew Waldemar (III), Duke of Schleswig, was elected king (1326–30). Gerhard himself took Schleswig. Christopher II was indeed recalled in 1330, but only to new contests. When he died in 1332, he had lost the entire royal demesne. There was now no king for eight years, while Gerhard ruled most of Denmark until in 1340 he was murdered, having by then incurred the hatred of nobles and people by his exactions.

Limitation of the Monarchy

This murder permitted the recall of the surviving son of Christopher from Germany, Waldemar III (1340–75). The new king had great qualities of statesmanship and persistence. His surname of Atterdag was drawn from his use of the hopeful phrase, " To-morrow is a new day." He restored by slow degrees the domain and power of the kingship. The Church, by now weary of the continual anarchy, was his ally, and he began his reign with the acquisition from the Bishop of Sealand of the town of Copenhagen on the Sound, which thus became for the first time the capital of Denmark. By the mediation of the Emperor Lewis IV he came to an agreement with his worst rivals. He married the sister of the other Waldemar, ex-king and Duke of Schleswig, who brought a dowry of land in Jutland, while he effected an exchange which gave Schleswig to the Counts of Holstein in return for Jutland proper. He raised money by sales of territory : Scania was ceded to Magnus of Sweden, who already possessed it, Esthonia, unprofitable and distant, to the Teutonic Order. Thus he was able to buy back lost land, the islands of Sealand and Fünen from the Counts of Holstein (1348), and, when the Black Death rendered land cheap, other portions of the royal domain. His taxes and power led to revolts of the nobles and the still mighty Counts of Holstein, but he kept the upper hand. At last, in 1360, he was able to hold a general Parliament which came to an agreement with him. The powers of the Parliament and the feudal structure of Denmark remained, but the king had recovered power and resources and the backing of his people. Renewed expansion could now be undertaken. Waldemar reconquered Scania from Sweden and in 1361 reduced the island of Gotland with the town of Wisby, the half-way port of the Baltic trade. By this time he was embroiled,

owing to his levy of customs duties in the Sound, with the great Hansa League of North German trading cities,[1] but he defeated both the Hansa and their allies, Sweden, Norway, and the Counts of Holstein. The peace of 1365 left him in possession of his gains, and he married his younger daughter Margaret to Hakon VI of Norway. The Hansa, however, were as resolute as he, and their trading prosperity was at stake. In 1367 they allied with Albert, Duke of Mecklen-

---

[1] See above, Chap. IX, pp. 186–87.

burg, whose son Albert had driven Magnus from the throne
of Sweden. Only Norway was on Waldemar's side. This
war the Hansa won. Waldemar went in vain to Germany
for allies; the Counts of Holstein and the disloyal nobles
of Jutland sided against him. In his absence Copenhagen
and Helsingborg in Scania were captured; Hakon VI made
peace. In 1370 the Danish Council made terms, confirmed
later by Waldemar himself, at the peace of Stralsund. By
this the commercial demands of the Hansa for freedom of
trade were fully conceded. The chief places in Scania and
two-thirds of its revenues were given up to them for sixteen
years. Worst of all, no new king of Denmark could be
elected without the Hansa's consent. Waldemar died in
1375 still shackled by his defeat. He had, after all, restored
the monarchy from the lowest depths. With the election
of his grandson Olaf, the son of Hakon VI of Norway, as
King of Denmark, by the successful diplomacy and under
the regency of a woman of genius, Margaret, the Queen of
Norway, a new era began for Denmark and the other Scandinavian kingdoms, that of the Union of Kalmar.

In the contemporary history of Norway, the same ele- Norway
ments, the Church, the feudalizing nobles, and the German
Hansa, play their parts with less complete victories and
reverses. Eric II the Priesthater (1280–99), who came to
a compromise with the prelates, challenged the growing power
of the Hansa towns, whose trading privileges he restricted.
The towns proceeded to a commercial blockade, which brought
the king to reason. Sweden arbitrated in 1285, and in 1294
the treaty of Tönsberg embodied a settlement which
granted the Hansa's demands. As a result, the Hansa in
the next reigns was able from its Norwegian headquarters
at Bergen to monopolize the cod-fisheries and trade of Norway. Eric's brother Hakon V, who lived at peace with the
Church and had its support, made a vain effort in 1308 to
put back the clock with regard to the unruly lay nobles.
He resumed all fiefs and abolished feudal powers. But this
edict demanded different conditions than obtained in Norway
and a stronger character than the king's. It was quite
fruitless. He had better fortune in his scheme for the succession to the crown. Although he could not induce the
Norwegians to give it to his daughter Ingeborg, yet her son

by Duke Eric of Sweden, Magnus II Smek (1319–63), was
elected king at his death, perhaps because he was an infant,
for the nobles were in full control.

Sweden   Sweden, after the death of Magnus Barnlock, was ruled
by the Marshal Torgils Knutsson, both before and after his
son Birger (1290–1318) came of age. East Finland was
added to the kingdom. But the old egotism reappeared.
The king's brothers, of whom the leading spirit was Duke
Eric, popular and unprincipled, persuaded him to compass
Torgils' death (1305), and then attacked him in wars in
which Denmark and Norway took part, and Birger lost most
of Sweden. Then with the treachery which characterized
these struggles Birger in 1317 captured and put to death
his brothers. But Eric's son was heir to Norway, and with
Norwegian help the Swedish nobles drove Birger into exile.
The infant Magnus II Smek (1319–63) was elected King of
Sweden.

Domination   There now began in both kingdoms a period of the un-
of the Nobles checked rule of the great nobles. Magnus Smek, when he
came of age, showed a keen perception of the national needs
of Sweden. He carried through in 1347 a codification of the
law for the whole country, which, besides improvement in
the substance of law, did much to merge the isolated provinces in one State. One code applied to the countryside,
another to the towns. But also the Crown was effectually
fettered by the Council of nobles. Magnus, too, saw that
the Danish province of Scania, with its fisheries, was by
geographical position a necessary complement to Sweden,
which could give his kingdom a western portal. In 1333 he
was called in by the Scanians then in revolt against the
Count of Holstein. To avoid a war, he made the mistake
of buying the territory for 34,000 silver marks. This overstrained the small resources of the Swedish monarchy : the
rest of his reign was crippled by financial embarrassment.
He sold and mortgaged the royal demesne, and became
heavily in debt to his own nobles. Troubles thickened as
his sons grew up and the separatism of Norway and Sweden
reasserted itself. His younger son, Hakon VI (1343–80),
was elected King of Norway, although Magnus himself remained regent till he was of age. The elder son Eric was
elected heir to Sweden. Scania remained a centre of dis-

turbance : Waldemar of Denmark desired it, the Swedish
nobles resented their king's preoccupation with its retention
and the taxes that followed therefrom. Unfortunately for
Magnus, a saint arose in Sweden, St. Bridget (Birgetta), who
used all her influence on the side of the nobles, to vilify the
king. The young Eric ended by being jealous of his father's
chief counsellor, Duke Bengt Algotsson, and raised revolt
with the aid of Waldemar and Duke Albert of Mecklenburg,
the king's treacherous and intriguing brother-in-law. The
revolt was meeting with great success when Eric died in
1359 of a recrudescence of the Black Death. Waldemar now
made war (1360) on his own account and conquered Scania
and Gotland. Magnus helplessly accepted the situation, while
his nobles, egged on by Duke Albert, to whom the fishery
revenue of Scania had been granted, turned against him.
In 1363 they elected Duke Albert's younger son, Albert, as
their king. Magnus himself was captured in 1365 in a
defeat. When his son Hakon VI obtained his release in
1371, he retired to Norway.

The reign of Albert of Mecklenburg marked the nadir
of the royal power. Threatened by Hakon VI, unpopular
because of his German following, he was obliged to agree
to the transfer of the government to the Council of nobles,
which co-opted its members. The chief authority was wielded
by the Steward, Bo Jonsson, who possessed half the kingdom including all Finland. But a new power was rising in
Margaret, Queen of Norway. Her son Olaf, already King
of Denmark, succeeded to Norway under her regency in
1380. When Bo Jonsson died in 1386, Albert fell out with
his nobles by endeavouring to appropriate his estates. They
appealed to Olaf, who died next year, and was replaced by
his formidable mother. It was not long before she overthrew Albert, and united the rule of all the Scandinavian
kingdoms. This " Union of Kalmar " had been foreshadowed
by the constant intermarriages and common class interests
of the nobles of the three kingdoms, and the progress in all
three towards a noble oligarchy. If feudal institutions and
serfdom were most developed in Denmark, they were also
present in a less advanced form in Norway and Sweden and
the peasants there were oppressed if not serfs. A class of
trading burghers could not really arise, for trade and the

fisheries for export had become a monopoly of the German Hansa.

Russia under the Tartar Yoke   While Scandinavia was following with delateb steps the evolution in organization and culture of Western Europe, the Russians under the " Tartar Yoke " were slowly developing on more original lines and expanding in an almost automatic fashion towards the north and east.   Their relations with the Tartars of the Golden Horde were those of humble vassals and tributaries.   The Great Prince of Vladímir, the senior prince of the house of Rurik, was appointed from among the lesser princes by the *yarlyk* or charter of the Khan of the Golden Horde, and to him was entrusted the levying of the annual tribute.   To obtain this *yarlyk* was a matter of intrigue and bribery.   Meanwhile, the principalities kept splitting up, as they were divided on the death of each prince among his sons.   But in the fourteenth century this fissiparous tendency was countered by the growing custom of petty princes becoming by treaty " younger brothers " of their greater kinsmen, thus in practice joining the ranks of the *boyars* or ordinary nobles.   The prince governed his principality by the council of his *boyars*, who ruled their lands in feudal independence.   Prince and *boyar* depended on their retainers for armed force.   The free peasants and the serfs were there to be ruled and taxed : they were the " black people."

The Russian Church   In this period the Church became both wholly Russian and independent.   Bishops and monasteries possessed vast estates : the Tartars treated them as a separate power who had influence with the unseen world.   The Metropolitan received his office by a *yarlyk* of the Khan.   Meantime the personnel of the clergy lost its Greek elements and leaders. Shortly after the metropolitan see was moved from ruined Kiev to Vladímir in the heart of Great Russia, the first Russian Metropolitan, St. Peter (1308–26), was chosen.   He fixed his residence in a minor town of his diocese, Moscow, and this location of the Metropolitan of the Russian Church perhaps more than anything else made Moscow the eventual capital of Russia.   For a long time the Metropolitans were more important than the Great Princes.   It was the monasteries, too, which were largely responsible for the colonization towards the north and east in the primeval forest.

Ascetic monks were the pioneers. Round their monasteries under great organizers grew the peasant settlements. Thus St. Sergius founded c. 1335 the Troitsa monastery north-east of Moscow. A new strength was coming to Russia by this overflow of men.

The secular importance of Moscow began with George (Yuri) (1304–24), the son of Daniel, the first prince of the town. Daniel had enlarged Muscovy by the acquisition of Pereyaslavl. George instigated in 1319 the execution by the Tartars of his rival, the Great Prince of Vladímir, Michael of Tver, his brother Ivan I Kalitá (John of the purse) (1324–41) obtained the *yarlyk* as Great Prince (1328) and the privilege of collecting the Tartar tribute. Ivan was a servile and astute vassal of the Golden Horde. With the wealth derived from his pickings from the tribute, backed on occasion by the Khan's armies, he bought up fresh lands and forced treaties of submission as " younger brothers " on other princes of the house of Rurik. At the same time he held fast to the alliance with the Church, offered him by the residence in his capital of the Metropolitan, in his day the Greek Theognostos (1328–53). Muscovy, with the Church's aid, became the centre of what unity there was in Russia.

The Rise of Moscow

When Ivan Kalitá divided his dominions among his sons, the new central power did not decay. Both Simeon (1341–53) and Ivan II (1353–9) were Great Princes of Vladímir by the Khan's appointment. Both the personal insignificance of Ivan II and the ten years' minority of his son Dimitri (1359–89) were more than supported by the great Metropolitan, St. Alexis (1354–78), who used his immense influence in favour of Muscovite supremacy. Although Dimitri, Prince of Suzdal, obtained the *yarlyk* as Great Prince on Ivan II's death, St. Alexis and the Muscovite *boyars* succeeded in procuring its revocation and the appointment of his protégé. Lithuania, indeed, was annexing parts of western and southern Russia, but the rival Princes of Tver and Ryazan became vassals of Moscow. Meanwhile the Golden Horde was fortunately breaking up. The Blue Horde of the west and the White Horde of the east separated. After 1359 there was a rapid succession and co-existence of Khans of rival families in the Blue Horde, which paralysed its action till the Vizier

Decline of the Golden Horde

Mamay became Khan in 1378 and imparted a temporary vigour. He resolved to punish the insubordinate Russians, but a first defeat at the hands of Dimitri at Pereyaslavl in 1378 was followed by a crushing overthrow on September 8, 1380, at Kulikovo on the River Don. The Great Prince, now really chief of the Russians, became known as Dimitri of the Don (Donskoi). Yet this victory of his was more important as a symptom of Russian growing strength and Tartar decline than as a decisive event. Within two years the Blue and White Hordes were reunited by Tuktamish, who captured Moscow in a terrible raid and reimposed the Tartar Yoke (1382). Russia was to wait many years for final deliverance.

Battle of the Don

Lithuania

While Russia to the east was a prey to disintegration and the Tartars, to the west it was dismembered by the heathen Lithuanians. After the death of the Great Prince Mindovg in 1263, Lithuania suffered an eclipse through internal dissensions, but the formidable warlike character of its people, barricaded against invasion by marsh and forest, remained unimpaired. On the defensive against the Teutonic Order to the north, the Lithuanians found an easy sphere of conquest to the east and south, where they appeared preferable to the Tartars. Black Russia, immediately to the south of Lithuania proper, was first absorbed. Polotsk and Vitebsk on the Dvina, in White Russia, were annexed under Viten (1293-1315). Prince Gedymin (1315-41) founded a new dynasty with its chief capital at Vilna. He occupied Podlasia, and by his victory on the River Irpen in 1320 became lord of Kiev, the ancient Russian capital, and its territory. The next step in expansion was offered by the destruction of the princes of Red Russia by the Tartars in 1324. A Polish prince, Boleslav of Mazovia, held the land till he was assassinated in 1340 for tyranny. Then Lubart, son of Gedymin, seized Volhynia while Casimir III of Poland took Galicia, the two main provinces. A war between Poland and Lithuania for the possession of the whole began. Lithuania, which was always a confederation of principalities rather than a single State, was hampered at first by civil war. When Olgierd (1345-77), a son of Gedymin, became Great Prince, Volhynia could be secured in 1352, and Lithuania further extended by the conquest of Podolia and the Ukraine from the Tartars. Meantime, Olgierd's brother Keystut fought the Teutonic Knights on the north. In spite of disunion among its princes Lithuania was a great power, when Olgierd was succeeded by his son Jagiello (1377–1434), whose adoption of Catholic Christianity ended its age-long heathenism and allowed the personal union of Lithuania with Poland. Even so, the Grand Principality contained two religions and two varieties of civilization, for the Russian majority remained Orthodox, the heirs of Kiev, while the dominant Lithuanians became Catholic, the pupils of Poland and the West. *Jagiello and Union with Poland*

The fourteenth century was the time of the greatest prosperity of the Teutonic Order. In 1310 it already possessed the south-east coast of the Baltic Sea—Prussia, Pomerella, a part of Samogitia, Semigallia, and Livonia. Into Prussia and Pomerella German immigrants, nobles and peasants, were pouring. But there were two strong and bitter foes, Poland and Lithuania; it was the latter that the Order coveted and dreaded most. The marshy interior of Prussia, never very populous, had become a wilderness in the last century's wars of extirpation. Thus the advance of the Order was partly dependent on colonization by means of fortified towns. Along the border raged a fierce guerrilla warfare with the Lithuanians, punctuated by wide-reaching raids which were campaigns. Prince Keystut (1342–82) led the Lithuanian defence, but the Great Prince Olgierd also took part. The Knights endeavoured to conquer both inland Samogitia up to the Niemen and thence Lithuania proper. They were aided by groups of crusaders from all countries, for to make the crusade in Prussia was a fashion: John of Bohemia, Lewis of Hungary, and Henry of Derby, later Henry IV of England, furnish instances among many. Under the Grand Master Winrich von Kniprode (1351–82) the Order reached the height of its power. In 1346 its territory had been rounded off to the north by the purchase of Esthonia from Denmark. With Lithuania he waged a never-ceasing war. Yet Samogitia was never really conquered: his greatest victory was won in 1370 at Rudau in the heart of Prussia. The year after he died Jagiello was converted and became King of Poland. The occupation of the Teutonic Order, the impulse of the crusade, was gone. *Teutonic Order*

Its Govern-
ment   In the meantime the Knights had done great things
for the expansion of Germany. The successful seizure of
Pomerella (1309) shut off Poland from the sea, and neither
repeated papal decisions in Poland's favour (1321, 1337)
nor wars (1326–43), in which Vladislav Lokietik won the
victory of Plowce (1331), took either that province or Kulm
from the Order's grasp. In 1343 at the final peace of
Kalisz, Casimir the Great was only able to keep the Knights
out of Kujavia and Dobrzyn on the south while he abandoned Pomerella. The Order's territory owed a vassalage
little more than nominal to both Pope and Emperor : in
practice it was a sovereign State under its Grand Master
and the annual Chapter of the Knights, who from the start
were military monks. Bound to send contingents in war,
but otherwise autonomous were the eight bishops headed by
the Archbishop of Riga. Prussia and Livonia were each
ruled by a Landmeister, and the German endowments of
the Order by the Deutschmeister. Prussia and Livonia were
subdivided into *Komtureien.* Under their sway were the
German German colonists. In Livonia these were mainly nobles
Colonization ruling over oppressed Lettish and Esthonian serfs, who in
1343–5 waged a fierce peasant war against them, and at odds
with the bishops from whom they held many of their fiefs.
They were able to hold Landtags from 1315 onwards, which
limited the power of both the bishops and the Knights. In
Prussia, besides the immigrant German nobles, there were
villages of free German peasants, who, led by contractors
(*locatores*), rented their land and were among the best off
of their class in the fourteenth century. Beside them were
the remnants of the natives held in serfdom. But the growth
of German privileged towns was not less. Some sixty were
founded between 1233 and 1416. They enjoyed internal
autonomy and mostly belonged to the Hansa League, in
whose ample commerce they shared. At the end of the
century Prussia was mainly Germanized. In this way, save
for later infiltrations of a minor character, the expansion of
Germany east of the Elbe, which had made its first tenta-
tive progress under Otto the Great and had come to its full
vigour in the twelfth century, reached a conclusion, which
was to affect profoundly the later history of Europe.

The advance of the Teutonic Order had been favoured

by the dislocated condition of the vast Slav country of Poland
Poland, divided into separate provinces under different
branches of the Piast dynasty, permeated in the west by
German settlers, and partially conquered by the half Slav,
half German King of Bohemia, Wenceslas III. It was the
death of Wenceslas and the extinction of his dynasty in
1306 which gave at last an opportunity for a Piast prince
to reunite Poland. This was Vladislav (Władysław) the Vladislav I
Dwarf (Lokietik) of Kujavia, who during the Bohemian Lokietik
ascendancy was already a claimant of the Great Princedom.
He now obtained recognition from Lesser Poland in the
south as well as Kujavia. In 1307, on the death of the
Silesian Piast, Henry of Glogau, Greater Poland in the centre
followed suit. But besides the hostility of the Piasts of
Mazovia to the east, Vladislav had to meet three formidable
foes, the German settlers in alliance with the Piasts of Silesia,
the Teutonic Order, and the new King of Bohemia, John
of Luxemburg. In 1310 the Germans of Posen, in 1311 those
of Lesser Poland, rose on behalf of the Silesian Piasts, and
were subdued by Vladislav, now supported more and more
by the revived national patriotism of Poland. Meantime he
made his worst mistake by calling in the Teutonic Knights
to assist him in making good his claims to Pomerella. They
came, massacred the Polish garrison of Danzig and seized
the land in permanency. To regain it and defend himself
against John of Bohemia, Vladislav sought allies : he married his daughter to Charles Robert of Hungary and his son
Casimir to the daughter of Gedymin of Lithuania. With
the approval of Pope John XXII, who sided with him, he
renewed the kingship in Poland in 1320 by his coronation
at Cracow. But this was followed by the bitter war (1323–33)
in which Vladislav with his two allies fought the Knights,
Bohemia, and the hostile Piasts of Silesia and Mazovia. He
had lost Kujavia when he died at the age of seventy-three.

Distinguished as Vladislav I had been for his magnificent Casimir III
persistence and patriotism, his son Casimir III the Great the Great
(1333–70) was a shrewder statesman, who resolved on peace
with the Knights and John, so as to unite Poland and expand
towards the less formidable east. By the Peace of Višehrad
(1335) he surrendered the suzerainty of Silesia to John, a
loss never retrieved, as well as Plock in Mazovia. Eight years

after at Kalisz he resigned himself to the loss of Pomerella. But, after a long Lithuanian war, he secured possession of Galicia to the south-east (1340–52). At the second treaty of Višehrad (1339) and that of Buda (1355) he cemented the alliance with Hungary by the choice of his successor. He had no son and his sister was married to Charles Robert of Hungary. Their son Lewis was made heir to Poland and a new great power created for the future. But the terms began the decline of monarchical power in Poland. Lewis was to regain Pomerella, govern only through Poles, and raise no fresh taxes. In every other way, however, Casimir worked for the union and central government of Poland. Fortunately, the old tribal provinces had been already broken up among the branches of the Piasts, but the older officials, the *voivodes*, were great local nobles. Now Casimir put in new royal officers, the *starostas*, corresponding to the French *baillis*, who ruled the *woyewodztwa* and the royal demesne, much increased by reclamations, therein. The *voivodes* found compensation for their lost functions by heading the local assembly or *Wiec* of their sub-province, which as yet was the only parliamentary creation of Poland. The sole common power connecting these local institutions was the person of the king, and even he was only suzerain, not ruler, of the great province of Mazovia, but his officials in Lesser Poland at the capital of Cracow, the Chancellor, Vice-Chancellor, and Treasurer, took on the functions of a central administration. His greatest service to national unity and civilization, however, was the issue of Poland's first written code of laws. The Statute of Wislica, which codified and harmonized the customary provincial laws and the king's decrees, was promulgated in 1347, and twenty years later (1368) finally accepted as Poland's national code. A similar national intention was shown in the erection of a university at Cracow in 1364, which was to supplant for Poland both Bologna and Prague.

Casimir's reign, under the remarkably consistent and all-embracing direction of the king, saw a general increase of prosperity which affected every class. " He found Poland of wood and left it of stone " was the later saying. First and foremost the nobles benefited. The line was drawn between them and other classes by noble birth, and great

Margin notes: Internal Reorganization; Prosperity

and petty nobles were equally privileged as *Szlachta*. The peasants, too, under the influence of German immigration and internal peace were no mere serfs. They were not tied to the soil and were protected by the royal courts. Not only German but Jewish influence was marked in the prosperity of the towns. The Jews, ever more persecuted elsewhere, thronged to Poland, where in 1334 they were placed under the exclusive jurisdiction of the king. But the privileges of the towns were not allowed to be any longer anti-Polish. Casimir established a supreme mercantile court at Cracow, and no appeal was allowed as formerly to German cities, like Magdeburg, whose customs the towns had been granted. The medley of races in Poland was made compatible with a nation-State. A similar policy of toleration and absorption was followed by Casimir in his Russian conquest of Galicia. The Orthodox Church received full liberty, and the native princes and *boyars* retained their lands and rights. But a Catholic hierarchy was introduced side by side with the Orthodox, while Polish immigration was encouraged. The towns were given the customs of Magdeburg.

When Casimir died of a hunting accident, his dynastic scheme, which was to enhance the power of Poland, did not work well. The new Angevin king, Lewis the Great (1370–82), was a Hungarian who saw little of Poland. He resided there but little, he annexed Galicia to Hungary, and he had only daughters, not the male heir to whom the succession was guaranteed. To placate the Poles and secure the throne for his descendants, he was obliged to make in 1374 the Pact of Koszyce, which inflicted a severe blow on the monarchy. In return for the Crown being entailed on one of his daughters, he made fatal concessions to the *Szlachta* : they were declared free from taxation, and offices could only be conferred on them. Thus the Crown was impoverished and limited in a way which showed how the crowd of Polish nobles were unable to rise above their narrow class interests. It was an evil precedent followed, when Lewis died, by civil war. The outcome was the succession of his daughter Jadwiga and her marriage with Jagiello of Lithuania which brought about the personal union of his land with Poland. Greatness for the new permanent combination was to come, but greatness with fatal flaws.

Lewis the Great

Pact of Koszyce

Bohemia

Parallel to the history of Poland under Vladislav and Casimir runs that of the other West Slav kingdom, Bohemia, under John and Charles of Luxemburg, both of them curiously typical of their respective generations. As was natural, too, from its geographical situation and its close connexion with the Holy Roman Empire, Bohemia was in far nearer relations than Poland with the life of the West and with its civilization. The extinction of the native house of Přemysl in 1306 left the throne open to conflicting claims. The Bohemian nobles had the right of electing their king ; Albert of Austria, the reigning King of the Romans, claimed to dispose of the kingdom as a vacant fief. He set up his son Rudolf as king (1306–7), while Duke Henry of Carinthia, who had married Anne, the eldest daughter of King Wenceslas II, was the candidate of the more national party. Rudolf gained the upper hand, but his early death frustrated this attempt of King Albert to renew the wide dominion of King Ottokar II. Henry (1307–10) was installed by his party in Bohemia. Yet Albert's second son, Frederick the Handsome, who had been guaranteed the succession, held out in Moravia, where the German element was strong in the towns, until he was weakened by his father's murder and allowed himself to be bought out. The country, however, remained disturbed by the enmity between the Czechs and the German section of the population, which Henry of Carinthia proved incompetent to quell. A new expedient was thereupon tried. The hand of the second daughter of Wenceslas II, Elizabeth, with the crown was offered to John, the only son of Henry VII of Luxemburg, the new King of the Romans. Henry VII eagerly accepted the offer of the Bohemian nobles, celebrated the marriage, and sent the bridegroom to be king, thus exalting his family, hitherto of small importance, to be one of the great houses of the Empire.

The Succession to Wenceslas III

John of Luxemburg

King John (1310–46), who was only fourteen at his accession, was all his life a splendid, glittering, irresponsible knight of chivalry, permeated by the French culture in which he had been bred, living by preference in France or his neighbouring county of Luxemburg, unimpeachably brave and warlike, and only by accident profitable to his kingdom of Bohemia. His life seems modelled on an Arthurian romance. His first years were occupied by struggles with the Czech

nobles for the control of affairs. But in 1315 he was compelled to put only Czechs in office, and after a civil war he
concluded peace in 1318 on the same terms. The Czech
leader, Henry of Lipa, acquired the government of both
king and people; in fact, after 1319 John was rarely in
Bohemia, which became for him a source of much needed
supplies for his adventures. Yet it was to him that Bohemia
owed a considerable expansion of territory. In 1822 he
obtained the German district of Eger from Lewis IV the
Bavarian. Between 1320 and 1346 he annexed Upper
Lusatia, which had been lost to Bohemia for seventy years.
More important was the suzerainty of Silesia, which had
been temporarily won by Wenceslas II when he was King
of Poland. The Germanized Piasts of Silesia preferred John
to their upstart kinsman, Vladislav of Poland, and after some
years of warfare Casimir III, as we have seen, abandoned
the province to John and to Germany (1335). At John's
death only two of the petty Silesian princes were not his
vassals.

Most of John's career—his Lithuanian crusades—his
Italian expedition, his interventions in Germany, his death
in the battle of Crécy—belongs to the history of other countries. His relations with his queen were never cordial, and
he had their eldest son Wenceslas educated at Paris, where
he exchanged his name for that of Charles. In 1333 his
father created him Margrave of Moravia with the administration of Bohemia, which was suffering from lack of govern-
ance. Although John revoked his act in jealousy of his
more popular son, they were reconciled and Charles restored
in 1338 when John had gone blind in his second Lithuanian
crusade, and in 1341 the margrave was elected heir to the
throne with hereditary rights. This really ended John's
absentee reign, although he remained king till his death at
Crécy.

Charles I of Bohemia (1346–78)—Charles IV as Emperor Charles of
—was in utter contrast to his father. Cool, unchivalrous, Luxemburg
diplomatic, a born administrator, he was devoted to Bohemia,
whose greatest king he was. To the French knight succeeded the Czech patriot. While still his father's vicegerent,
although already King of the Romans, he had secured his
country's ecclesiastical autonomy. Hitherto Bohemia and

Moravia had been dioceses in the province of Mainz, controlled therefore by the leading German archbishop. Now (1344) Charles obtained from the Pope the erection of Prague into an archbishopric with the two lands as its province. As king he used his double position to confirm Bohemia's privileged position in the Empire. Moravia, Silesia (the remaining northern principalities of which he annexed in 1369), Upper Lusatia, and Lower Lusatia (which he also acquired in 1369) were declared by him united to the Bohemian Crown, although they might he held as fiefs from it. No appeal was to lie from the King of Bohemia to the Emperor. While in 1348 and 1355 he enacted that the Bohemian throne was hereditary in the male and female lines of the house of Luxemburg, in case of their extinction the sole right of electing a new monarch was reserved to the Bohemian Estates. The unity of the Bohemian realm, too, was occasionally emphasized by the holding of general Diets from all provinces, although he enfeoffed (1349) his brother John Henry with the margravate of Moravia, and his own youngest son John with the duchy of Görlitz in Lusatia. The kingdom of Bohemia was to be a self-contained unit attached to the Empire of which it was to be the leading power.

National
Prosperity

The development of the kingdom in all departments of the national life was Charles's chief aim. Before his father's death he had been already busily engaged in recovering the royal demesne, which had been mostly mortgaged to the nobles. In the time of disorder Bohemia had fallen a prey to brigands : these Charles by repeated efforts extirpated without mercy. He revived the public law-courts and in 1356 enacted that the peasants should be able to appeal to them from the feudal courts of their lords. His attempt, however, to introduce a codification and revision of the law in the compilation called the *Maiestas Carolina* failed before the opposition of the Estates, who preferred their more primitive and more national customary laws. Equally important was his work in the economic sphere. He spread the culture of the vine and constructed fish ponds. He restricted retail trade to born Bohemians, and enlarged Prague, the capital, by the founding of the New Town (Nové Město), to which other than Germans were admitted, unlike the

older towns of Bohemia. For intellectual life and culture
he founded in 1348 the University of Prague, which quickly
became famous. Students from all central Europe thronged
to it, and for years it was more German than Czech. Yet
the Czech element increased in the University, and Charles
sedulously favoured the Czech tongue, as the language of
his household and the law-courts. He was a patron of
architecture and art, and in his reign Bohemia definitely
turned from the Byzantine to the Western tradition. French
Gothic entered the country, French and Italian influences
transformed painting. Early humanism made its first steps
in Bohemia in the court and chancery of Charles.

So pious a prince was a pillar of the Church, whose first Religious
archbishop, Ernest of Pardubice, enjoyed his special favour. Revival
But here he was not so successful. The Bohemian Church
was extremely wealthy—it owned half the land of the country
—and was very corrupt. Not unnaturally, too, heresy, both
Catharan and Waldensian and mixtures of the two, was rife
in south Bohemia amid the Czech-speaking population. Well-
meant official efforts of reform and persecution did little
good, but a national religious movement sprang up, which
later had momentous consequences. Conrad Waldhauser,
an Austin canon from Austria, became famous as a preacher
at Prague for the reform of manners. He was followed by
a native Czech, the fervent evangelist John Milíc, who from
1364 to his death in 1374 exerted an extraordinary influence
on Czechs and Germans, however much at enmity with
wealthy monks and clergy. Although orthodox, Milíc, by
his apocalyptic belief in the coming of Anti-Christ—whom
he once identified with the worthy Charles—and his demands
for the general reform of a corrupted Church did much to
prepare the way for the Hussite revolt from Catholicism in
the next century. The nationalism that Charles fostered
was bearing unexpected fruits. When Charles died in 1378
an opportunity had already been given by the outbreak of
the Great Schism of the West for momentous and radical
innovation.

Like Poland and Bohemia, the kingdom of Hungary Hungary
recovered unity and strength and made advances in civilization during the fourteenth century. The extinction of
the house of Árpád in 1301 left it under the sway of great

provincial dynasts and the prey of civil war between claimants
of the crown.   At first Wenceslas (III) of Bohemia, with the
support of his father Wenceslas II, had the upper hand, but
his rival Charles Robert of Anjou, the son of the pretender
Charles Martel, maintained himself in Croatia and the south,
backed by the Pope and his legates.   It was indeed the
pretension of the Pope as suzerain to nominate the King
of Hungary which gave most popularity to the claims
of Wenceslas among the Hungarian nobles.   But Wenceslas II
was attacked by King Albert of Habsburg and then died.
Wenceslas III found it best to withdraw (1305) his claim
to Hungary in favour of Otto of Bavaria, another connexion
of the house of Árpád.   Otto, however, was no match for
Charles Robert.   In 1307 an assembly near Pest elected
the Angevin their hereditary king without recognizing the
previous papal nomination.   Charles I (1308–42) was duly
crowned next year.

Charles I
Robert.
His Reforms

It took Charles Robert fifteen years to break down the
power of the dynasts who had shared up Hungary, but the
task was done effectively.   He inherited the great qualities
of his Capetian ancestors, and reorganized the crumbling
monarchy.   Both clan and great local dynast were now
obsolete ; they were replaced by a feudal nobility.   The
prelates and the greater nobles formed the magnates of
Hungary.   In war they led from their estates, as the king
did from the royal demesne, their *banderia* of knights and
men-at-arms, the nerve of the army.   But below them and
counterbalancing them came the numerous and powerful
class of lesser nobles, who possessed identical legal privileges
with the magnates, were members of the administrative
county assemblies, under the count nominated by the king,
and served in their county's *banderium*.   Beside them, as in
France or England, were the free bourgeois of the towns,
which were favoured and increased in number and population by the king.   There were even districts of free peasants, largely settlers from abroad, who were systematically
attracted to fill the wide vacant spaces of the thinly-peopled
realm.   Below these, however, there was the mass of the
peasants, serfs (*jobbágy*) bound to the soil and crushed under
the yoke of the feudal lords.   The whole population together preserved its extraordinarily variegated character :

outside the central plain of Hungary proper there was a broad fringe of different races and languages, Slovak, Roumanian, German, Serb, besides the compact group of Croatians who formed a separate realm south of the River Save.

Over this medley Charles Robert revived the central power of the kingship. He nominated the royal officials and the counts. He established a royal court of justice, the Curia. After 1324 he no longer summoned a real parliament, although the Estates met formally once a year at Székes-fehérvar. The nobles' share in government was exercised in the county courts. Still more important for the strength of the kingship was Charles's reorganization and fostering of its economic resources. The still wide demesne lands were made more productive by immigration and careful farming, so that the king was the wealthiest landowner. Besides this, he derived a large income from the customs (*regale*), which he increased by abolishing internal tolls and levying duties at the frontier, much to the benefit of the trading class. He concluded, too, commercial treaties with his neighbours for the same purpose, and gave Hungary a stable currency with a gold florin of invariable value which facilitated foreign commerce. He improved the gold mines, a chief asset of the country's wealth. All this national prosperity redounded to the wealth of the Crown, and not only in customs duties. The townsmen paid a levy called the *census*, while the country dwellers contributed a hearth-tax (*collecta*). The Church did not escape, for when the Papacy collected a tenth from the clergy, the king took a third of the proceeds.

The fruits of this revival of Hungary were reaped by Lewis I the Charles's son, Lewis I the Great (1342–82), who brought the Great chivalrous French culture of the West to half barbarous Hungary. His justice was renowned, and he did something to civilize the law. Like his neighbours he founded a national University, that of Pécs (1367). He was a collector of manuscripts illuminated in the reigning French style, and under him and his father French Gothic cathedrals were built in Hungary. The ideals of chivalry pervaded the court and the new court literature.

Lewis inherited friendly relations with the rulers to the north and west, Casimir of Poland—whom he was to succeed—and the Emperor Charles IV : all three were men of

similar aims. To the south, however, he had rivals. Tsar
Stephen Dushan was creating the great Yugo-Slav kingdom
of Serbia and coveted Croatia; Venice possessed the Dalmatian coast towns and dominated Hungary's outlet in the
Adriatic. After a long aberration caused by his attempt to
conquer Naples while revenging the murder of his brother
Andrew,[1] Lewis turned to these essential interests of his
kingdom. In 1356–8 he conquered Dalmatia from Venice.
Dushan had more than repelled the Hungarian attacks, but
after his death (1355) the Serbian realm broke up and Lewis
was able to erect a province in Serbia and Bulgaria south
of the Danube. This did not last—racial and religious
aversions were too strong—and after 1370 only a nominal
suzerainty remained to Lewis south of the Danube and in
Roumanian Wallachia. In the Adriatic, however, he continued to prosper. Always hostile to Venice, partly to
break her trade monopoly, he was Genoa's ally in the War
of Chioggia, and his possession of Dalmatia as well as the
access of Hungarian ships to the Italian rivers was confirmed
in 1381 by the peace of Turin.[2] When he died, the King
of Hungary and Poland seemed the greatest power in East
Europe. Yet nothing had been done to save the crumbling
Balkans from the insistent Turkish conquest.

Summary   If North and East Europe is viewed as a whole in the
fourteenth century, it is obvious that the expansion of
Western civilization, which was at work in the thirteenth
century, was accelerating and deepening, with the sole exception of Russia which remained isolated in a slow, indigenous
progress under the Tartar Yoke. As feudalism, town-life
and serfdom grew in the thirteenth century, so did centralizing, legislating, and civilizing monarchy in the fourteenth.
Scandinavia was really the most conservative. The spirit
of local particularism and personal independence native to
it played into the hands of the nobles and did not allow
monarchy to take firm root. Yet the same spirit in the
people restricted serfdom to Denmark and checked the
growth of typical feudalism itself. To the south of the
Baltic the predominance of the Teutonic Knights and the
Hansa League was a victory for the West. It brough

[1] See above, Chap. XVI, pp 848–49.
[2] See above, Chap. XVI, pp. 855–56.

Germany eastward, a Germany of feudal lords and free, bourgeois, trading towns, two main ingredients of Western civilization. In the three central kingdoms, Poland, Bohemia and Hungary, the same process took a form more original and more fertile. Under their three great dynasties they developed not only feudal monarchies on the Western pattern but national institutions and national cultures, Slav or Magyar. They did not only borrow, they created, and their native inheritance continued to differentiate their history from that of the true West. None the less their links with the West grew closer and stronger. Their destiny was decided. Their religion was the Catholic Church, their institutions were feudalized, their monarchies of the Western type, their civilization was Latin and Western, one of the many sequels which have made the Roman Empire of antiquity the parent of the modern world.

SUGGESTIONS FOR READING ON CHAPTER XVIII

I. SCANDINAVIA

Cambridge Medieval History, vols. vi and vii, relevant chapters, and the books listed for Chapter VIII.

II. RUSSIA

The works listed for Chapter VIII.

III. POLAND, LITHUANIA, AND THE TEUTONIC KNIGHTS

Cambridge Medieval History, vol. vii, chapters ix and xxiv ; vol. viii, chapter xviii.
Cambridge History of Poland, vol. i. 1950.

IV. BOHEMIA

Cambridge Medieval History, vol. vii, chapter vi.
Jarrett, Dom Bede : *The Emperor Charles IV*. London, 1935.
Lutzow, Count F. : *Bohemia*. Everyman's Library. London, 1909.

V. HUNGARY

Cambridge Medieval History, vol. viii, chapter xix ; vol. iv, chapters xvii, xviii, and xxi ; and the books listed for Chapter VIII.

CHAPTER XIX

THE BALKANS AND THE TURKISH ADVANCE, 1282–1380

**Hetero-
geneity of
the Balkans**

WHILE in Western and Central Europe in the fourteenth century there was a continuous tendency
to organization of some sort and the development
of institutions, the Balkan peninsula seemed to remain
incapable of fresh advance in that department of civilization
and indeed to be losing in personal and racial rivalries that
which it had inherited. In the intertangled condition of the
races and languages of the land and the vivid contrasts of
its geography, varying from the plains of the Danube basin and
Macedonia to the great ranges of the centre and the split-
up cantons of Greece proper, diverse and mutually secluded,
only a great civilized and military power, such as the Eastern
Empire had once been, could, and that by long, uninterrupted effort, have given unity and strength. As it was,
Greek jostled Slav and Frank in the south, Albanian, Vlach,
and Slav in the centre; the Vlachs beyond the Danube
were only just forming elementary principalities; south of
it, not only were Bulgars and Serbs separate with an in-
definable disputed zone between them, but the Yugo-Slavs
of whom the Serbs were the chief division, were irremediably
broken up into rival sections by habitat, religion, and history
The Serbs proper, centring round the River Morava, were
Orthodox; the Croats and Dalmatians were Catholic; the
Bosnians, besides numbering both Orthodox and Catholic
among them, also included a large and generally persecuted
group of Bogomils, those Manichæan heretics whose offshoot
in the West had given rise to the Catharan or Albigensian
religion.

**The Eastern
Empire.
Andronicus
II**

It was in this seething confusion of discordant element
that Andronicus II in 1282 succeeded his father Michael
Palaeologus. No one more unfit for his task could have
been found than this pious and feeble prince, and he aggra-

404

vated his incompetence by the length of years during which
he displayed it. At the same time his inheritance was
deplorable. The remnant of the Empire was overtaxed and
misgoverned ; it was constantly exposed to the ravages of
its neighbours and foes ; it was without a navy or native
army ; and the energy of its population was spent in ecclesiastical feuds born of Michael VIII's politic " re-union " with
the Western Church. Andronicus shared these theological
passions, and was a slave to his quarrelling clergy. Yet this
exhausted realm and race were not all degenerate : the era
of the Palaeologi was a period of intellectual renaissance.
Scholarship and literature revived in a movement that was
to be of immense value for the rise of humanism in the
West. More original was the new phase of Byzantine art.
In mosaic and fresco a charming style of realistic grace was
created, which replaced the tradition of stiff symbolism. It
was parallel to the contemporary movement in Italy, to
which it was rather a parent influence than a pupil. In
their fall the Byzantines sought refuge in a far past and
were inspired anew.

In 1282 the Eastern Empire extended in Europe over
Thrace and Macedonia ; there its enemies were the Serbs
and Bulgarians. In addition, it possessed the new conquest
of Mistra in the southern Morea ; there it was at odds with
the Franks of Achaia. In Asia Minor it still ruled the old
provinces on the sea-coast from the Maeander to the Black
Sea, but here its territory was shrinking before a more formidable enemy. The Seljūk Turks of Rūm were indeed decadent, Turkish
and little more than Mongol governors since the defeat of Emirs of
Kuza-Dagh, but their lands were divided among a number Rūm
of Turkish tribes under Emirs, vigorous and aggressive, who
swarmed in from the East. The most powerful of these
chiefs, the Emir of Karaman in the centre, was for the most
part remote from the Byzantine frontier. Others, however,
raided and conquered the Greek lowlands. The Emirs of
Aidin, Germiyan, and Karasi were steadily encroaching.
The Turks took to the sea and plundered in the Ægean.
Most fatal of all was a little tribe settled in once Greek The
territory on the River Sangarius, none too far from Nicæa Osmanlis
itself, a district to which they gave the name of Sultanöni.
They were in the most favourable position for expansion,

and under the leadership of Ertoghrul rapidly gained recruits from other Turks.   In 1281 Ertoghrul died, and was succeeded by his son Osman, from whom his subjects took the soon dreaded name of Osmanlis, the Ottoman Turks.

Against these swarming foes Andronicus relied mainly on mercenaries, for the old peasant militia was disappearing. Many were Turks ; others were called Alans, Christians from north of the Danube, Vlachs or Russians.   But his general, Philanthropenos, revolted, though vainly, and his son and co-regent Michael IX failed to rescue the city of Magnesia. In 1303 a new experiment was tried.   The Catalan mercenaries, who had fought for Sicily in the War of the Vespers, were unemployed after the peace of Caltabellotta, and some 6,000 of them took service under Andronicus.   Their leader was a German, Roger de Flor, who received the title, first of Grand Duke (i.e. admiral) and then of Cæsar, as well as the hand of the Emperor's niece.   The Asiatic campaign of the " Grand Company " of the Catalans was marked by brilliant victories, but they proved worse than Turks to the unhappy Greeks.   The Emperor could not continue to pay them, and, like the Free Companies later in France, they pillaged country and town with ruthless brutality.   Cyzicus never recovered from the ruin they wrought.   Summoned back to Europe to repulse the Bulgarians, they occupied Gallipoli, the key of the Dardanelles, and pursued their horrible ravages in Thrace.   They received reinforcements, both Catalan and Turk.   The murder of Roger de Flor by Michael IX in 1306 only increased their ferocity.   Under Berenguer de Rocafort they moved to Macedonia committing their usual atrocities, till in 1309 they descended on Thessaly and thus left the Empire.

Meantime the Empire was losing Asia Minor to the Turkish emirs.   The Seljūks of Rūm were now extinct, but Osman and his allies advanced continuously.   Only the corner of land on the Sea of Marmora and the isolated city of Philadelphia in Lydia were left to the Greeks.   A new defence of Christendom, however, had been erected at Rhodes. In 1308 the Knights Hospitallers quitted their temporary headquarters in Cyprus, and with the Pope's sanction attacked the Greek pirates of the island of Rhodes.   They achieved the conquest in 1310 ; thenceforward, their fleet was used

The Catalan Grand Company

Turkish Advance

Knights of Rhodes

to check the swarming pirates of the Ægean, whether Greek or Turk.

Civil war was added to the disasters of the Eastern Empire. When the co-regent Michael IX died in 1320, his son Andronicus was at first proclaimed heir by his grandfather. But the young man, though filled with profitless energy, was a rake and a prodigal. He caused the death of his brother, and, in fear of disinheritance, revolted. Three wars, in which Bulgarians and Serbs took part, between the two Andronicus wasted the resources of the Empire. In the third war Andronicus II in 1328 abdicated the government, and while retaining the title of Emperor became a monk till his death. *Byzantine Civil Wars*

No situation could have been more favourable for the advance of the Ottoman Turks, who were now the immediate neighbours of the remnants of the Empire in Asia. Osman, though the extent of his conquests seems small, deserved his fame as the founder of a State and dynasty. At the head of his mounted nomads he crossed the ill-defended passes of Bithynia, and isolated by systematic ravage and nomad occupation the few fortified towns. In the end, although the process was long, they were starved into surrender. In 1308, at a time when Ephesus to the south fell to a fellow Emir, he was receiving blackmail from Brūsa, one of the chief frontier cities. In November 1326, just before he died, his son Orkhan took Brūsa and made it the Ottoman capital. *Osman. The Ottoman Turks* *Orkhan*

Orkhan, who was the first Sultan of the Osmanlis, gradually reached the Sea of Marmora. In 1329 Nicæa itself fell after a defeat of Andronicus III at Philocrene ; in 1337 Nicomedia followed suit. About the same time the Ottoman dominions were doubled by the absorption of the Turkish emirate of Karasi to the south.

Besides the fact of conquest, the rule of Orkhan was recommended to his Christian subjects by its general justice and tolerance : it was indeed an improvement on that of the decrepit and extortionate Empire. The *rayahs*, as the Christians were called, paid their poll-tax and kept their churches and customs : their bishops were their representatives towards the Turkish government. Orkhan could even count on their assistance in war. The Ottoman army was reformed by the new Sultan on the advice of his brother and vizier Ala-ettin. The general levy of Osmanli horse- *Ottoman Government* men was largely replaced by more organized troops. An efficient cavalry was provided by the fief-holders, who in return for their land were called up for each campaign. But a more important innovation was the establishment of a standing corps of disciplined infantry. The best of these

The Janizzaries were the uniformed Janizzaries (" new troops "), who were recruited from Orkhan's Christian subjects. A paid Turkish infantry was levied as well for each campaign. It was this solid body of foot, of which the best were Christian, which won the Ottoman Sultans their most decisive victories over their Christian enemies.

Byzantine Dissensions and Decadence The miserable state of the Greek Empire in Europe continued till the death of Andronicus III in 1341 : it suffered by land from Serbs, Bulgarians, and even Tartars from the Ukraine, and by sea from descents of Orkhan and the other Turkish emirs of the Asiatic coast. Worse came, however, when the child, his son John V, ascended the throne. The regency was disputed between the Great Domestic (the commander-in-chief), John Cantacuzene, who had been the main support of Andronicus III, and the Empress-mother, Anne of Savoy, egged on by the Grand Duke Apocaucos. Driven from Constantinople, Cantacuzene proclaimed himself co-Emperor. Able as he undoubtedly was, and restrained by genuine scruples from aiming at the dethronement of his ex-ward, he could not have done a more unfortunate thing for the Empire. In the six years' civil war which followed Macedonia was lost to the Serbs and Philippopolis to the Bulgarians, the result of dubious alliances. It was partly owing to the death of Apocaucos and partly to the assistance of Orkhan, to whom he gave a daughter to wife, the first Byzantine princess to enter a Turkish harem, that John Cantacuzene secured a temporary triumph in 1347 by a treaty which made him Emperor-regent for his other son-in-law John V Palaeologus. But Cantacuzene's reign continued the disasters of the Empire. He fell out with the Genoese, who since 1261 had held in complete independence the suburb of Galata on the harbour of the Golden Horn, and, when his little impromptu navy was destroyed and his allies, the Venetians, were defeated, was compelled in 1352 to grant his enemies something like a monopoly of Byzantine trade.

A gleam of hope had shone meantime in the Crusade of the Archipelago (the Ægean), which was organized by Pope Clement VI. Venice was now alarmed by the Turkish piracy in the Ægean and joined the papal league. In 1344 the combined fleet furnished by the Pope, Venice, the Hospitallers, and the King of Cyprus captured Smyrna from Omur Beg, the Emir of Aidin. The town was given to the Hospitallers to defend, and a new champion was engaged in the person of the Dauphin Humbert II, but, though Omur Beg was killed in an attempt to recover Smyrna, Humbert was quite incapable and soon withdrew. The great hopes of the Crusade dwindled to the useful possession of Smyrna by the Knights of Rhodes.

Crusade of the Archipelago

This gain was more than counterbalanced by a loss to the Osmanlis. Cantacuzene was unable to keep on good terms with his legitimate colleague, John V, as the young Emperor grew up. The elder Emperor may have stood for better government than his unruly son-in-law, but certainly not for success. In the new civil war, which began in 1353, the unpopular Cantacuzene called in his Ottoman allies under Suleyman, son of Orkhan. They won him a temporary victory, but seized on Gallipoli, the key of the Dardanelles. In the increased disfavour which followed this and the elevation of his son Matthew to the imperial purple Cantacuzene gave up the struggle. In 1355 he abdicated in favour of John V, who was already welcomed by the capital, and became a monk. The harm to the Empire, however, was irreparable, for Orkhan, at war with John V, fortified and retained Gallipoli. The Ottomans had gained the gateway into the Balkans and Europe.

The Osmanlis seize Gallipoli

The entrance of the Ottomans into Europe, no longer as raiders but as permanent settlers and rulers, was to prove fatal to the Byzantine Empire. Yet it still seemed possible that Constantinople might fall to Christian, if barbaric neighbours, who might in the long run absorb and continue the East Roman civilization, the Slavs of the Balkans. Bulgaria, indeed, was losing the faculty of aggression. After the Tsar Constantine Asên had been slain in 1277 by the swineherd Ivailo, Michael VIII succeeded in intruding his son-in-law John Asên III as ruler, but his protégé was soon driven out by a new usurper, George Terteri.

Bulgaria's Decline

This Tsar finally repelled Ivailo's last attempt to regain the throne, but in 1292 himself fled to the Greeks before a fresh Tartar invasion, sent by Nogai Khan, chief of the Patzinaks in the Ukraine, who replaced him by a certain Smilets.   Then, in 1295, Theodore Svetslav, son of Terteri, with the help of a Tartar chief whom he betrayed, seized the crown and kept it, in spite of Greek support to two pretenders, for twenty-seven years.   But Bulgaria, lacerated by the Tartar invasions, the Greek wars, and civil strife, did not recover the formidable strength of a century earlier.

Serbia's Ascendancy   Her rôle as the expanding Slav State was taken by Serbia.   Incomplete though Serbia was without the two divisions of Bosnia and the banate of Machva on the Danube which were under Hungarian suzerainty, it was still powerful. King Stephen Dragutin (1276–81) soon abdicated, and governed Machva as a Catholic and Hungarian vassal.   His brother Stephen Urosh II (1281–1321), debauched, pious, and ambitious, aimed at higher things.   He seized Skoplie from the Byzantines, and after his marriage to a Byzantine princess dreamed of ascending the imperial throne.   But in spite of oscillations to Catholicism he did not even succeed in retaining Machva, which he conquered.   On his death a civil war between rival claimants resulted in the victory of his bastard son, the fierce Stephen Urosh III (Dechanski). New complications arose with the founder of a new Bulgarian dynasty, Michael Shishmanich, on the extinction of the house of Terteri in 1322.   Tsar Michael repudiated his wife, Stephen Urosh's sister, to marry a Byzantine princess.   In alliance with Andronicus III he attacked Serbia, but on June 28, 1330, the Serbians won the decisive battle of Velbuzhd (Köstendil), in which Michael was killed.   Thereby Bulgaria became a Serbian dependency.   Even Andronicus III gained some Bulgarian territory.

Tsar Stephen Dushan   It was not long, however, before the victorious Serbian was dethroned and murdered (1331) by his son Stephen Urosh IV, known as Dushan, the favourite of the nobles.   Dushan was the greatest of the Serbian kings, with whom their ambitions seemed near fulfilment.   Bred in Constantinople, he was a legislator, as well as a warrior.   He took advantage of the civil wars of the Byzantines over Cantacuzene to conquer all Macedonia, save Thessalonica, while his Bulgarian

THE BALKANS c. 1340

vassal, John Alexander (1331–65), obtained Philippopolis.
Albania was already Dushan's, and in 1346 he unmasked his
objective by having himself crowned at Skoplie as " Emperor
of the Serbs and Greeks," while a Serbian Patriarchate was
erected at Ipek. The conquest of Thessaly and Epirus followed.   An almost successful counter-attack of Cantacuzene
was frustrated by the revolution which put John V Palaeologus in power, and Belgrade was won from Hungary, if
Bosnia held out under its *bans*.   In 1355 Dushan was preparing to besiege Constantinople itself, when he suddenly
died.   With him the project of a Serbo-Greek Empire and
the chance of preventing the Turkish invasion also expired.
Serbia, an agricultural and pastoral land, held by barbaric
nobles and subject peasants, advanced slowly in civilization
under him ; he codified the laws and encouraged trade and
culture.   But he had neither time nor the means to give
any real unity to the diverse races and provinces he ruled.
The institutions of the South Slavs and Byzantines had,
indeed, much in common, for the former borrowed from the
latter.   There were the nobles of varying power, who were
all free landed proprietors ; there were the free peasants and
free tenants ; there was the mass of mere serfs at their
lord's mercy.   The Tsar had his imitation of Byzantine
court officials. He gave out fiefs, charged with military
service. He could tax and summon his subjects to war.
He had a right to *corvées* and dues for the upkeep of his
estates and administration.   This autocrat, however, had
always to reckon with resistance or revolt.   He governed
with the advice of the great nobles, among whom racial,
clannish, and local instincts far transcended any common
interest of the Balkans or the State.

The Vlach   Dushan had maintained friendly relations with the new
principalities Vlach principalities beyond the Danube. Somewhere about
1290 the Vlachs of Transylvania were moving south into
the plain of Wallachia, where Slav and Tartar and Cuman
had so long inhabited. The Vlachs were Orthodox, and
religious persecution from the Catholic Hungarians seems
to have been one motive for the migration. Radou Negrou,
who established the first principality of Wallachia (Vlachia)
between the Carpathians and the Danube, was a Transylvanian noble with his band of warriors. Besides conquer-

ing the peoples he found, he maintained his independence of the King of Hungary, as did his successor Ivanko Besaraba (1310–30). Alexander Besaraba, the third prince, defeated an attempt of Charles Robert of Hungary to subdue him, and if he became the vassal of Lewis the Great, this subjection was thrown off before Lewis died. Contemporaneously with the foundation of Wallachia, other Transylvanian emigrants had established settlements subject to Hungary to the north by the River Moldau. One chief, Bogdan, in 1349 revolted and made these lands into the principality of Moldavia. He and his successors, however, were obliged to profess themselves vassals of Poland.

These principalities, largely Slav in blood, although increasingly Vlach (i.e. romance) in language, were drawn by situation, religion, and interest towards the Slavs, Bulgarian and Serb, south of the Danube, their natural allies against the common foe, Hungary. Their institutions and civilization were Bulgarian. The prince was a despot, richly endowed with land ; his *boyars* or nobles held free land on terms of military service. Service was also due from the free peasants, but the largest class was that of serfs, holding hereditary land and owing a poll-tax and labour to their lords. As a whole, the people were prosperous and warlike cattle-breeders, primitive and unruly. Unlike their neighbours, they had no literature ; even the language of their liturgy was Bulgarian.

The Serbian Empire at once broke up on Dushan's death. Division His son Tsar Stephen Urosh V was speedily thrust aside to of Serbia remain a cipher till his death. Thessaly and Epirus at once obtained independence. Among the great nobles Vukashin was master of South Serbia with his capital at Prizren and in 1366 took the title of king ; his brother Ugliesha ruled Macedonia ; while Lazar held Machva and the north. Nor was Bulgaria less divided. The Tsar John Alexander married as his second wife a converted Jewess and declared her son John Shishman his successor. His elder son John Sratsimir revolted thereon at Vidin on the Danube, while on the Black Sea coast another prince, Dobrotich, carved out a state, known from his name as the Dobrudzha. The Byzantines and Hungarians each invaded the dislocated land and made their profit. When

John V Palaeologus came in 1365, returning from Hungary, to negotiate an alliance against the Turks, John Shishman, not unnaturally if unwisely, took his revenge and kept him imprisoned until the crusading Amadeus VI of Savoy enforced his liberation by the capture of the Bulgarian ports.

Sultan Murat I

Union among the Christians was never more needed. In 1360 Sultan Murat I succeeded his father Orkhan, and proceeded to the conquest of the Balkans.   He improved

The tribute of Christian boys

on his father's institution of the Janizzaries by recruiting them from the sons of the conquered.   This began the tribute of Christian boys.   The strongest and most promising were taken from their parents at the age of twelve, and bred under strict discipline as fervent Moslems for the Sultan's service.   The famous corps of infantry which thus formed the Sultan's bodyguard and the best of his army became the arbiter of the Ottoman Empire.   The fighting populations of the Balkans, unable to act together as Christians, provided as Moslems the instrument of their own conquest.

Ottoman conquest of Thrace

Murat began by the conquest of Byzantine Thrace, Adrianople and Philippopolis fell to him : the former city became his capital, and a large immigration of Osmanlis, who abandoned their nomadic habits, took place.   Only a small set-back to the Ottoman progress was effected   by the crusade of Amadeus, " the Green Count " of Savoy, promoted by the Pope, who received a promise of submission to the Roman Church from John V.   The count, indeed, captured Gallipoli in 1366 and rescued John from the Bulgarians, but his funds were exhausted and on his departure Gallipoli was retroceded at the Turkish threats.   Vukashin of Serbia now made a great effort.   The Serbs had already

Battle of the Maritza

been defeated and Macedonia ravaged.   In 1371, on September 26, Vukashin and Ugliesha at the head of all their forces met Murat on the River Maritza.   Their defeat was crushing, and they were both slain.   The disaster entailed the annexation of Macedonia, and the subjection of the Southern Serbs, while the Tsar of Bulgaria became a Turkish vassal.   His example was followed in 1373 by John Palaeologus, whose dominions now hardly reached beyond the walls of Constantinople.

John V had meantime made a journey to the West to appeal for aid.   In 1369 he submitted at Avignon to the

papal supremacy and the Western creed. But the poten- Vassalage of Constantinople
tates of the West had their own concerns and ambitions
to occupy them : no aid was forthcoming and the unlucky
John was detained at Venice by his creditors. Since his
eldest son, the regent Andronicus, declined to rescue him,
he associated his younger son, Manuel II, who had raised
his ransom, with him on the throne. This justifiable choice
relit the flame of civil war which cursed the Palaeologi. The
ex-regent Andronicus IV revolted and in 1376 seized the
capital and his father. Another revolution in 1379 restored
John and Manuel to Constantinople, while Andronicus
retained a town or so on the Sea of Marmora. The result
of the suicidal conflict was an increase of the Turkish tribute
and the cession of Philadelphia in Lydia, which with Skutari
was the only Asiatic town retained by the Byzantines, to
the Turks. Meanwhile Manuel II, worthy of a better
fate, led the Byzantine contingent in the Ottoman armies
till the death of his dissolute father in 1391. If the times
were desperate, the dynasty provided no remedy.

After the disaster of the Maritza, two Serb states remained Serbian States
unconquered, the kingdom of Serbia under Lazar (1371–89)
and that of Bosnia under Tvrtko (1353–91). Tvrtko enlarged his territory at Lazar's expense and gained part of
the Dalmatian coast. Lazar, like the rival rulers of Bulgaria,
was a Turkish vassal. He revolted, won a victory with
Tvrtko's help at Toplica (1387), and formed a Balkan league
against the enemy. But when Murat attacked, the allies
did not unite. Bulgaria was first reduced to submission ; First Battle of Kossovo
then on June 15, 1389, Lazar with his Serbs and auxiliaries
was overthrown at the fatal battle of Kossovo. Although
Murat himself was killed as well as Lazar, this battle decided
the fate of the Balkans. Though vassal principalities, divided
and weak, lingered on, the Osmanli Empire reached the
Danube. Islam was established in Europe under a military
despotism of terrible efficiency.

The interests of Christendom in the Levant were upheld Little Armenia
after the fall of Acre not only by the republics of Venice
and Genoa and the Knights of Rhodes but by the two
Christian States of Little Armenia or Cilicia and Cyprus.
Each provided a much-needed base of trade and shipping,
and Armenia was as well at the head of a trade-route,

debouching at Ayas or Laiazzo, which led into the Mongol dominions. Armenia under its native dynasty put up a gallant, but ruinous fight against its Moslem neighbours, the Mamlūks of Egypt and Syria and the Turks of Rūm, repelling devastating invasions. At first the kingdom could count on the alliance of the Mongol Īl-khans of Persia, but when after 1302 the Īl-khan became a Moslem, he too became a foe. To woo the West was the only resource, and the Armenian kings, already allied by marriage with the Latins, adopted the Catholic faith and endeavoured to convert their Monophysite subjects. This produced some papal help, but also civil war and more Mamlūk invasions. When Leo V, last of the native dynasty, died in 1342, little was left to him save the coast town of Gorigos. A troubled period of foreign kings, invasion, and religious discord ended with the accession of Leo VI of Lusignan in 1373. Two years later he was conquered and led captive to Cairo by the Mamlūks. Except as a title of the Kings of Cyprus Little Armenia ceased to exist.

Cyprus   Cyprus, guarded by the sea, had a better fate under the Lusignans. But Amaury, Prince of Tyre, introduced a growing evil when in 1306 he usurped the regency from his brother King Henry II. He conferred trading privileges on the Venetians, who thus rivalled the hitherto dominant Genoese, and the wars of the two republics reacted to the injury of Cyprus. King Peter I (1359–69), an adventurous knight of the type of his century, made vigorous efforts for the Crusade. In 1361, with the help of the Hospitallers he captured the town of Attalia (Satalie) in Lycia from its Turkish emir, a famous exploit, but his tour in the West for a fresh expedition only produced individual crusaders and the support of Venice. He sacked Alexandria by surprise in 1365 and some Syrian coast-towns later. But Venice could not wish the ruin of the oriental commerce and mediated a settlement with the Mamlūks. When Peter was murdered by his own nobles, who hated him, the regency for his son Peter II was a time of civil war. The mob sacked the Genoese quarter at Famagosta and brought on an invasion in reprisal. In 1374 Famagosta was ceded to Genoa as the only privileged port in the island. Cyprus did not recover from this blow to its prosperity.

After the death of William, the last Villehardouin Prince Achaia
of Achaia, in 1278, Greece proper was tethered to the policy
of the Kings of Naples, and suffered from their absenteeism
and schemes. Six bailies of Achaia, one of whom was
William Duke of Athens, succeeded one another in eleven
years. Yet there was a respite of good government, 1289–97,
under Florent d'Avesnes, the husband of Isabelle de Villehardouin, who was enfeoffed with the principality, on condition that, if he died without male heirs, the fief should
revert to the Kings of Naples in case the princess or her
female descendants married without the suzerain's consent,
a proviso which ended in constant Neapolitan intervention.
Meantime there continued to be a Greek Despot of Epirus Byzantines
and Duke of Neopatras, and the Byzantine province of in the
Mistra in the south of the Morea, while the Latin duchy of Morea
Athens under Guy II de la Roche was at the height of its Athens
prosperity and showed a curious mixture of Greek and Latin
civilization. Charles II of Naples endeavoured to provide
both for the government of his Greek dependencies and their
expansion by consolidating all his claims in the person of
his son Philip, Prince of Taranto, who was to be the vanquished general of Falconaria. In 1294 Philip was married to
an Epirote princess, and given Corfu with the suzerainty of
Achaia, Athens, and the rest. The widowed Isabelle was
married in 1301 to a prince of Savoy, Philip, who thus
became for a few years an unpopular resident Prince of Achaia,
until he was deprived by Charles II and Philip of Taranto
entered on the principality. But Philip of Taranto was
himself an absentee, whose real interests lay in Italy.

A new revolution in the affairs of Greece was caused by The Catalans
the invasion of the Catalan Grand Company, which with a conquer
band of Turkish allies quitted Macedonia to ravage Thessaly Athens
in 1309. Unimpeded by the Duke of Neopatras but defeated by a Byzantine army sent in pursuit of them, they
next reached the duchy of Athens. The duke there was now
Walter of Brienne, who objected to Byzantine rule in Thessaly and hired the redoubtable freebooters to fight for him.
They ravaged Thessaly once more till Walter had obtained
his terms, and then the duke dismissed them unpaid. The
desperate Company entrenched itself on the River Cephisus
in Bœotia, where on March 15, 1311, Duke Walter assaulted

27

them with a reckless charge in the best manner of feudal
chivalry.   But the Catalans had turned the ground into a
marsh sodden by the river.   Walter and his knights were
helplessly bogged and then shot, hewn, or trampled down.
Only four or five escaped.   It was one more victory of the
professional soldier over unteachable feudalism.   The Company took possession of the duchy and shared up the widows
and lands of the slain.   To legalize their conquest, they
accepted an absentee duke in a son of Frederick of Sicily,
but real power was exercised by local vicars-general who
presided over an organization Catalan in institutions and
language.   They failed to gain a footing in Achaia, but
Neopatras with most of Thessaly was annexed on the death of
the last Greek duke in 1318.   Negropont, which had been
re-won for the Eastern Empire by Michael VIII, had already
been re-acquired by Venice at the turn of the century to
become one of her chief bases in the Levant.

Achaia and
Mistra
During this time Achaia was bandied from one Angevin
grantee to another by means of complicated marriage treaties
with Villehardouin heiresses.   A Louis of Burgundy defeated
and slew (1316) the Majorcan prince Ferdinand, and was
himself poisoned soon after.   The Angevin John of Gravina
(1318-33) even governed for a while in person.   Then Robert
of Taranto, son of the titular Latin Empress Catherine, was
nominal ruler (1333-64).   The strongest power in the land
was the Empress's factotum, the Florentine merchant Niccolò
Acciaiuoli, who in Greece was a feudal lord.   The older
Frankish nobility of Achaia was mainly extinct and its place
taken by a newer set of adventurers.   The Franks had lost
ground to the Greeks.   The Greek governors of Mistra were
appointed for long terms of office—the Despot Manuel Cantacuzene for life (1348-80)—and their enlarged province was
not only prosperous but becoming one of the last centres of
Greek culture.   It contrasted with Achaia under the absentee
Angevins.   In Epirus, where the line of Angeli had given
place to half Italian Orsini (1318), the Byzantines succeeded
in restoring their rule, till it was conquered by Stephen
Dushan in 1349 together with Thessaly.   When Dushan's
empire dissolved, a local Serbian dynasty remained.

In this situation, ever more threatened by the Osmanlis
from the north, we leave Greece proper.   Hopeless disunion

of races, religions, and restless dynasts was its main feature.
The Franks never took healthy root ; the Greeks could not
expel them. The Venetians in chief and their Genoese
rivals exploited the rich commerce from their colonies
and fortresses. Angevin and Aragonese, without establishing any effective rule, increased the confusion. Yet the
vitality of the Greeks was shown in art and literature. The
Balkans as a whole were teeming with hardy warriors. They
and Christendom were paying for the blind greed and ignorant
racial hatreds of the Fourth Crusade.

SUGGESTIONS FOR READING FOR CHAPTER XIX

A. Sources

Chalcocondyles, L. : *Historiae.* Ed. Bekker, I. Corpus Scriptorum
Historiae Byzantinae. Bonn, 1843.
Phrantzes, G. : *Chronicon.* Ed. Bekker, I. Corpus Scriptorum Historiae
Byzantinae. Bonn, 1838.

B. Modern Works

Atiya, A. S. : *The Crusade in the later Middle Ages.* London, 1938.
Baynes, N. H. : *The Byzantine Empire.* London, 1925.
Bréhier, L. : *L'église et l'Orient au Moyen Âge.* 5th edn. Paris, 1928.
Cambridge Medieval History, vol. iv, relevant chapters.
Finlay, G. : *History of Greece.* Ed. Tozer, H. F. Oxford, 1877.
Miller, W. : *The Latins in the Levant.* London, 1908.
Gibbon, E. : *History of the Decline and Fall of the Roman Empire.* Ed.
Bury, J. B. London, 1909–14.
Miller, W. : *Trebizond, the last Greek Empire.* London, 1926.
Diehl, C. : *Histoire de l'empire Byzantin.* Paris, 1919.
Diehl, C. : *Byzance, grandeur et décadence.* Paris, 1919.
Diehl, C. : *Manuel de l'art Byzantin.* Paris, 1910.
Dalton, O. M. : *Byzantine Art and Archaeology.* Oxford, 1911.
Hill, G. : As given for Chapter VI.
Pears, E. : *Destruction of the Greek Empire.* London, 1903.
Jorga, N. : *The Byzantine Empire.* Trans. Powles, A. H. Temple
Primers. London, 1907.
Spinka, M. : *A History of Christianity in the Balkans.* Chicago, 1933.
Temperley, H. : *History of Serbia.* London, 1919.
Seton-Watson : *History of Roumania.* London, 1935.
Gibbons, H. A. : *The Foundation of the Ottoman Empire.* Oxford, 1916.

CHAPTER XX

CHIVALRY, WARFARE, AND DAILY LIFE

The Code of Chivalry

EACH of the four classes which made up medieval society, the clerk, the knight, the bourgeois, and the peasant, had its own set of duties corresponding to its occupation, but only in the first two were those duties formulated into an ideal of conduct. The ecclesiastic was to pray and even to preach, and to practise at least the lower grades of asceticism: chastity, obedience, and poverty. The knight came to have an analogous code of chivalry, knightliness. And as we have seen that the generality of clerks made but poor progress in attaining to the ideal allotted to them, so it was with the chivalric class. The ideal of chivalry was " more honoured in the breach than in the observance ". Yet the existence and inculcation of the ideal did have their effect in taming slowly the little mitigated barbarity of earlier times and introducing a higher standard of conduct among the fighting nobles in an age that, even in its advance, was still rough and fierce and crudely passionate. The Middle Ages were only learning civilization, but they were creative ; they conceived a better world than that they lived in ; and their small realization of their dreams is less wonderful than the indubitable improvement under conditions of disorder, brutality, and ignorance which would seem to make it impossible.

Its Development

The ideal of chivalry, however, was the product of a long period of development, most of which falls outside the limits of this volume. As may be seen in the *Chansons de Geste* of the eleventh and twelfth centuries, the primal conception was one of manliness, the reckless and stubborn courage, the fierce independence, and the honest faith towards lord, kinsman, and comrade, befitting a vassal who held his land on military tenure by fealty and homage, and whose occupation was war. To these essential elements, the influence of the Church added another, the protection of

Christendom, and the duty to fight in the Christian cause and for Christian purposes. The Crusades exercised a The Crusades powerful influence so far as religious warfare went. To defeat and slay the infidel and compel him to be converted, and to restore to Christendom the Holy Land, the scene of the life and crucifixion of Christ, was a sacred vocation leading to Heaven, and as congenial to a race of warriors as the unremitting pursuit of personal and family feuds and feudal warfare, which as the Churchmen reminded them led to Hell. When the crusade against heretics was invented in the thirteenth century along with that against the obstinate heathen of Prussia and the Baltic lands, this Holy War, if less really religious, became more attractive still, for the profits were greater ; it competed with its older version, the long effort of reconquest in Spain against the Moors, where indeed much of its spirit was bred. To fight for Holy Church and to extend the frontiers of Christendom became the most laudable part of the knight's profession.

When the Military Orders of Knighthood were founded for the defence of the Holy Land and pilgrims, the semi-monastic life to which they were vowed contributed to the growth of the ideal. So, too, did the influence on the side of self-restraint and rightful dealing which emanated from the magnetic St. Bernard and others of his like. A quasi-religious devotion to women, a vocation to champion widows and orphans and the oppressed were added to the prescription of turbulent manliness. In the late twelfth century we find the idea of knight-errantry embodied in the lays of the Arthurian cycle. The knight is still absorbed in the quest for adventure, but he defends ladies in peril and abolishes evil customs. So, too, for the first time he becomes a lover. *Amour* This transformation was earliest effected in South France *courtois* and gives the inspiration to the poetry of the troubadours of Langue d'oc. That district and language had become too civilized and luxurious to be content with the fierce virility of the older ideal alone. Wealth and the chances of inheritance and the frequent absence of the feudal noble on adventure had given the feudal lady more independence and had for the first time imparted a feministic outlook to medieval society. The Provençals' neighbourhood to and their dealings with the Arabs of Spain, with their quasi-refinement, their

civilized treatment of their womenfolk, and their preoccupation with impassioned love-poetry, must have had their
effect. The Provençal troubadour, who was often a Provençal knight, erected a science of courtly love (*amour
courtois*), which became a necessary ingredient of the knightly
character. The lover chose the sovereign lady of his heart,
worshipped her with unremitting devotion, and was inspired
by her to feats of arms and chivalrous behaviour. In a
society, where the unmarried girl was kept largely in seclusion and where marriages were contracted by family arrangement at an early age, the lady of the *amour courtois* was
almost always married and, in theory, unobtainable. The
knight's love was platonic by convention, however much
this may have been belied by the facts of life. Hence to
passion and constancy was added the chivalrous virtue of
secrecy in love. The knight must endure any pain or shame
rather than reveal his lady's favour, even platonic. But
other virtues followed, too, in this perplexed morality. The
barbaric knight had been generous to profusion, a quality
dear to dependent minstrels ; the new knight must be courteous to all, wise, and self-restrained. His deeds and his
manners must be worthy of the unknown, yet famous, lady
of his heart. He seeks honour ; his actions must be honourable in a wider sense than that of good faith.

This feministic ethos, with its mixture of delicate, high-
strung idealism, of discreet playing with fire, of refinement,
and of free love, was not long in journeying northward as
the north began to quit its rude barbarism. A great lady is

Marie of
Champagne

the protagonist. Marie, Countess of Champagne (1145–98),
was the daughter of Louis VII of France and the gay Eleanor,
heiress of Aquitaine and later wife of Henry II of England.
In her court at Troyes, her husband's capital, she brought
the new chivalry and science of love into the land and literature of Langue d'oïl, whence it spread over Europe. The
Arthurian lays of Chrestien de Troyes and his fellows, recited or
read to a society of knights and ladies, acted as propaganda.
In this new atmosphere and diffusion the *amour courtois*
definitely abandoned the conventional platonism of the
troubadours. It might be the exalted love for an unwed girl
which ended in a happy marriage. More generally it is
represented as the same devotion for the married woman ;

Lancelot and Guinevere become the models for the chivalric class, for a knight who was not a lover was unequal to his calling.

Hunting and the mimic warfare of the tournament were the recreations of this aristocratic society. There was a science of venery and falconry as well as of love. Here again may be noted the greater part that the noble dame was playing. She could take part in flying the hawk as she rarely could in the violent sport of hunting the stag or boar. She was the privileged spectator of the tournament, in whose Tourna-honour lances were broken and men killed, and whose favours ments were borne by her champion in the lists. The institution of tournaments, in which knights fully armed fought for victory, was a beneficial invention of the eleventh century which had reached its apogee in the year 1200. It gave the chivalrous class their dearest pleasure and the occupation which was their *raison d'être* ; it made and kept them expert in arms and horsemanship without the misery of non-combatants, the ruin and devastation of the countryside, which accompanied the private wars and feuds of the fierce baronage. Naturally denounced and forbidden by the Church for its un-Christian character and the deaths which were its inevitable incidents, it acted, as did distant crusades, as a safety-valve for the fighting instincts of a turbulent race. For the fighting of the tournament in the thirteenth century was fully real. Whether in the single combat or in the *mêlée* with hundreds of knights on each side the weapons were those of warfare, and death and wounds were freely dealt. It had its profits, too, which took the place of booty. The arms and armour and the person of the defeated stood at the disposal of the victor, and were redeemed by ransom. An expert and invincible jouster, like William Marshall, Earl of Pembroke (*ob.* 1219), in his younger, poorer days, could make a living by the spoils of his vanquished adversaries as he passed from tournament to tournament.

William Marshall himself might be given as a favourable Completion instance of the improvement in the morale of knighthood of the Ideal which was taking place. Of unquestioned honour, of inviolable fidelity to the lord to whom he had done homage, of self-restraint and even unselfishness in victory, he contrasts with the ungovernable heroes of the *Chansons de*

Geste. And he represents a tendency visible among a host of men whose record is much inferior. But the ideal of knighthood was still being heightened. This change was represented in literature by the Romances of the Holy Grail, the vessel which, whatever its origins in heathen tradition, was associated with the Last Supper and the loftiest conception of chivalry. Here the hero was the virgin knight, Sir Galahad, who was free from sinful and earthly love and therefore worthy of the beatific vision. By this creation chivalry received the completion of its ideal and its closest connexion with religion. It is no mere coincidence that in the thirteenth century a king reigned who was the living embodiment of the ideal. Apart from the ascetic virginity of Sir Galahad, which no medieval writer could omit when he drew a portrait of absolute perfection, St. Louis obeyed without contradiction the precepts of chivalry when it was still new-found and fresh. Fervently religious, chaste, just, kindly, truthful, courteous, and brave, a foe to heretics and infidels, a lover of peace and faith, the protector of the poor and weak,

> " he lovëd chivalrye,
> Trouthe and honour, fredom and curteisye."

The history of the times shows how exceptional he was, but chivalry was one of the forces which had made him possible, and he testifies to an amelioration of contemporary standards of knightly behaviour. It must be confessed that the conduct of the noble class among which he lived, and to which he was a congenial hero, was immeasurably below his: it was still violent, brutal, dissolute, pitiless. But, in varying degrees over the West, it felt the curb and listened to the incitements of chivalry. The average knight was no longer the mere creature of impulse, redeemed by valour and fidelity, which his ancestor had been.

It was natural that the diffusion and general acceptance of the ideal of chivalry by the feudal class over Western Europe should result in the formalizing of the ideal. The creative, spontaneous age of chivalry ends with St. Louis as that of asceticism ends with St. Francis. As a discipline for ordinary nobles, chivalry inevitably became a code, a thing of cut-and-dried rules, a matter of good form adapted to the normal capacity. In the process it became too often an external manifestation of good breeding with but a

St. Louis

Fourteenth-century Chivalry

moderate effect on the man within. The knight of the fourteenth century, more frequently than his predecessor, did the proper thing. He fought the infidel somewhere—in Spain, in Prussia, in the Levant—and got that duty over. He frequented tournaments under rules which lessened the death-roll and made it a matter of dextrous horsemanship. He gave largess to minstrel and herald on the due occasions. He had his sentimental love-affairs with high-wrought, conventional fancy. He observed a code of formal courtesy to ladies. He took fantastic vows which could be kept without great difficulty. In war, he fought challenged battles at a set place, and charged with reckless, brainless courage. He thanked his enemy for a good fight. He gave mercy to the vanquished and filled his purse with the ransom. He played with great spirit the part of the knight of romance.

Two things strike one in this later chivalry, its addiction to show, and its narrow class spirit. Never was chivalry more splendid and profuse than in the tournaments, processions, and banquets of the fourteenth century. The knight, with his armour and its blazoned trappings, his golden spurs and ring, his cloak of scarlet and vair, was a gorgeous, indeed a gaudy, figure. Pompous ceremonial and rich costume were the essential feature of the new orders of the Garter, or the Star, or the Collar, founded by warlike potentates with enigmatic mottoes. If it could be afforded, the ceremony of his knighthood, once the girding on of the sword, and the giving of the blow on the neck, with the words " Be valiant," was enhanced by vigils and symbolic bathing, prayers, vows, and benedictions, ending with the sumptuous array in his knightly garb. His necessary love affair might be a convention, harmless enough like that of the last troubadour, Theobald of Champagne, for the spotless Queen Blanche of France, while more earthly loves engaged him. The form, indeed, such was the strength of the ideal, might be both passionate and overruling. In such ways Dante loved Beatrice and Petrarch Laura, continuing in Italy the tradition of the troubadours. But these were supreme poets, to whom the world of vision was more real and deeper in the spirit than the world of fact. Their truth in other men was a routine of hyperbole. They made living and immortal what their world wished to believe it was.

Its Pomp and Conventions

Heraldry   The knight's coat of arms, the subject of the so-called science of heraldry, had become of the first importance in this age of class ostentation. The usage of coloured devices on the shield, apart from mere ornamentation, had begun in the first half of the twelfth century. The famous cross of Savoy appears in 1137 ; Geoffrey Plantagenet, Count of Anjou (*ob.* 1150), used a design afterwards borne by his illegitimate grandson, the Earl of Salisbury ; the fleur-de-lys of France was adopted as a badge by Louis VI (*ob.* 1137). The concealment of the face in the helmet in battle or tournament made these marks of identification a necessity. By 1200 the designs, once assumed, were becoming hereditary and by 1300 were universal for knights. They were embroidered on the surcoat and painted on the lance's pennon as well as depicted on their original home, the shield. The designs or " charges " on the shields were composed from geometrical forms, in which varieties of the Cross were predominant, and from natural objects, like animals and plants.[1] The need to identify each individual and to indicate inheritance and intermarriage introduced further refinements ; dimidiation (the halves of two shields set side by side) appears *c.* 1200, impalement (the whole of two coats side by side in the same shield) a little later, quartering (two coats repeated alternately, 1, 2, 2, 1, in the four quarters of the shield) in the mid-thirteenth century ; the younger sons of a family used small additions to its coat to show their " cadency." As might be expected, the thirteenth-century coats in their simplicity and grace are the most beautiful ; besides the need of innumerable different coats, the fourteenth century increased the oddity and fantastic elaboration of the designs. To know how to describe (blazon) a coat and identify it became a necessary branch of a knight's education, and a group of expert officials, the heralds, grew up, sacrosanct intermediaries in war and tournament, the custodians of the usages of chivalry and the knowledge of armorial bearings. Their " science " was a curious mixture of indispensable information, ingenious and useful rules, trifling pedantry, and pompous display.

----

[1] Punning on the name was frequent (*armes parlantes*), e.g. the King of Castile bore a castle, the King of Leon a lion, Louis (Loys) of France a fleur-de-lys.

No less marked than the taste for show was the narrow- Class
ness of the chivalric sphere of duties. The good bourgeois Limitation
was at best tolerated. The peasant was always derided and of Chivalry
despised—villain and churl were terms of reproach. In
the practice, if not the pure theory of chivalry, he was
no subject for courtesy, mercy, or generosity. He was
without the pale, born to serve and suffer. To his women
were due neither the respect nor the protection nor the self-
restraint which were to be observed towards ladies of gentle
birth. It is often quoted how the Black Prince, who guarded
his captive King John with splendid hospitality, could
massacre without pity the ignoble inhabitants of revolted
Limoges, and how Edward III nearly did the same to the
gallant *bourgeoisie* of Calais, guilty of the crime of heroic
resistance. The father and son were models of the chivalry
of their day, not ferocious exceptions, although it is to be
remembered that all his knights interceded with Edward III.
Chivalry was obligatory between knight and knight, noble
and noble, not to uncouth plebeians. In the next age it was
to become more hollow and fall lower still. Yet the rise in
the standard of behaviour remained. The chivalric class had
acquired convictions of honour, loyalty, fair play, and
courtesy, the practice of which, even if formal and imperfect,
was the badge of their rank. The fulfilment of the ideal
brought praise and admiration, gross transgression of it
discredit and a stain. Even though the savage instincts
would break out, a barbarized society had become one tinged,
and often more than tinged, with culture. There was a " good
life " by which actions were measured and towards which
men ought to strive.

The daily life of the chivalric class of the thirteenth and Daily Life
fourteenth centuries combined elements of both splendour of the
and luxury and primitive hardness and discomfort. Of course, Chivalric
Class
it not only grew somewhat less rude by the close of the period,
but it varied immensely from country to country and from
grade to grade among the aristocracy. The Italian or
Spaniard did not live like the North Frenchman or English-
man ; the baronial household was very different from that
of the lord of a single manor. Still there were certain very
general features of the life of the age which appeared in
similar forms in each country and in diverse degrees of

wealth or importance. One of these features was the lack of privacy whether in castle or manor house. The great lady might retire from the hall full of retainers and guests, to the solar, but even that was more of a family living-room than a private apartment. The habit of entertaining friends in a new room, the parlour, which became frequent in the fourteenth century, might make her company more select, yet not the less present. The bedroom, if she was of consequence to have one of her own, was shared by day with her waiting women. The vaunted secrecy of her lover, if she had one, was at the mercy of confidantes or spies. And the men's life was as little private as that of a public-school boy. A second

feature was the rude equipment of the feudal household. Glass windows were, even at the end of the fourteenth century, a luxury of the great. Ill-lit, draughty, and smoky in the north, or in the fireless south deadly cold in winter, the hall or room might be gay with paintings or arras hangings for the wealthy, but the floor was rush-strewn or bare save perhaps in Spain or Provence, where carpets for solar or parlour had been borrowed from the Moors. Benches, settles, stools, chests, and a rare chair were the furniture. The best comfort was to sit on a cushion or the foot of the bed. Eating was accomplished, except in luxurious Italy, without forks. Two diners shared the same platter or the slab of coarse bread (the trencher) which served the same purpose. Sugar, pepper, and spices, which disguised the coarse meats, were costly luxuries, the source of merchants' fortunes. Comfort is a relative term, but in the modern interpretation the age

had little or none. The third feature, which characterized the noble and his inferiors, was the time spent in the open air. Not only did sport or war occupy the daylight hours, but the garden and the orchard were the natural escape from the gloomy, chilly dwelling. If rain or snow did not drive them in, it was the best place for leisure and even business hours, the safest for a private interview. Winter was one of the evils of life ; the coming of May—" Sumer is icumen in "— was welcomed with a joy that rings through all medieval

secular literature, courtly or simple. Fourthly, we may remark the shortness of life. Commonly, the medieval knight could not look forward to fifty years—battle or disease, in an age when medical knowledge was scanty and

mainly fallacious, carried him off. His lady's lot was no
better. To die in childbirth was a likely event for any bride.
The frequency of second and third marriages, even allowing
for the annullations which the wide circle of forbidden
degrees permitted to interest or fickleness, testifies to the
brief life of one or other wedded partner.

The life of the lady was naturally more stay-at-home than Life of the
that of the knight. To manage her household, to spin and Ladies
weave, occupied the country dame ; to embroider with her
damsels at the window or to be read to and to read, to listen
to the minstrel, were the employments of the great lady,
besides the devotions that were common to both. Dances,
singing, games, festivals, and hawking were her recreations.
Her marriage was usually arranged by parent or guardian, and
was often an undisguised sale ; in theory she owed complete
submission to her husband, a submission which contemporary
opinion, at variance with the convention of chivalry, allowed
to be enforced with blows. The frankness of ordinary speech
in both sexes reached coarseness and verged on brutality.
In dress she followed her own wishes and the prevailing Dress
fashion in spite of the sermons of friars or the laments of the
elderly. If fashions changed but slowly, their evolution over
the period was marked enough. Buttons were welcomed
with a kind of rapture when they came in after 1300 ; their
use allowed garments to fit the wearer in a fashion hitherto
unknown. The simpler, graceful dress of the thirteenth
century, in harmony with its architecture, gave way to the
more elaborate and varied costume of the fourteenth, and then
degenerated into fantastic, garish oddities as the year 1400
drew nearer. Men's dress went through an analogous
change ; a buttoned *cotehardie* succeeded the tunic, and after
1350 taste began to degenerate towards a foolish, *outré*
fantasy. The showiness which characterized the later
chivalry appeared in this, too. As a girl the lady had been
taught her accomplishments and kept in the background
save when she went with downcast eyes to church, in the
south the common beginning of the lover's enthralment. But
we may doubt whether the seclusion was always so strict or
never evaded. Nature and youth were strong.

The training of the knight was more varied, like his later Education
life. Primarily, it was still the education of a feudal vassal of the Men

with everyday duties to perform as a member of the fighting, governing class.   The ideal of chivalry was a sublimation of those essential duties and that ethos, the carving on the pillar and capital which did not disguise and was not an absolutely necessary adjunct to their social function.   The knight had to be able to take his part in a feudal complex.

The Page The boy of gentle birth, the *damoiseau*, began his career away from home somewhere about the age of seven or eight in the household of some noble, great or small.   There he learnt his manners in attendance on the ladies, as a kind of upper servant, and was trained in physical exercises and sports, riding and the management of mimic weapons.   He would learn French, if it was not his native tongue, for it was the language of chivalry and vernacular literature.   In the fourteenth century, reading became a common accomplishment, and writing increasingly frequent—Edward III's autograph has survived.   A knowledge of Latin, even, is to be noted occasionally towards the close of the period, and so is the royal or noble author in vernacular prose.   If we go south to Italy and Spain, Latin is there, especially in Italy, an easier and frequent acquirement.   The town-loving nobles of Italy were literate in 1300, even if only in the vulgar tongue, and a king in Spain in 1270 could be Alfonso the Learned.   A petty noble in the north might still be unlettered much later.   We must never forget the wide variations over Europe in the general picture.

The Squire The next stage in the gentleman's career was that of the squire.   At an average age of fourteen he entered on his apprenticeship in arms.   His duties were now more about the person of his lord, to arm and attend him and follow him to hunt and war, to become an expert in the difficult management of horse and weapons.   By the age of twenty Chaucer's Squire in the *Canterbury Tales* had already fought in France.

> "Wel coude he sitte on hors, and fairë ryde.
> He coudë songës make and well endyte,
> Juste and eek daunce, and wel purtreye and wryte. . . .
> Curteys he was, lowly, and servisable,
> And carf biforn his fader at the table."

The domestic duties of the squire included waiting on the ladies as well as carving at table.   The romances of real life, often unedifying, as well as the ideal, began in squireship.

The squire was now qualified to assume the more inde- The Knight pendent position of the knight, to " take on him the order of knighthood." What this meant in the theory of chivalry we have seen. In real life it meant that he was qualified for command and employment, for serving in the host with a full array of squires and sergeants of his own. But far from every squire proceeded to the degree of knighthood : its obligations and expenses were too heavy. He might remain a squire in some great household, or more likely, if an elder son, return to his manor to live the life of a country noble, with not infrequent intervals of war and adventure. The numerous younger sons were eager for royal employment or that of duke and count. They swelled the army of officials and adventurous warriors, ending their career in France as a " chevalier du roi." In North Italy, indeed, the rank of knight was almost a civic dignity which marked the greatness of a family and its noble status. In Florence, it was the touchstone by which a noble house incurred the disabilities and penalties of the " Grandi."

Chivalry had grown up with a particular method of fighting Arms and and a particular military organization, that of the mounted Armour man-at-arms who served by feudal tenure for a specified period per year. Its repute depended on the superiority of the mounted, armoured knight so trained and levied, over opponents on foot or with lighter armament. The weapons he must learn to use required both strength and skill. First and foremost was the long and cumbrous lance used in the charge. Then there was the heavy sword for closer fighting. And these were supplemented by the ruder battleaxe and mace and the dagger for dispatching the foe. These weapons changed but little, but the defensive armour improved. In 1200 the knight wore a flat-topped helmet of beaten steel which covered the face. Underneath this came the hood of chain mail (interlaced steel rings) covering head, neck, and shoulders. The main defence was the hauberk or sleeved shirt of mail, either chain or rows of little plates or rings, which was worn over a padded leather jerkin. Footed hose of mail completed the body armour. Over all was worn the surcoat which kept the mail from rust and displayed the coat of arms to identify the wearer. On his left arm the knight carried the small " heater-shaped " shield, also emblazoned with his coat of arms, to ward off the blow of sword or lance. The heavy horse or destrier that he rode in battle or tournament was in its turn often partly covered with mail or hardened leather.

Their development

This equipment, weighty and clogging as it was, was, except for the shield, a better defence against actual cuts than against bruises and broken bones, and it was against these that thirteenth-century developments were directed. The knees and elbows, which the shield could not guard, were defended by jointed plate-armour or *cuir-bouilli* over the mail, and the use spread from the south of strips of plate down the legs and arms to safeguard the bones. The helmet of war became conical, as it had been earlier, so that blows should glance off. The deadliness of archery in the fourteenth century and the increase of the armourer's skill produced a further advance. Now the legs and arms were sheathed in jointed plate-armour, a breast-plate was superimposed on the chain-mail shirt, gauntlets and shoes of jointed plate covered hands and feet, bands of steel hung from the breast-plate. The day was not far distant when knight and horse would be cased in plate-armour. The knight and his horse were becoming barely vulnerable towers of steel, irresistible if they could get their tumultuous charge home, but almost helpless if thrown or held up by pike or stake. The practice of the tournament only prepared them against one another in a fossilized fashion.

The decline of the feudal array and of chivalry was hastened by the rise of a more efficient fighting force, the mercenary soldier. The military service of the feudal knight was after all a part-time occupation, especially when private war diminished. He was invincible partly because of his armament and splendid courage, partly because the footmen he lorded over were likewise part-timers, less eager for battle, worse-equipped, and not tempered for combat by the regulated conflict of the tournament. But in the thirteenth century *The Professional Soldier* there was steadily growing the employment of professional mercenary soldiers. Although from the start they might consist of adventurers of any rank, these were largely poor nobles and younger sons. Frederick II and his sons had recruited nobles and *ministeriales* from Swabia, and the practice was continued by the Italian tyrants with Frederick's permission, and later with that of Rudolf of Habsburg—Guido della Torre of Milan, like Ezzelin da Romano before him, had a guard of German troopers. Henry VII led to Italy not only feudal forces but mercenary Brabantines. A fresh source of supply, both mailed horse and foot, was opened by the levy of Catalans in the War of the Vespers. With little pretence to nobility, they served in Italy, and conquered Athens as the Grand Company. Lewis the Bavarian and John of Bohemia let loose new swarms of German adventurers on Italy, who ended by forming the terrible Free Companies there. Meanwhile the Hundred Years' War, as we have seen, led to the creation of similar Free Companies, horse and foot, out of nobles and peasants practised in continual war. These soldiers were commonly unmitigated ruffians, but their valour was enhanced by a professional competence that was not ornamental, and they were open to considerations of tactics and even strategy that the knight with his chivalry did not imagine.

As we have seen, new weapons were ready, which the seasoned warrior did not disdain, and which neutralized much of the advantage of the old chivalric training in horse and lance. The Pike and the Long-bow The Flemish pikemen found at Courtrai that they could beat off and rout the most furious charge of feudal knights if they kept together in a chosen position. In the same way, or one but little different, the Swiss overcame German chivalry at Sempach. The lesson was applied by knights themselves when they dismounted and made pikes of their lances at Dupplin Muir and Crécy. The Catalan light infantry of the Almugàvers, with their short swords, when supported by knights, could dispatch the horses and cumbered riders of the packed enemy squadrons by flank attacks. As epochmaking, at least, was the English employment of the longbow, begun by Edward I. The cross-bow was deadly, yet excessively slow in a field of action. But if covered by mounted and dismounted knights on a chosen ground from the impact of the enemy charge, the long-bowmen could cut up and ruin with their swift volleys the wildly attacking feudal array as it lumbered onwards on its heavy destriers. Hitherto tactics had been mainly confined to the use of a

concealed reserve. Now there were opportunities for a plan
of battle, even if it were only workable on the defensive.
The adoption of complete plate-armour only alleviated the
knight's disadvantage by practically shortening the effective
range of the clothyard shaft. The English system could be
met by a plan of campaign, like that of Bertrand du Guesclin,
which declined to attack and eschewed pitched battles. But
it will be noticed that in neither case were the conventions of
chivalry, with its challenges to battle on a fixed place and day,
or the unthinking charges of the feudal knight trained in the
clash of the tournament, of more than subordinate use.
Craft and forethought were counting more and more, and the
day of manœuvre was near at hand.

Gunpowder   The invention of gunpowder and of cannon was another
novelty in the warfare of the fourteenth century, which
appears in its third decade. Excessive slowness and uncertainty of fire, clumsiness and immobility as extreme, made
cannon for many years of little use save for their effect on the
enemies' morale, but in the last ten years of the period, though
still in their infancy, they could slowly breach town-wall or
castle. They were in the charge of professional plebeians.
The knight's training was no help here. Like the professional
soldiery and peasant archers they were making the feudal
host and the training and methods of chivalry out of date.
The heavy-armed horseman had his place in war ; he was not
its master. Even in fifteenth-century Italy, where foot came
to be neglected, he was a professional mercenary, not a
knight of chivalry.

The Clerical   A considerable overlapping of functions between class and
Order   class was given to later medieval society by the wide extension
of the clerical order. The reception of the tonsure and a
smattering of Latin made a man a clerk, however profane his
life and occupation might be. Clerks of noble or plebeian
extraction filled the royal and feudal and town administra-
tions as well as the universities. If they wished to be
rewarded with ecclesiastical benefices, which required them
either to take or to be able to take the higher orders, they were
obliged to remain celibate, but otherwise there was no
necessity for them to take orders at all, or they could be
content with the lower orders, below that of sub-deacon,
which were compatible with marriage. It was among these

amphibious persons, who, if they took church endowment, took it as a salary for other services or as a maintenance for a life of study, that the most zealous and able defenders of the lay powers, the " clercs " and even the " chevaliers du roi " were found. It was only in the fourteenth century that we find the mere layman cropping up among them. They formed a link between classes ; it was the snapping of it by the increase of unequivocally lay literacy which at the close of this period was tending to isolate the ecclesiastical hierarchy as it had not been isolated since the rise of the universities. The life of the majority of clerks, therefore, apart from their literate profession and their lack of the warlike exercises of the laity, differed very little from that of the class of society in which they happened to be. The church dignitary would probably live in rather greater comfort than his lay counter-part. The town or country parish priest occupied the same position with regard to bourgeois or peasant. Celibacy was ineffectively enforced. Pretty generally the parish priest formed a connexion with an *amica* to manage his house. If he did not, he was likely to be regarded as a danger to the families of his parishioners. Yet there was still the eagerness of parents to provide for a clever son amid the ranks of the ecclesiastics, against whom they railed with virulent hatred. The chaste priest was naturally all the more admired if little imitated.

Unless he was a Carthusian, the life of the well-conducted The Monks monk was differentiated from his lay neighbours rather by its regular, community discipline and the time passed in the *opus Dei* in the choir than by any great severity of asceticism in the fourteenth century. The monks lived according to the scale of their endowments, which of course varied from monastery to monastery. Learning, though still existent and encouraged by legislation, was the vocation of but few. The monks, too, saw a good deal of the outer world. They had numerous guests—hospitality was a favourite duty —they had property to manage and much business in the world. Manual labour was on the way to disappearance. Even the Cistercian lay brother, who worked in the fields, was superseded by hired labourers and by lease-holders. A monk could be as devout, learned, and ascetic as he chose, but usually there was little to compel him to be so. Ill-conducted,

lax, and corrupt monasteries merely added crying sins to this
undistinguished life.   Save for the austere Carthusians, the
monk might well enter the monastery as a youth, sometimes
from his parents' devoutness, sometimes because he seemed
unfit for the rough and tumble of the world.   He might well
be unsuited for the religious life in either case.   He received
his education from the master of the novices.   When he was
of sufficient age, he would be professed a monk, and enter on
the normal routine to continue as plain monk or obedientiary
(official).   If he rose to be abbot, he had a separate dwelling
in the abbey precincts, and according to the wealth of the
foundation lived as a great or small landowner.   The mendi-
The Friars cant friars varied between comfort and indigence just as they
numbered among them more devout or learned men and
more rogues (among the Franciscans at least) than the monks.
They were more of the people than the monks and took the
colour of their surroundings.   Yet there was no mistaking the
religious fervour of the time.   External and superstitious as
Religious it largely was, men believed in the Christian faith with an
Mentality ardour proportioned to the violence, oppression, fraud, and
of the Age cruelty which they saw and practised.   The solemn rites of
daily worship, the consolations of religion, the sermons and
legends which depicted a higher life and appealed to higher
instincts were ever present.   It required devotion and
courage to be a heretic.   Ignorance and barbarism perverted
these instincts to the fashion of the age.   On the news of
the captivity of St. Louis the shepherds and wandering rabble
of North France followed an adventurous impostor, who produced a letter from the Virgin Mary, in the plundering,
insensate Crusade of the *Pastoureaux*.   By the time they got
to Bourges the authorities, at first impressed, had had enough
of their outrages—they were suppressed and dispersed.   In
the same century the terrible crusades against the heretics
and heathen were admired and organized.   But yet hospitals
were founded, penniless girls dowered, alms given, and works
of charity done.   The leaven of Christianity did not cease to
work among men for all the formalism and corruption with
which it was surrounded.

Daily Life Differences in wealth varied the life of the townsmen from
of the such luxury as the age afforded to poverty or destitution.
Townsmen Town-life, except at times in the south, did not necessarily

imply such an absence of rural surroundings as might appear
from their occupations. The country was at their doors and
the well-to-do had their gardens. It did imply, however, the
narrow, filthy street on which the houses were built, and into
which refuse of all sorts was cast. It did imply the constant
risk of fire in the lath and plaster and even the stone dwellings.
Perhaps the greater part of a town's habitations might have
a life of twenty or thirty years. The shop or counting house
on the ground floor corresponded to the hall of the manor, and
was open to the street in business hours : outside might be
the bench for gossip. Above the shop was the family living-
room. The wealthier the merchant, the more rooms he
would have in the fourteenth century, and the accessories of
tapestries, beds, and cushions would not be inferior to those
of the wealthy knight, but he would be more crowded than
the latter. The poorer the artisan, the more narrow was
his dwelling and the ruder and scantier his furniture. In this
class, too, as you went south, the more were the refinement
and convenience, and also the privacy of the well-to-do—the
house might be built round a court—but a prevailing
simplicity of domestic apparatus, however costly and colour-
ful, was universal. The grades of the induction into craft
and business have already been described,[1] but in the fourteenth century the children of a prosperous bourgeois, boys Education
and girls, went to school together, where they were taught to
read and write and the elements of Latin. Such might, like
Froissart, become clerks, but they mostly continued in their
father's business. In Italy, indeed, the literary bourgeois,
like Villani or Sacchetti, was common. Latin and the
vernacular were open to them, even if they made no pretence
to learning. Bourgeois morals were no better or worse than
those of the nobles. To guess from the facts of later centuries,
infant mortality was far higher among them than in the
countryside, and the enlargement of the towns may partly
account for the slowing down of the increase of the population
in the fourteenth century. Poor as the inferior townsmen
might be, they lacked neither holidays nor amusements.
The Church's holidays were numerous, and made life tolerable.
Of drinking (especially in the north), singing, dancing, games,
and rough sports the year was full. A boisterous, thriftless

[1] See above, Chap. IX, p. 178.

cheerfulness pervaded this rude society. Miserable in evil times, they enjoyed the day and did not look forward to the morrow which they knew would come for good or ill in spite of them.

The life of the peasant was even more the sport of war and famine. Owing to torrential rains there was from 1315 to 1317 a terrible famine, only a little relieved by importation from Sicily and Naples, which devastated Germany, the Netherlands, and northern France with effects comparable to those of the Black Death forty years later; and local and less deadly dearths were not infrequent. In the fourteenth century, as we have seen,[1] the peasant's lot grew worse, and the sufferings of the French and Italian peasant from the Free Companies were atrocious. In better times, the prosperity of the rural population varied much from country to country according to local conditions, and indeed from year to year, according to the seasons. The vineyards of the south, the pastures of Switzerland, the polders of Flanders, the rich ploughlands of Normandy gave a very different subsistence than did the barren uplands of Castile or the heaths of Saxony and Brandenburg. In Catalonia and other districts serfdom was still rampant; in lands where personal freedom was widespread there was generally the poor class of landless cottars who lived on the edge of beggary. At their best, the circumstances of well-to-do peasants—and there were many such in France and North Italy—who had escaped from serfdom were far from intolerable. Their ignorance was profound; their civilization primitive and full of heathen survivals. There was hard work. The houses were ill-built, two-roomed cottages in the north, in the south larger buildings but the dwelling of several families, in both cases shared with the domestic animals. The poorer villagers lived in wretched hovels or apartments, with a pot, a straw bed, and a stool for furniture. They all suffered from the exactions and insults of the ruling classes. But in average seasons there was enough to eat; there were holidays; there was only too much sour ale and bitter wine; there were dances, sports, and games; they lived in the open air. Life was rude and monotonous, brawling and limited, but the sameness of to-day and to-morrow was a blessing. It was

---

[1] See above, Chap. IX, pp. 192–94.

the variety of flood and famine, pestilence and war, which was the ever-present dread of the Middle Ages.

SUGGESTIONS FOR READING FOR CHAPTER XX

A. Sources

The suggestions for Chapter IX are useful for this chapter also, as well as those under Literature for Chapter X. To these may be added such chronicles as Froissart and Joinville, Dante's *Divina Commedia*, the *Histoire de Guillaume le Maréchal*, ed. Meyer, P., 3 vols., Paris, 1891-1901, and the early Italian poets together with Dante's *Vita Nuova*, trans. Rossetti, D. G., ed. Gardiner, E. G. (Temple Classics), London, 1904. *Le Novelle* of F. Sacchetti, 2 vols., Florence, 1888, give familiar Tuscan life.

B. Modern Works

in addition to those suggested for Chapters IX and X

Ashdown, C. H. : *British and Foreign Arms and Armour*. London, 1909.
Biagi, G. : *Men and Manners of Old Florence*. London, 1909.
Cambridge Medieval History, vol. v, chapters xx, xxii ; vol. vi, chapters xxiv, xxv ; vol. viii, chapters xxi, xxiii.
Chaytor, H. J. : *The Troubadours*. Cambridge, 1912.
Coulton, G. G. : *Chaucer and his England*. London, 1908.
Coulton, G. G. : *The Chronicler of European Chivalry*. London, 1930.
Dal Lungo, I. : *Women of Florence*. Trans. Seligmann, M. G. London, 1907.
Evans, J. : *The Unconquered Knight, Pero Niño*. London, 1928.
ffoulkes, C. J. : *Armour and Weapons*. 3 vols. London, 1909.
Galbraith, V. H. : *The Literacy of the English Kings*. Proc. Brit. Acad., 1936.
Gautier, L. : *La chevalerie*. Paris, 1890.
Langlois, C. V. : *La société française au XIII* siècle d'après dix romans d'aventure*. Paris, 1904.
Lavisse, E., ed. : *Histoire de France*. Vols. iii, iv, relevant chapters.
Luchaire, A. : *Social France under Philip Augustus*. Trans. Krehbiel, E. B. London, 1912.
Molmenti, P. : *Venice, the Middle Ages*. Trans. Brown, H. 2 vols. London, 1906.
Niccolini di Camugliano, G. : *The Chronicles of a Florentine Family*. London, 1933.
Oman, C. W. C. : *History of the Art of War in the Middle Ages*. 2 vols. London, 1924.
Painter, S. : *Chivalric Ideas and Practices in Mediaeval France*. Johns Hopkins University Press, 1940.
Prestage, E., ed. : *Chivalry*. London, 1928.
Quennell, M. and C. H. B. : *History of Everyday Things in England*. Pt. I. London, 1918.
Traill, H., ed. : *Social England*. London, 1901 ff.
Woodward, J. : *A Treatise on Heraldry, British and Foreign*. 2 vols. Edinburgh, 1896.
Wright, Thomas : *Homes of Other Days*. London, 1871.

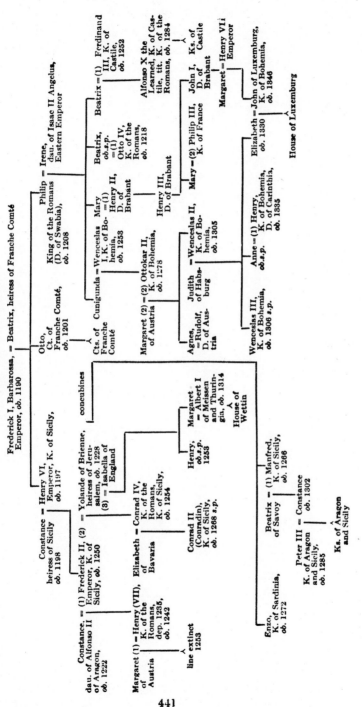

THE HOUSE OF HOHENSTAUFEN

HOUSE OF CAPET

Philip II, Augustus, K. of France, *ob.* 1223

Louis VIII = **Blanche,** dau. of Alfonso VIII of Castile, *ob.* 1252 / K. of France, *ob.* 1226

Robert, Ct. of Artois, / Cts. of Artois

Charles I, = **Beatrix, heiress of Provence,** Ct. of Anjou and Provence, K. of Sicily, *ob.* 1285 / House of Anjou

Alphonse = **Jeanne,** dau. of Raymond VII, Ct. of Poitou and Toulouse, *ob. s.p.* 1271 / Ct. of Toulouse

Margaret of Provence = **St. Louis IX,** K. of France, *ob.* 1270

Isabella = (1) **Philip III** (2) = **Mary of Brabant,** K. of France, *ob.* 1285 / of Aragon

Margaret = (2) **Edward I,** K. of England, *ob.* 1307 / Es. of Norfolk and Kent

Charles (1) = **Margaret of Anjou-Naples,** Ct. of Valois, *ob.* 1325

Louis, Ct. of Evreux, *ob.* 1319

Philip, Ct. of Evreux, K. of Navarre, *ob.* 1343 (*see across*)

Philip IV, K. of France and Navarre, *ob.* 1314

Ferdinand = **Blanche de la Cerda of Castile**

Joanna, = **Philip IV,** heiress of Champagne and Navarre

Philip VI (1) = **Jeanne, heiress of Duchy of Burgundy,** K. of France, *ob.* 1350

John II (1) = **Bona of Bohemia,** K. of France, *ob.* 1364

Philip, D. of Burgundy, etc., Ct. of Flanders, etc., *ob.* 1404 (*see across*) / Ds. of Burgundy

John, D. of Berry

Louis I, D. of Anjou, Ct. of Provence, tit. K. of Naples, *ob.* 1385 / Ds. of Anjou, tit. Ks. of Naples

Charles V, K. of France (Dauphin), *ob.* 1380 / Ks. of France

Charles IV, K. of France and Navarre, *ob.* 1328

Philip V, K. of France and Navarre, *ob.* 1322

Jeanne, heiress of Franche Comté

Louis X, K. of France and Navarre, *ob.* 1316

Joanna, = **Philip,** heiress of Champagne and Navarre

Edward II = **Isabella,** *ob.* 1357, K. of England

Margaret, = **Louis II, Ct. of Flanders,** *ob.* 1346, eventual heiress of Franche Comté, *ob.* 1882

Louis III of Maele, Ct. of Flanders, *ob.* 1383

Margaret (2) = **Philip, D. of Burgundy,** *ob.* 1404, heiress of Flanders and Franche Comté, *ob.* 1405 / Ds. of Burgundy

John I, K. of France, and Navarre, *ob.* 1316 *s.p.*

Philip, = **Joanna, Q. of Navarre,** *ob.* 1349, Ct. of Evreux, K. of Navarre, *ob.* 1343

Edward III, K. of England, *ob.* 1377

John, D. of Lancaster, *ob.* 1399

Edward, P. of Wales, *ob.* 1376

Henry IV, K. of England, *ob.* 1413

Richard II, K. of England, *ob.* 1400 *s.p.*

Charles II, K. of Navarre, *ob.* 1387

Charles III, K. of Navarre, *ob.* 1425

HOUSE OF ANJOU

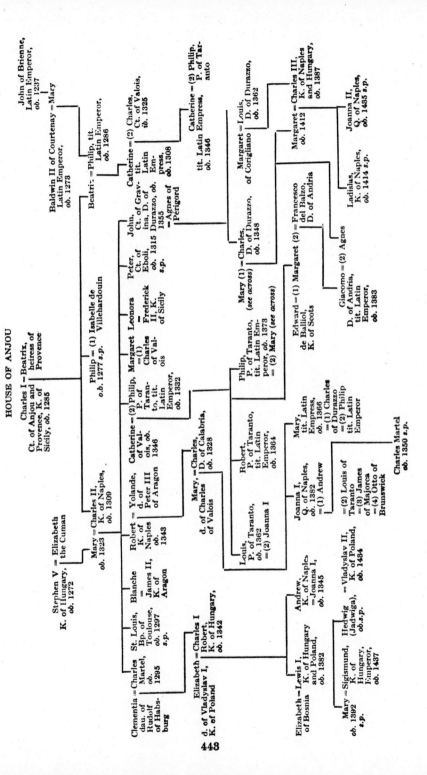

448

HOUSE OF LUXEMBURG

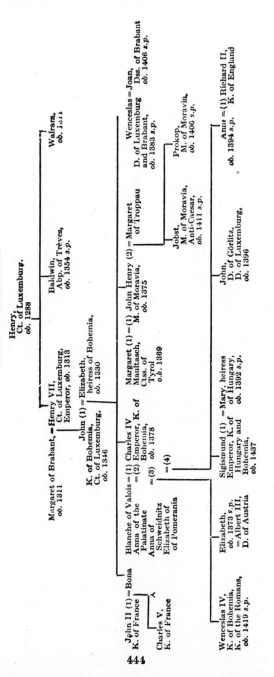

HOUSE OF HABSBURG

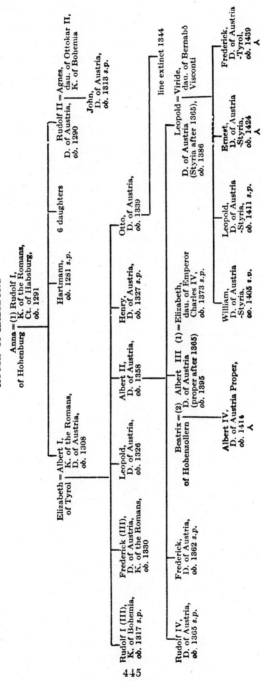

Anna = (1) Rudolf I,
of Hohenburg   K. of the Romans,
   Ct. of Habsburg,
   ob. 1291

- Elizabeth = Albert I, K. of the Romans, D. of Austria, *ob.* 1308 / of Tyrol
- Hartmann, *ob.* 1281 *s.p.*
- 6 daughters
- Rudolf II = Agnes, dau. of Ottokar II, D. of Austria, *ob.* 1290 / K. of Bohemia
    - John, D. of Austria, *ob.* 1313 *s.p.*

Descendants of Elizabeth and Albert I:

- Frederick (III), D. of Austria, K. of the Romans, *ob.* 1330
    - Rudolf I (III), K. of Bohemia, *ob.* 1317 *s.p.*
- Leopold, D. of Austria, *ob.* 1326
    - Frederick, D. of Austria, *ob.* 1362 *s.p.*
- Albert II, D. of Austria, *ob.* 1358
    - Rudolf IV, D. of Austria, *ob.* 1365 *s.p.*
    - Albert III (1) = Elizabeth, dau. of Emperor Charles IV, *ob.* 1373 *s.p.*
      Beatrix = (2) Albert III, D. of Austria (proper after 1365), *ob.* 1395
      of Hohenzollern
        - Albert IV, D. of Austria Proper, *ob.* 1414
    - Leopold = Viride, dau. of Bernabò Visconti, D. of Austria (Styria after 1365), *ob.* 1386
        - William, D. of Austria -Styria, *ob.* 1405 *s.p.*
        - Leopold, D. of Austria -Styria, *ob.* 1411 *s.p.*
        - Ernest, D. of Austria -Styria, *ob.* 1424
        - Frederick, D. of Austria -Tyrol, *ob.* 1439
- Otto, D. of Austria, *ob.* 1339
    - Henry, D. of Austria, *ob.* 1327 *s.p.*
    - line extinct 1344

HOUSE OF ARAGON

Maria = Peter II, K. of Aragon, Ct. of Barcelona, ob. 1213
heiress of Montpellier

James I (2) = Yolande of Hungary
K. of Aragon and Majorca, ob. 1276

Constance = Peter III, K. of Aragon and Sicily, ob. 1285
dau. of Manfred of Sicily, ob. 1302

James II = Esclarmonde of Foix
K. of Majorca, ob. 1311

Yolande = Alfonso X, K. of Castile, ob. 1284

Isabelle = Philip III, K. of France

Sancho, K. of Majorca, ob. 1324 s.p.

Ferdinand, ob. 1318

James III, K. of Majorca, ob. 1349

James (IV), ob. 1375

Blanche = Ferdinand de la Cerda, ob. 1275
dau. of St. Louis of France

Sancho IV, K. of Castile, ob. 1295

Ferdinand, ob. 1333 Λ

Alfonso, ob. 1333 Λ

Charles, constable, ob. 1354 Λ

Ferdinand IV, K. of Castile, ob. 1312

Alfonso XI, K. of Castile, ob. 1350

Henry II = Joanna, descended from Ferdinand de la Cerda
K. of Castile of Trastamara, ob. 1379

Blanche = Peter, K. of Castile, ob. 1368
of Bourbon, ob. 1361 s.p.

John (2) = Constance
D. of Lancaster, ob. 1399

John I, K. of Castile, ob. 1390

Catherine = Henry III, K. of Castile

Alfonso III, K. of Aragon, ob. 1291 s.p.

Isabella = Dinis, K. of Portugal, ob. 1328

Yolande, = Robert, K. of Naples

James II = Blanche, dau. of Charles II, K. of Aragon, K. of Naples ob. 1327

Frederick II = Leonora, K. of Sicily, dau. of Charles II, ob. 1337 K. of Naples

Peter II, K. of Sicily, ob. 1342

Successive, Ds. of Athens

Louis, K. of Sicily, ob. 1355 s.p.

Frederick III, k. of Sicily, ob. 1377

Maria, Q. of Sicily, ob. 1402 s.p. = Martin of Aragon

Leonora

Beatrix = Afonso IV, K. of Portugal, ob. 1357
dau. of Sancho IV of Castile

Alfonso IV, K. of Aragon, ob. 1336

Peter IV (3) = K. of Aragon, ob. 1387 Λ

Peter, K. of Portugal, ob. 1367

Ferdinand, K. of Portugal, ob. 1383

446

INDEX

Printed in Great Britain by Lithography by Jarrold & Sons Ltd., Norwich.